S0-BIF-383

GUILTY MONEY: THE CITY OF LONDON IN VICTORIAN AND EDWARDIAN CULTURE, 1815–1914

FINANCIAL HISTORY

Series Editor: Robert E. Wright

www.pickeringchatto.com/financialhistory

GUILTY MONEY: THE CITY OF LONDON IN VICTORIAN AND EDWARDIAN CULTURE, 1815–1914

BY

Ranald C. Michie

LONDON
PICKERING & CHATTO
2009

Published by Pickering & Chatto (Publishers) Limited
21 Bloomsbury Way, London WC1A 2TH

2252 Ridge Road, Brookfield, Vermont 05036-9704, USA

www.pickeringchatto.com

All rights reserved.
No part of this publication may be reproduced,
stored in a retrieval system, or transmitted in any form or by any means,
electronic, mechanical, photocopying, recording, or otherwise
without prior permission of the publisher.

© Pickering & Chatto (Publishers) Ltd 2009
© Ranald C. Michie 2009

BRITISH LIBRARY CATALOGUING IN PUBLICATION DATA

Michie, R. C., 1949–
Guilty money : the City of London in Victorian and
Edwardian culture, 1815–1914. – (Financial history)
1. Financial institutions – England – London – History –
19th century 2. English fiction – 19th century – History
and criticism 3. Capitalists and financiers in literature
4. London (England) – In literature
I. Title
332.1'09421'09034

ISBN-13: 9781851968923

This publication is printed on acid-free paper that conforms to the American
National Standard for the Permanence of Paper for Printed Library Materials.

Typeset by Pickering & Chatto (Publishers) Limited
Printed in the UK by the MPG Books Group

CONTENTS

PREFACE

This book is the product of obsession and rejection and its writing has been akin to an exorcism! The obsession has been to try and discover, over the course of the last twenty-five years, how the City of London was seen by those who lived before 1914. The rejection was the hostility this faced from funding bodies, publishers and fellow academics. On quite a number of occasions I was tempted to abandon the task, given the other demands on my time, but I did not. Conversation with non-academics convinced me that there was a genuine interest in the results of my research. The project thus grew and grew until it became a book-length monograph. It is for that reason I am so grateful to Pickering and Chatto, and Robert Wright, the editor of their series on Financial History, for their advice and making my findings available. I am also grateful to all those who have suggested novels and novelists I might read, in the hope that they might deal with the City of London. In this I would single out the bookseller Richard Beaton for his suggestions. Many valuable finds resulted, and even when none were made, the voyage of discovery has been an enjoyable one. The depth and diversity of the culture of the Victorian and Edwardian eras has been an astonishment to me, and all I have been able to do is skim the surface. I would also like to thank Francis Pritchard and Paul Lee for help they provided during the final production stages of this book.

How my book will be received remains an unknown as it is unlike anything I have ever produced before. Though its theme is the City of London as a financial and commercial centre, it is not a factual account. Though it relies heavily on novels it is not an exercise in literary criticism. Though it attempts to identify ideas and images it is not a cultural history. The fact that it does not fit into any obvious category may explain why referees for journals and publishers found it easy to be critical rather than understand what I was trying to achieve. This book sets out to test one simple theory and that is whether it is possible to establish, with any degree of precision, the place occupied by a financial centre in the culture of a nation, and the degree to which that changed over time. From that stems all the other questions I seek to answer and the conclusions I reach. The financial centre is the City of London; the country is Britain, the period is from

1815 to 1914; and the material used is mainly the novels written in those years. I believe both the City of London and the question are of sufficient importance to justify what I have tried to do and hope that the reader may find the subject as fascinating as I have.

In the hope that I have been successful in this task I dedicate this book to my youngest son, Jonathan Michie. Like me he is driven by an obsession, though in his case it is Japanese cartoon art, or Manga.

Ranald Michie
7th August 2008

INTRODUCTION

The City of London has been one of the leading financial centres in the world for over 300 years, playing an essential role in the mobilization and distribution of credit and capital. Over that time the business conducted within its confines has generated vast wealth for the British people and provided an essential service for successive British governments through the ability to borrow and tax. For those reasons alone it might be assumed that the City would be regarded as the brightest jewel in the British crown, treasured by all because of the riches it generated. Such a view, though, runs contrary to both the culture of envy, created by the sight of the large fortunes generated in the City, and a fundamental mistrust of money that was made through manipulating money itself rather than productive toil. As the inaugural issue of a magazine devoted to wealth observed in 2008, 'There is a widespread belief in a distinction between the deserving and the undeserving rich. And it goes far beyond the ancient debate over egalitarianism or socialism. Even for those who are happy to accept capitalism, and the idea that some will be richer than others, there is still a sense that some of the wealthy do not deserve their status'.[1] Among those perceived as the least deserving were bankers who, in the words of a respected BBC journalist in 2008, 'Were making obscene fortunes for themselves by gambling with other people's money'.[2] This meant that the City of London, as a financial centre, had major barriers to overcome if it was to achieve a favourable status within British society. Compounding this problem of gaining acceptance was the fact that much of the business undertaken in the City was of an international nature and was conducted by people who were seen to be foreign, either because of race or religion. This gave them the status of outsiders, erecting another barrier between those in the City and the rest of society. As the respected financial journalist, Hartley Withers, noted in 1916, 'Much of the prejudice against financiers is based on, or connected with, anti-Semitic feelings, that miserable relic of medieval barbarism'.[3] None of this was confined to either the Victorian and Edwardian eras or to Britain for evidence of an anti-money culture could be found from earlier and later periods and other countries. As Rubinstein concluded in his book on capitalism and culture, '...the thrust of intellectuals throughout the western world over the past 150 years has been consistently and persuasively anti-capitalistic'.[4] Similarly, Rosenberg has traced the portrayal of Jews as moneylenders and thus villains through the ages.[5]

Certainly such views did not disappear in the Victorian and Edwardian eras as this comment by J. A. Hobson, in his 1902 classic study of Imperialism, reveals,

> In large measure the rank and file of the investors are, both for business and for politics, the cats' paws of the great financial houses, who use stocks and shares not so much for investments to yield them interest, but as material for speculation in the money market. In handling large masses of stocks and shares, in floating companies, in manipulating fluctuations of values, the magnates of the Bourse find their gain. These great businesses – banking, broking, bill discounting, loan floating, company promoting – form the central ganglion of international capitalism. United by the strongest bonds of organization, always in closest and quickest touch with one another, situated in the very heart of the business capital of every state, controlled, so far as Europe is concerned, chiefly by men of a single and peculiar race, they are in a unique position to manipulate the policy of nations. No great quick direction of capital is possible save by their consent and through their agency. Does any one seriously suppose that a great war could be undertaken by any European State, or a great State loan subscribed, if the house of Rothschild and its connexions set their face against it?'[6]

The fact that hostility towards the City of London remained, because of its association with money, foreigners and Jews, is not the central question as these are perpetual prejudices within society. Evidence that they existed at this time reveals little about the place of the City within British culture, unless what can be shown is that no change took place. This is where the debate begins. There are those who suggest that hostility towards the City within Britain began to fade after the mid-nineteenth century onwards whereas an anti-industrial culture remained. 'Traditional prejudices against financiers (although not against industrialists) were gradually being eroded' is one such recent view expressed by Robinson.[7] This is also the central message of Weiner's influential view that Britain's economic decline was the product of a cultural preference for parasitic services rather than productive manufacturing, though others have found a singular lack of convincing evidence to support the thesis.[8] Only recently have historians attempted to discover whether a pro-City culture developed in Britain during the course of the nineteenth century. Paul Johnson, for example, has suggested that City bankers and financiers achieved growing acceptance within society, as their business practices became better understood and thus viewed with less hostility over time.[9] Similarly, Cain and Hopkins identified a growing alliance in this period between those in the City and the landed elite, creating a group of 'gentlemanly capitalists' whose power and influence lasted well into the twentieth century.[10] All this suggests that the barriers to cultural acceptance faced by the City, because of its personnel and activities, were steadily overcome in the Victorian and Edwardian period, in contrast to the industrialists who remained perpetual outsiders. Nineteenth-century manufacturing was undertaken in the North, and thus far from the cultural centre of the country in London, and involved dirt, noise and the risk of violent death from the machinery, whereas finance was a metropolitan activity and involved nothing more than reading, writing and arithmetic.

There is no doubt that the City of London grew in importance and changed in composition over the Victorian and Edwardian eras. In the mid-nineteenth century the City of London was primarily a British commercial and financial centre providing services for the British economy and the British government. Even those international transactions that it handled were largely generated by the need to provide for Britain's own external trade and investment. From then on, activity in the City of London was increasingly driven by global challenges and opportunities. The rapid growth of international trade generated a simultaneous demand for organization and shipping on the one hand and credit on the other, with the result that the provision of these services in the City was greatly boosted in the fifty years before the First World War. The development of banking systems across the world had a similar effect as the supply of funds seeking temporary employment grew enormously at the same time as the financial requirements of governments and businesses both expanded and changed with, again, profound consequences for the City. London merchants and markets increasingly served international markets whether it involved the supply of colonial produce to European consumers or European manufactures to colonial consumers. The London money market became the central intermediary in the mobilization and distribution of credit internationally, drawing money from around the world to finance international trade and to provide business with the short-term funds its daily operations required. The London capital market not only handled the issue of securities on behalf of governments and corporations from all over the world but also sold these securities to investors from across Europe. Many of the firms involved in these commercial, credit and capital operations were themselves of foreign origin and employed a cosmopolitan staff. Illustrative of the global role played by the City of London on the eve of the First World War was the fact that the London Stock Exchange increasingly quoted securities from around the world and provided a market that attracted investors from across the globe. Over half the value of the stocks and bonds quoted on the London Stock Exchange in 1913 was foreign in origin. This external orientation was found throughout the activities undertaken in the City. The Lloyds insurance market insured ships and cargoes irrespective of ownership and routes. Around two-thirds of world marine insurance was handled in the City of London by the time of the First World War, while British fire insurance companies were heavily involved in providing cover abroad. The revolution in communications that had begun with the telegraph in the 1850s, and then extended to the telephone from the 1890s, had permitted a growing physical separation between transport, trade and finance, so that the City of London could emerge as an intermediary centre for all types of international transactions.[11]

Lying behind this success was the size and specialization that existed in the City of London, whether it involved merchants and markets or bankers and brokers. In 1913 there were a total of 227 different banks operating in the City of London. These ranged from the large commercial banks with their domestic branch networks, through the specialist merchant banks to the British overseas banks providing banking services around the world and the branches of major foreign banks. Collectively, these comprised a dense financial cluster that was capable of providing the expertise and capacity required for any financial operation anywhere in the world. Supported by an equally dense cluster of other financial intermediaries, such as the 5,000-plus strong membership of the London Stock Exchange, they were able to either absorb the floating balances from banks around the world and employ it in the finance of international trade or mobilize the capital required to build entire railway systems and urban infrastructure projects.[12] Overall, it was estimated in 1911 that those employed in financial services in the City had reached almost 50,000 people out of 350,000. The fact that it was only a seventh of the total indicated the continued diversity of the activities undertaken there, with trading and transport being the most important.[13]

Connecting those financial and commercial clusters to the rest of the world were links between those operating in London and their equivalents in countries abroad. The Lloyds marine insurance markets had agents in every port in the world while many stock and commodity brokers had agreements with foreign counterparts under which each bought and sold on their own markets on receipt of a telegram or telephone call from abroad. The same was true for merchants who relied upon extensive contacts abroad in order to obtain the commodities and manufactures they bought or to distribute the products that they sold. This business was conducted on the basis of trust, leaving all in the City vulnerable to the default of a counterparty upon which reliance had been placed. The size and growth of these networks can be seen most clearly in banking. Between 1860 and 1913 the number of foreign banks with London branches rose from three to seventy-one, while there was also a group of British overseas banks with London head offices but branches spread around the world, especially Asia, Africa, Australia and Latin America. By 1913 these overseas banks operated 1,387 branches compared to only 132 in 1860.[14] These were only the most visible manifestations of the links that existed between banks in the City of London and their overseas counterparts. The most common link was a correspondent connection in which a bank that had a London office acted on behalf of those that had not. By 1912 a total of 1,211 banks from around the world had a presence in London through these correspondent links.[15] It was this combination of markets, businesses and connections that gave the City of London its core strength in commercial and financial services before 1914 and made it into a global centre. The effect of this was to make the City of London a magnet for financial and commercial services, and so attract personnel from throughout the world. On the eve of the First World War the City of London was the largest, most specialized, most diverse, and most cosmopolitan financial and commercial centre in the world.[16]

What this suggests is the existence of a direct relationship between the development of the City of London as a financial centre between 1800 and 1914 and its growing cultural acceptance, in which the former drove the latter. However, given the complexity of the link between economy and culture there remain strong doubts that such a relationship actually existed. It is particularly difficult to establish causality as both economy and culture changed considerably in the course of the nineteenth century not least because the relationship was transformed with urbanization, which fostered both interaction and separation.[17] This was especially the case for the City as it was at the forefront of these changes, as the residential population relocated to other parts of London and its vicinity, and manufacturing moved even further away. In the first volume of his popular and influential history of England, published in 1848, the eminent Victorian historian, Lord Macauley (Thomas Babbington Macauley) contrasted the City in the mid-nineteenth century with what it had been two centuries before, in the mid-seventeenth century. As he so eloquently wrote,

> In the seventeenth century the City was the merchant's residence ... In such abodes, under the last Stuarts, the heads of the great firms lived splendidly and hospitably. To their dwelling place they were bound by the strongest ties of interest and affection ... The whole character of the City has, since that time, undergone a complete change. At present the bankers, the merchants, and the chief shopkeepers repair thither on six mornings of every week for the transaction of business but they reside in other quarters of the metropolis, or at suburban country seats surrounded by shrubberies and flower gardens. This revolution in private habits has produced a political revolution of no small importance. The City is no longer regarded by the wealthiest traders with that attachment which everyman naturally feels for his home. It is no longer associated in their minds with domestic affections and endearments. The fireside, the nursery, the social table, the quiet bed are not there. Lombard Street and Threadneedle Street are merely places where men toil and accumulate. They go elsewhere to enjoy and to expend'.[18]

What was happening in the nineteenth century was that the City of London was emerging as a specialized business district bereft of its residential population, as well as many subsidiary economic activities. The era of commuting, for example, had been inaugurated whether from the areas immediately adjacent to the City or, increasingly, further away as mass transport facilitated greater mobility. In earlier centuries particular parts of the City had been singled out as representing specific activities and those who conducted them. Such was the case with Exchange (or 'Change') Alley, in which was found those who bought and sold stocks and shares. However, as the City ceased to be a diverse and populated community it came to possess a collective identity. The characteristics once attributed to specific places, people and activities in the City were increasingly acquired by the City as a whole during the nineteenth century. In this process it did not matter that the City remained as much a commercial centre as a financial one right up to the First World War. What mattered was what people thought happened in the City rather than what actually took place there. The outcome was that the City could become the physical manifestation of capitalism itself as people struggled to come to terms with that concept and the economic changes that were taking place, as they created winners and losers in their wake. [19] Under these circumstances there may be no link between the City and culture as each occupied separate worlds. The division between home and work in a modern society could allow individuals to escape the moral dilemmas involved in a clash between cultural beliefs and economic imperatives. Even for those in the City the commute to work operated as a physical divide between the two worlds, allowing them to distinguish between what they did to earn a living and what they did in their hours of leisure, whether in beliefs or actions. However, there is also the possibility that it was culture that was a critical determinant of economic behaviour. The set of beliefs adhered to by a nation's population could influence the direction and performance of a modern economy. This could extend far beyond the presence or absence of a work ethic to a culture that embraced or rejected capitalism. It could even determine the preferred form of capitalism, such as an anti-industrial culture leading to a switch away from manufacturing and a switch to more service-orientated pursuits.[20] Complicating the task of isolating the direct influence of culture on the economy is its indirect influence on government economic policies. Governments could be driven to adopt policies based on cultural beliefs that may or may not be mistaken, and these could have far reaching consequences for the pace and pattern of economic growth.[21] The problem with the relationship between culture and economy through the instrument of government is that the economic policies implemented were driven by numerous, diverse and often conflicting influences and objectives. This makes it difficult to disentangle those that were the product of a common culture and those driven by party-political ideology, military necessity, international obligations, social requirements, administrative considerations or simple expediency.[22]

This makes the Victorian and Edwardian period before 1914 an ideal one in which to explore the relationship between economy and culture, especially through the use of the City of London as an interface. Generally, this was a time when there was very limited government intervention in the economy. The

City of London was left to operate largely unfettered by government control or regulation, with even the central bank, the Bank of England, being controlled by shareholders rather than the state. Similarly, the changes to the Companies Acts, despite evidence of abuse, were fairly limited. Wynne-Bennett, writing as late as 1924, was of the opinion that, 'There has been more systematized fraud and complete financial loss connected with mining propositions than with any other industry'. A. E. Davies reflected in 1926 that a company prospectus was a product of fiction not fact. In neither case was much action taken by the government to deal with either problem, despite periodic outcries from the public and the press.[23] This leads to a series of pathways which need to be followed if a connection is to be established between economy and culture in the specific case of the City of London before 1914. The first pathway is to establish whether Britain did, in fact, develop a pro-City culture in the course of the Victorian and Edwardian years. If it did, was this the consequence of economic change or the cause of it? By establishing a chronology for cultural change it should be possible to separate cause and effect and so identify whether culture was driven by the economy or the economy by culture. The second pathway emerges if a pro-City culture is found not to exist in Britain and the public were indifferent to finance. If that was the case it suggests that the cultural world and the economic world existed in different spheres. The third pathway is the one taken if Britain is discovered to have an anti-City culture, akin to the anti-industrial one that other historians have identified. As the City of London flourished throughout this period it suggests that what people believed to be true may not have prevented them from pursuing objectives directly opposed to those beliefs, such as living on earnings considered immoral or profiting from unethical investments. Each of these pathways needs to be explored before it becomes possible to draw conclusions about the relationship between culture and economy.

To answer these questions fully requires some precision in identifying culture and then measuring change. 'Culture' is taken to mean the collective ideas, beliefs and values of the population at a particular moment in time. Collective culture is not easy to establish, especially if the attempt is made to capture a broad spectrum of views rather than take as representative the opinions of a small number of the rich or powerful or that expressed in official government reports. The problem with that is such evidence may entirely misrepresent the prevailing collective culture or attribute a momentary view as representative of an entire age. F. M. L. Thompson has observed, for example, that the identification of an anti-industrial culture was based upon the '...unreliable foundations of selective quotations from literary sources...'.[24] Nevertheless, novels do offer one means of establishing some sense of contemporary culture and tracing change over time. In an increasingly literate society the novel can be seen as both a reflection of the time in which it was written and an influence upon those who read it. By using novels the historian can capture what people at the time said, thought and believed. Though clearly contrived and structured the reported conversations do give an insight into contemporary views and concerns. Nowhere else is it possible to recapture the actual dialogue of the Victorian era. The storylines used in novels also indicate what mattered to people and how they interpreted the world they lived in. Novels thus offer the potential for unearthing the true tenor of Victorian and Edwardian culture and establishing its priorities and direction.[25] As one Victorian novelist, Frederick Wicks, observed in 1892,

> While the historian deals with the growth of peoples and the movement of nations, it is the province of the novelist to exhibit the domestic life of his contemporaries. His object should be to give pictures of the life of the day, reflecting the most striking phases and the most startling developments of social relationship, that the strength and weakness of the nation may be seen in the detail.[26]

Given the steady production of novels over this period, they also provide a means of continually monitoring changing cultural values. In contrast, other evidence of contemporary culture lacks either the continuity or depth necessary to observe trends over time. Cartoons do provide useful snapshots, such as during the Railway Mania, while there was a brief flurry of paintings with a City theme in the late 1870s, but finance only rarely lends itself to visual display.[27] Plays do provide an alternative to novels as they also take up contemporary concerns and so supply a continuous commentary on current cultural values and attitudes. However, they lack the detail to be found in novels, especially when financial matters arose, as they relied on either dialogue or display. As it was, what appeared on the stage was usually a reflection of the ideas, attitudes and interests that were also to be found in contemporaneous novels, especially as there was an overlap between writers and playwrights in either personnel or subject matter.[28]

This does not mean that there are not serious disadvantages and limitations in using novels as items of historical evidence. Novels are works of fiction in which writers manipulate the characters, plots, dialogue and circumstances in order to achieve the end they want. They are the product of the author's interests, beliefs and imagination, unrestrained by the need to examine and assess hard evidence and substantiate the conclusions reached. In addition, they are driven by the desire of the author for material gain and the publisher for commercial success. Thus, they cannot be used as substitutes for facts; these must be sought from other sources uncorrupted by the need to entertain. Also, by their very nature, novels were not produced by a cross-section of society but by those who were creative and literate. Those who wrote novels were probably those in society least sympathetic to the humdrum world of work or the single-minded pursuit of wealth, and this must be allowed for. Novels also have an element of escapism or nostalgia in them, allowing those who read them to enter, however briefly, a different world from that of their own, free from everyday cares and complexities. Kenneth Grahame, the author of *The Wind in the Willows*, chose to portray an imaginary world of animals rather than the routine of the City life with which he was familiar.[29] Conversely, this does make novels useful as historical evidence as they were written for an audience and produced for sale. Whatever the opinions of novelists, their living depended upon writing books that interested their readers and this included both the plot and the contents. Similarly, publishers of such novels had to sell the books they produced if they were to cover their costs and make a profit, as did the booksellers that stocked them. Unlike tracts and broadsheets that were written and distributed in support of a cause, novelists and their publishers had to achieve a level of public acceptability if they were to survive. In that way novels do provide ideal material from which to judge prevailing culture as they were the product of a two way relationship between producer and consumer.[30]

Another problem, however, does exist and that is the representative nature of the novels used as historical sources. The Victorian and Edwardian eras witnessed a huge outpouring of literature most of which is now forgotten, being deemed as not worthy of lasting merit. However, it was these popular novels as well as the literary classics that the public read on a regular basis, and so it is important to examine what they were saying and how that changed over time. If the attempt is to capture contemporary culture the study cannot be confined to a few giants of the past, as is the approach of the literary specialist.[31] It is not the verdict of today on a work's literary merit that is significant but rather the words and opinions being expressed at a particular moment by those who caught the mood of the time. Thus, it is critical that the novel enjoyed both a wide circulation and was written in the specific time period under consideration, and not afterwards, when hindsight may very well have influenced what was being said. Novels written after the First World War, for example, cannot be used as evidence of views prevailing before that event, given the power it possessed to change attitudes. This is true even of the work of a single author than spans the First World War. Only the first book, *The Man of Property,* in Galsworthy's triple trilogy, *The Forsyte Saga,* can, for example, be used as a piece of historical evidence as the others were written and published after the First World War. That makes them ineligible as historical evidence of the pre-war culture, despite temptations to do so because of the slow unfolding of a family saga over the period.[32] It is what is being said and when it is being said that matters, not who says it and the purpose for which it was written. Only contemporary fiction provides an authentic mirror on the past, if the objective is to establish contemporary culture. In this context, novelists, playwrights, poets and artists are used as reporters of the time they lived in, not as historians interpreting the past for a later generation. Victorian and Edwardian writers relied heavily on characters, locations and events drawn from real life, so establishing a close connection between the literary world and the real world.[33] In turn, the fact that these novels were widely read meant their views and opinions were absorbed by both their own and subsequent generations, so giving writers the power to shape the culture of the society within which they lived, and more widely, given the borrowing of storylines in the English-speaking world and across Western Europe.[34]

Luckily for the historian money and finance do feature in novels from throughout the Victorian and Edwardian eras and from the pen of numerous novelists, not only the literary giants of the early years. Petch observed that '...money is everywhere in Victorian Literature...'; Crosby that, 'To note that money looms large in Victorian fiction is to observe the obvious,...'; Knezevic that 'There is hardly a Victorian novel that is not about money, and hardly a Victorian novelist without some grasp of the operations of contemporary finance capitalism'; while Weiss noted '...the pre-eminence of money in the Victorian imagination.'[35] London also looms large in Victorian and Edwardian literature, as its size and complexity offered so many opportunities for the imagination of the novelist while it was also the place where so many of them lived and worked.[36] However, much of this refers not to the activities of the City of London, or high finance, but the everyday concerns of getting and spending in what was the largest urban area in the world at the time.[37] The actual novels that devote considerable space to the activities and personnel of the City of London are relatively few, being numbered in hundreds rather than thousands, but they do include the work of some of the most popular writers of the day. These included novelists of lasting literary merit, such as Dickens and Conrad, whose work was read extensively both at the time and since. It also includes others like Trollope and Galsworthy whose popularity rose and fell over time but whose output was extensively read then and subsequently. There are also other writers who enjoyed an enormous following when their work first appeared but then sunk into relative obscurity, such as Marie Corelli or E. Phillips Oppenheim. Finally, there were those who established a niche for themselves which meant that each novel they wrote attracted a loyal following, as was the case of Charlotte Riddell with the City itself; Walter Besant on London generally; fulfilled a moral purpose, as with Annie Swan; provided a political commentary like Hilaire Belloc or provided the excitement of African adventure, as was the case with H. Rider Haggard. The novels of all these writers sold extensively in the years before the First World War, whatever the later judgements of literary scholars. Given that the readership of the work of these authors was not confined to the actual novels, but frequently included the prior serial publication in the weekly journals, it is fairly evident that the views they expressed received a wide circulation. Overall, there are a sufficient number of novels and novelists to provide an evolving commentary on contemporary culture, with each being seen as a proxy for the beliefs and attitudes of their own generation.[38]

By using novels in this way the historian takes a fundamentally different approach to that of the literary critic. The literary critic seeks to explain the novel in terms of what the author achieves as part of a creative process and so reads meaning into what is being said. The historian uses contemporary novels as receptacles of contemporary beliefs which can provide insights into contemporary culture. The material each uses may be the same, in terms of literary output, but the interests and objectives of each are totally different. Though the novel is seen to be the preserve of the literary scholar this does not mean it cannot be used by the historian as a valuable tool of analysis, if particular care is taken to identify the questions being asked of this type of evidence. If such care is not taken a circularity is created. Historians do not write in a vacuum but under the influence of the culture within which they live. In turn that culture owes much to fiction through which ideas, beliefs and values are both broadcast among the population as a whole and conveyed from one generation to the next. When a literary critic cites the views of a historian as confirmation of their interpretation of the views of a particular novelist, they may be doing nothing more than identifying the influence the novelist has had in determining how the period in which they lived has been interpreted through the questions asked and the emphasis given. The historian must not read meaning into a novel which is not there while the literary critic must see the novel as a work of fiction not fact. If these divisions are adhered to novels can be used by both historians and literary historians to the advantage of both. If these divisions are not adhered to both the historian and the literary scholar risks basing conclusions on flawed evidence.

1 CAPITALISM AND CULTURE: 1800–1856

From at least the seventeenth century onwards the City of London was widely regarded as a place where a man and his money were easily parted and usually by the most villainous means imaginable. The place it occupied within contemporary culture was one that varied from amazement, because of its size and population, to distrust as a result of the activities conducted there. Such a view was driven both by the longstanding Christian antipathy towards usury, which inevitably brought any financial centre into disrepute, and the general suspicion of the middleman in any transaction, as the differential price led both buyer and seller to believe they had been cheated. In addition, there were specific events in the City of London that fuelled public hostility. The speculative boom in 1720, with the Mississippi Bubble in Paris and the South Sea Bubble in London, convinced many that there was something rotten associated with the rise and fall of stock and share prices, and the promotion of joint stock companies. Those events continued to colour popular perceptions from then on, and certainly way into the nineteenth century.[1] At the time of another speculative boom in 1864 the British historical novelist, W. H. Ainsworth, thought it worthwhile to write a story based around John Law, the great Scottish financier whose schemes lay at the heart of the events in Paris.[2] However, other aspects of the City's activities did experience a slow rehabilitation during the course of the eighteenth century, which was evident by the beginning of the nineteenth. Increasingly the City merchant was regarded by contemporaries as being an honourable person, having accumulated wealth through legitimate means. The business being conducted by merchants had relevance to most people, as they ranged from retailing through wholesaling to international trade, and so was accepted as necessary. If that business was then conducted in such a way as permitted the slow accumulation of a fortune, without the use of practices that appeared to cheat suppliers and customers, then the successful merchant could command the respect of their peers. Such a verdict was personified by the popular story of Dick Whittington, who had risen from rags to riches as a City merchant. The City was a place of opportunity where even the humblest person could succeed to such an extent that he could purchase a landed estate and challenge the established gentry of the country.[3]

Evidence of the growing regard for the City merchant in the contemporary culture of the early nineteenth century can be found in Jane Austen's *Pride and Prejudice,* published in 1813. This novel painted a very positive picture of Mr Gardiner, the uncle of Elizabeth Bennet, even though he was a wealthy and successful London merchant. It was accepted that many might have '...difficulty in believing that a man who lived by trade, and within view of his own warehouses, could have been so well bred and agreeable'. However, that was the case though the fact that her uncle was in trade was seen as a barrier to Elizabeth making a good marriage among the landed gentry. That did not prove to be so as she married a large and well-connected landowner, who developed a close and friendly relationship with the Gardiners.[4] A similar impression is conveyed in the novel *Rob Roy* by Sir Walter Scott, dating from 1818. The father of Frank Osbaldistone was a respected wine merchant in the City. He had arrived in London from Northumberland with nothing, but became successful and wealthy through hard work and skill. Initially Frank looked down on trade and did not want to join the family firm because of the endless routine that the work of the counting house involved. His place was therefore taken by a cousin from Northumberland, Rashleigh Osbaldistone, who had been intended for the priesthood. He turned out to be untrustworthy and brought the business close to ruin, forcing Frank to step in out of loyalty to his father. Frank then became a partner, and continued in the business despite the fact that he had inherited the family estate in Northumberland and so had no need to do so.[5] Similarly, in Ainsworth's 1841 novel, set in London at the time of the Great Plague and Great Fire, Stephen Bloundell, a wholesale grocer in the City, was praised because 'His integrity and fairness of dealing, never once called in question for a period of thirty years, had won him the esteem of all who knew him; while his prudence and economy had enabled him, during that time, to amass a tolerable fortune'. Nevertheless, his apprentice, Leonard Holt, was rejected by Lord Argentine as a suitable suitor for his sister. However, he did eventually marry her, after saving the King's life and gaining an estate and title. Their son then married the granddaughter of Stephen Bloundell, whose father, also called Stephen, had inherited the City grocer's business from his father. This suggests that City merchants had achieved a position within British culture where their fortunes could bring acceptance from the established landed gentry, leading even to marriage.[6] The same was not yet generally true for those in the City who made their living by finance, though private bankers located in the West End of London were beginning to join merchants in possessing social acceptability.[7]

Reinforcing popular prejudice against finance was the speculative mania of the mid-1820s which centred on loans issued on behalf of foreign governments, especially from Latin America, and the promotion of a large number of joint stock companies, many being engaged in mining at home and abroad. Most of the foreign governments defaulted on their loans after a few years, especially the newly independent Latin American republics while one state, Poyais, turned out to be entirely fictitious. Most of the mining companies were also abandoned, after exhausting all the money raised, though a few did return large profits.[8] This episode confirmed the existing prejudices against the City of London despite the fact that the main security held and traded was the National Debt, on which interest was regularly paid and whose value, in real terms, was growing. Illustrating the prevailing belief that those in the City were, at best, driven by avarice or, at worst, criminality, is Thomas Peacock's *Crotchet Castle,* published in 1831. The reader is first introduced Ebenezer MacCrotchet, who had been born in London of a Scottish father and a Jewish mother. This conjures up an image of expertise in money combined with meanness. Ebenezer's maternal grandfather had been a City merchant and it was this business that he inherited, using it to create a fortune. 'Mr MacCrotchet had derived from his mother the instinct, and his father the rational principle of enriching himself at the expense of the rest of mankind, by all the recognized modes of accumulation on the windy side of the law'. With this fortune he had become a respectable member of society through marriage to an English Christian, losing his Scottish accent, changing his name to E. M. Crotchet, and, finally, purchasing a country estate. All this confirmed the view that, by then, City merchants were able to integrate successfully into respectable society. However, such a course was not open to those whose activities lay in finance, as could be seen from the career of young Mr Crotchet. After an Oxford education Crotchet joined '... the eminent loan-jobbing firm of Catchflat and Company' as a junior partner, where he enjoyed rapid success but only at the expense of numerous innocent investors. The following reported conversation suggests how City financiers were seen in the aftermath of the 1820s speculative boom.

> Stranger. 'Young Mr Crotchet, Sir, has been, like his father, the architect of his own fortune, has he not? An illustrious example of the reward of honesty and industry?'
>
> The Reverend Doctor Folliot. 'As to honesty, sir, he made his fortune in the City of London; and if that commodity be of any value there, you will find it in the price current. I believe it is below par, like the shares of young Crotchet's fifty companies. But his progress has not been exactly like his father's: it has been more rapid, and he started with more advantages. He began with a fine capital from his father ... But, sir, young Crotchet doubled, trebled, and quadrupled it, and is, as you say, a striking example of the reward of industry; not that I think his labour has been so great as his luck.'
>
> The Stranger. 'But, sir, is all this solid? Is there no danger of reaction? No day of reckoning, to cut down in an hour prosperity that has grown up like a mushroom.'

The City was seen as a place where fortunes could be made quickly and easily by those with little ability and even less breeding, through the duping of those gullible enough to trust them, but the wealth so gained could just as easily evaporate. In the short-term those who profited from their success in the City were able to gain whatever they wanted, even marriage to the daughter of a Lord. Young Crotchet had been engaged to the daughter of a banker, Touchandgo, but when the banker absconded after the collapse of his bank, it had been broken off. Instead he was now engaged to Lady Clarinda, the daughter of the impoverished Lord Foolincourt, who was in need of money. Lady Clarinda's view on this arrangement was very pragmatic, as she told her previous suitor. 'If I take him, it will be to please my father, and to have a town and country-house, and plenty of servants, and a carriage and an opera-box, and to make some of my acquaintances who have married for love, or for rank, or anything but money, die for envy of my jewels'. This was despite the fact that she did not love young Crotchet and found him ugly, his bubble schemes having '... stamped him with the physiognomy of a desperate gambler'. Lady Clarinda was saved from this fate because, with the inevitable bankruptcy of Catchflat & Co., young Crotchet fled to America with the money he had made. Lady Clarinda then married her poor but honest suitor, Captain Fitzchrome, so conveying the message that those who made their money in the City through finance could not expect to enjoy the rewards for long.[9]

Further undermining the City in the eyes of the public were the monetary and banking problems that occurred after 1815. These were blamed on the City, especially the Bank of England, as it was '...the greatest bank of deposit and circulation in the world...' Such an attitude can be seen in the novel written by Harriet Martineau, *Berkeley the Banker*, which was published in parts between 1832 and 1834. The story revolved around two rival provincial banks. One was sound and well managed while the other was neither, but both collapsed with serious consequences for the community. When unfounded rumours started to circulate about Berkeley's bank, which was sound, depositors rushed to withdraw their money. This led it to draw on a London bank, where Berkeley's son Horace was a partner, for gold and silver coins and Bank of England notes. This succeeded in calming the depositors and withdrawals abated but when the London bank was itself put under pressure it withdrew support. On hearing this, the depositors once again besieged Berkeley's bank to withdraw their money, forcing it to close. This was regretted as it was recognized that a trustworthy banker like Mr Berkeley provided a real service to the community. His bank had been solvent but had been let down by its London banker and the monetary stringency created by the Bank of England. The London bank survived but Mr Berkeley was rendered penniless. He had to give up his large house, only surviving on the charity of his creditors, while his two daughters became governesses. Mr Berkeley was an 'honourable' man who then worked hard to salvage something for these creditors by realizing the bank's assets. This proved an impossible task under the circumstances. Post-war deflation made it difficult for those who had borrowed money from the bank to repay it, as the real value of their debts was rising, whereas in the previous inflationary era they had fallen over time. In contrast, Mr Cavendish had set up his bank in full expectation that it would eventually collapse. His intention was to lend extensively through issuing his own banknotes and to accept as much in deposit as possible in the form of gold coin. He then placed all the assets he accumulated in his wife's name, and thus beyond the reach of creditors when the collapse eventually came. When rumours that Cavendish's bank was in trouble started to spread, he fled town with his family and all the cash and other assets he could carry. The bank then collapsed causing pandemonium.

> The excitement was indeed dreadful. If an earthquake had opened a chasm in the centre of the town, the consternation of the people could scarcely have been greater. It was folly to talk of holding a market, for not one buyer in twenty had any money but Cavendish's notes and unless that one happened to have coin, he could achieve no purchase. The indignant people spurned bank-paper of every kind, even Bank of England notes.

Those holding the bank's notes or whose savings were in the bank lost it all. Cavendish 'had acted knavishly, and thus injured commercial credit'. He eventually reappeared in London under an assumed name. By then he was part of a gang forging Bank of England one pound notes, as these were in short supply because of the post-war credit restriction. When the forgers were discovered he fled to New York, leaving his fellow conspirators to be hung, though there was some sympathy for them as they were supplying a demand that the Bank of England was ignoring.[10] The provincial banker was seen to be a valuable member of society, if he conducted a sound business, but was vulnerable to rumour and financial and monetary problems emanating from London.

In the early Victorian years public perception of the City continued to be largely determined by those of its activities involving money, in contrast to those involving trade.[11] City merchants continued to grow in stature. In another of Ainsworth's historical novels, *Old St. Paul's*, set in London at the time of the Great Plague, the City grocer, Stephen Bloundel, was the subject of high praise. 'His integrity and fairness of dealing, never once called in question for a period of thirty years, had won him the esteem of all who knew him; while his prudence and economy had enabled him, during that time, to amass a tolerable fortune'.[12] Similarly, in Charles Dickens's work a positive impression of City merchants is conveyed whether they were the Cheeryble Brothers (German merchants), Anthony Chuzzlewit & Son (Manchester warehousemen), Scrooge & Marley (foreign merchants) and Dombey & Son (West India merchants). Even Scrooge was ultimately portrayed as a fundamentally kind and respectable member of the community once he overcame his meanness.[13] This can be seen clearly in *Dombey and Son,* dating from the mid-1840s. In that novel Dickens captured the global importance of the business these City merchants did, generating pride in their achievements. 'The earth was made for Dombey and Son to trade in, and the sun and moon were made to give them light. Rivers and seas were formed to float their ships; rainbows gave them promise of fair weather; winds blew for or against their enterprises; stars and planets circled in their orbits, to preserve inviolate a system of which they were the centre'. The commercial importance of the City was plain to all and was at the very heart of Britain's success as a maritime nation. When Dombey's daughter Florence strays into the City she experienced 'the clash and clangour of a narrow street full of carts and wagons' and 'peeped into a kind of wharf or landing – place upon the river – side, where there were a great many packages, casks, and boxes, strewn about...' All this activity was directed from the office of firms like Dombey and Son. Jem Carker, the office manager, 'saw many visitors; overlooked a number of documents; went in and out, to and from, sundry places of mercantile resort...' There was also a large a varied correspondence to be attended to. 'The letters were in various languages, but Mr Carker the manager read them all ... He read almost at a glance, and made combinations of one letter with another and one business with another as he went on, ...' Though Dombey is eventually ruined through the unauthorized speculations and subsequent flight of the office manager, there is no suggestion that he was not an honourable man and that the business that he undertook was not of importance. He is thus left to enjoy his release from business worries through finding a home with his daughter and her husband.[14] The City merchant was recognized as a central figure in British life, especially if their business was both international and conducted on a grand scale. British culture had taken on board the fact that Britain was the greatest trading nation in the world, and that much was owed to City merchants for this success.

This admiration of the merchant did not spill over in the other aspects of the City's activities, especially if they involved speculation and company promotion, though the level of hostility had faded somewhat by the early 1840s. Thackeray's 1841 novel, *The History of Samuel Titmarsh and the Great Hoggarty Diamond* focused on fraud and company promotion in the City, but the views were more light-hearted as such events were seen as having taken place sometime in the past. 'there was great mania in the City of London for establishing companies of all sorts; by which many people made pretty fortunes'. Among those were a number of insurance companies, and Samuel Titmarsh was clerk to one of these, the Independent West Diddlesex Fire and Life Insurance Company. This was located in 'a splendid stone mansion in Cornhill' and had been promoted by Mr. Brough, a City merchant whose firm, Brough and Hoff, specialized in the Turkey trade. Whereas the senior partner, Hoff, stuck to trade, Brough became heavily engaged in speculating in foreign government bonds and domestic company promotion. Initially, this brought success, making him 'one of the richest men in the City of London'. He became MP for Rottenburgh, and entertained 'the great people of the land at his villa at Fulham'. This further reinforced the social acceptability of the City merchant. Brough himself confidently proclaimed, 'The daughter of a British Merchant need not be ashamed of the means by which her father gets his bread. I'm not ashamed – I'm not proud. Those who know John Brough, know that ten years ago he was a poor clerk like my friend Titmarsh here, and is now worth half a million'. It was Brough's financial activities that undermined this status, as doubts began to emerge about the solvency of the companies he had promoted, including The Ginger Beer Company, The Patent Pump Company and The Consolidated Baffin's Bay Muff and Tippet Company. Directors resigned from his companies and the partnership with Hoff was dissolved. Finally, the West Diddlesex came under pressure as those whose lives had been assured died and buildings it had insured against fire burnt down, some under suspicious circumstances attributed to the actions of Jewish businessmen. '[L]ife insurance companies go on excellently for a year or two after their establishment, but ... it is much more difficult to make them profitable when the assured parties begin to die'. Brough fled to France leaving Titmarsh to take the blame. 'The failure of the great Diddlesex Association speedily became the theme of all the newspapers, and every person concerned in it soon held up to public abhorrence as a rascal and a swindler. It was said that Brough had gone off with a million of money'. As it was Titmarsh ended up bankrupt and in prison, from which he was rescued by his wife, his mother and other relatives. Brough was left with nothing, his house and all his possessions having been sold to pay his creditors. Those who had invested in his companies also lost all. The impression generated was that the City was seen as a place which rewarded those who worked hard, as in trade, but punished those who speculated, as in corporate stocks and shares, whether they were company promoters or investors.[15]

What also emerges from Thackeray's work is the sense that those in the City remained socially inferior, gaining acceptance solely because of their money. This emerges in *The Book of Snobs,* which appeared in 1846. In a chapter devoted to 'Great City Snobs' those in the City were seen to have 'a mania for aristocratic marriages'. Such marriages were seen as purely financial transactions through which the coffers of impoverished nobility were replenished, while those who had made money in the City gained instant status for themselves. However, the point was made that it was only the offspring of these City/Nobility marriages that gained full acceptance within aristocratic circles. In the meantime, the City man who married a noble wife had to accept that he would be looked down upon despite his wealth and business success. 'Fancy the domestic enjoyments of a man who has a wife who scorns him; who cannot see his own friends in his own house; who having deserted the middle rank of life, is not yet admitted to the higher; but who is resigned to rebuffs and delay and humiliation, contented to think that his son will be more fortunate'.[16] Such a view is developed in Thackeray's 1847–8 novel,

Vanity Fair, which also emphasised how transitory were fortunes and relation-ships in the City.[17] Amelia Sedley's father was a stockbroker, who '...conducted his mysterious operations in the City'. Eventually he failed. 'All his speculations had of late gone wrong with the luckless old gentleman. Ventures had failed, mer-chants had broken, funds had risen when he calculated they would fall. What need to particularize?' The result was that John Sedley was transformed almost overnight from a wealthy City man into a pauper, dependent upon the charity of his son in India and deserted by almost all his business associates. He was forced to move in with his ex-clerk while all his possessions were sold at public auction to pay his creditors. 'Good old John Sedley was a ruined man. His name had been proclaimed a defaulter on the Stock Exchange, and his bankruptcy and commer-cial extermination had followed'. Amelia's engagement to George Osborne, the son of a successful merchant, was broken off by the father, John Osborne, and when it took place against his wishes he disinherited the son, such was his desire to sever all connection with failure. The message was clear – the City was a cruel place in which there was no room for sentiment.

What is also apparent is that the public were aware of a hierarchy within the City and the place such people occupied within society as a whole. According to Thackeray, retail merchants were at the bottom of the City's social classes, being akin to servants. William Dobbin was looked down upon by other boys at school, being referred to as 'grocer's boy', because his father was a partner in Dobbin & Rudge, grocers and oilmen, who supplied large houses with such items as tea, sugar, candles, and soap. 'the selling of goods by retail is a shameful and infamous practice, meriting the contempt and scorn of all real gentlemen'. Above the retail merchant was the merchant who traded with distant countries in exotic commodities, for this had a touch of mystery about it as well as pro-ducing greater wealth because of the greater risks run. John Osborne was one of these, and proud of it, declaring that, compared to those from the West End, 'I am a plain British merchant, I am, and I could buy the beggarly hounds over and over. Lords indeed!' Ranking along with foreign merchants, but a little below, were stockbrokers like John Sedley, but above them both were private bankers such as Hulker, Bullock & Co. They were referred to as 'a high family of the City aristocracy, and connected with the 'nobs' at the West End'. In turn, marriage linked these groups of City merchants, bankers and brokers closely to each other. It was only a small number of the wealthiest and most prominent who formed connections with non-City families living in the West End of London. Judging from *Vanity Fair* there was an underlying tension between the City and the West End rather than a bond formed through marriage and wealth.[18]

By the early 1840s there also appeared to be a greater acceptability of Jewish financiers in British culture. In his 1844 novel, *Coningsby,* Benjamin Disraeli introduced a character based on the Rothschilds, namely the Jewish financier Sidonia. Sidonia was not only rich, powerful and successful but was also respected for his intelligence and integrity. He is referred to as 'lord and master of the money-market of the world' and this was a mantle that had descended from father to son. When Sidonia entertained it was a lavish and well attended event that 'exceeded in splendour and luxury every entertainment that had yet been given. The highest rank, even Princes of the blood, beauty, fashion, fame, all assembled in a magnificent and illuminated palace, resounding with exquisite melody'.[19] In a subsequent novel, *Tancred* (1847), Disraeli indicated that Sidonia's financial activities were directed from a large house near the Bank of England in Sequin Court in the City. It was there that Sidonia 'deals with the fortunes of kings and empires, and regulates the most important affairs of nations, for it is the counting-house in the greatest of modern cities of the most celebrated of modern financiers'. The British public could take pride in the City as it was home to the most powerful financiers in the world, such as the Rothschilds and Barings.[20] Nevertheless, there remained an ambiguity about the way the City was regarded. This is seen in Smedley's 1850 tale of young men making their way in the world, *Frank Fairleigh,* as the City is seen in both lights. The respectable and hardworking Frank Fairleigh nearly ends up working for a relative in the office of a London merchant, as this required an ability to learn foreign languages and bookkeeping. In contrast, the thief and gambler, Richard Cumberland, did end up in the City but in a firm of bill-brokers on whose behalf he lent money to friends and acquaintances.[21]

It is thus evident that there was neither a full nor permanent realignment of the City in British culture in the early Victorian years. This can be seen from a reading of one of the publishing sensations of the time, G. W. M. Reynolds, *Mysteries of London,* which appeared in serial form between 1844 and 1856. In a series of interlinked episodes these stories touched upon many aspects of the City of London at the time. Though the City of London was recognized as 'the emporium of the world's commerce' it was not its trade and shipping that was the focus of Reynolds's attention. Instead it was the City's role in the promotion of new companies, the buying and selling of securities, and the fortunes made and lost as a result. Organising and manipulating all this were a 'multitudinous class called "City men", who possess no regular offices, but have their letters addressed to the Auction Mart or Garraway's, and who make their appointments at such places as "the front of the Bank", "the Custom-house wharf", and "under the clock at the Docks"'. One such was George Montague Greenwood.

> He was a City man : but if the reader be anxious to know what sort of business he transacted to obtain his living; whether he dabbled in the funds, sold wines upon commission, effected loans and discounts, speculated in shares, got up joint-stock companies, shipped goods to the colonies, purchased land in Australia at eighteen-pence an acre and sold it again at one-and-nine, conducted compromises for insolvent

tradesmen, made out the accounts of bankrupts, arbitrated between partners who disagreed, or bought in things in a friendly way at public sales; whether he followed any of these pursuits, or meddled a little with them all, we can no more satisfy our readers than if we attempted the biography of the man in the moon, – all we can say is, that he was invariably in the City from eleven to four; that he usually had 'an excellent thing in hand just at that moment'; and, in a word, that he belonged to the class denominated City men.[22]

What is conjured up by Reynolds is a view of the City as a place where a vast fortune could be made by those who began 'without a farthing', though how this was done remained rather mysterious. However, these fortunes were also very transitory if they involved company promotion or speculation, with those who failed becoming outcasts in the City, shunned or mocked by their ex-associates. The City was seen as a place where human feelings were absent and fraud was commonplace and acceptable. A career in the City led inevitably to failure or death. Greenwood is killed by his French ex-valet, while his brother, who had not gone into the City, enjoyed a happy, prosperous and rewarding life.[23]

It did appear impossible for the City to free itself from its association with financial fraud, no matter the regard accorded to merchants, the recognition that certain bankers were trustworthy, and the admiration of the power it possessed as the leading commercial and financial centre in the world. This ambiguity can be seen from Charlotte Brontë's 1853 novel, *Vilette* in which Lucy Snowe expressed her admiration of what she found in the City.

> Descending, I went wandering whither chance might lead, in a still ecstasy of freedom and enjoyment; and I got – I know not how – I got into the heart of city life. I saw and felt London at last: I got into the strand; I went up Cornhill; I mixed with the life passing along; I dared the perils of crossings. To do this, and to do it utterly alone, gave me, perhaps an irrational, but real pleasure. Since those days, I have seen the West-end, the parks, the fine squares; but I love the city far better. The City seems so much more in earnest: its business, its rush, its roar, are such serious things, sights, and sounds. The City is getting its living – the west-end but enjoying its pleasure. At the west-end you may be amused, but in the city you are deeply excited.

Conversely, in the same novel Mrs Bretton's relative poverty was explained by the fact that 'the handsome property of which she was left guardian for her son, and which had been chiefly invested in some joint-stock undertaking, had melted, it was said, to a fraction of its original amount'.[24] Similarly, in Thackeray's 1853–5 novel, *The Newcomes*, financial fraud and bank collapses are central themes, though a distinction is drawn between the different banks involved. On the one hand there were the cautious and respectable dealings of a well-established City bank, Hobson and Newcome, which had its origins in the cloth trade, and the more recent arrival, the rather mysterious Bundelcund Banking Company, that grew out of India and the activities of Rummun Loll of Calcutta. Hobson and

Newcome was run by Sir Barnes Newcome. 'though Sir Barnes Newcome was certainly neither amiable nor popular in the City of London, his reputation as a most intelligent man of business still stood; the credit of his house was deservedly high, and people banked with him, and traded with him, in spite of faithless wives and hostile colonels'. The Bundelcund Bank was run by an Indian, Rummun Loll, and a number of Anglo-Indian associates, including a cousin of Sir Barnes Newcome, Colonel Thomas Newcome. Unlike Sir Barnes the Colonel knew little about banking but was well liked and trusted by the investing public. Sir Barnes, as an experienced and clever banker, knew both when to get involved with the Bundelcund Bank and when to pull out, without letting sentiment or rivalry influence him. As he observed,

> 'Of course we will do these peoples' business as long as we are covered; but I have always told their manager that we would run no risks whatever, and to close the account the very moment it did not suit us to keep it: and so we parted company six weeks ago, since when there has been a panic in the Company, a panic increased by Colonel Newcome's absurd swagger and folly. He says I am his enemy; enemy indeed! So I am in private life, but what has that to do with business? In business, begad, there are no friends and no enemies at all. I leave all my sentiment on the other side of Temple Bar'.

Sentiment was not something that the public expected to find in the City as it was driven solely by established business practice. Thus Sir Barnes escaped untouched when the Bundelcund Bank was exposed as a fraud on the sudden death of Rummun Loll, as did the Anglo-Indian directors who had sold their shares in the Bank before the public had realized they were worthless. In contrast, the colonel lost all his money and possessions as did many innocent investors, who had been persuaded to buy shares because of their trust in him. The City was seen as a ruthless place where some made money and others lost.[25]

It was the City's ability to simultaneously enrich and impoverish people, and the social consequences of that, which continued to fascinate the public in the middle of the nineteenth century. This fascination was further fuelled by the nationwide frenzy for joint-stock company promotion and share dealing during the railway mania in the mid 1840s.[26] The positive side is captured in Thackeray's *The Diary of C. Jeames de la Pluche, esq*, which appeared in 1854, as one of the pieces is entitled *A Lucky Speculator*. It concerns a footman, James Plush, who made a fortune through speculating in railway shares. His employer was Sir George Flimsy, a banker who was a partner in the City firm of Flimsy, Diddler and Flash. Once Sir George realized that his footman had made £30,000 through his speculations all social barriers disappeared. The footman was invited to sit with the family, attend their social gatherings and court their daughter, Miss Emily Flimsy, while he became director of thirty-three railway companies and was chosen to stand for Parliament.[27] The dark side can be seen in *Yeast*, a novel by Charles Kingsley that was published in 1851. This condemned the entire system of finance conducted in the City of London, as exposed by the railway mania, though the main criticism was reserved for the banks. Lancelot Smith had been 'ruined to my last shilling' by the collapse of the London bank run by his uncle. As a result of rumours in the City that the bank was in trouble, depositors rushed to withdraw their savings. 'The house has sustained a frightful blow this week – railway speculations, so they say – and is hardly expected to survive the day. So we are all getting our money out as fast as possible ... every man for himself. A man is under no obligation to his banker that I know of'. The bank ran out of cash to meet those who wanted to make withdrawals and so was forced to close. 'The ancient firm of Smith, Brown, Jones, Robinson & Co., which had been for some years past expanding from a solid golden organism into a cobweb-tissue and huge balloon of threadbare paper, had at last worn through and collapsed, dropping its car and human contents miserably into the Thames mud'. Its collapse converted Lancelot from a rich man to a pauper overnight, as his savings had been deposited there. This led him to view the whole system of credit as practised in the City as fundamentally unstable and flawed. He told his uncle, 'Look at your credit system, how – not in its abuse, but its very essence – it carries the seeds of self-destruction. In the first place, a man's credit depends not upon his real worth and property, but upon his reputation for property; daily and hourly he is tempted, he is forced, to puff himself, to pretend that he is richer than he is'. In contrast, his uncle blamed it all on 'foreign railways'. This indicates that the place of the City in contemporary culture had become part of a wider debate about the growing materialism present in society, for it represented an obvious target for those who believed that individuals should focus more on the spiritual. A stranger present during this exchange of views, for example, suggested that what the City did was against the teachings of Christianity. 'Did I not warn you of the folly and sin of sinking capital in foreign countries while English land was crying out for tillage, and English poor for employment'. The stranger turned out to be Jesus in disguise gathering disciples for a new campaign to restore faith in traditional doctrines, with reform of the City being a priority. As the City was driven by self-interest rather than the common good, it was condemned as a proxy for all greedy and selfish behaviour.[28]

Nevertheless, unlike the 1820s, when little of value remained, the railway mania did leave a permanent reminder of what had been achieved. This was visible to all in the shape of railway lines that became an integral part of everyday life. As such it was impossible to ignore the beneficial legacy that the speculative outburst had produced. Even Kingsley's criticism attacked the City's promotion of foreign railways, which deprived British agriculture of investment and British workers of employment, even though this was a late and minor component of the mania. Consequently, there was no outright condemnation of the City in the wake of the railway mania in the same way as had happened in the past. The result was a much more balanced view of the City of London from contemporaries as the excesses, disappointments and losses of the mania faded and the benefits produced by railways became clear. Such a verdict can be seen from the 1850 novel by Robert Bell, *The Ladder of Gold*. This had the railway mania as its theme with the central character being modelled on Hudson, 'The Railway King', who was the most prominent promoter of the time, and experienced a dramatic rise and fall in the public's esteem. The novel did contain the usual attacks on the corrupting power of money as with the statement, 'Gold will buy up the consciences of men, and purchase homage for wealthy knavery, while honesty goes begging through the world', as well as expressing the traditional dislike of Jewish moneylenders. It also captured the mixed impression of London that the visitor from the country was left with because of its immense size, as it was both 'an extremely disagreeable and uncomfortable place' with its 'vast number of streets, the crowds, the din, the uproar' and a recognition that it was 'the great heart of commerce'. London could be all things to all men and this repelled some and impressed others.

The principal character in Bell's book, Richard Rawlings, lived in a provincial town, Yarlton, which was some distance from London, but he used a London lawyer, Tom Chippendale, to handle his financial affairs, after he became wealthy through an inheritance of his wife's.[29] Rawlings was a man who had begun with nothing and then amassed great wealth through hard work and the marriage to the rich widow of a local businessman. Despite his wealth, he spent only moderately and managed his investments very successfully. In contrast, the local landowner, the Earl of Dragonfelt and his son, Lord Valentine, were seen as spendthrift aristocrats. However, there was a sense that Rawlings was too much in love with making money, for the point was made that 'Men who regard money as a means to an end, seeking in other sources the true satisfaction of life, seldom grow rich … But men who regard money as the end itself, seldom fail'. The story began in 1830 when the repercussions of the 1825 speculative boom were still being felt. The leading local bank, Sarkens Brothers, had been weakened as a result of a series of bad loans contracted at that time, and this nearly brought them down when customers drew out savings during a subsequent poor harvest. The Bank of England had refused assistance, suggestive again of a continuing antagonism between provincial and metropolitan banking, and Sarkens Brothers had only been saved by borrowing extensively in London on mortgage.[30] Into this situation came railways.

> The whole country, from coast to coast, was to be traversed and dissected by iron roads; wherever there was a hamlet or a cattle-track, a market or a manufactory, there was to be a railroad; physical obstacles and private rights were straws under the chariot-wheels of the Fire-King; mountains were to be cut through as you would cut a

cheese; valleys were to be lifted; the skies were to be scaled; the earth was to be tun-
nelled; parks , gardens, and ornamental grounds were to be broken into; the shrieking
engine was to carry the riot of the town into the sylvan retreats of pastoral life; swel-
tering trains were to penetrate solitudes hitherto sacred to the ruins of antiquity;
hissing locomotives were to rush over the tops of houses; and it was not quite decided
whether an attempt would be made to run a railway to the moon.

Central to this process was the City of London as it was only there that the
finance and expertise was to be found that would bring these railway lines into
being.

A colony of solicitors, engineers, and seedy accountants had settled in the purlieus of
Threadneedle. Every town and parish in the kingdom blazed out in zinc plates on the
doorways. From the cellars to the roofs, every fragment of a room held its committee,
busy over maps and surveys, allotment and scrip ... to this focal centre were attracted
the rank and wealth, the beggary and the villainy of three respectable kingdoms. Men
who were never seen east of Temple-bar before, were now as familiar to the pavement
of Moorgate-street as the stockbrokers who flew about like messengers of doom, with
the fate of thousands clutched in scraps of dirty paper in their hands. Ladies of title,
lords, members of parliament, and fashionable loungers, thronged the noisy passages,
and were jostled by adventurers and gamblers, rogues and imposters.

Taking his opportunity Rawlings bought up the stock of an isolated local railway
and then, by linking it to other lines, transformed its prospects. In the process he
had to force the Earl of Dragonfelt to let the railway cross his land. This he did by
buying up the mortgages on the estate and then threatening to foreclose. By these
means he also acquired sufficient influence to become MP for the town, and
so moved to London, taking a house in Park Lane. Once in London Rawlings
became a focal point for the promotion of railway companies and speculation
in the shares that surrounded them. 'Railways at that moment occupied more
attention than any other topic, foreign or domestic, that was before the country,
because everybody hoped to make money out of them'. He was regarded as an
expert on the subject, 'the lion of the share-market ... every line with which Mr
Rawlings connected himself was up at a great premium'. This was attributed to
his skill and knowledge and so he was feted both by company promoters, who
wanted him to join their board, and by investors who bought shares in the companies with which he was associated. 'Whatever he touched turned to profit,
and the mines of wealth he ploughed seemed illimitable and inexhaustible'. As
a result of the widespread belief that Rawlings had become fabulously wealthy
because of his railway dealings, rapid social advancement followed. His wife was
invited to all the grand social gatherings and his two daughters were courted
by aristocratic young men, with a view to marriage. Those whom railways had
made wealthy were seen as fair game for those with aristocratic connections but
no money. In exchange, those who had become wealthy saw profit through an

alliance with the older gentry as it gave them a social position and respectability. One of those who courted Rawlings's daughters was Lord Charles Eton, who lacked a fortune of his own. This was a barrier to his political career as his uncle, Lord William Eton, explained. 'No man can aspire to a high position in England without the command of adequate resources. It is the vice of our system. The power of our aristocracy does not reside simply in a tradition – it is preserved and fortified by wealth'. As he had no fortune of his own until his uncle died and he inherited the estate his solution was to marry someone with wealth who would provide him with the means to advance his political career.

The woman he chose was Margaret, the younger daughter of Rawlings, but he had to justify his choice to a sceptical uncle.

> Mr. Rawlings has the command of enormous wealth; he is one of the richest commoners in England. I admit at once that his origin is obscure, but I never heard a breath against his reputation; he is shrewd, clever, and practical. I have met people of the highest rank at his house. Reflect upon these circumstances, and do not decide hastily upon a measure involving my future happiness and success in public life.

The uncle's response was,

> 'Now listen to me. I have heard you patiently. The daughter of this railway jobber has a large fortune. Well? Granted. There are fifty as good baking at this moment in the smoke of Manchester or Liverpool, who would average you a hundred thousand pounds, and would walk barefoot up to London for the chance of becoming Lady Charles Eton. Do you hold your station so cheap as to sell yourself in such a market as that? Are there no women in the aristocracy whose alliance would bring you wealth and influence, that you must fling yourself away upon a – it chokes me to think of it. I tell you at once, that such a degradation would put an end to our intercourse for ever! ... What! Marry the daughter of a railway gambler, picked up, probably, in the train, proposed for in a refreshment room, and the banns published at all the stations for the glorification of the chairman and directors. I shouldn't be half so outraged if you married a common girl out of the Opera'.

Nevertheless, Lord Charles was determined to marry the youngest daughter of Rawlings, claiming to love her, and so his uncle agreed to the match. Lord Charles then asked Rawlings for permission to marry his younger daughter, to which he agreed, despite the fact that Margaret was opposed, being in love with an old friend from Yarlton. However, Rawlings wanted the aristocratic connection and would accept no refusal, offering to settle a fortune of £50,000 on her when she married. He had already bought a country estate in Norfolk, Ravensdale, for himself.[31]

At that stage all was going well with Rawlings's railway schemes and he was reaping the financial and social benefits of success. However, the public became increasingly aware of a number of dubious practices associated with railway promotion. One was including on the committee those with titles but little wealth, in order to make the company appear well-supported by influential people. Another was to rig the markets so as to give the impression that that the shares were in demand. This was done through simultaneously issuing shares and then buying them back in the market at a premium. A final device was to pack share-holders' meetings with supporters so as to intimidate those likely to ask awkward questions. Knowing that such methods were in use to persuade investors to take up the issues of shares made insiders like Rawlings aware that their supposed wealth was based on fictitious values. Hence his desire to form an alliance with the aristocracy as he believed this would help him when the crash came, as well as settling money on his daughter and the purchase of land. As it was the inevitable collapse of the speculative bubble came. 'The crash was as instantaneous as the collapse of a balloon', and it had the usual consequences. 'The mass of the specula-tors were ruined; and a few crafty hands had amassed enormous wealth'. Rawlings was now seen as a villain and those who had lost money or resented his rapid advance wanted him punished. This led Lord Charles to try and prevent his wife from having any connection with her family as he believed his reputation was being damaged by association with Rawlings. However, she refused and Rawl-ings refuted all allegations, regarding them as 'malicious rumours set afloat by a mob of disappointed speculators, who are turning round upon every man that happened to be more fortunate or sagacious than themselves'. What Rawlings saw was the hypocrisy of Lord Charles and his uncle, who now wanted to disas-sociate themselves from him, because of the whiff of scandal, whereas before they were happy to be associated because of the wealth and connections it brought. Rawlings was not dropped by all those who had courted his acquaintance when he was successful, despite the fact that he had lost most of his fortune when the bubble burst. Mr Farquhar, who possessed an established fortune of his own, still wanted to marry Rawlings's other daughter, Clara, whether she came with money or not. By now Rawlings greatly regretted forcing his other daughter, Margaret, to marry Lord Charles rather than her childhood sweetheart, Henry Winston. He thus readily agreed to this marriage as it secured Clara's future. Eventually Lord Charles is challenged to a duel by Margaret's childhood sweetheart because of the way she was being treated by her husband. Lord Charles was killed in the duel leaving Margaret free to marry Winston in the future. The story ended with Rawlings re-establishing himself as a successful businessman through hard work and perseverance while avoiding all speculative schemes.[32]

What emerges from Bell's fictional account of the railway mania was an attack on speculation, which was seen as corrupting or destroying all involved. However, this was not a condemnation of the City of London as a whole, only certain of the processes associated with the promotion of companies and dealing in securities, while the concern over banking failures was more provincial than metropolitan. British culture had taken on board the advantages that flowed from trade and industry, and so respected those who conducted it, while the landed aristocracy were seen as wasteful in the way they spent money that they neither earned nor even possessed, leading to debt and decline. They were also seen as obstacles to progress, in opposing the construction of railway lines over their land, but hypocritical in their willingness to benefit from the money they received when granting such rights. This hypocrisy also extended to the speed with which they embraced the new men of wealth, including marriage, and then disowned the connections when they no longer served their purpose. The railway mania did appear to represent a change in attitude towards the City. The City of London was not fully rehabilitated as a result, because of the excesses of the mania and the losses experienced by many investors, but there was an acceptance that it was not entirely populated with rogues, even among those involved in money and finance, while spendthrift aristocrats were fully deserving of criticism. Such a verdict can also be found in the 1854 novel by Mrs Gore, *The Money Lender*. A central character in the novel was Abednego Osalez, who operated as both a common moneylender and an international banker, occupying simultaneously a dilapidated house in the East End of London and a fine mansion in the West End. This reflected the enormous disparity to be found in London on each side of the City. To the west were to be found the homes of the wealthy while, to the east, 'the wilds of Moorgate', was an area consisting of dirty and unkempt slum dwellings and second hand shops and populated by poor, working-class people. This also reflected the polarized views on the City as it was populated by both despised money lenders and respected international financiers.

Osalez was commonly supposed to be a Jew and despised by all accordingly, as Jews were regarded as little better than 'fish-women, chickweed-boys, scavengers' carts and letter carriers' Even worse was the fact that Osalez was a moneylender, a 'detestable' occupation, but one which he was happy to pursue because of the wealth and power it gave him. To Osalez, 'Everything is to be had for money, if applied with the same intelligence that gathered it together'. His was the philosophy of the middleman. 'I buy whatever I can buy cheap, and sell it whenever I can sell it dear'. He lent money at high rates of interest to individuals, secured on the deposit of possessions like jewels and works of art, which he would then sell for much more than the loan when it was not repaid. This made him despised by all, including those to whom he lent money, such the Duke of Rochester, who was now in his power because of constant borrowing to maintain an extravagant lifestyle. In return, Osalez despised those to whom he lent money. They were unable to live within their ample means because of an addiction to a profligate lifestyle and to gambling. As long as such people spent freely they had numerous friends and were well thought of. However, once the money ran out it ended in bankruptcy with the mortgaged estates being sold, the houses let, and the family moving abroad to live a cheaper and quieter life on the money they were able to salvage, once all the debts had been paid. The Duke of Rochester, with a rent-roll of £50,000 per annum, could not live within it and so fled to Italy when he had exhausted all sources of borrowing. He left behind numerous unpaid debts to small tradespeople, who suffered badly as a result. British culture in the 1850s was turning against the aristocracy because of its excesses rather than finding its usual villains in the City of London.

Basil Annesley, an army officer from an aristocratic family, also began to see another aspect of Osalez as he got to know him. This aspect was not only Osalez's discretionary lending to those in need but also, and more importantly, his operations in international finance. Annesley recognized that 'Money is indeed power'. Bankers, not kings or politicians, were seen as the 'real potentates of modern times who sway the destinies of nations and individuals with a rod of gold, and issue their decrees in bank-notes and Exchequer bills'. From the City, Osalez conducted an extensive business in international finance. Annesley visited him there, passing through the constant traffic in Cheapside, and the 'narrow, dirty, dingy' streets leading to offices and warehouses. Having been directed to Osalez's office in Old Jewry,

Basil proceeded through the gorge of a narrow court into a larger one, surrounded by high buildings, one side of which seemed occupied by a handsome old-fashioned dwelling house, and the other by a range of buildings, the basement story of which was appropriated to counting-houses. Of this portion of the mansion, the huge swing-doors seemed in continual vibration to admit or emit a perpetual string of human beings – the sort of careworn, sallow-cheeked people who walk with their coats closely buttoned over their pockets, and their blank visages indicating a mind wandering at many miles' distance, whom one recognizes at first sight as the children of Mammon. Unnoticed, – for such people proceed straight to their place of rendezvous, without a vacant thought to bestow on auguries of the flight of crows or sight of strange faces, – Basil pushed his way through the swing-doors among the rest; and, after passing a second swing-door, found himself in a vast sky-lighted chamber, containing by way of furniture, a large timepiece against the wall, three long ranges of wooden counters, forty wooden stools, and forty wooden clerks seated calculating thereupon; each with his parchment-bound ledger before him, each with his multiplication-table engraved on his soul in characters effacing even those of the tables of the law. In the centre of the hall, was a single mahogany desk and stool loftier than the rest, apparently destined to the use of the high-priest of the temple of Mammon. But it was vacant. Clerks were hustling backwards and forwards, with chequebooks, or pocket-books, or printed papers in their hands; apparently as mechanical in operations involving the disposal of millions, as the timepiece against the wall in admeasurement of the still more valuable currency assigned its computation. A buzz of whispers, never rising into unbusiness-like tumult, seemed to form a portion of the heated and unsavoury atmosphere of the place; the money shovelled backwards and forwards across the gated pay-counter, being of no more account in the eyes of

the individuals occupied in promoting its circulation, than barley-sugar in those of
the confectioner's boy to whom prohibition has ceased to be irksome.

Despite the appearance of buildings in the City, and the anonymity of most of
those carrying on business there, Annesley felt ' – it is probable that a larger
amount of capital passed through every one of those shabby doorways in the
course of a week than into any mansion in St. James's square in the period of a
year'.

However, Annesley was even more impressed when he visited Osalez in his
townhouse in Russell Square, where he entertained important visitors from the
highest political circles in Britain and the most important people in continental
finance. Osalez was in direct contact with Downing Street, for example. After a
meal at Osalez's house Annesley comprehended the wealth and power of those
in the City. It was those in the City who could afford the finest food and wine,
and the staff to prepare and organize it, rather than those in the West End. 'Billingsgate, Smithfield, and Farringdon, despatched to the West End only their
refuse produce, after dedicating the finest to the heavier purses of the aristocracy
of Guildhall'. Similarly, from listening to the conversation of City financiers at
the dinner, Annesley understood the global reach of the City.

> Hitherto his notions of 'the world' might have been geographically defined as
> 'bounded on the north by Marylebone, on the south by Lambeth, the east by St. Mar-
> tin's-lane, the west by Kensington gardens. But he now heard Australia, America and
> China familiarly talked of as lying within the ring-fence of the kingdom of Mammon.
> India seemed regarded as a home farm by these old gentlemen; and the Spice Islands
> as their flower-garden. Their caravans were traversing the wilderness, like the private
> post of some lordly establishment. As to Europe, – poor, commonplace, domes-
> tic Europe, – each had his courier galloping homewards from Petersburg, Vienna,
> Berlin, like Horse Guards' estafettes, trotting backwards and forwards to Hampton
> Court or Hounslow. As to Paris, it was a toy; a snuff-box that seemed to lie in the
> waistcoat-pocket.

It became apparent that it was those in City who were

> the master hands that move the wires of kingly puppets; the mainsprings of aris-
> tocratic action; without whom, privy-councils and parliaments might mouth and
> gibber in vain; the veritable monarchs who make peace and war; the potentates who
> created the independence of America, who rendered France a citizen kingdom, and
> would do as much for the British Empire, had peer-ridden England the smallest taste
> for enfranchisement'. Such people as these '...continued to treat of kings and minis-
> ters in all quarters of the globe, as so many implements for coining in the hands of
> those real masters of the world, the money-mongers of its various exchanges.

By the mid-1850s the British people had become impressed by the power that
the City wielded. Annesley was almost awestruck to be in the company of 'great

financial operators, whose electric wires communicated from one end of the world to the other'. Suddenly, he met in real life people he had only read about before.

> The names by which he heard his companions addressed, were familiar to him attached to loans and other gigantic financial operations, announced by the papers as having audiences of the Chancellor of the Exchequer; men whose signatures, inscribed on a sheet of paper, create a railroad that is to facilitate the intercommunication of kingdoms, – an Argentine Republic, – a county hospital, – or an insurrection in Cochin China!

He listened with amazement as

> They talked of the politics of Europe as men talk of the moves of a game of chess; of sovereigns, as if the ivory or ebony or boxwood pieces of the board. The identity of such privileged portions of human nature was evidently unimportant to their calculations. To the high priest of Mammon, there was no Nicholas, – no Francis, – no Frederick William, – but in their places – Prussia, Hardenberg and Co., – Austria, Metternich and Co., Prussia, Nesselrode, et hoc. Of money itself, under the august name of Capital, they treated as he had never heard it treated before, as an end and not a mean; and millions sounded in their mouths less than the ponies or pounds, he was accustomed to hear betted elsewhere. In the arguments of that singular coterie, there was matter to drive thrice as many political economists to distraction!

All this was in great contrast to the trivial nature of a normal dinner conversation which consisted of political news, stock exchange tips and general gossip.[33]

These City financiers were largely of foreign origin and all were equally familiar with the main European languages, French, Italian, German, as they were with English. Osalez's father and grandfather had been very successful merchants in Cadiz. His grandfather had been a Jew but became a Christian on his marriage to a protestant. However, bearing a Jewish name and with a Jewish appearance, the family continued to be regarded as Jewish, and so was ostracized by the Christian community, while the Jewish community did the same because of the conversion. To escape this dual persecution Osalez was sent to Eton to be educated, especially as the family's main business was trading between Spain and England. This was prompted by a belief that commerce was more respected in England than in Spain, and thus those who made their fortune that way would be more respected. Though Osalez gained admittance to Eton and then Oxford, eventually becoming an MP, his father having bought him a seat, he was never accepted into society. He was continually labelled a Jew and suffered constant insults as a result, being excluded from the normal participation in social circles, whether at school, university or afterwards. This included aristocratic families refusing to countenance marriage with any of their daughters. Stung by these repeated slights Osalez decided to forgo society and concentrate on making money. On the death of his father he had disposed of his Spanish property and opened an office in London as a stockbroker. In addition, he started operating as a money lender. This was only a pastime but it gave him power over those who had treated him badly. As he grew older Osalez became reconciled to his position, and decided to forgive both those who had persecuted him and his family, with whom he had become estranged. By giving one niece, Salome, a large dowry, she was able to marry an Austrian count, Count von Ehrenstein. He did the same for another, Ester, who married Basil Annesley, whose mother was the daughter of a Duke and whose father had been a general. It was Basil's mother's family that had rejected Osalez as a prospective son-in-law many years before, because of his Jewish origins, whereas now such a marriage was considered acceptable.[34]

Though the presence of both Jews and foreigners in the City continued to damn it in the eyes of many, a change did appear to have occurred in the mid-nineteenth century. At the very least those Jews who had settled in Britain and converted to Christianity were deemed acceptable, leading even to intermarriage. Even a case could be made out for money lending, though it, along with stock exchange speculation, remained of dubious value and not to be undertaken by respectable people.[35] In contrast, the association of the City with international finance, and the power and influence that gave to England, was seen in a positive light. The Rothschilds may have been both foreign and Jewish but their financial activities benefited England, and that was now recognized. A similar change in attitude towards City banking in general as can be seen in the 1856 novel by Emma Robinson, *The City Banker*. Though being set in London, and involving a City banker and his family, there is a noticeable absence of any obvious antagonism because of their involvement with the world of money. In fact, they come across more as sinned against than sinning. The story revolved around the Mulgrave family. Sir Peter Mulgrave was the sole partner in a private City bank, which he had made very successful 'by bold and fortunate speculation'. The result was he became very wealthy, a millionaire, being referred to 'one of the wealthiest money-traders in England'. This gave him social aspirations, acquiring a large country estate as well as a house in town. Having achieved that he set his sights on contracting a good marriage for his eldest son.

> Like many other representatives of the great moneyed class in this country, Sir Peter Mulgrave had no sooner attained wealth, than he desired to ally it with aristocracy. He formed a purpose, that finally became a fanatic resolve, and the main object of his life – to become himself the founder of a family which should rank with the proudest in the land. He thought it necessary to begin with an exaggeration of the injustice, without which, it is said, an aristocracy cannot flourish long. He determined to make his eldest son the centre of his grand aims, and the principal depository of his accumulated wealth. Oliver Mulgrave, the younger son, was accordingly condemned to the training and drudgery of a person but little raised above the condition of a clerk in his father's establishment. His elder brother was brought up, meanwhile, in all

the notions and profuse habits of expense and luxury of the heir of a great family. A commission was procured for him in the Guards, and every species of indulgence and liberty was accorded to him. This plan succeeded equally ill with both brothers. Valentine Mulgrave became a spendthrift and prodigal, and perhaps something worse than either. And though his habits and necessities kept him a slave of his father's will, it was with no very good result. He married against his own inclinations, in accordance with his father's commands and selection, a lady of very high birth and connexions – with whom he led a most unhappy life for a few years; and was finally killed in a duel which her provoking manner and arrogance compelled him to fight with a German Count of equal pretensions; without leaving any acknowledged lawful issue behind him. Meanwhile, Oliver, naturally indignant at the preference shown to his brother, with views so unfair, broke into a rebellion, which he completed by an act the most offensive possible to his aspiring sire. He married the daughter of a bankrupt City merchant, to whom he had been permitted to pay his addresses at a time when the father was reputed nearly as rich as his own. And this he did shortly after the unexpected death of Captain Mulgrave had transferred all Sir Peter's ambitious hopes and purposes of fulfilment upon him. The result was an estrangement and separation between the father and son; which had now lasted so long a period, that scarcely an idea could be entertained of their ever coming to a reconciliation. Such might have been possible, however, had not Oliver's five children most unfortunately persisted in all being girls![36]

Having been cast out by his father, Oliver Mulgrave had joined a London joint stock bank, which was much less prestigious than being owner of a private bank. This led his father to resent him even more as he was now a business rival. Though Sir Peter's bank was in Lombard Street, in the City, it did a mainly personal business, lending money to individual customers, and so was vulnerable to competition from the growing number of joint stock banks. In Sir Peter's opinion Oliver was an 'unnatural son who has even attempted to rival me in my own walk, and has established an opposition house that prospers against me, principally by means of his knowledge of the secrets of my business and connexions'. 'Oliver Mulgrave had, indeed, become the chairman of a flourishing joint-stock bank in the immediate neighbourhood of his father's, but this was merely an accident of the limited locality in which offices of the kind are usually established in the City, and the confidence placed in his skill and integrity by large classes of the mercantile community'. As a result, Sir Peter, who was a widower, had decided to remarry in the hope of producing an heir, as he did not want Oliver to inherit. Being a wealthy banker, it was suggested that Sir Peter could have his pick of any unmarried women.

There was not a mother among the wealthy and even titled circles in which he moved, who would not willingly have offered the pick of their daughters to the rich banker. Scarcely a daughter among those youthful bevies, who would not have been the willing *Danae*, to be exposed and carried off in the clutches of the monster of gold, to whatever devouring doom. The inordinate worship and admiration among us, has withered even the dewy freshness and sweetness of our virgins' hearts. They sell themselves – that is their only distinction from their sisters standing at a price in the marketplaces of the east. However, Sir Peter ended up being ensnared in a plot devised by his confidential clerk, Rignol Blackadder. He introduced Sir Peter to a Mrs Snareswell, who appeared in the guise of a respectable widow, whose two children had drowned in a tragic accident. In reality she was an actress with an illegitimate daughter, fathered by Blackadder. They expected to profit from the arrangement when Sir Peter died, as he was already over 70, leaving Mrs Snarewell a wealthy widow.[37]

However, the plan failed when it was discovered that Blackadder had been embezzling money from the bank and using it to make loans to individuals at very high rates of interest. As the managing clerk he was in a position to steal, especially as Sir Peter had become too infirm in body and mind to pay attention to the details of the business. When this was discovered Blackadder was apprehended by the police. Having fallen out with Mrs Snarewell, who fled to the Continent with a young admirer, he confessed to the whole plan. The shock killed Sir Peter but not before making his son Oliver 'the head of the firm of Mulgrave and Holtwhistle, one of the most flourishing private banking establishments in England'. In the meantime it had been discovered that Sir Peter's other son, Valentine, had secretly married a country girl called Clarice Avery and this produced a male child, also called Valentine. This wife had died, leaving him free to make the marriage that his father had insisted on. The son had been brought up in ignorance of his real father by his wife's family in Devon. He became wealthy overnight, when he discovered pirate treasure on a shipping expedition to Madagascar. He then married Florence Sufton, whose father was a wealthy London merchant who had bought, on retirement, the estate of Apple Florey, in Devon, including the village where Valentine lived. Sir Peter also recognized Valentine as his grandson on his deathbed.[38] What emerges from a story of this kind is a City of London that is both stable and respectable. This view can be supported by the fact that in *A Rogue's Life*, which was published in 1856, Wilkie Collins omitted any potential areas of wrongdoing associated with the City.[39] Banking, in particular was now seen to be a necessary business, especially a well-run private bank as opposed to the new upstarts, the joint stock banks. Both City merchants and bankers were seen as people who had amassed wealth through legitimate means and used it to secure both their family's future and their place in society by purchasing country estates and intermarrying with the established gentry. Not only was the City merchant seen as conservative and trustworthy but the banker was now perceived in the same way. The international financier, also located in the City, was seen as bringing power and prestige to Britain. Money lending remained beyond the pale, and Jews had yet to receive full acceptance, but even they did not provoke the hostility found in the past.

This suggests that by the mid-1850s British culture was mirroring the economy in making the transition from having an inward-looking, rural and agricultural bias to one that accepted the reality of urban and industrial life and the importance of global connections. In the process the City of London was recognized as performing a useful and important role, though the excesses of company promotion and speculation remained a scar on its collective reputation. The focus of hostility shifted from the City to the aristocracy, because of their extravagant lifestyles and their willingness to prostitute themselves for the sake of material gain, while criticizing those who were making the money that they themselves spent so freely. There was also a recognition that poverty existed among plenty and that many people continued to experience hard and difficult lives, as in the workshops and putting-out trades in London or the industrial workers in northern England. No group within society appeared to be absolved from blame for current difficulties, with the City of London being included among a number of possible candidates. This suggests that economy drove culture rather than the reverse, and that the City of London was not viewed with indifference but in a positive light as an integral part of British life, for all its faults. However, if this was the case it would be expected that there would be a steady improvement in the position of the City of London within British culture in the decades to come. In particular, the likes of the Stock Exchange and joint-stock banking would rise in public esteem as they became ever more central to the activities conducted in the City.

2 FINANCIERS AND MERCHANTS, 1856–1870

By the mid-1850s the City of London had established itself as the most important financial centre in the world, though it continued to face rivalry from Amsterdam and, especially, Paris. It also remained a very important commercial centre, being the world's largest port, benefiting from Britain's dominant position in international trade. Domestically, the railways and the telegraph permitted those in London to receive and transmit news and orders to and from all parts of the kingdom, facilitating the integration of markets to a degree never before attained. Generally, fundamental forces were working to enhance the importance of the City in the country's external and internal commercial, financial and business affairs. Banking, for example, was increasingly conducted through branches directed from London head offices. Tangible evidence of the impact made by London on the entire British population, rather than those living within its vicinity or the small aristocratic elite who were regular visitors, was the Great Exhibition of 1851. This received a huge number of visitors from across the country, as well as generating vast publicity. Local enterprise and local business did continue to flourish, as with the continuing importance of locally-run banks and stock exchanges, but they were increasingly responsive to a lead from London. In terms of culture this could have a number of repercussions. On the one hand it might generate an admiration for the City as the most powerful and successful commercial and financial centre in the world. On the other hand the growing influence of the City over the nation's well being might stimulate resentment because the loss of local autonomy. Both reactions were possible and so it is important to determine which came to dominate. Conversely, it is possible that neither of these fundamental changes in the City's international and domestic role were responsible for its place in contemporary culture. Instead, it could be events that determined attitudes. In particular, this period saw the spread of joint stock enterprise away from the likes of railways into other types of business, such as mining and manufacturing, in response to the passing of the Limited Liability Acts. A number of the companies formed in London proved a great disappointment to investors. The period also witnessed not only a speculative boom, focusing especially on the shares of joint stock companies, but also a banking crisis in 1866 with the collapse of Overend Gurney. This was a firm of discount brokers whose operations placed them at the heart of the London money market, and so their collapse had devastating consequences for banking both at home and abroad. As the partners in Overend Gurney had converted their business into a joint stock company with limited liability only the year before, leaving the new investors to bear the loss, its collapse did much to damage the emerging reputation of the City as a place of stability and honesty. Finally, neither positive fundamentals nor negative events might have had any impact on altering the position of the City within contemporary British culture between 1856 and 1870. Instead, the continuing association of the City with the likes of money and speculation, and the presence there of foreigners and Jews, might preclude any real change in attitudes, suggesting that culture was impermeable to economic influences of any kind, apart from at a very transitory and superficial level.[1]

One author whose work provides some clues to the answer was Charles Dickens, though his novels rarely address the activities of those in the City with any detail. In *Our Mutual Friend*, which dated from 1864–5, he described the working day of Mr Podsnap, who was in marine insurance, as 'got up at eight, shaved close at a quarter past, breakfasted at nine, went to the City at ten, came home at half-past five, and dined at seven'.[2] Beyond that the City activities of Mr Podsnap were a mystery. It was only in dealing with the activities of bankers and company promoters in this period that Dickens touched upon the City though, again, with little detail, as with Mr Merdle in the 1857 novel, *Little Dorrit*. Merdle was admired because of his global power and influence. '[H]is daily occupation of causing the British name to be more and more respected in all parts of the civilized globe capable of the appreciation of world wide commercial enterprise and gigantic combinations of skill and capital'. Conversely, he was distrusted because 'nobody knew with the least precision what Mr Merdle's business was, except that it was to coin money'. With the use of the word 'coin' the suggestion is made that a City financier was akin to a forger, whose products were fake. This latter judgement is confirmed when Merdle's bank failed, resulting in numerous small investors losing their money, and Merdle being exposed as a crooked financier. He committed suicide, so as to avoid public humiliation, leaving a note to explain his actions. 'The Inquest was over, the letter was public, the Bank was broken, the other model structures of straw had taken fire and were turned to smoke'. The final verdict on Merdle was left to his butler: 'Mr Merdle never was the gentleman'.[3] The view was certainly being expressed that certain practices of those in the City did not bear close inspection.

As it was not only Dickens who took up the themes of speculation, company promotion and banking collapse in the City from the mid-1850s, this suggests that it was events such as the rise, fall and suicide of a prominent City financier like Sadlier that were instrumental in determining the prevailing view of the City.[4] This was central to Charles Lever's 1859 novel, *Davenport Dunn*. The character, Davenport Dunn, was a company promoter whose activities took him from his native Ireland to London, as was the case with Sadlier. Davenport Dunn, through hard word and sheer ability, carved out for himself a successful position as a lawyer in Dublin. He then branched out into finance, including property speculation and joint stock company promotion 'starting thus from an humble attorney in a country town, he gradually grew to be known as a most capable adviser in all monetary matters; rich men consulted him about profitable investments and safe employment of their capital; embarrassed men confided to him their difficulties, and sought his aid to meet them; speculators asked his advice as to this or that venture; and even those who gambled on the eventful fortunes of a ministry were fain to be guided by his wise predictions'. What emerges is the continuing view that money had the power to surmount social barriers. According to Lady Lackington, 'Now one knows horrid people when they are very rich, or very well versed in some speculation or other – mines, or railroads, or the like'. One such person was Davenport Dunn who had given Lady Lackington valuable advice on her investments, with the result that she had made money speculating in mining shares and Guatemala State bonds. This encouraged others of her class to cultivate his acquaintance, invite him to dinner and accept his invitations in return, in the expectation of profiting similarly from his knowledge and advice. Though he was seen to be socially inferior, and lacking in taste, the fact that he had money and the ability to enrich others, overcame all such obstacles.[5]

Dunn was believed to be able to work magic with his ability to float a company, raise the finance, and make fortunes for all. This led the impoverished Lord Glengarriff to invite him to stay at his country house in the hope that he would take up a pet scheme of his, which was to turn the area into a tourist resort and harbour rivalling anything on the Continent. So impressed was Lord Glengariff with Dunn's plans to float a company, The Grand Glengariff Villa Allotment and Marine Residence Company, that he agreed to let his daughter, Lady Augusta, marry Dunn. This was in spite of his original belief that somebody like Dunn could not buy his way into the top ranks of society, which was occupied by himself and his children. The daughter had a different view, having given up hope of securing a favourable marriage from within her own social group, and seeing Dunn as an acceptable alternative. Dunn believed a marriage such as this would secure his position in society, allowing him not only to enter the landowning classes but be accepted there. He also calculated that it would improve his business by providing him with a wider circle of connections. Powerful connections could 'make a swindling railroad contractor the first man in London'. Initially the scheme was a success with £723,000 being raised when the company was floated in London. There were grandiose plans for a hydropathic establishment and a casino on the site, along with a lead mine and a marble quarry, while stories spread that a variety of important lords and ladies, including the Queen, were rushing to commission houses for themselves in such a spot. This encouraged others to commission their own houses and the shares reached a premium in the market.[6]

By this stage Dunn was based in London, from where he was directing his operations. He had rented a splendid house in Piccadilly and entertained lavishly, attracting the titled in society.

> Dunn's house was a sort of Bourse, where shares were trafficked in, and securities bought and sold, with an eagerness none the less that the fingers that held them wore gloves fastened with rubies and emeralds. In those gorgeous drawing-rooms, filled with objects of high art, statues stolen from the Vatican, gems obtained by Heaven knows what stratagems from Italian and Spanish convents, none deigned to notice by even a passing look the treasures that surrounded them. In vain the heavenly beauty of Raphael beamed from the walls – in vain the seductive glances of Greuze in all their languishing voluptuousness – in vain the haughty nobility of Van Dyck claimed the homage of a passing look. All were eagerly bent upon lists of stocks and shares, and no words were heard save such as told of rise or fall – the alternations of that chance which makes or mars humanity.

All in society who could obtain an invitation came to Dunn's London house in the hope of hearing something to their advantage, as in this reported conversation. "'Chimbarago Artesian Well and Water Company'", lisped out a very pale, sickly-looking Countess. "Shares are rising, Mr. Dunn; may I venture upon them?'" Dunn also possessed great influence in political circles through his ability to finance projects, especially those in his native Ireland. As the Prime Minister told Dunn, when he let him know that the award of a title was possible, 'we honour the industrial spirit of our country by ennobling one who has acquired a colossal fortune by his own unaided abilities' but added that it was a matter of balancing conflicting demands as 'Manchester and Birmingham have also their "millionaires"'.[7]

Dunn had made the transition from provincial to metropolitan finance, established himself as a successful company promoter in the City, and brought to fruition a number of schemes that contributed to the prosperity of the country. This suggests that the position of the City within British culture was continuing to be cemented. The City was seen as a means through which dynamic individuals like Davenport Dunn could rise quickly to positions of wealth and influence, displacing the likes of penniless aristocrats like Lord Glengariff in the process. Money alone secured the acceptance of such people while the projects they promoted were solid, beneficial, and British, involving such laudable aims as land irrigation, port development, tin and lead mining, strawberry growing and holiday resorts. However, the story of Davenport Dunn also reveals a reawakening of a view of the City as a centre of wasteful speculation akin to gambling, the creation of bubble companies that soon disappeared leaving investors with nothing, and the collapse of banks bringing losses to all involved. Reference is made to London financiers whose frauds had been exposed, such as a railway promoter, Lionel Redlines, caught as he tried to flee the country on a Liverpool steamer bound for the USA, and the banker, Sir John Chesham, sentenced to be transported to Australia. What increasingly dominates the novel, *Davenport Dunn*, is the seamy side of finance in which the public were being duped through false claims in prospectuses and false markets in shares. The comment was made that, 'The imaginative literature of speculation – industrial fiction it might be called – has reached a very high development in our day'. Generally, company promotion and share speculation was seen as analogous to horse-racing and gambling, with stories about the two being juxtaposed. This led to the final verdict that,

> So intensely had the money-getting passion taken possession of the national mind – so associated had national prosperity seemed to be with individual wealth – that nothing appeared great, noble, or desirable but gold, and the standard of material value was constituted to be the standard of all moral excellence; intending to honour industry, the nation paid its homage to Money![8]

The result was a gradual unravelling of all Dunn's projects as rumours started to circulate that they were not securely based but involved a pyramid of credit. In order to forestall the collapse of one of his main companies, the Ossory Bank, located not in London but Kilkenny in Ireland, Dunn himself arranged to have rumours circulated stating that this bank was in trouble. These rumours led to a run on the bank as depositors rushed to withdraw their savings, with a vivid description being given of a huge crowd assembling in front of the bank in a desperate attempt to withdraw savings and convert the bank's notes into gold before the bank closed its doors forever. However, having made preparations for such an event, by secretly shipping in cash over the previous days, the bank was able to pay everybody and the crowd melted away. The bank's reputation was enhanced, and Dunn emerged a hero. When new fears about the financial state of the bank circulated again they were not believed, even though they were true. Though clearly dishonest, Dunn believed that any action he took was justified because his schemes were undertaken for the benefit of Ireland rather than to make money for himself. The Ossory Bank, for example, flourished after the first crisis, with deposits growing and lending increasing, to the benefit of all. The problem was that Dunn had used the bank for his own purposes, and so jeopardized its long-term survival. In particular, he was supporting a false market in the shares of his other companies by employing the bank's money to purchase those being sold by worried investors. Thus the bank was heavily dependent upon the price of shares as most of its money was tied up either in holding these shares or in providing loans where such shares acted as collateral.

The vast number of those enterprises in which Dunn was engaged had eventually blended and mingled all their interests together. Estates and shipping, and banks, mines, railroads, and dock companies, had so often interchanged their securities, each bolstering up the credit of the other in turn, that the whole resembled some immense fortress, where the garrison, too weak for a general defence, was always hastening to some point or other – the seat of immediate attack. And thus an Irish draining fund was one day called upon to liquidate the demands upon a sub-Alpine railroad, while a Mexican tin mine flew to the rescue of a hosiery scheme in Balbriggan.

Only Dunn could master the '...complicated details of figures, intricate and tangled schemes of finance...' This made the tangled web of finance dependent upon him, with any crack in the edifice bringing the whole structure down.[9]

What Lever reveals is a contemporary belief that nothing in the City was substantial and all was dependent upon the skill of one man, who employed increasingly dishonest techniques in order to obscure the real state of affairs. If he failed, collapse and exposure was inevitable, followed by flight or prison. At one stage Dunn had taken a berth on the *Artic*, a ship bound from Liverpool to the USA, in case problems arose that he could not deal with. It was important for Dunn to maintain the façade that all was well. He assured everyone that he had no problems raising money as 'Baring, Hope, Rothschild, any of them would assist me with millions, if I needed them' However, his schemes were being jeopardized by a sudden tightening of credit in the money market. 'Down goes credit, and up go the discounts; the mighty men of millions have drawn their purse-strings, and not a guinea is to be had; the City is full of sad-visaged men in black, presaging every manner of misfortune'. Dunn confessed to his father, 'Well, Sir, last week was a very threatening one for us. No money to be had on any terms, discounts all suspended, shares falling everywhere, good houses crashing on all sides, nothing but disasters with every post, but we've worked through it, Sir'. Dunn received financial aid from his associate on the Continent, Glumthal, and political support from the Prime Minister for the Glengariff scheme. In addition, he resorted to more criminal measures in order to shore up his position, as he needed more money to support the share prices of his companies. As a lawyer he held the title deeds of a number of estates, and he used these without the owners' consent. He used Lord Glengariff's estate as collateral for a loan of £36,000, while he sold an estate belonging to Lord Lackington, an Anglo-Irish peer, who was abroad at the time, and paid the money into his own account.[10]

By marshalling all these resources, whether legal or illegal, Dunn survived the financial crisis. In the process he managed to secure around £2 million for himself, had the promise of a peerage from the Prime Minister, and was on the verge of marrying the daughter of an Irish Lord. The fact that his companies were on the verge of collapse, ruining numerous people as a result, did not concern him as he had now achieved the position that he had long worked for. This achievement drew admiration from his confidential agent, Simeon Hankes, in conversation with a friend. He referred to Dunn as a 'genius' and 'the cleverest man in England'.

> 'Just think for a moment what a head it must have been that kept that machinery at work for years back without a flaw or a crack to be detected, started companies, opened banks, worked mines, railroads, and telegraphs, built refuge harbours, drained whole counties, brought vast tracks of waste land into cultivation, equalizing the chances of all enterprises by making the success of this come to the aid of the failure of that: the grand secret of the whole being the dexterous application of what is called "Credit".'

Even when it all collapsed he predicted that Dunn would escape unscathed.

> 'When the crash comes – it will be in less than a month from this day – the world will discover that they're done to the tune of between three and four millions sterling, and I defy the best accountant that ever stepped to trace out where the frauds originated, whether it was the Railways smashed the Mines, the Mines that ruined the Great Ossory, the Great Ossory that dipped the Drainage, or the Drainage that swamped the Glengariff, not to speak of all the accidental confusion about estates never paid for, and sums advanced on mock mortgage, together with cancelled scrip re-issued, preference shares circulated before the current ones, and dock warrants for goods that never existed ... there isn't a class nor condition in life, from the peer to the labouring man, that he hasn't in some way involved in his rogueries, and made him a partner in the success. Each speculation being dependent for its solvency on the ruin of some other, Ossory will hate Glengariff, Drainage detest mines, Railways curse Patent Fuel, and so on. I'll give the Equity Court and the Bankrupt Commissioners fifty years and they'll not wind up the concern.'

All that would happen was that Dunn would have to live abroad in Paris, Rome or Naples until the storm blew over, and he might lose a few bad shares, bonds and properties, but his fortune would be intact. If it came to a court case Dunn would be defended by Mr Linklater, who would plead that his client was ill and had himself suffered a large reversal of fortune. Hankes firmly believed that Dunn would then return.

> 'Davenport Dunn will be back here, in London, before two years are over, with the grandest house and the finest retinue in town. His dinners will be the best, and his balls the most splendid of the season. No club will rival his cook, no equipage beat his in the Park. When he rises in the Lords – which he'll do only seldom – there will be a most courteous attention to his words; above all, you'll never read one disparaging word about him in the papers. I give him two years, but it's just as likely he'll do it in less'.

However, according to Hankes, what Dunn had done was no different from what went on all the time in the financial world, only that Dunn was better at it than most.

'Glumthal himself is not too clean-handed; lords and fine ladies that lent their names to this or that company, chairmen of committees in the House that didn't disdain to accept five hundred or a thousand shares as a mark of grateful recognition for pushing a bill through its second reading; aye, and great mercantile houses that discounted freely on forged acceptances, owning that they thought the best of all security was the sight of a convict-hulk and a felon's jacket, and that no man was such prompt pay as he that took a loan of a friend's signature. What a knock-down blow for all that lath-and-plaster edifice we dignify by the name of Credit, when the world sees that it is a loaf the rogue can take a slice out of as well as the honest man!'

Hankes had realized the game was nearly up and so threatened to expose the illicit activities that had been going on if Dunn did not buy him off. Dunn got him a well-paid government post in the West Indies, through the good offices of the Prime Minister. Hankes was both Jewish and a willing participant in all that went on but he was basically honest, being bowled along by the latter's brilliance.[11]

On the eve of succeeding in his plans, whatever the cost to others, Dunn was killed in his private railway carriage by a fellow Irishman, Kit Davies, who believed he stood between him and the title and lands that his daughter would come into through marriage to the new Lord Lackington. Davies escaped being hung for his crime by pleading that he had acted in self-defence, as Dunn had shot at him first. With Dunn's death his whole financial empire quickly crumbled. 'For weeks the newspapers had no other theme than the misery of this man's cruel frauds'. The phrase 'Dunn's Frauds' passed into regular usage among journalists. The Ossory Bank failed and Dunn's companies collapsed, including The Grand Glengariff, where the treasurer had absconded with £50,000. Glengariff and his daughter were forced abroad to live in reduced circumstances in Bruges. As more and more of Dunn's activities came to light there was a realization that society had for years back been the dupe of the most crafty and unprincipled knave of all Europe, that the great idol of its worship, the venerated and respected in all enterprises of industry, the man of large philanthropy and wide benevolence, was a schemer and a swindler, unprincipled and unfeeling. The fatal machinery of deception and falsehood which his life maintained crumbled to ruin at the very moment of his death; he himself was the mainspring of all fraud, and when he ceased to dictate, the game of roguery was over. While, therefore, many deplored the awful crime which had just been committed, and sorrowed over the stain cast upon our age and our civilization, there arose amidst their grief the wilder and more heart-rending cry of thousands brought to destitution and beggary by this bold, bad man. Of the vast numbers who had dealings with him, scarcely any escaped; false title deeds, counterfeited shares, forged scrip abounded. The securities entrusted to his keeping in all the trustfulness of an unlimited confidence had been pledged for loans of money; vast sums alleged to have been advanced on mortgage were embezzled without a shadow of security. From the highest in the peerage to the poorest peasant, all were involved in the same scheme of ruin, and the great fortunes of the rich and the hardly-saved pittance of the poor alike engulfed. So suddenly did the news break upon the world that it actually seemed incredible. It was not alone a shock given to mercantile credit and commercial honesty, but it seemed an outrage against whatever assumed to be high-principled and honourable. It could not be denied that this man had been the world's choicest favourite. Upon him had been lavished all the honours and rewards usually reserved for the greatest benefactors of their kind. The favours of the Crown, the friendship and intimacy with the highest in station, immense influence with the members of the Government, power and patronage to any extent , and, greater than all these, because more widespread and far-reaching, a sort of acceptance that all he said and did, and planned and projected, was certain to be for the best, and that they who opposed his views or disparaged his conceptions were sure to be mean-minded and envious men, jealous of the noble ascendancy of his great nature. And all this because he was rich and could enrich others! Had the insane estimate of this man been formed by those fighting the hard battle of fortune, and so crushed by poverty that even a glimpse of Paradise, it might have been more pardonable; but far from it. Davenport Dunn's chief adherents and his primest flatterers were themselves great in station and rolling in wealth; they were many of them the princes of the land. The richest Banker in Europe – he whose influence has often decided the fate of contending nations – was Dunn's tried and tested friend. The great Minister whose opening speech of a session was a mot d'ordre for half the globe had taken counsel with him, stooping to ask his advice, and condescending to endorse his opinions. A proud old noble, as haughty a member of his order as the Peerage possessed, did not disdain to accept him for a son-in-law; and now the great Banker was to find himself defrauded, the great Minister disgraced, and the noble lord who had stooped to his alliance was to see his estate dissipated and his fortune lost![12]

Dunn was seen as a man who had risen from poverty, through success in banking and company promotion, to a position of power and influence in society and politics. This suggests that the ability of the City to reward the talented and hardworking was widely appreciated. However, a negative side of the City of London is also observed. This was the double dealing, fraud and corruption through which Dunn and his kind enriched themselves at the expense of others. In addition, the apparently solid domestic enterprises being promoted turned out to be nothing more than puff and paper, disappearing when the manipulation ended and bringing ruin in their wake. Responsible for all this were largely homegrown financiers, like Dunn, rather than foreigners, while Jews also avoided blame. This view of the City as being domestically orientated also comes across in a somewhat later novel by Charles Lever, *That Boy of Norcott's*, which appeared in 1869. It was Paris that was seen to lie at the heart of international trade and finance, with Jewish firms central to its operations. Jews '...were the warriors of commerce; and they brought to the battle of trade, resolution and boldness and persistence and daring not a whit inferior to what their ancestors had carried into personal conflict'. The firm of Hodnig and Oppovich, for example, traded across Europe and were an offshoot of the Jewish merchants, Nathanheimer of Paris.

The Nathanheimers own all Europe and a very considerable share of America ... these great potentates of finance and trade had agencies in every great centre of Europe, who reported to them everything that went on ... If a country needed a railroad, if a city required a boulevard, if a seaport wanted a dock, they were ready to furnish each and all of them. The conditions, too, were never, unfair, never ungenerous, but still they bargained always for something besides money. They desired that this man would aid such a project here, or oppose that other there. Their interests were so various and widespread that they needed political power everywhere, and they had it ... from one end of Europe to the other the whole financial system was in the hands of a few crafty men of immense wealth, who unthroned dynasties, and controlled the fate of nations with a word.

Digby, the son of Sir Roger Norcott, married the Jewish heiress, Sara Oppovich, so restoring the family fortunes that had been dissipated by his father through gambling and a lavish lifestyle. He then used the money to develop the coal deposits on the family estates near Hexham.[13]

In the 1850s and 60s the City continued to be seen as a largely British financial centre, in contrast to Paris, and this is confirmed by other writers. One such at this time was Anthony Trollope, as in *The Three Clerks*, which was published in 1857. The speculative venture that attracts the attention of Alaric Tudor, a London civil servant, was a new Cornish tin mine, the Wheal Mary Jane, which was returning rich profits to its shareholders. He had been sent down from London to draw up a report on this mine and, while there, he was persuaded by Undecimus (Undy) Scott, the eleventh son of Lord Gabelunzie, to speculate in its shares. Scott had used his position as an MP to engage extensively in company promotion and share dealing. 'Why are members of Parliament asked to be directors, and vice-governors, and presidents, and guardians, of all the joint-stock societies that are now a set agoing? Not because of their capital, for they generally have none; not for their votes, because one vote can be but of little use in any emergency. It is because the names of men of note are worth money. Men of note understand this, and enjoy the fat of the land accordingly'. He was Vice-President of the Caledonian, English, Irish, and General European, Oriental and American Fire and Life Assurance Society, and 'a director also of one or two minor railways, dabbled in mining shares, and, altogether, did a good deal of business in the private stock-jobbing line'. He used his connections to cultivate those out of whom he could make money by involving them in his share dealing.

> He could not afford to associate with his fellow-men on any other terms than those of making capital of them. It was not for him to walk and talk and eat and drink with a man because he liked him. How could the eleventh son of a needy Scotch peer, who had to maintain his rank and position by the force of his own wit, how could such a one live, if he did not turn to some profit even the convivialities of existence?

It was for this purpose that he struck up a friendship with Alaric Tudor because of the report he had to write. 'Alaric wrote a report which ... sent the Mary Jane shares up, and up, and up, till speculating men thought that they could not give too high a price to secure them'. Alaric was lent the money to buy the shares by a fellow clerk, Harry Norman, who disapproved of buying shares on principle. 'He disliked speculation altogether, and had an old-fashioned idea that men who do speculate, should have money wherewith to do it'. He disapproved even more when he learnt it was not railway, canal or gas company shares but mining ones, and especially those of the mine on which Alaric had written the report. As it was, Alaric bought shares for £205, and then sold them for more than £500, clearing a profit of over £300 for himself. Encouraged by this success, Alaric started to speculate in mining shares in partnership with Scott. He kept all this hidden from his wife, who was ignorant about money matters and disliked both Scott and his friends and relatives. She shared the general belief that investors with limited funds should stick to 3 per cent consols, as the safest investment.

One of Scott's brothers had married the widow of a London stockbroker. She was a wealthy woman with an income of a £1,000 a year, while her daughter, Clementina Golightly, possessed £20,000 in her own name, which produced an income of £800 per annum. Scott arranged for Alaric to become the trustee of this fortune when the daughter married a Frenchman, as this would allow them to use it for their own purposes. Having sold the mining shares they were now speculating in the shares of a new Irish railway, the Great West Cork, which was to run from Skibbereen to Bantry, with a branch to Ballydehob. 'Alaric had bought very cheaply a good many shares, which many people said were worth nothing, and had, by dint of Undy's machinations, been chosen a director of the board'. Through his political influence Scott was going to get the branch approved, in the expectation that this would greatly improve the prospects of the railway, and so allow them to sell their holding at a substantial profit. They also started speculating in the shares of a company being promoted to build a bridge across the Thames, at Limehouse. Again, Scott believed that he could use political influence to get it not only approved but also obtain a government grant, with the shares rising substantially as a result. For a while the shares did rise in the expectation that the Limehouse Bridge would get approval and support, despite the opposition from certain MP's. At that stage Alaric wanted to sell out, and repay the trust fund, but Scott would not, believing they would go higher still, despite the advice of their brokers, Blocks, Piles and Cofferdam, to sell. Throughout, Alaric was reluctant to use the trust fund for such doubtful investments, knowing it might be considered illegal, but he agreed to do so. 'Though he was a rogue, he could not yet bear his roguery with comfort to himself. It sat, however, as easy on Undy as though he had been to the manner born'. By constantly speculating in shares Alaric and Scott believed they would emerge substantial winners.

> If a man speculates but once and again, now and then, as it were, he must of course be a loser. He will be playing a game which he does not understand, and playing it against men who understand it. Men who so play always lose. But he who speculates daily puts himself exactly in the reversed position. He plays a game which experiences

teaches him to play well, and he plays generally against men who have no such advantage. Of course he wins.

As it was, the Limehouse Bridge failed to get approval and the shares became worthless. By the end, £10,000, or half the trust fund, had been used to buy these shares. When this was discovered Alaric, as the trustee, was put on trial and sentenced to six months in Milbank prison. This was the minimum for the crime of defrauding a trust fund, as the judge and jury had become convinced that he had been duped by Scott. Though Scott escaped punishment the publicity stemming from the trial had ruined his reputation, and he was forced to resign as an MP and live abroad, where he preyed on English tourists and ended up an alcoholic. A similar fate awaited Alaric on release from prison as his promising Civil Service career was over. He was left with no alternative but to emigrate to Australia with his wife and daughter, never to return.

What emerges from a novel such as *The Three Clerks* is a view that in the 1850s it was speculation rather than the City that was evil as it ruined people's lives, whether they were honourable and hardworking like Alaric or untrustworthy and idle, as in the case of Scott. The centre of such speculative activity was seen to be the financial district in the City of London and so it was condemned by association. 'Oh, the city, the weary city, where men go daily to look for money, but find none; where every heart is eaten up by an accursed famishing after gold; where dark, gloomy banks come thick on each other, like the black, ugly apertures to the realms below in a mining district, each of them a separate little pit-mouth into hell'. However, those to be found in the City never emerged from behind the doors of these banks to be condemned by society, and so the anti-Semitism of the past, for example, had largely disappeared. Instead, the problem lay with the individuals who gambled in shares and tried to manipulate the price or profit from inside information rather than those in the City who promoted the companies and provided a market. The companies all had merit, being promoted to provide railways and bridges or to mine tin within Britain.[14] Such a verdict about contemporary culture is reinforced by a novel from the pen of Mrs Henry Wood, author of one of the most widely read novels of the time, *East Lynne*, published in 1861. That novel ignored financial matters, apart from the briefest of mentions, but that theme is taken up in a later work.[15] In *Oswald Cray*, which appeared in 1864, speculation and the City were prominent features though the main theme was medical negligence. By the mid-1860s company promotion was all the rage, producing gains for some and losses for others. It was these losses that seemed to obsess contemporaries. When Lady Oswald died it was discovered that she had left only £6,000, which was much less than people expected. Her lawyer, Mr Wedderburn, explained why. 'It would have been considerably more, but that her ladyship, a few years ago, was persuaded by an evil counsellor to sell out a large sum from the funds and invest elsewhere, for the sake of higher interest'. This turned out to be a company newly promoted in the City. 'She put it into some bubble scheme, and it burst' observed Wedderburn, who suggested that 'Women should never dabble in business. They are safe to burn their fingers'. Dr Davenal, her medical adviser, replied, 'Men have burnt theirs sometimes'. Not only had she lost half her fortune, but so had friends and acquaintances, driven to take the risk because of the falling return on investments in the National Debt. Even though Mrs Henry Wood was aware of the continuing importance of trade, especially the warehouses and shops around St. Paul's and Cannon Street, it was its role in company promotion that defined the City at this time.[16]

One scheme, in particular, is described in detail, with particular emphasis on the human consequences of its rise and fall. This involved Dr Davenal's young and rather impulsive assistant, Mark Cray, and his friend from his student days at Guy's Hospital, Mr Barker. Barker had already dabbled unsuccessfully in financial activities and ended up in prison. He was now involved in trying to float a Welsh lead mine, the Great Chywddn, as a joint stock company.

> The previous autumn, in consequence of some trifling difficulty in London, Mr. Barker found it convenient to enter on a temporary sojourn at a distance; and he penetrated to a remote district of South Wales. Whilst there, with the good luck which that gentleman believed he was born to and should some time realize, a vein of lead was discovered of a promising nature. He contrived to secure a large interest in it, and undertook to get up a company for working it.

Mr Barker was an adventurer with little knowledge of or skill in either mining or finance. This did not prevent him from trying to float a mining company that would make his fortune. Mark Cray's wife, Caroline, who was a niece of Dr Davenal, had recently inherited £4,000 from her mother's estate in the West Indies. Instead of investing this money safely in buying a house and developing a medical practice in the country town of Hallingham where they lived, which was the advice they were given, it was to be used to develop the mine and float it in the City as The Great Wheal Bang Mining Company. It was only after a short initial hesitation that Caroline was persuaded to have her money used in this way, captivated by the promised riches and the entry it would give her into London society. The conversation that took place captures the flavour of those considering such an investment, especially for the naïve who were likely to be impressed by the projections found in prospectuses.

> Mark Cray 'Some of the mines yield fifty thousand pounds profit the first year of working. I declare when I first heard of Barker's prospects I was ready to eat my fingers off, feeling that I was tied down to the life of a paltry pitiful country surgeon....My share the first year would be three thousand pounds', he computes.

Caroline Cray 'But Mark, do you mean to say that Mr Barker has offered you three thousand a year for nothing. I don't comprehend at all'.

Mark 'Not for nothing. I should give my services, and I should have to advance, a certain sum at the outset. Talk about an investment for your money, Caroline, what investment would be equal to this?'

The words startled her for the moment. 'I promised poor Uncle Richard that the money should be settled upon me, Mark. He said he urged it as much for your sake as mine'

'Of course', said Mark, with suavity. 'Where there's nothing better to be done with money it always ought to be settled. But look at this opening! Were your Uncle Richard in life, he would be the first to advise the investment of the money in it. Such chances don't happen every day. Caroline, I can't and won't humdrum on here, buried alive and worked to death, when I may take my place in the London world, a wealthy man, looked up to by society. In your interest I will not do it'

'Are the mines in London?' asked Caroline.

'Good Gracious, no! But the office is, where all the money transactions are carried on'.

'And it is quite a safe thing, Mark'.

'It's as safe as the Bank of England. It wants a little capital to set it going, that's all. And that capital sum can be supplied by your money, Caroline, if you will agree to it. Hundreds of people would jump at the chance'.

An utter tyro in business matters, in the ways of a needy world, imbued with unbounded faith in her husband, Caroline Cray listened to all with eager and credulous ears. Little more than a child, she could be as easily persuaded as a child, and she became as anxious to realize the good fortune as Mark

'Yes, I should think it is what my uncle would advise were he alive', she said. 'And where should we live, Mark?'

'At the west end, Carine; somewhere about Hyde Park. You should have your open and close carriages, and your saddle-horses and servants – everything as it ought to be. No end of good things may be enjoyed with three thousand a year'.

'Would it stop at three thousand, Mark?' she questioned, with sparkling eyes.

'I don't expect it would stop at twenty', coolly asserted Mark 'How far it would really go on to, I am afraid to guess. In saying three thousand, I have taken quite the minimum of the first year's profits'.

'Oh, Mark, don't let it escape you. Write to-night and secure it. How do you know but Barker may be giving it to some one else?'

She was growing more eager than he. In her inexperience, she knew nothing of those miserable calamities – failure, deceit, hope deferred. Not that her husband was purposely deceiving her: he fully believed in the good he spoke of. Mark Cray's was one of those sanguine roving natures which see an immediate fortune in every new scheme brought to them – if it be only wild enough.

The upshot was that Oswald and Caroline moved to London, They took a mansion in Grosvenor Place while Barker occupied 'sumptuous' apartments in Piccadilly. The Company appeared to be flourishing, judging from the appearance of its offices in the City. 'The offices were undeniable in their appointments. Situation, width of staircase, size of rooms, decorations, furniture, attendants, all were of the first water'. As a warning to her readers Mrs Henry Wood made clear that,

> People who play with the money of others do not generally go to work sparingly; and speculative public schemes necessarily entail a great outlay. These schemes springing up now and again in London, to the beguilement of the unwary – one in about every ten of which may succeed in the end – have been so well described by abler pens than mine, that I might hesitate to touch upon them, were it not that the story cannot conveniently progress without my doing so, and that I have a true tale to tell. How many hearts have been made to ache from the misery entailed by these uncertain ventures, ushered in with so much pomp and flourish, so full a promise of prosperity; and how many heads, unable to bear the weight of the final ruin, have been laid low in the grave, God alone will know. They have ruined thousands in body; they have ruined some in soul; and the public is not yet tired of them, and perhaps will not be to the end of time.

However, such was very much the verdict of hindsight, not the opinion of those investors who were willing to wager a small amount of money on a mine in the hope that they would strike lucky and end up rich.

> If you never had the chance of going to bed at night a poor man, and waking up in the morning with a greater fortune than could be counted, you might have it now. You had only to enter largely into the Great Wheal Bang Mining Company, become the successful possessor of a number of its shares, and the thing was accomplished. For the world was running after it, and some of the applicants were successful in their request for allotments, and some were unsuccessful; and these last went away with a face as long as the Wheal Bang's own prospectus, growling out prophecies of all manner of ill-fortune for it. The grapes were sour. The shares were up in the market to a fabulous premium, and a man might take half-a-dozen into Capel Court, and come out of it with his pockets lined with gold.

Faced with prospects such as these how could the ordinary investor resist placing a small bet on the future of the mine by buying a few shares. The shares could always be sold if the risk got too great, hopefully at a nice profit. Otherwise they could be retained until the time when the mine proved its worth and made all the shareholders rich. Such was the opportunity that the City offered the investor.

Certainly, in its early stages all appeared to be going well with both the mine and the floating of the company.

> Mark Cray's money had effected wonders, or rather his wife's; for hers it was. A great many of these magnificent projects are nipped ignobly in the bud through want of a little ready-money to set them fairly going. But for Mrs. Cray's thousands, Mr Barker's gold mine might never have been heard of by the world, and Mr. Barker's name had not attained to its enviable pre-eminence. These thousands did it all. They got up the company, they set the mine a-working, they paid for the costly offices, they dazzled the eyes of the public, they gave earnest of present wealth, they seemed to assure future success. Certainly, if any mine had ever a fair prospect of realizing a golden

harvest, it appeared to be the Great Wheal Bang. The working had begun most promisingly, and every success was fairly looked for.

Caroline's money had given Barker the means to both explore the seams of lead in Wales and float the company in the City.

> How he would have accomplished this, or whether he ever would have accomplished it, is doubtful, had he not found a coadjutor in Mark Cray, and the aid in Mark's money. Mark resigned the control of the money to him, and Mr Barker did not spare it. No earthly adjunct was wanting to ensure the success of the scheme, provided the mine only realized its present promises.... Mark Cray's thousands went. But ere they had come quite to an end, the Great Wheal Bang Company was in full operation in London, the shareholders had answered to their calls, and the money was flowing in.

Judging from this description this company appeared to be the one in ten that did succeed. It was no mere bubble conjured up by some City financier of rather dubious origins, with no other purpose than to extract money from ignorant investors. In contrast this involved a real mine that did have rich veins of lead ore and in which the promoters had sufficient faith so as to risk their own money. 'The money flowed down to the mine, and the works went on beautifully, and the specimens of ore that came up to town were said to be more valuable than any ore ever was before'.

Confidence in the success of the mine was shared by all involved. 'the returns were certain to be without parallel, and Mr Barker was in a glow of triumph, and Mark Cray in a state of ecstatic delight, and the lucky shareholders leaped up many degrees in the scale of society'. Reports from Wales and visits to the mine all pointed to it being a great success.

> Mark had made several visits to the scene of the mines, and he came back each time with (if possible) renewed assurance of their brilliant future; with increased ardour. Had the Chancellor of the Exchequer obligingly made Mark an impromptu present of a hundred thousand pounds, Mark would have flung it broadcast into the mine, had the mine thirsted for it. He did not understand these things in the least; and the constant bustle going on, the number of the miners, even the money paid in wages and similar expenses, were to Mark only an earnest of the rich returns that were to come thereafter, Mark would go back to London in a glowing state, and send his friends the shareholders into a fever, longing to realize the prosperity that seemed so close at hand. The weekly reports filled other weekly reports with envy, and created a furore in the speculating world.

Anticipating this imminent wealth the shareholders embarked on a lavish lifestyle, financed from the credit that was extended to them by those who also had confidence in the riches soon to flow from the mine. 'How many set up carriages on the strength of their future riches cannot be told'. Naturally the creators of the company, who were now among its directors, shared in this extravagance, drawing upon the Company to finance expenses that were much more for social than business purposes, carried away as they were by the success they were enjoying. Mark and Caroline became the toast of London society and entertained on a grand scale. 'Mrs Cray, with her vanity and her love of display, was in seventh heaven'. As long as the prospects of the Company were bright the shareholders were happy to condone this use of their money in this way. Mr Barker and Mark Cray were also selling some of the shares they held to finance their expenditure, but did so only sparingly because they anticipated that they would rise much further in price once the mine started to produce lead in large quantities.

> This much must be said for the Great Wheal Bang Company – that its projectors were at least honest in their belief of its genuineness. In that they differed from some other companies we have heard of, which have turned out to be nothing but a swindle – if you will excuse the word – from the very earliest commencement, the very first dawning dream of their projectors. Mr. Barker was of that strangely sanguine nature which sees a fortune in the wildest scheme, and plunges head and heart and creed into the most improbable speculation; Mark, an utter tyro in mines and all that concerns them, including companies, saw only with Barker's eyes. When Mr. Barker assured the entranced shareholders that one hundred pounds put into the Great Wheal Bang would multiply tenfold and tenfold, he spoke only the sanguine belief of his heart. When Mark Cray declared to his brother Oswald that a thousand pounds embarked in it by him would make him a rich man for life, he asserted the honest truth according to his conviction.

Such were the prospects of the company, fuelled by daily reports from the mine regarding the quality of the lead ore being discovered, that the directors and the existing shareholders were reluctant to sell any of their holdings, anticipating even greater gains in price. At the same time those who were not yet shareholders clamoured to be able to buy some, frequenting the company's offices in the City in the hope of being able to persuade others to sell. The result was to suck in ever more investors, which pushed the price of the shares higher, so convincing existing shareholders not to sell, because they would rise more on the morrow, and persuading others to buy, so pushing the price up even more. 'Half London was ready to snap them up'. Despite the proven quality of the lead ore being discovered problems began to appear with the mine in the shape of an inrush of water, which could neither be stemmed nor pumped away. Cray and Barker decided to keep these problems secret, as it would adversely affect the company's prospects and thus depress the price of the shares. Mark Cray even sold shares to his stepbrother Oswald, for £1,000, in the full knowledge that the future of the mine was in doubt. Mark chided his brother, saying 'Oswald, old fellow, you were always inclined to be fanciful. The mine is a glorious mine, and you'll be a blind booby if you don't secure some benefit in it. I'll answer for the safety of the investment with – with – my life'. When one of the shareholders, Mr Brackenbury, a City investor who was having the mine watched, came to Mark Cray and threatened to reveal what he knew about the problems with water, he was persuaded to stay silent by Mark Cray buying back his holding of shares at the price he paid for them. City insiders were not going to get caught by any collapse as they kept themselves well informed about their investments and sold their shares as soon as they were aware of any sign of problems. It was the ordinary investor who would lose.

Barker had intended to sell his shares before the news broke, but held on too long. In contrast, Mark Cray, who was new to the field of company promotion, was worried about the repercussions that such an action might bring. He told Barker, 'They'd call it felony, or swindling, or some such ugly name. Do you suppose I'm going to put my head into that noose? I was born a gentleman'. Nevertheless, he agreed to share any money Barker got from his sales. However, the news about the difficulties being experienced at the mine could not be suppressed, and as it began to leak out worried investors began to gather at the Company's offices in the City. This put an immediate stop to the plans for disposing of the shares as the two men saw the crowd start to form on the street. '"Its all up", shouted Barker in Mark's ear. "The news is abroad, and they have heard of it. Look at their faces."' Barker stayed to face the shareholders, who stormed the company's offices, while Mark Cray slipped away. 'His hands shook with terror; his face as white as death'. He abandoned both the office and his home, leaving his wife in ignorance of what was happening. She had to face another mob of shareholders who besieged her house looking for him. With the collapse of the company Mark and Caroline were ruined and fled into hiding in a poor part of London, where they existed on what little cash they had and by selling her rings and his cuff links. The servants had first pick from what was in the house and the rest was sold on behalf of their creditors. Mark and Caroline escaped to France, beyond the reach of their creditors and the irate shareholders, but eventually returned to London, as they had run out of money and Caroline was dying.

Caroline died in London, while staying with her relatives, while Mark Cray and his friend Barker tried another company promotion scheme in Paris. This time it was going to be a success, according to Mark Cray, as they had learnt much from the previous experience.

> The mine was very good; but of course there was risk attending it, from water or other causes, and the danger was unfortunately realized. This is different. Once the company is formed, and the shares are taken, it can't fail. Barker and I went through the thing together over and over again when he was in London; we had it all down before in black and white. We allowed for every possible risk and contingency, and we proved that the thing could not fail, if once organized.

Barker and Cray had become serial promoters moving from scheme to scheme, market to market, in the hope of getting the next one right. The fault never lay with them but was attributed to bad luck or unfortunate timing. The switch to Paris, for example, was attributed by Mark to the fact that 'The money market was tight here, and men don't care to speculate when money's not plentiful'. It had nothing to do with past failures when the investors lost all their money! Needless to say, the French scheme collapsed.

> It appeared that Mr Barker's grand project, with 'finance' for its basis, had come to grief. At the very hour of its expected fruition, the thing had in some ingenious manner dropped through, and thereby entailed some temporary inconvenience, not to say an embarrassment, on its two warm supporters, Barker and Mark. Of course it was entirely undeserved; a most cruel stroke of adverse fate; nevertheless both of them had to bow to it. Mark Cray came over to England; and Barker was compelled to go into ignoble hiding, no one but himself knew where, whilst he smoothed his ruffled plumes, and gathered his forces for a fresh campaign.

Mark was now penniless and so took a medical post in Barbados until another opportunity in the field of company promotion would open up for himself and Barker. The current failure was but a temporary setback as both men remained convinced that the next great scheme would make their fortunes. However, neither Barker nor Mark Cray was depicted as a fraudulent financier, as they were also victims of the opportunities created by the Limited Liability Acts to lure investors into gambling in shares.[17]

In Ainsworth's 1864 historical novel, based on the life of John Law and his activities in Paris at the time of the Mississippi Bubble, the man himself is never condemned. Instead, the view was expressed that 'All financial operations on a grand scale savour of what is popularly called gambling'. The point is also made that events in Paris at that time were far worse than anything that was happening in London at the time he was writing. 'Even in our speculating times it is scarcely possible to form a notion of the frenzy which then prevailed – which spread like a contagion through Paris – through all the provinces of France, and indeed, throughout Europe'.[18]

In a series of stories that appeared in 1864, which all had an unambiguous moral message, the point was made repeatedly that the work people did was not what made them evil. Mr Constantine was a 'busy, calculating London tradesman', but he was also a loving and caring family man. In terms of financial activities there was an acceptance that bankers could be ruined through no fault of their own but 'By one of those sudden and unexpected reverses which sometimes in the course of Providence fall on commercial circles…' Instead, it was the opportunity that the City gave for both speculation and company promotion that was the undoing of the individual. In the most substantial of the tales, called *Geoffrey The Genius, and Percy the Plodder*, the careers of two friends are contrasted. One was Geoffrey Armitage, the son of a wealthy London merchant who had bought the Manor House in Nestlebury on his retirement. Through a family friend, Mr Needham, Geoffrey got a position as a clerk in a large mercantile establishment in the City, Longsyte and Gatherall. 'In the counting-house of some general merchant ... you will learn the details of the business, and find out where, a few years hence, you may form good connections for yourself'. This experience was not limited to trade as

> the dealings of general merchants are not always confined to the mere purchase and sale of goods at home and abroad. Some of the merchant princes of England, as they are not inaptly termed, dabble as much in the stocks, and in the transfer of bonds and shares, as any recognized speculator, only they do it less openly. You will have plenty of chances of being initiated into the secrets of the Money Market, as well as the mercantile one, if you enter the counting-house of an enterprising English merchant.

After gaining experience Geoffrey started up on his own as a merchant, making speculative investments in cargoes, financed through extensive borrowing. These were successful and he became rich. From that he moved into speculation in shares. This was at the time of the railway mania. Unlike others Geoffrey emerged unscathed and even wealthier. 'What recked he that the busting of the noxious bubble which he, and such as he, had helped to swell, drew tears of agony from the widow's heart, or dried up the last resources of a struggling husband and father?' Geoffrey then established himself as a company promoter with an office in the City to which 'Brokers, jobbers, active agents for needy patentees of clever inventions' came seeking his support. 'everything in which he embarked money, whether foreign or domestic, prospered'. This was not to last, though for, when the crash came Geoffrey was brought down along with the rest. '[F]earful pressure in the money market' was seen as the immediate cause but the underlying reason was speculation itself. Geoffrey became a City financier and enjoyed enormous monetary success but was eventually bankrupted and had to emigrate. In contrast, his friend, Percy Malcolm, who also lived in Nestlebury but with his widowed mother and an uncle, became a clerk in a cotton textile mill in Flaxborough. He worked hard, studied chemistry and learnt the art of making dyes. Such was his ability and perseverance that he ended up a partner in the business, bought the local manor house and married Geoffrey's sister.

Despite this criticism of the City and the financial activities that were undertaken there, it was recognized that not all that emerged was speculative froth. 'The railroads, for instance, were a mere speculation when first begun; now they are so necessary a part of our social intercourse, that the only source of wonder is, how we did so long without them'. The problem was to differentiate between those projects that were likely to be of benefit and those that were not. Again, the severest condemnation was reserved not for those in the City but those who gambled on the rise and fall of shares using money placed in their trust for the benefit of others. '[T]hose men who stake, not only their own money, but that entrusted to their charge, on the chance of doubling or trebling that amount by speculating in shares or trade, or practising on the ignorance, folly, or credulity of others, are amongst those whom God himself has denounced and disowned'. It was speculation that had ruined Mark Eveleigh, the banker. 'In his desire to increase that wealth (not for himself, but for the son whom he doted on), he had rashly and secretly speculated'. There were also those in the City who had grown wealthy through legitimate means, such as trade. One was Mr Cameron, who had come to the City from Scotland, and established himself as a Manchester warehouseman. He was 'as rich as a Jew, they say, and does a large business in the City'. He had a house in the country as well as one in London.[19] It does appear that in the wake of the railway mania a period of reflection had resulted in a more benign view of the City emerging from the mid 1850s until the early 1860s. This view recognized the major contribution that the City had made to the life of the nation through an improved banking system and the creation of railways, while it was those who speculated who were seen to be a fault rather than the brokers and jobbers of the Stock Exchange.

As well as the condemnation of speculation there was a continuing distrust of bankers as evidenced by Charles Reade's 1863 novel, *Hard Cash*, but the location had switched from the City to the country, as the Bank of England now commanded total confidence. The story centred round a ship's captain. After surviving numerous difficulties on his final journey home to England from China, including a hurricane, pirates, two robberies and a shipwreck, he was swindled out of his life's savings by the local banker to whom he entrusted it all on his return. Captain Dodd had invested his savings in India, where the rate of interest was higher, but as he was to return to England he wanted to take his money with him. The sum was £14,000. Not wanting to risk the money any longer than necessary, after all his experiences, he immediately deposited it with the local banker, Richard Hardie, in the small town of Barkington. However, Hardie was insolvent as he had made large losses during the railway mania, through unwise speculations.

> Mr Richard Hardie was born and bred in a bank; one where no wild thyme blows ... nor cowslips nor the nodding violet grows; but gold and silver chink, and Things are discounted, and men grow rich, slowly but surely, by lawful use of other people's money.

Having withstood the temptation of the 1825 bubble in his youth, and saved the family bank, Hardie had fallen prey to the temptations of the railway mania in 1845. At first he resisted the speculative urge and had even reminded people of what had happened in the 1820s. 'But, when he saw that shares invariably mounted; that even those who, for want of interest, had to buy them at a premium, sold them at a profit; when he saw paupers making large fortunes in a few months, by buying into every venture and selling the next week – he itched for his share of the booty, and determined to profit in act by the credulity of mankind, as well as expose it in words. He made use of his large connections to purchase shares, which he took care to part with speedily. He cleared a good deal of money, and that made him hungrier: he went deeper and deeper into what he called Flat-catching, till one day he stood to win thirty thousand pounds at a coup'.

He was still holding these shares when the bubble burst after a damning article in *The Times*. To cover the money he had borrowed for his speculations he robbed the trust funds of his own two children of £5,000. This had been set-tled on them by his wife's father, a successful businessman who did not trust his son-in-law. As this would be exposed if they ever married he tried to ensure that they did not, so blighting their happiness. At the same time he used money in the accounts of wealthy clients to cover the bank's outgoings creating a false set of accounts in the process to cover what he was doing. Noah Skinner, the chief cashier of the bank, knew what he was doing and felt that Hardie had only him-self to blame for the mess he had got into.

> You had only to take the money of a lot of fools that fancy they can't keep it them-selves; invest it in Consols and Exchequer bills, live on half the profits, put by the rest, and roll in wealth. But this was too slow and too sure for you: you must be a Roth-schild in a day: so you went into blind speculation, and flung old Mr. Hardie's savings into a well. And now for the last eight months you have been doctoring the ledger ... You have put down our gains in white, our losses in black, and so you keep feeding your pocket-book and empty our tills; the pear will soon be ripe, and then you will let it drop, and into the Bankruptcy Court we go.

If the theft from the customer accounts was discovered Hardie would end up in prison or worse. Skinner used his knowledge to demand and receive a payment of £1,000 not to expose Hardie, as he had kept a full set of the real accounts. As it was, the amount deposited by Captain Dodd would allow Hardie to replace the money he had misappropriated from the customer accounts as well as safe-guard his own future when the bank eventually failed. He was able to do all this because nobody knew that Captain Dodd had deposited the money, having gone straight to the Bank on his return to England, then suffered from a seizure that made him lose his memory. He had no receipt to show he had deposited the money, trusting the entry made in the bank ledger by Hardie.

Local people looked to a local bank rather than a London bank for safety and security as they knew and believed in the local banker. Thus it came as a great shock when the bank collapsed, leaving customers stunned 'so great was the con-fidence inspired by the old bank'. On the day the bank closed the scene at the bank door was heart rending: respectable persons, reduced to pauperism in that one day, kept arriving and telling their fellow-sufferers their little all was with Hardie, and nothing before them but the workhouse or the almshouse: ruined mothers came and held up their ruined children for the banker to see: and the doors were hammered at, and the house as well as the bank was beleagured by a weeping, wailing, despairing crowd.

Hardie's house was stoned by a mob leaving the windows broken.

Towards afternoon the banker's cool contempt for his benefactors, whose lives he had darkened, received a temporary check. A heavy stone was flung at the bank's shutters: this ferocious blow made him start and the place rattle; it was the signal for a shower; and presently tink, tink, went the windows of the house, and in came the stones, starring the mirrors, upsetting the chairs, denting the papered walls, chipping the mantlepieces, shivering the bell glasses and statuettes, and strewing the room with dirty pebbles, and painted fragments, and glittering ruin.

Not only did those with deposits in the bank lose everything but so did those holding the bank's notes as these were now worthless. Hardie's children, Alfred and Jane, were heartbroken about what had happened as their lives in Barkington were now ruined. However, their despair was the least of it. Faced with ruin customers of the bank fled abroad, hanged themselves, went mad, ended up in prison for debt, died of shock or despair, were forced into the workhouse or had to depend on charity. One of these distressed and deranged customers even attacked Hardie's daughter, Jane, in the street and she died of the resulting injuries. Not content with what he had done, Hardie had his son abducted and committed to a lunatic asylum on the eve of his marriage, so as to prevent the fact that he had plundered his children's trust fund being exposed. There seemed no end to the depths that Hardie would stoop to in order to conceal what he had done. The impression is clearly conveyed that bankers lacked the normal feelings towards family and mankind in general, for otherwise they would not behave as they did. This was attributed to an obsession with money which was valued above all else.

Captain Dodd's wife, with her husband in an asylum and the money lost, was forced to leave Barkington. She moved to London with her family and got a job in London making cloaks for '...one of those great miscellaneous houses in the City'. Again, this indicates a continuing awareness of the important role played by the City merchant in the nation's prosperity. Conversely, this awareness was matched by the unsavoury aspects attached to company promotion and speculation. An uncle, who would have helped the family, had been ruined by railway speculation and was in no position to do so. Noah Skinner also lost the £1,000 he had been paid to keep quiet, through speculating on the London Stock Exchange. Whether he was a bull and bought for a rise or a bear and sold for a fall 'certain foxes called brokers and jobbers got the profit and he the loss'. In the end the truth came out, helped by a written confession from Noah Skinner found after his death. Captain Dodd recovered his memory and his daughter Julia married Hardie's son, Alfred. It was also discovered that Richard Hardie had accumulated a fortune of £60,000 through the careful management of the money he had secreted away, which had been safely invested in land and houses in London and in consols. This allowed him to repay the trust fund and Alfred Hardie used that money to repay the bank's customers, so re-establishing the family's reputation as bankers. Along with Edward Dodd, who was now his brother-in-law, Alfred reopened the bank in Barkington. The running of the bank was left to Edward while Alfred went on to become MP for the town. What thus emerges is a somewhat mixed message. The overriding one is that only cash, property and consols were safe investments, while both provincial bank deposits and joint-stock company shares were liable to fluctuate in value or become worthless, with disastrous consequences for all. Nevertheless, the provincial bank re-established itself under new management, suggesting a faith in the value of a sound and well managed local bank. Similarly, though speculation in shares was condemned because of the ease with which money could be lost, the reverse was also noted. The main reason that Richard Hardie could repay the money he had embezzled was because he had gone to London and speculated successfully on Turkish bonds on the Stock Exchange. He made £49,000 on an investment of £5,000 helped by an announcement that the Sultan was to repay part of the loan, as they had been in default. From this it is possible to identify joint stock company promotion, and subsequent speculation in the shares issued, as the particular aspect of the City that attracted widespread public condemnation in the early 1860s. Nevertheless, compared to the Railway Mania, contemporary speculation in foreign government debt was profitable. This, along with the position of the Bank of England and the National Debt, suggests that the City had established a sound reputation for itself within British culture.[20]

Such a verdict also emerges from another of Charles Reade's novels, *Foul Play*, co-authored with Dion Boucicault, and published towards the end of the decade in 1868. Emphasizing the continuing importance of commercial activities in the City the action centres round a merchant, John Wardlaw and his son Arthur. Wardlaw and Son had an office in the City but the family lived in a house in Russell Square, indicating that the City was no longer a place of residence. Arthur Wardlaw had been groomed to take over the firm from his father: 'at school till fifteen, and then clerk in his father's office till twenty-two, and showed an aptitude so remarkable, that John Wardlaw, who was getting tired, determined, sooner or later, to put the reins of government into his hands'. In the meantime Arthur had been sent to Oxford University and provided with a private tutor, the Reverend Robert Penfold, who was the son of Michael Penfold, the chief clerk in the firm. However, he was now back in London having replaced his father in the active management of the family business. City merchants were seen as large firms with international operations, employing clerks specializing in 'one department only', and possessing agents across the world, such as in Sydney, Australia, where White and Co. acted for them. Goods were regularly shipped between these two firms. However, despite his training, Arthur was not managing the business very well and it was losing money. He was overambitious, insufficiently cautious and had been unlucky with the agents and correspondents he used. 'He had concealed his whole condition from his father, by false bookkeeping'. His father drew £4,000 annually from the business to fund his life at Elmtrees, the country mansion he had bought on his retirement. The result was that Arthur was left 'battling for his commercial existence, under accumulated difficulties and dangers'. This suggests an appreciation of not only the profits to be generated by a successful City merchant but also the dangers involved whether from taking too many risks, a lack of ability or simple bad fortune. To remedy the situation Arthur devised a scheme to defraud the City underwriters who insured his ships and cargoes. White and Co. was to despatch from Australia to Wardlaw and Son in London gold on one ship and lead and copper on another. However, Arthur paid the mate of one of the ships £2,000 to switch the two cargoes secretly before loading. The ship, believed to be carrying gold, would then be deliberately sunk by the mate on the journey home. The intention was to claim on the insurance for the gold, which was worth £160,000, while disposing of it himself, as it would be in the firm's warehouse disguised as lead.

Making Wardlaw and Son's precarious position even worse was the collapse of the discount house, Overend and Gurney.

> At this very crisis came the panic of '66. Overend and Gurney broke; and [Arthur] Wardlaw's experience led him to fear that, sooner or later, there would be a run on every bank in London. Now, he had borrowed £80,000 at one bank, and £35,000 at another: and, without his ships, could not possibly pay a quarter of the money. If the banks in question were run upon, and obliged to call in all their resources, his credit must go; and this, in his precarious position, was ruin

This is exactly what happened as one day Mr Burtenshaw, of Morland's bank called to ask for repayment of the £80,000 loan as they were experiencing a run. If Wardlaw could not repay, the bank would have to suspend, as it could not meet the withdrawals being made by depositors. This would then focus attention on Wardlaw and Son, and its precarious position would be quickly exposed. 'Morland's suspension, on account of money lost by Wardlaw and Son, would at once bring old Wardlaw to London, and the affairs of the firm would be investigated, and the son's false system of bookkeeping be discovered'. As it was, the ship carrying the supposed lead, which in reality was the gold, arrived in Liverpool while the other was confirmed lost. This allowed Arthur to claim the insurance money and so repay his loans. In the meantime his father, who had come up to London because of the panic in the money market, let Arthur draw on his private account at the Bank of England until the insurance money came through. The firm was saved but the plot came to light from the testimony of a survivor from the ship that had sunk. John Wardlaw, shocked to hear what had been going on, made good the loss and handed the firm over to his chief clerk, telling him that 'the house of Wardlaw exists no more. It was built on honesty, and cannot survive a fraud. Wardlaw and Son were partners at will. I had decided to dissolve the partnership, wind up the accounts, and put up the shutters. But now, if you like, I will value the effects, and hand the business over to Penfold and Son, on easy terms'. This is what he did, dying three days later while Arthur ended up in a lunatic asylum, having become insane as a result of the strain.[21]

In *Foul Play* Reade and Boucicault avoided the usual criticism of the City, as the crime being committed is not perpetrated on innocent investors through fraudulent company promotions or market manipulation. Instead it was a crime undertaken by one group in the City, the merchants and shippers, against another, the marine underwriters. The only losses sustained were upon City professionals whose very business was to assess risk. There appeared to be no general condemnation of either City merchants and shipowners on the one hand or the insurers on the other. All were seen to be undertaking necessary activities without which international trade could not take place, which would be a loss to Britain. Even bankers were seen as essential as they provided the credit without which business could not take place. What emerges is the vulnerability of those in the City to sudden changes in financial and commercial life. Events internal to business, or a general panic, could quickly and easily transform success into failure, with disastrous consequences for all concerned. John Wardlaw died of shock and shame, when the plot was uncovered, while his son Arthur was driven mad as a result of the pressure he had to endure. Nevertheless, business continued as normal with Wardlaw and Son operating under a new name while Morland's bank survived, after the repayment of the loan. Throughout the Bank of England appeared as solid and dependable while a successful City merchant had every right to purchase a country estate for his retirement. The high regard expressed for the City merchant was becoming universal. In the 1867 novel, *No Thoroughfare*, written by Charles Dickens in collaboration with Wilkie Collins, the principal character was a respectable City wine merchant.[22] In his 1870 novel, *Lothair*, Disraeli referred to Cantacuzene, a Greek merchant operating out of London, as not only possessed of great wealth but also 'a thorough gentleman'.[23] Hence the fact that stealing from such people was a crime that could not be excused, as in *Levison's Victim*, by M. E. Braddon, which was published in 1870.[24]

However, the ongoing speculative boom of the 1860s was slowly beginning to change attitudes towards the City, as can be seen from the work of Charlotte

Riddell. In her 1864 novel, *George Geith of Fen Court,* the City escaped strong criticism, even where company promotion and share speculation was concerned, for it was up to investors to act cautiously, especially if they bought shares in companies where liability was not limited to the amount they had paid. The story revolved around George Geith, who was a self-employed accountant in the City, operating from rooms in Fen Court, where he both lived and worked. Such work was 'drudgery' but through it he and many more were responsible for the millions made in the City. When his sister-in-law visited 'George opened his books, and showed her the means by which he made money; showed her the endless columns, the interminable entries, the weary writing, the lines and lines of figures'. His was 'an existence like that of hundreds of business men, who are sufficiently well off to be uninteresting, and so thoroughly content and self-satisfied that the most daring of authors would never venture to put them in a book'. George Geith was originally from a gentry family in Bedfordshire, being a cousin of Sir Mark Geith of Snareham Castle. He had been a vicar but came to London, so as to escape an unfortunate marriage and to make his fortune, having forsaken God.

> To London he came to seek his fortune. In a feigned name he sought employment, which he found at last in the offices of Horne Brothers, accountants, Prince's Street, City. For five weary years he stayed there, wandering through labyrinths of figures, and applying himself so closely to learn his business thoroughly, that, when at length he summoned up courage to start on his own account, he carried with him to Fen Court a very respectable number of clients, profitable to him, but so small in the estimation of the great house, that Horne's suffered them to drop through the meshes of their trade-net without a regret.

He drew up balance sheets for London businessmen, such as retailers, and landowners from the country who needed an account of their financial affairs. In this he prospered. 'The more money he made, the larger his connection grew; the higher the stake he was playing for, the more cautious George Geith became in business, the more earnestly he buckled to his work'. Though such business was 'uninteresting to outsiders', because of the dull routine of work, it was

> the back-bone of England, only that which furnishes heiresses for younger sons; only that which sends forth fleets of merchantmen, and brings home the products of all countries; only that which feeds the poor, and educates the middle classes, and keeps the nobility of the land from sinking to the same low level as the nobility of all other lands has done; it is only this, I say, which can find no writer worthy of it, no one who does not jeer at business and treat with contempt that which is holy in God's sight, because it is useful, and proves beneficial to millions and millions of His creatures.

Here was real recognition of the importance of the City to Britain. It was also recognized that in the City class counted for little: 'the peer and the peasant stand on an equality in a City office, if they bring work in their hands with them'.[25]

Another aspect of the City that emerges from Charlotte Riddell's insights was the tension that existed between those who did business there. On the one hand there were the small traders like George Geith and his various clients, like Mr Bemmidge, a retail wine merchant. On the other hand there were the bankers that provided them with the short-term credit they needed to operate. In the eyes of Mr Bemmidge, 'London bankers are Herods ... they strangle all the young businesses they can lay their hands on. The fact is that in another generation or two, there will be no small traders at all. Every business will belong to a millionaire, or a company, and men like ourselves will have to be clerks or porters'. To such people bankers were no better than Jewish moneylenders. What he was complaining about was high rates of interest these banks charged and the stiff conditions they imposed. This led George Geith to switch his account from the Merchant's and Tradesman's bank to an old established firm of private bankers, Nortons, of Size Lane in the City. This bank was classed alongside Coutts and was extensively used by the country gentry. This was despite the fact that 'Externally, the bank was dingy; internally, it was dirty. Further, it was dark, small, and unimposing. At the Merchant's and Tradesman's all was plate-glass, frescoes, mouldings, handsome flooring, elaborate ceilings. Behind counters, the highly-polished mahogany whereof shone like a mirror, were ranged rows of clerks, who made themselves as generally disagreeable as it was in the power of bank clerks to do; and its remoter regions, separated by glazed partitions from the vulgar herd, was the sanctum of the manager – a gentleman who united the conciliating manners of a bear with the appearance of a fop. In Size Lane, how different! Through a narrow doorway the visitors squeezed themselves into the bank, which was dark even in the summertime, by reason of unclean windows, dingy walls, a pervading presence of green baize, and the absence of even the most ordinary cleanliness. ...The dust of years lay thick on the shelves; ink, spilled by generations of clerks, stained the desks and floor. The once green baize, which covered the door leading to Mr. Norton's private room, had faded to a yellowish brown; ...' This shabbiness impressed Geith who felt it must reflect the fact that Nortons' did not need to impress clients as their name alone did that, having been in existence for over a century. 'Drawing his cheques on Norton gave him a certain standing amongst his clients; and though George knew it was all humbug, though he knew his bills would have been just as good paper if Aldgate Pump had been written on them, he was still glad to be able to fall in with popular ideas, and endeavoured to humour popular prejudices to the fullest extent'. Through the issue of bills drawn on Norton's Geith was able to obtain temporary credit until the date of payment. In return he deposited all his clients' money with Norton's, and the money he was making from his business and careful speculation in colonial produce. However,

Nortons Bank failed and Geith heard too late to withdraw both his own money and that belonging to clients but in his name. He had £10,000 on deposit and all was lost. 'He had believed Nortons' bank to be as safe as the Bank of England, and behold! His belief had ruined him'. Luckily, through his friendship with Mr Tettin, a solicitor, Geith was able to raize enough money to meet the bills coming due and repay his clients' money. However, he was left with nothing and it took him 15 months to clear the debt. In contrast to Mr Norton, who retired to Devonshire where he had an estate in his wife's name, George Geith was forced to cut his expenditure greatly.[26]

One of George's country clients was Ambrose Alfred Molozane of Molozane Park in Hertfordshire, who consulted him because he was worried about his financial affairs. He had bought 100 £50 shares in a Cornish mining company, the Sythlow Mines, which had been promoted by a crook called Punt. They were now worthless and unsaleable, leaving Molozane with a large debt as the company did not possess unlimited liability and the shares were only partially paid. He had fallen prey to 'Mines, and railways, and speculations of all sorts...', with events being compared to the South Sea Bubble. Molozane asked Geith to visit him in the country and sort out his finances, in the hope of avoiding ruin. When there, the Molozane family treated him as an equal, but that was not the case with most of their relatives and neighbours. George was looked down upon by the country gentry because he had made his money in the City. Molozane's daughter Beryl told him that.

> We have some neighbours who talk about the City as if it were a den of thieves; and who, although every sixpence they have was made in trade, 'could not think of putting their sons to business'. They were happy to have had fathers who were not ashamed of trade. But for that, they would now be poor enough. ...The outer world can know nothing of business, except what it hears from the initiated; and if the initiated declare it is all roguery and vulgarity from chapter to chapter, what is society to say?'

Beryl's own aunt, Mrs Elsenham, referred to George Geith as 'A poor accountant in the City. A person whom, had he called to speak to me on business, I should not have allowed to sit down in my presence'. In response, George Geith considered himself an equal of them all.

> 'I am still less ashamed of being an accountant in the City....The City has given me a home; my business has provided bread and cheese; and I am not going to follow the examples of the citizens, and despise that which has kept me off the parish. Business is a capital invention, and the City is a place where any man with courage and industry may push his way. The City is the proper land for younger sons to emigrate to, if younger sons could but be induced to think so'.

The City was seen as an 'El Dorado' where fortunes could be made, and this money brought social standing in its wake. A number of the estates bordering

Molozane Park were let to people from the City, such as Mr Werne, a manufacturing chemist, and Mr Finch, a merchant, because their aristocratic owners
could not afford the upkeep of the houses. These City people were slowly gaining
social acceptance through their hospitality to the local gentry. 'In this country,
you know, great people are not so inaccessible as they seem to be in the City'. As it
was, the losses sustained by Molozane through his investments forced him to sell
his estate to Mr Werne, come to London, and seek employment. He got a post
as a clerk with the shipping house of Murphy, Dowsett and Raikes in Leadenhall
Street, which was only a short walk from the small house he had rented just off
the Caledonian Road. This brought him and his family into regular contact with
George Geith. Eventually his daughter Beryl married George and they rented an
apartment in Catherine Court, within five minutes walk of his office. [27]

   After his financial reverse, when Norton's bank failed, George and Beryl had
to give up this apartment and live at the back of the office in Fen Court. This
introduced Beryl to the work of an accountant but when she offered to help
George he refused. '[H]e ridiculed the idea of his little girl, his own Beryl, developing into a hard-headed, business-woman, with City phrases ready on the tip of
her tongue, and no subjects of conversation except the price of money, and the
chances of lower discounts'. However, Geith was finding that he was no longer
so quick and accurate as he had been in the past but could no longer afford to
employ a clerk to help him. Faced with the prospect that her husband could not
continue forever as an accountant Beryl approached one of her country friends
for advice about what he could do. This was Mr Finch, who ran a large warehouse
in Fore Street in the City. He recommended that Geith became the London
agent for a manufacturer, Mr Bidwell, from Stockport, who had approached
him about handling the business. Mr Finch was too busy to undertake it and
was thus happy to pass it on to Geith. With capital advanced by his aunt, Lady
Geith, and with his cousin Mark as an active partner, George established a huge
warehouse in London and became very wealthy. 'George Geith made money in
handfuls' ending up as a 'City magnate' while the business, 'Geith and Geith is
at the present time one of the largest and most respectable in the City'. Beryl
increasingly played an active role in the business. 'By degrees, she learnt how to
arrange his papers, how to keep his bills, his invoices, his receipt-notes, and his
letters, so that at any minute she could find him a particular account, or tell him
where such and such a proposal was put'. However, she died after bearing George
a son. George bought Snareham Castle from his cousin and left his son, Walter,
there to be looked after by Lady Geith. [28]

   From this novel emerges a complex but generally positive picture of the City.
City people continued to be seen as socially inferior, but now without cause,
and they were in the ascendancy, buying up the country estates of those who
could no longer afford their upkeep. However, anything and anyone in the City

associated with company promotion continued to be disapproved of and that aspect receives greater emphasis in her 1866 novel, *The Race for Wealth*. The City continues to be viewed as a mixed community whose inhabitants were engaged in a constant race for either wealth or bread. This could also be seen spatially, with Cannon Street in the west being described as 'the handsomest thoroughfare in London, though it is in the City' whereas the area to the east, around Billingsgate in Lower Thames Street, was a place where many lived in overcrowded and squalid conditions. Though the wealthy City merchants and bankers had moved to houses in the West End, and their clerks to the East End, the City was still a place were the poor lived so as to be near their work. Similarly, the City was not only a centre of finance but also a place of domestic trade, being where London got its fresh fish and foreign fruit, as well as a centre for international trade. However, descriptions of these mercantile activities, though acknowledged, are not noteworthy compared to the ability London possessed to make people wealthy. That is why Lawrence Barbour, the descendant of an old Norman family now reduced to the level of small farmers, came to London. Like others he recognized the position to which the family had fallen, reflecting, 'What is the use of blood without money? What is the good of birth unless a man have gold also?' A distant relative, Josiah Perkins, lived in London, in Limehouse, and he offered to employ Lawrence in his business as a manufacturing chemist. Lawrence's father regarded the Perkinses as inferior people, despite his own reduced circumstances, but Lawrence saw it as an opportunity to better himself. An ancestor of the Barbours had married the daughter of a drysalter in the City, Isaac Perkins.

> All the gold that Isaac Perkins had scraped together in the course of a long and industrious life took to itself wings and fled away, when the young Barbours came to lay hands upon it. Mrs. Stafford Barbour's fortune proved indeed a perfect curse to her descendants. On the strength of it they gambled, they betted, they trained horses that always lost, they purchased pictures – they married aristocratic paupers.

This all conjures up a continuity of contact between the country and the City in which the country only survived through regular influxes of metropolitan money, whether through marriage or land purchase. The Barbours' own mansion and estate, Mallingford End, had been bought on each occasion by people who had made money in trade in London, much to Lawrence's disgust. 'I saw a vulgar, illiterate snob buy the place where we had lived for centuries, and then I saw that snob sell Mallingord End to a worse snob; and I saw the whole countryside bow down and worship Mammon'. This made him determined to 'come to London to conquer it, to make money out of its inhabitants, to earn a place for himself among the merchant princes of the Modern Babylon'.

Initially Lawrence was content to concentrate upon becoming a successful manufacturing chemist, observing that 'Business is the one occupation in which a man may rise, no thanks to anybody but himself'. In that he has as his model a Mr Sondes, who was a successful chemical manufacturer and sugar refiner in the East End, where he both lived and worked. However, he then met Mr Alwyn 'a business man, with Money written on every line, on every wrinkle, on every feature, on every fold of his attire, and yet who aped the fashionable man of solid West-End standing all the time'. Mr Alwyn was the latest owner of Mallingford End, having inherited the family business, started by his grandfather. It was a firm of colonial brokers, Alwyn and Alwyn, with offices in the City, where Mr Alwyn directed operations from the 'inner office'. In the outer office were clerks like Percy Forbes, who found the work dull, boring and routine and 'grew day by day more hateful to him'. 'Percy knew a great deal more about flower-shows and regattas, operas, and the latest novels, than about banking business, custom house clearances, protested bills, and legitimate acceptances'. Despite the hope that one day he might inherit the business by marrying Alwyn's only child, a daughter called Henrietta. Forbes left the firm and used a small inheritance to become the managing partner in a sugar-refining business in the East End of London. Manufacturing was portrayed as not only a much more interesting and worthwhile business than the City, but also one where money could be made with modest amounts of capital.[29]

Alwyn was in financial trouble having taken too many risks in business, including fraudulent trading. 'Mr. Alwyn was rich, very rich; but the world called him a millionaire, and therein the world was wrong. He had not made his money easily, he had not made it perfectly honestly'. In a last attempt to save himself from ruin, Alwyn forced his daughter to marry one of his business associates, a Mr Gainswoode, who was reputed to be as rich 'as Rothschild'. As a wedding present for Henrietta, Gainswoode bought Mallingford End from her father, who then placed the money beyond the reach of his creditors if he failed, which happened shortly afterwards.

> Great was the astonishment expressed in mercantile circles when the failure of Alwyn and Alwyn, Colonial brokers, was announced; but this astonishment proved as nothing in comparison to the dismay felt when it came to be understood the house had not merely stopped payment, but was rotten and bankrupt to the core. Some few persons, indeed, had been doubtful of the firm's solvency for a considerable time previously, but then in such cases a few persons always are wise before their time.

Most were unaware that the firm had long been on the verge of collapse, apart the domestic servants, as they were in a position to pick up the most intimate gossip.

It is the penalty people have to pay for civilization – this utter want of domestic and social freedom; this dwelling continually in the midst of a great army which keeps its sentinels always on the alert; this sleeping, and eating, and walking, and driving, for ever surrounded by guards who are cognizant of every look; who take account of every word; who know the weaknesses, the sins, the anxieties, the hopes of their betters, as their betters never know the weaknesses, sins, anxieties, hopes, fears, of the men and women who compose this modern inquisition.

The other group that had a strong idea of the true state of affairs were the clerks. 'And in like manner your clerks, knowing all about your affairs, tell what they suspect one to another; and before you clearly see the end, they have talked it over, and wonder how you will bear it, and what you will do. So with Mr. Alwyn at any rate. There was not a subordinate about his establishment who felt surprised when the order came to close the place'. However, this did not spell the end of Alwyn's career in the City, for he soon returned as a successful company promoter, working in partnership with Lawrence Barbour. Clearly, a record of fraud and failure was no barrier in the City as long as the result was the making of money.

Lawrence's manufacturing business in the East End had taken him regularly to the City. That made him acquainted with company promotion and share speculation where he saw the possibility of making much more money than was ever possible in manufacturing. 'There are various kinds of business which a man may find to take him into the City; but of these only two are now necessary to be specified – legitimate and illegitimate – one connected with his regular trade, and another that had no sort of concern with it'. Spotting the opportunities created by the passing of the Limited Liability Acts for company promotion, the likes of Alwyn and Barbour were quick to enter the field. 'These were the palmy days of limited liability and unlimited speculation ... There were companies for everything – for banking, for dining, for diving, for drinking, for bathing, and burying, and clothing, and washing, and furnishing. No person who has not studied the statistics of companies can have the faintest idea of the deluge which came upon the earth for its wickedness when once Parliament opened the sluice-gates by doing away with Unlimited Responsibility. The thing was never thought of or imagined by man which did not, in the days of which I am speaking, find some one to make it into a body, with a tail of secretaries, directors, solicitors, brokers, bankers, managers, agents'. What took place was seen as being akin to the South Sea bubble and the railway mania but took the form of a series of small speculative surges rather than one large single event, but prayed on a widespread belief that the way business was to be done was going to be transformed through limited liability. Thus all wanted to share in the potential profits to be made, including vicars, widows, spinsters, curates, squires 'all sorts and descriptions of people, who swallowed the bait as greedily as hungry fishes, and who feel the hook that bait covered tormenting to this very day'.

Concerned about the risks he was taking, and the morality of what he was doing, Lawrence decided to abandon his work as a company promoter in the City. He became a partner with Forbes in a sugar refinery and returned to the East End 'where fortunes are made by hard work instead of by sleight of hand'. However, he got bored with that and so returned to the City and company promotion.

> At last he had found the true El Dorada – the alchemist's secret. Under his touch, the most unpromising ventures became perfect mines of gold. He was regarded as a lucky man – one of those with whom the former Rothschild would have loved to be associated. Speculators sought him, capitalists bore him off in triumph to dinner, clerks were deferential to him, plodding business-folks discoursed to one another of Lawrence Barbour's rise, and sighed. How he had entered London at twenty without a sovereign in his pocket, and risen long before middle age to the position he had attained – these things were talked of in omnibus or steamer, in counting-houses and coffee-rooms; and yet – the old friends who had given him their hands and bade him God speed in the days of his struggling apprenticeship to business, would scarcely acknowledge him now. He had sinned, and not even his reputed wealth could cover that sin away from the sight of those in whose eyes he most of all he desired to stand well.

The sin that he had committed was not so much giving in to the lure of money in the City but that, though a married man with children, he was now living with Henrietta Alwyn, who was now a rich widow, as Mr Gainswoode had died. If she remarried she would lose her fortune, and so turned down Lawrence's offer of marriage after his wife had agreed to a divorce. She told Lawrence 'I like something more substantial to depend on than shares in companies. It is very profitable while the companies are good for anything, doubtless, but I have seen so much of business ups and downs, that, now I am independent of trade, I should like to keep so, thank you'. She then walked out on him.

Eventually Lawrence suffered the fate of all company promoters through overreaching himself. When his last venture, The British and Continental Provision Company, collapsed it brought down the Conqueror Fire and Life Office and then all the others because of the way the finances were linked. The stress made him delirious as he realized his 'Race for Wealth' had ended in failure because of his involvement with company promotion in the City. He had lost not only lost all his money but his wife and family and the respect of those who once cared for him. His wife did take him back but he died shortly afterwards. She then married Percy Forbes, who was now a well established sugar refiner in the East End. With the money Forbes had made there he bought back the family estate and he and his family lived there in happiness.[30] However, it did not apply that the ambition of all in London was to buy an estate and establish themselves in country society. Henrietta had disliked living in the country, much preferring London. Her husband had only purchased a country house so as to display his art collection, especially his old masters, as that could not be done in a London house. Like his wife he did not like country society, considering it inferior to London. Their friends who came down from London remarked that 'they thought the country dull, and preferred town'. This feeling was reciprocated in the country as the people there disliked them, especially someone like Gainswoode, whose father had been a London moneylender, and his wife, as she was the daughter of a bankrupt merchant. Those in the country considered themselves superior to those who had made their money more recently, even though, like Lawrence's father, they had lost it all and much of what they once had had come from trade in the past. Mrs Gainswoode remarked, sarcastically, that 'Birth never mates with wealth in this country, you understand; of course, great people never marry for money, never did'. She went on to describe Mr Barbour as part of a 'decaying race', pointing out that 'money is power'. What is conveyed is a sense that only a few City people bought country houses, because of the cost of purchase and upkeep, and those that did so largely recreated London society there, rather than mixing with the local population. It took someone such as Percy Forbes, with strong country connections and whose fortune came from a respectable line of business, to achieve ready acceptance. Lawrence Barbour could have had all that if he had only stuck to manufacturing and not dabbled in company promotion and share speculation in the City.[31]

Despite all that took place in the mid-1860s, with the bursting of the speculative bubble and bank collapses, the City retained its admirers though that was now reserved for its mercantile aspects. It was in 1870 that Mrs Riddell produced what was almost a eulogy to the commercial City in her novel, *Austin Friars*. This novel was largely set in the City. 'what a view of the City is to be had from Bankside! ...a place of churches, houses, streets, lanes, bridges of old as well as recent developments like the Cannon Street railway terminus and new wharves and warehouses'. There was an acceptance that this was a changing City. 'Where the great City station and the great City hotel now are, there stood formerly a City bank and a City insurance company'. These changes were having an effect beyond the City as the large mansions, set in their own grounds in places like Denmark Hill, were being demolished to make way for smaller and more numerous houses. These mansions had been owned by rich merchants and it was these mercantile firms that were facing greater competition in the City. One such was Alexander Monteith, who operated from an office in Leadenhall Street. 'every one tells me the battle is fiercer, the struggle harder, than it used to be'. As a result many smaller mercantile firms, where the partners and staff still lived in cramped and unhygienic conditions on the premises, were disappearing. For those that remained, the partners and staff were now living further and further out. Luke Ross, a 'book-keeper in a third-rate City house' was living in Homerton, where the rents were lower. Nevertheless, it was the activities of these merchants and their staff that took centre stage. The adversities they have to overcome could be trivial, such as the 'meagre luncheon city folks have to put up with, and eat, like the Israelites, in haste, as well as frequently standing'. They could also be major, as with the uncertainties of credit, where any restriction caused severe difficulties. 'one of those periods of "tightness" in the City, when apparently no person has money and no person can get any; when the people who discount are as "short" and as much put to it for capital as those who require discount; when bankers find their money flowing out too rapidly, and are themselves as anxious and embarrassed in their great way as the pettiest tradesman, who finds a difficulty in scraping together ten pounds to meet his engagements'. Why these occur 'is a mystery even to the elders in Israel'.

The focus of the story was a woman who ran her own business in the City. After being abandoned by the man she was living with, Austin Friars, Yorke Forde (her married name), took up the business herself as she was already handling the foreign correspondence and managing the office. As she told Luke Ross, 'Very few of the people with whom business was transacted in London ever saw Mr. Friars. His fleshly representative was always a clerk or a boy – his spiritual representative was myself'. Austin had become engaged to the daughter of a City merchant, Monteith, who had invited him to join him in his business. He thus decided to abandon Yorke, with whom he had been living as man and wife, and the business they ran together, even though she had invested an inheritance of £1,000 in it. Being cast off in this way made her determined to succeed on her own but she needed a partner to assist her and to act as the public face of the firm. For this she selected Luke Ross as he knew the business. As Yorke explained to him.

> Do you not know that the sort of education I have had for years past has made me feel like a man, judge like a man? Do you imagine I am going to be either dependent upon the Monteiths for my daily bread, or satisfied with the thirty-five or forty pounds a year I should get from my thousand pounds if I invested it safely? Listen, I am willing to risk the thousand pounds for the sake of indulging my whim. If I do not lose it, well and good; if I do, well and good still. I have been a governess and a companion, and those two brilliant careers would still remain open to me, if the worst came to the worst. But there are parts of that business to which it would be impossible for me to attend. I could work, I could do the correspondence, I could see nothing was neglected; but I could not receive the people who called, neither could I go about with draggled petticoats calling upon them. That is just the point where the fact of my being a woman comes in as an impediment; but if you will help me, if you will take that part, there need be no difficulty.

Despite this defiant statement of female independence, Yorke was also of the opinion that women were 'now less useful and more extravagant than has ever been the case before in the chronicles of England'. As Luke was in love with her he agreed to her request. [32]

More generally, the contrast is made between the respected and valuable commercial City, and the rewards that brought to those who pursued it, and the speculative nature of the financial City, and the consequences for those who followed that path. There was the experienced and successful merchant Alexander Monteith, who operated to the highest standards: 'Mr Monteith had not lived in the City of London all his working days of his life for nothing; and when the necessity arose for him to obtain information, he knew exactly where to seek with the assurance of receiving it'. This information revealed that his son-in-law and partner, Austin Friars had borrowed extensively on bills in order to support a lavish lifestyle, but had not repaid them when they became due. This was bringing the firm into disrepute and so Monteith dissolved the partnership, knowing that reputation and trust was the basis of success in the City. Riddell observed,

> There is cheating enough, and lying in abundance, and swindling and close-shaving too, in this great city, God knows! More is the pity; but there is honest toil and straightforward dealing likewise. There are men whose word would be better than another's bond; who would not wrong you or me of sixpence; who would work themselves to death in order to pay their just debts; who look upon the doors of the Bankruptcy Court as the gates of hell; and who, if ruin through misadventure overtook them, would rather give up to their creditors the beds they lay on than defraud a man through any 'composition-deed' of his just demand.

In her view the criticisms made of those in the City were based on ignorance:

> the majority of writers who have undertaken to portray business know nothing on earth about it, and know, if that be possible, a trifle less about the men who work hard to keep wife and children above want while they live, and to leave an unsullied name behind them when the hour comes that closes the books of time and opens those of eternity ... if fair dealing, honest trading, honourable feeling, were not more common than the reverse, commerce would soon come to a standstill.

The ideal could be found in Luke Ross, who worked hard and steadily and dealt fairly with all. His reward was to marry Yorke Forde after her husband died, leaving her a rich widow and the owner of a country estate.[33]

The behaviour of these merchants was contrasted with Austin Friars. His uncle was a rich and successful merchant but he was the illegitimate son of his half-sister, and so was not going to inherit. He was not willing to build up a business slowly, in the way that Yorke Forde and Luke Ross were doing, or work steadily to maintain an existing one, as was the case with Alexander Monteith. Instead, he wanted to make a quick fortune and then retire to the country, and saw speculation as the means of doing it. However, his speculations lost him money, forcing him to borrow more and more. Austin would borrow from friends and business acquaintances, giving them bills in return, which they would discount at either private banks such as Howe and Lavery or joint stock banks like the United Kingdom Banking Company. It was made to appear that the bill was the product of a commercial transaction between two firms while it was simply a loan, or accommodation bill. As these bills were always being renewed and never repaid they became more and more difficult to discount, eventually forcing those who held the bills to ask Austin for payment, which he was unable to do. He then started to forge the signature of his father in law, among others, so as to replace his own bills with fresh ones that could be discounted. When this was discovered Austin blamed it all on the Jews. 'when a Christian gets amongst Jews, what can he expect but to have his teeth drawn-by way of reprisal, I suppose?' Monteith paid off his son-in-law's bills to avoid disgrace. This allowed Austin to start up again in business, backed by an old business friend, Mr Turner. Mr Turner had been left a small estate in Warwickshire, and wanted '...to make money enough to retire to that estate, and spend the rest of his days as an idle country gentleman'. Their business prospered allowing Austin to occupy 'large grand offices in Billiter Square, lots of clerks, plenty of business, his bank balance was always satisfactory, his payments duly met. He had a house at Highgate, where he entertained much City and other Company'. However, that was not enough for Austin as he continued to speculate in the hope of making a large fortune, but again lost money. To cover his losses he went back to forging bills of exchange. When this was discovered he was forced to flee the country, with Mr Turner taking over the business and agreeing to meet all the forged bills. Mr Turner wanted to be rid of Austin as he discovered that he was untrustworthy. The impression is clearly conveyed that the commercial City was regarded as a respectable route to success and wealth compared to the financial City which involved risk and dishonesty.[34]

In this novel Riddell again addresses the question of City–Country relations. Some merchants, like Austin Friars and Turner, saw the City simply as a means to an end, and that end was to retire to an estate in the country with sufficient wealth to live on comfortably. London could be compared unfavourably with the country, leading many who worked there to long to escape.

> In lieu of scorching pavements, moss, grass, ferns, and wildflowers. Instead of great warehouses, shops filled with goods set out to the best advantage, stuccoed porticoes, and mile after mile of bricks and mortar; hedgerows made up of the dark glossy-leaved evergreen oak, hawthorn on which the berries were just turning colour, brambles trailing in picturesque wildness, convolvuli climbing from branch to branch and starring the abundant foliage with pure white buds. In place of crowds of anxious-faced hurrying men and women, stray children returning from the village school, a few labourers stretched on the turf sheltering under the trees from the heat of the summer-sun, eating the while their frugal dinner ...Whilst in exchange for the rattle of cabs and the thunder of Pickford's vans, for the ceaseless roar and rumble and the hoarse growl of the metropolitan thoroughfares, which ceaseth not completely either by day or night, a wonderful virtue of stillness, the blessed rest and

repose whereof could be likened unto nothing save that peace of God, which passeth all understanding.

There were also many, though, who had no desire to swap London for a country estate, such as the successful merchant, Mr Collis, who could well afford to purchase one if he wanted.

> As a change, I like the country; as a sanitary institution, I admire it; for there can be no question about the good a 'change' does the Londoner; but for a residence-good Lord! ...,the mental pace of London life unfits a man for this sort of stagnated existence. I once asked a friend what he did when he went into the country, and I have treasured up his reply ever since. 'I consult Bradshaw', he said, 'for the first train back to town'. And if all Londoners spoke out their minds, you would find that is what the bulk of them would like to do also.

People were keen to leave London to escape 'the heat, and the work, and the dust' and go to a place 'without duns, without masters, without bills to meet, without business payments to make'. Once there, in his opinion, they quickly missed all that urban living provided when living in the country, namely company, restaurants, good food and drink, reviews and newspapers, and instead, had to endure 'the miserable monotony of a country existence'. Also, in the country class and connections were important whereas in London, 'Provided a man be wealthy, I do not imagine they care particularly who his father may have been, or whether indeed he ever had one'.[35] Appalled as were many contemporaries by the City as a place and the business done there, others saw it positively in terms of the opportunities it offered compared to the country. The City allowed conventions to be challenged as it provided a refuge for the likes of Yorke, an adulteress, and allowed her to succeed as a businesswoman.

A transition was taking place in the City in the middle years of the nineteenth century and this was picked up on by contemporaries and influenced its place in British culture. There was an exodus in which the City's residential population was decamping to the suburbs. This was undermining the perception of the City as a mixed residential and working community and converting it into one based on the functions it performed. Here again change was taking place. Though the City's commercial activities did continue to grow, the impression that many had was that it was those associated with money in all its forms that were coming to dominate the City. Such a view was fuelled by the prominence given not just to the growth of joint stock banking but also the promotion of joint stock companies and the trading in stocks and shares on the Stock Exchange. Both these were widely reported in the press as the public became fascinated by the rise and fall in share prices and the appearance of new forms of business. Though bringing the City to prominence, this was not entirely beneficial to its reputation as it tended to emphasize the speculative and fraudulent. This was especially the case after the conversion of Overend Gurney into a joint stock company and then its collapse a year later, with large losses for investors and destabilizing consequences for the entire financial system. The consequence was that the place of the City in British culture that emerged in these years was a rather mixed one. To some it remained a commercial City to be lauded as the greatest of its kind in the world, as with Charlotte Riddell. To others it was where financial fraud took place with those undertaking it escaping any form of punishment, as expressed by Wilkie Collins in his classic detective novel, *The Moonstone*, which was published in 1868. 'The upshot of it was, that Rosanna Spearman had been a thief, and not being of the sort that gets up Companies in the City, and robs from thousands, instead of only robbing from one, the law laid hold of her, and the prison and the reformatory followed the lead of the law'.[36] Conversely, it was also recognized that the City was home to the nation's foremost financial institutions and that they were the victims of crime rather than the perpetrators. Even Dickens was aware of this, as in *Hunted Down* in 1859, where an attempt to defraud an insurance company was described.[37] This makes generalization about the position of the City of London in British culture rather difficult. Different aspects could be highlighted to produce different results such as the growing respect for merchants and bankers compared to the suspicion that surrounded company promoters and Stock Exchange jobbers.[38] As the exodus from the City was to accelerate after 1870, and its commercial activities were increasingly overshadowed by those involving credit and capital, its place in British culture in the future was going to be determined by its role as a financial centre.

3 DAMNATION AND FORGIVENESS, 1870–1885

From 1870 onwards the City of London was judged by contemporaries more and more on the functions it performed. This meant that its position in British culture increasingly relied upon which of these functions caught the public's imagination at any particular moment rather than the actual range and importance of the activities conducted within its boundaries. During the years after 1870 the City of London consolidated its position as the dominant financial centre in Britain. Domestically, London-based joint stock banks extended their influence throughout England and Wales by opening ever more branches and taking over provincial banks. Provincial banks followed the same route by taking over London banks and then gradually transferring the centre of their operations to the City. The result was a nationwide branch banking system in England and Wales that was capable of withstanding any financial crises or monetary disturbance. Increasingly, all the City's joint stock banks were seen to possess the stability that was once the exclusive privilege of the Bank of England. City-based joint stock banking became a highly disciplined service conducted according to strict principles and careful monitoring. The last collapse of a major British bank in the nineteenth century took place in 1878 and concerned a Scottish bank, the City of Glasgow Bank, rather than one in the City. This was highly symbolic as Scotland had long been home to best practice in banking and possessed a reputation for thrift and prudence. At the same time the railway and the telegraph, with the telephone appearing from 1879, helped to integrate British financial and commercial markets so that all looked instantly to London for prices and conditions. Again, such activities became routine as bankers, brokers and merchants throughout the country were in constant contact with each other. Finally, joint stock enterprise had passed through a learning curve, making it easier for financiers in the City to provide a realistic valuation of the businesses created. It was now evident that joint stock would not sweep all before it but it was also clear that corporate enterprise could make a real contribution in certain areas of the economy, as well as providing a safe and remunerative investment. The transformation of British railway companies into businesses which provided an essential service, while also paying interest and dividends, did much to change public perception regarding domestic joint stock enterprise. In addition, there was a widening range of other joint stock companies providing essential goods and services such as banking, insurance, tramways, telephones and electricity supply.

However, there was another element to the functions performed by the City that undermined the impression created by all those that the public increasingly took for granted. These related to the growing importance of the City as a global financial centre serving not only Britain's own international trade and finance but also those of other countries. In addition to a small number of London based banks operating in distant countries, foreign banks increasingly established contacts, agencies and even branches in the City to facilitate the transfer of money between each other, so helping to create a London based payments network for the entire world. All this was greatly aided by the maturity of the international telegraph network with London as its hub. The attractions of the City for foreign bankers extended far beyond the facility they found there to make and receive payments. A direct or indirect presence in the City gave them access to the London money market, where they could profitably employ temporarily idle funds, as well as the ability to participate in investment opportunities from around the world that were increasingly found there. It was some of these overseas investment opportunities that were also responsible for undermining public confidence in the City. Though those issuing and buying sovereign loans were increasingly able to assess their true worth, recognizing that not all government guarantees were alike, some foreign governments failed to honour the debt and repayment commitments they made. This brought the whole process into disrepute. Similarly, though many of the major joint stock companies promoted with the objective of operating abroad were eventually successful, especially the railways, there were a number that failed. This left the investors involved angry at what had happened and generated a general feeling that there was something devious and corrupt about those in the City who had been involved. Foreign mining projects were a perpetual source of friction between the City and the investing public as success remained a matter of luck rather than judgement, with the many companies that failed far outnumbering the few making spectacular profits. Even the building and running of a railway in a foreign country involved a high degree of risk. It was especially difficult to estimate construction costs and likely revenue, for example. When such calculations were honestly made and expenditure strictly controlled, it was inevitable that a delay would occur between the completion of the line and the ability to pay interest on the debt, let alone declare dividends. In the meantime there was ample scope for criticism of those in the City who had persuaded the public to buy shares. There was not even the justification that these railways benefited the public generally, whatever the return to investors, as had been largely the case with the 1840s mania, as they were now located abroad, not at home. However, it was not this increasing professionalization of the City's investment community that impinged upon the public but, rather, the constant ups and downs of the market bringing losses to some and gains to others, the transgressions of individual financiers especially when they resulted in prominent legal cases, and the presence of highly risky investments, such as mines and new technologies, that possessed a high probability of failure. All these had the potential to highlight particular activities in the City and so influence the position it occupied in contemporary culture.

The other feature of the post-1870 years was the arrival in the City of an increasing number of foreign financiers and merchants. This reflected the pivotal position of the City in international trade and finance, making it essential for many conducting such operations to have a London base, especially as the need to interact with others in their own line of business or gain access to the global communications network, was becoming an essential prerequisite for business success from 1870 onwards. Whether to buy or sell, borrow or lend, receive or send a presence in the City became essential for the conduct of many commercial and financial operations around the world. However, it was not only these fundamental developments that attracted foreigners to the City for events also played their part. The eclipse of Paris as a financial centre in 1870–1, because of war and insurrection, made London the undisputed international financial centre, bringing a rush of foreign financiers and banks. A number of French banks opened offices in the City at this time, for example. Similarly, German unification led to the eclipse of Frankfurt as a financial centre, and the migration of key personnel to London. This had the effect of emphasizing the cosmopolitan element of the City and reawaken somewhat dormant fears that Jews and foreigners were undermining Britain with dangerous and dubious financial practices. Whereas lapses in business behaviour in the City might be excused by some if committed by British nationals, especially if the eventual results were of benefit to the domestic economy, such was not the case when the money was directed abroad by those perceived to be alien. The result was that the position of the City in British culture remained clouded by ambiguity in the 1870s and early 1880s, as it completed the transition from community to business district, from commerce to finance, and from domestic to global. Throughout, certain of its activities became so routine that they became almost invisible while others came to feature prominently, so distorting the image of the City in the eyes of the public.[1]

This ambiguity in attitudes towards the City can be seen in the 1871 novel by Sheridan Le Fanu, *Checkmate*. On the one hand there was the wealthy and respectable stockbroker, David Arden, whose family owned landed estates in Yorkshire and Devon and lived in Mortlake Hall in Middlesex. On the other hand there was the powerful City banker, Walter Longcluse, with a fortune of £2 million and an income of around £100,000 per annum. He was seen to be a cultured European and a member of the 'City notability'. On a visit to the offices of the stockbrokers Childers and Ballard where 'Most men would have been per-emptorily denied' and 'the more fortunate would have had to wait the result of an application to Mr Ballard' but 'to Mr Longcluse all doors flew open'. In reality Walter Longcluse was a British murderer, operating under an assumed identity, who had made his fortune through lending money to spendthrift members of the landed gentry on exorbitant terms.[2] There was an acceptance that stockbrok-ing had become respectable but moneylending was not, and the recognition of a growing Continental influence in the City. It was this influence that was seen to have grown considerably by 1874–5, when Anthony Trollope's novel, *The Way We Live Now*, was published. Trollope had already made brief references to the City in earlier novels, taking up the recurring theme of the volatility of fortunes made there. As well as *The Three Clerks,* in *The Last Chronicle of Barset,* which came out in 1867, it was observed

> 'But don't you feel now, really, that City money is always very chancy? It comes and goes so quick'.
>
>   'As regards the going, I think that's the same with all money', said Johnny. 'Not with land, or the funds. Mamma has every shilling laid out in first-class mortgage on land at four per cent. That does make one feel so secure! The land can't run away'.[3]

This was written in the wake of the financial difficulties of the mid-1860s and before the long depreciation of land values that began with the problems experi-enced by agriculture from the 1870s onwards. However, *The Way We Live Now* highlights the seamy side of City practices, as revealed in the revelations associ-ated with the 1875 government inquiry into foreign loans. One of the central characters was the banker and company promoter, Augustus Melmotte. His ori-gins were shadowy but he was thought to be both foreign and Jewish, which was no bar to success in the City. 'in the City Mr Melmotte's name was worth any money, – though his character was perhaps worth but little'. This suggests an immediate gulf between City morals and those existing generally in society.

The particular business that Melmotte was involved in was to raise the money to build a railway from Salt Lake City to Vera Cruz, the South Central Pacific and Mexican Railway. There was considered to be no substance to this project, as it was 'built upon the sands'. Its only purpose was to allow the promot-ers to make money by continually buying and selling the shares. At the numerous meetings and lunches held in clubs, and when dealing with a constant stream of visitors, Melmotte 'played the part of the big City man to perfection, standing about the room with his hat on, and talking loudly to a dozen men at once'. The City was seen as being at the very centre of international finance. 'Melmotte had the telegraph at his command, and had been able to make as close inquiries as though San Francisco and Salt Lake City had been suburbs of London'. When the company failed and Melmotte was exposed as a crooked financier, he was immediately deserted by his business associates. The City had no loyalty even to its own. 'he could do no good by going into the City. His pecuniary downfall had now become too much a matter of certainty'. The City was a place of brutal and callous relationships being more of a jungle than a civilized society, and Melmotte had made the mistake of being caught. 'Melmotte had committed various forgeries ... his speculations had gone so much against him as to leave him a ruined man, and, in short, ... the great Melmotte bubble was on the very point of bursting'. Faced with prison, Melmotte had only suicide available to him, and this he accomplished by taking prussic acid.

The City was a place that operated on its own moral code, which included cheating the investing public and abandoning those who were caught. Neither honour nor loyalty operated there. However, City men were no longer seen as a race apart, for the exodus of the leading merchants and bankers to homes elsewhere had placed them among the rest of society in London. Georgiana Longestaffe, whose father had an estate in the country, observed that, 'As for City people, you know as well as I do, that that kind of thing is all over now. City people are just as good as West End people'. This even extended to Jewish bankers as she had every intention of marrying Ezekiel Brehgert, even though he made no pretence to being other than a practising Jew. 'The man was absolutely a Jew; – not a Jew that had been, as to whom there might possibly be a doubt whether he or his father or his grandfather had been the last Jew of the family; but a Jew that was'. The marriage only failed to take place when Brehgert's bank, Todd, Brehgert, & Goldsheiner lost £60,000 through the collapse of Melmotte's railway project. This meant that he could not provide her with the town house she demanded. Despite being Jewish and a City banker, Brehgert was accepted in the highest reaches of society. 'Mr Brehgert was considered to be a very good man of business, and was now regarded as being, in a commercial point of view, the leading member of the great financial firm of which he was second partner'. It was the foreign company promoter, Melmotte, who was not, apart from a brief spell when his wealth and lavish expenditure bought him entry. Even Brehgert was of the opinion that Melmotte's 'business was quite irregular, but there was very much of it, and some of it immensely profitable. He took us in completely'.[4] This suggests that the public differentiated between the safe and respectable aspects of the City and the risky and dubious, with the former being associated with long established British bankers, including Jews, while the latter took the shape of more recent arrivals from the Continent. Such a theme recurred again in Trollope's 1876 novel, *The Prime Minster*, as it featured the City financier, Ferdinand Lopez. He was Jewish, of Portuguese descent, and began his career in a stockbroker's office after education in England and Germany. However, he did not stay there long, preferring instead to operate independently in the City. As he told his wife, 'I buy and sell on speculation. The world, which is shy of new words, has not yet given it a name. I am a good deal at present in the South American trade'. That could be either commercial, as in the guano trade, or financial, such as in the shares of the San Juan Mining Company. The problem was he lacked capital and hoped to remedy that shortage by marrying Edith Wharton, the daughter of a rich London lawyer. Though he did marry her it was with the disapproval of her father, who refused to provide the large settlement that Lopez hoped for or lend him the money he wanted. Eventually, as his marriage began to fall apart and his creditors demanded payment, he committed suicide by stepping in front of a train.[5] Lopez was clearly a very marginal City figure being a lone operator, rather than a major company promoter, as with Melmotte, or an established City banker, like Brehgert. What is revealed in Trollope's writings is that though contemporaries were aware of a range of financiers operating in the City it was those who were foreign and Jewish that most captured the public's attention, being associated with its growing international orientation.

It was this external orientation, combined with company promotion, foreign loans, and speculation that did most to condemn the City among contemporaries in the mid-1870s, as can be seen the 1875 novel, *Ye Vampyres*, subtitled *A Legend or The National Betting- Ring, Showing What Became of It*. The author was the Spectre, and it used an imaginary setting though it would have been obvious to contemporaries what was being referred to. England was the Old Countree, Fernland was the USA, London was the city of Undone, and the stock exchange was the Vortex. Though highly critical of the City the author does recognize the honesty of many who did business there. 'Now Undone City contained some very wealthy bankers, traders, and merchants of high standing and of every conceivable description'. That said, the author then directed his venom on the members of the Vortex, as they even cheated others in the City. 'There were very many honourable men in Undone City who had long been sick and tired of the doings in the Vortex. These men could not see why the City should be any longer disgraced and polluted by a perpetuation of such evils. It was talked over again and again but nothing ever came of it. Occasionally Swindlers were prosecuted, but very seldom punished'. This belief that the Stock Exchange was the source of all corruption in the City was fostered by the fact that it was closed to non-members, conducting its business in secret. Non-members had to stand outside the door and give orders to members, who then went inside to buy and sell on their behalf. This meant that non-members had no way of knowing whether the prices they paid or received were the product of open and fair bargaining or arrived at through the collusion of members who profited at the expense of outsiders. The Spectre, standing outside the Vortex, 'saw many inhabitants running to and fro, in and out of this "house" of the world, engaged in what they called "doing bargains" for those they termed "outsiders". I listened attentively, and I soon discovered some who were called "brokers" doing "outsiders" as well as doing "bargains". One of these brokers was Nimrod Myrabolanes, who employed two clerks, Raskall Clencher and Alick Goodheart, while one of his clients was Meteor Cowries, who stood outside while the clerks ran in and out with orders for the dealers, or jobbers.

The Vortex thus fostered the gambling instinct among the public as they placed bets on the rise and fall of prices, which all took place due to mysterious forces, creating gains for some and losses for others. The Spectre told his readers that

> The Undone Vortex was quite different from all other marts. There was a fascination about its doings which so allured 'outsiders', that once they had tasted its wild enslaving thralls they never could desist. Even while they were being ruined the brokers so excited them with the vain hope of the tide turning in their favour that they plunged deeper and deeper! Sometimes their dupes made a little plunder – for it was always plunder, what one made another lost. There was no good done there, no one ever produced anything of any benefit to the rest of Undone City, or the Old Countree round. Some called it The Undone Betting-ring, while by others it was named the National Disgrace! The flower of the youth of Undone City and of the Old Countree were always to be found congregating about the portals of the Vortex, hoping to win something for which they had never toiled, but they nearly always lost and were 'cleared out'. And then they went away beggars, and looked so pale and woe-begone, for which the brokers did not care one bit! The victims, if they did not die of heart disease, generally took to drink, or poisoned or shot themselves, while many had to be confined in lunatic asylums for the remainder of their wretched lives'. What took place on the Stock Exchange was considered to be nothing more than gambling and this became uncontrollable during a speculative boom and collapse. 'At times there were what used to be called 'panics', and then nearly everybody in Undone City, and in the Old Countree round, suffered more or less; because the insiders used to concoct and spread false reports, and frighten the poor outsiders out of their stocks, scrip, and shares, for which they had worked full many a livelong day and year. By means of what were called 'operations' on the market, dependence could never be placed on its steadiness at any time....During the prevalence of those 'panics', however, the fluctuations were so violent that far greater loss and ruin inevitably ensued. As everything in the Vortex was conducted within closed doors, and with the utmost secrecy, no one could ever tell whether what they heard was true or false. They never could satisfy themselves by going into the Vortex – that was not allowed. The 'insiders' grew very rich indeed; and the 'outsiders', many of them, very poor indeed. The Vortex possessed a committee to regulate its affairs; but as it was composed of brokers and jobbers, everything they did was to their exclusive benefit[6]

Bad as the Stock Exchange was, others in the City were implicated in cheating the public, as revealed in the experiences there of two stepbrothers, Ralph and Walter Osborne, who came to England from America at a time when the latter was still a colony of the former. When Walter arrived in England he was introduced, through a mutual friend, Linksigh Dooum, a land shark, to the 'great banking firm of Grab Brothers, in Money Street'. They got him membership of the Stock Exchange so that he could be their inside agent. The chief partner in Grab Brothers was Todigrab. As a member of the Stock Exchange, Walter's role was to help Todigrab float companies, such as the Metal Mountains Debenture Swindle, Empirical Land Company of Southville, and The Wee Countree Public Robbery Company. One of the companies they floated was a silver mine in the USA, the Beloved Silver Mining Company. Despite the endorsement of the US ambassador to Britain, General Poker, it turned out to be a swindle as those promoting it knew there was no silver in it. This had echoes of Baron Grant's Emma Silver Mine promotion of 1871.[7] After his training with Todigrab, Walter launched out on his own as a company promoter, joined by Raskall Clencher, who had been expelled from the Stock Exchange. The investors that Walter persuaded to take shares in the companies he floated were drawn mainly from the army and West End clubs as this was his own family background. In contrast, Raskall had a strong country connection, and so brought them in as investors. Using the services of brokers such as Catzpore and Fleasum, of Aurum Factors, Dooum Easy Lane, Walter and Raskall floated companies and issued loans, which were then given an official listing on the London Stock Exchange, without any scrutiny regarding their true worth. 'swindling loans were foisted upon the unwary inhabitants of Undone City and of the Old Countree, which loans were endorsed by the Committee, and sanctioned by them, and countless thousands were ruined by these and similar undertakings. Widows and orphans who placed reliance in the character and judgement of the Committee were thus reduced to poverty, and obliged to eat the bread of carefulness all the remainder of their days! ... These Spoilers were masters in the art of monetary strategy, building palaces with the spoils of their victims; lavishing money upon any object which their whim or caprice suggested, and indulging in costly entertainments – for they had no heart to feel the sorrows and ruin occasioned by misdeeds which told of the spoilation upon which they fattened, the legalized robbery by which they had grown rich'. Again, the Stock Exchange was seen to be at the centre of all that was wrong with the City because the promotion of these worthless companies and the issue of worthless loans could not have taken place without the apparent respectability of an official quotation and the facilities provided to buy and sell the securities created. The comment was made that 'Everything was to be done by Companies.

When Walter's stepbrother, Ralph, came to England, he started speculating in shares. Whereas betting on a horse race was seen as gambling, speculating on the rise and fall of stocks and shares could be disguised as a legitimate business, and thus attract those who would never normally wager, like Ralph. Brokers were believed to spread false information so as to encourage their clients to buy and sell frequently. They also employed dummy clients in order to encourage genuine investors to speculate and it was their actions that led to both speculative booms and panics. Finally, the advice that they gave benefited them rather than their clients. It was the money that the investors lost that enriched the brokers, and allowed them to live lavish lifestyles

in those big houses at Loud Park – at Queen's gate – in Swell's quarter, or in that highly-respectable, God-fearing neighbourhood, Tranquil Vale; who keep their second establishments at Triton, Fopville, Hillsborough, or Bracing Wells; who keep their dozen hunters, their Yachts, at Buttsgate or Bulls, and who take their box at the opera for the season! These are the men who are supposed to live upon nominal rates of commission, and yet go in for the most expensive houses, and indulge in well-appointed equipages and costly entertainments!

Even when Ralph discovered that he was being cheated by his broker, John Brokum of Dirt Alley, he found he had no recourse to law as the Vortex was not a public institution. Similarly, a complaint to the Vortex Committee would achieve nothing as they only represented their members. However, this was seen as some kind of rough justice. 'You hoped to rob somebody when you gambled, and it ended in their robbing you'. In particular, as Ralph had operated as a bear, selling in the expectation of a fall in price, rather than as a bull buying for a rise, he deserved to lose. Selling what one did not own was seen as especially evil compared to buying what you could not pay for. Despite these reverses Ralph persevered with his speculations, learning how to take advantage of the market and the activities of the company promoters, brokers and jobbers. His success was achieved not at the expense of innocent investors but others in the City, such as Todigrab and the brokers Catspore and Fleasum, whose offices eventually went up in flames. Todigrab died as result while Fleasum was killed by a disgruntled investor. As a result Ralph became so rich and powerful that he was regarded as 'quite a City man', and in a position to contemplate marriage to Lady Beatrice Violet Playfair, the daughter of a landed aristocrat. Having made his fortune Ralph decided to give up speculation but could not. Such was the power of the Vortex that even an honourable person like Ralph was never free from its spell.[8]

It thus appeared to some in the 1870s that neither action against company promoters nor against brokers would be sufficient to eradicate the evils of speculation that was rife in Britain at the time. Though both Todigrab and Fleasum were dead, and their offices burnt down, the City continued to flourish. Newer, grander and even more far-fetched schemes were promoted. Similarly, Ralph and his prospective father-in-law, Lord Playfair, were now facing ruin, as they had lost heavily in new speculations. The implication was that the corruption present in the City could not be tackled by punishing a few of the most prominent bankers and brokers because 'it is the System which corrupts'. At the heart of the system was the closed nature of the Vortex as it operated solely for the benefit of insiders and to prevent outsiders getting justice. What was required was the closure of the Stock Exchange, and there was a growing demand for this from its victims as more and more faced ruin. They wanted an inquiry into the Vortex 'with a view to its immediate and absolute abolition on its present footing, and to the substitution in its place of an Open National Stock and Share Market, free to all'. In the end the Vortex exploded.

> The Vortex was in flames. Books, ledgers, telegrams, contacts, accounts, bonds, shares, scrip, etc., were scattered on the pavement, or flying in the air half consumed, and the whole atmosphere was darkened with ashes from the burning contents … now and then a boot, with a bit of a leg in it, shot up high in the air, or an arm in the attitude of making a bid for some wretched swindle; but that was all that was ever seen of them. Owing to the instantaneous nature of the catastrophe, the amount of the destruction to life and property was awful to contemplate. A huge wave of Retribution had shot in one moment from its centre to a distance of many miles before its force was wholly expended. It was now known that the whole of the vaults of the Vortex had exploded with terrific effect.

There was massive destruction and loss of life all around forcing thousands to flee in order to escape with their lives. One of the dead was Raskall Clencher, who had been beheaded in the blast.

Taking advantage of the sudden destruction of the Vortex, Ralph, accompanied by Beatrice, led a mob to the Houses of Parliament where they demanded admittance. There they were opposed by the Members of Parliament, especially a Railway Director, but to no avail. Ralph and Beatrice, supported by various members of the House of Lords, forced the House of Commons to debate the concerns of the mob. Ralph spoke about how he now realized the evils of speculation and that action must be taken. In response, a law was passed abolishing the Vortex. On hearing this news 'the bells of every town and village rang', Ralph urged a meeting to

> Open the markets. Stamp out gambling; no carrying over; pay for everything you buy. Sell nothing you have not got. Form an influential body of men whose names shall be unsullied, through whom alone all Loans and Undertakings can be placed upon the market. Let every project be submitted to the keenest and most searching scrutiny. Don't allow such a scandal as Foreign Loans to be foisted upon the gaping multitude, merely to fill the pockets of the knowing ones, who in the course of two or three days succeed, by devilish acts, in entrapping the unwary, and filling the subscription lists! If Countrees, Near and Far, require money, they must exercise the patience and undergo the scrutiny and the examination of ordinary mortals, to say the least, and be content to wait until they can satisfy the would-be lenders of their ability to pay both interest and capital at stated periods. Treat them with no more consideration than you would bestow upon private individuals! Deal a home-thrust at Speculation and Peculation simultaneously! You will thus restore that confidence in the monetary classes which is now so deservedly wanting!

His advice was taken.

> An association was at once formed upon a grand scale ... it comprised, among its members, all the leading bankers, capitalists, and merchants of Undone City, which was then the Emporium of the World. These had long been desirous of dissociating themselves from the Great national swindling house, which still continued to emit smoke and flame whenever an unfortunate Vortex broker approached it, in a state of drivelling insanity, to search for his strong box of securities.

This new association proved to be a great success despite efforts to destroy it. Branches were opened throughout the country, connected by telegraph. Ralph then married Lady Beatrice Playfair, having conquered the scourge of specula-tion.[9] Despite the virulence of this attack on the City, there was an acceptance that most of what took place there was necessary, and that this included such financial activities as issuing loans and trading securities. What people disliked was the way certain of these activities were conducted, especially the closed and secret business of the London Stock Exchange and the lack of protection it provided for those investors who bought and sold shares. This was a common complaint at this time along with the general belief that speculation in stocks and shares was nothing more than gambling.[10] Nevertheless, the City was now seen as a necessary part of a modern economy even though certain of its prac-tices and facilities were regarded as immoral and even dangerous, and should be suppressed either by government intervention or direct action.

Such views continued to linger into the later 1870s though the anger tended to abate as the most blatant abuses both faded from memory and faded from use, as their exposure limited their value to those who had used them. In a still highly critical account of the relationship between the members of the London Stock and the investing public, the semi-fictional book by Erasmus Pinto, *Ye Outside Fools!*, of which a new edition appeared in 1877, warned against any investment in British industrial shares, foreign mines and the issues of most foreign govern-ments, but recommended domestic railways.[11] An even more benign view of the City also appeared in that year in the shape of the novel, *The Golden Butterfly*, written by Walter Besant in collaboration with James Rice. Again, the focus was on company promotion and stock exchange speculation, with which the City was increasingly identified. Though still antagonistic towards those involved in the promotion of mining companies and speculation, it did not condemn those in the City as evil people. Rather it depicted them as dull and uncultured, having been made that way by a life devoted to money-making '...young City men but just beginning the worship of Mammon,...'. One of them, Gabriel Cassilis, who was an eminent City financier, told a dinner guest that 'Modern history begins with the Fuggers' as he measured everything by its monetary importance. Cas-silis was 'a very rich man ... His house was in Kensington Palace Gardens – a fact which speaks volumes; its furnishing was a miracle of modern art; his paintings were undoubted; his portfolios of water-colours were worth many thousands; and his horses were perfect ... He had married at sixty-three, because he wanted an establishment in his old age. He was too old to expect love from a woman, and too young to fall in love with a girl'. He had married Victoria Pengelly, who was twenty-eight. She came from a good but impoverished family and had decided that

> it is better to be rich and married than poor and single ... He was a director of many companies – but you cannot live in Kensington Palace Gardens by directing companies – and he had an office in the City which consisted of three rooms. In the first were four or five clerks. Always writing; in the second was a secretary, always writing; in the third was Mr. Gabriel Cassilis himself, always giving audience.

In these few words Besant summed up the contemporary perception of a City financier as a man who had made himself rich through his own efforts and an understanding of the ways of finance but had sacrificed, in the process, both his youth and a loving family life. Cassilis's wife had married him for his money but quickly grew to despise this 'man of shares, companies, and stocks'.[12]

Into Cassilis's office in the City came Gilead Beck, an American who had made millions through finding oil in Canada. He had an annual income of £500,000 and a letter from a New York bank that gave him unlimited credit. He wanted Cassilis to invest this fortune for him. On Cassilis's advice the money was to be placed in the shares issued by companies that Cassilis himself was floating, fuelling the suspicion that Beck was going to be defrauded by this City financier. Beck drew the line at taking shares in a silver mine, illustrating the continuing resonance of the Emma Silver mine scandal on the City's reputation. Only land and 3 per cent consols were seen as safe investments, whereas all shares were considered very risky. Another character, Phillis Fleming, had a fortune of £50,000, all invested in consols and producing a steady income of £1,500 per annum, making her a very attractive catch for any man, young or old. Nevertheless, it was made clear that Cassilis had to work hard for the money he expected to make from handling Beck's investments. Cassilis 'spent the day locked up in his inner office. He saw no one, except the secretary, and he covered an acre or so of paper with calculations. His clerks went away at five; his secretary left him at six; at ten he was still at work; feverishly at work, making combinations and calculating results'. Beck was not Cassilis's only client whose money he put into the shares of his own companies, because he did the same for them all. One was Lawrence Colquhoun, who not only entrusted his money to Gabriel Cassilis but also that of his ward, Phillis Fleming. 'Colquhoun was not the man to trouble about money. He was safe in the hands of this great and successful capitalist; he gave no thought to any risk; he congratulated himself on his cleverness in persuading the financier to take the money for him' Colquhoun's lawyer, Joseph Jagenal, advised him against placing his money in Cassilis's hands when he learnt what he had done. All Colquhoun could tell him was that Cassilis had 'talked me into an ambition for good investments which I never felt before ... after all, why not get eight and nine per cent., if you can?' Jagenal response was, 'Because it isn't safe, and because you ought not to expect it' advising him to place it in consols and railways. Colquhoun agreed to take his lawyer's advice. 'I will ask him to sell out for me, and go back to the old three per cents. And railway shares ... which is what I have been brought up to'. It was now recognized that the City had made a major contribution to the British economy as UK railway companies provided both essential transport and a safe investment. In contrast, the City's direction of funds abroad was not so well received, partly because of the losses being sustained by investors in companies operating abroad or foreign governments. 'Happy for this country that Honduras, Turkey, and a few other places exist to plunder the British capitalist, or we should indeed perish of wealth-plethora. Thousands of things all round us wait to be done; things which must be done by rich men, and cannot be done by trading men, because they would not pay'.[13]

Cassilis was a clever financier with a plan to make himself immensely rich, not at the expense of his clients but others in the City. Using the £250,000 entrusted to him by Beck, and the ability to ensure that he got allocated all the shares he applied for, as he was one of the promoters, he was able to control the market in the shares of certain companies. Those who sold shares in these companies in expectation of getting an allotment, which was common practice at the time, would be forced to buy them in the market instead, as he would have allocated them all to himself and his associates. The effect of this would be to force up the price allowing Cassilis to sell out at a profit, at the expense of his fellow speculators. Cassilis was uninterested in the companies themselves, only in whether he could buy and the sell at a premium. 'The wise man distrusts all companies, but puts his hope in a rise or fall'. As Beck became worried by the risks involved in holding company shares Cassilis agreed to buy them all back from him at cost price, netting a large profit for himself as they had risen in price through his operations in the market. He then invested Beck's money in government stocks, not the National Debt but those issued by Latin American republics. Even there Cassilis had a plan to make a great deal of money by operating in the market through the control he had over his clients' money. His first action was to pay Oliver Wylie £50 to produce a pamphlet warning the public of the inability of the government of the Republic of Eldorado to ever pay interest on its bonds. After the publication of the pamphlet the price of the bonds fell. At that stage he used all the money at his disposal to buy these bonds. This was his own £300,000, Beck's £250,000 and that of clients for whom he had power of attorney, such as Lawrence Colquhoun and Phillis Fleming. In all, he was able to employ £2 million in cornering the market in Eldorado bonds. In response to the pamphlet the ambassador of the Republic of Eldorado published a rebuttal that suggested that the country was in a prosperous condition and could easily resume payment on its bonds. That then encouraged buying. 'Half the country clergy who had a few hundreds in the bank wanted to put them in Eldorado Stock'. As a result the price started to rise. With the funds now at his disposal he had cornered the market in the bonds and as the settlement day approached those who had sold in the expectation of buying back at a higher price found there were none to buy. This drove the price higher and higher.

> Gabriel Cassilis was a gamester who played to win. His game was not the roulette-table, where the bank holds one chance out of thirty, and must win in the long-run; it was a game in which he staked his foresight, knowledge of events, financial connec-tions, and calm judgement against greed, panic, enthusiasm, and ignorance. It was his business to be prepared against any turn of the tide. He would have stood calmly in the Rue Quincampoix, buying in and selling out up to an hour before the smash. And that would have found him without a single share in Law's great scheme. A great game, but a difficult one. It requires many qualities, and when you have got these, it requires a steady watchfulness and attention to the smallest cloud appearing on the horizon.

That reference to the Mississippi bubble in Paris in 1720 illustrates the enduring legacy of spectacular speculative booms and crashes on the cultural perception of the City of London. It also indicates that perceptions of the City were influenced by events that took place in other countries and for which it was not responsible, suggesting that the way it was viewed was also a product of its function.

As it was, the stratagem adopted by Cassilis appeared to be working as the price of the bonds kept rising. Those in the City, such as the jobbers on the Stock Exchange, who had sold them in expectation of a fall, had now to buy them back if they were to honour their commitments. If they did not they would be declared defaulters, so destroying their reputation and thus their ability to do business in the City, where trust was of critical importance. However, on the very eve of his triumph, Cassilis took his eye off the market and the rumours that were circulating. Instead of the calculating City financier of old, on which his fortune and reputation had been made, he let personal feelings get in the way of business. Through certain actions of his wife, and the receipt of anony-mous letters, he believed she was having an affair with another man, and this distracted him at a critical time. 'It should have been a busy day in the City. To begin with, it only wanted four days to settling-day. Telegrams and letters poured in, and they lay unopened on the desk at which Gabriel Cassilis sat, with the letter before him, mad with jealousy and rage'. Under the strain of what he believed was his wife's infidelity Cassilis did not pay attention to his business affairs and eventually suffered a stroke that mentally incapacitated him. He missed the opportunity to sell out the Eldorado bonds at a huge profit before settlement day. 'Had he done so at the right moment, he would have realized the very handsome sum of two hundred and sixty thousand pounds; but the trouble of the letters came, and prevented him from acting'. In the meantime the government of Eldorado had made a statement that they could not pay interest on the loans with the result that they collapsed in price as those holding them rushed to sell for whatever they could get. This meant that those in the City who had sold them in expectation of a fall were able to buy them at a low price and so make good their bargains. This destroyed Cassilis's corner on the market. Even worse, he had to pay for all the shares he had agreed to buy despite the fact that they now had no value. As he had invested all his own money and that of his clients in these bonds, they were all ruined. There was a fine line between success and failure in the City as it all depended upon the course of events and the need to remain ever vigilant. Cassilis was not an evil person defrauding his clients, promoting worthless companies and valueless foreign loans. Instead he was a normal person exposed to the worries and distractions of all married men. Unfortunately, as he operated in the City the consequences were disastrous as he had played for high stakes and lost. It was the place, and what went on there, that created the problems not the people themselves.[14]

This can be seen from the fact that the greatest casualty of what had happened was Cassilis himself. 'For sixty years of his life, this man of the City, whose whole desire was to make money, to win in the game which he played with rare success and skill, regarded bankruptcy as the one thing to be dreaded, or at least to be looked upon, because it was absurd to dread it, as a thing bringing with it the whole of dishonour. Not to meet your engagements was to be in some sort a criminal. And now he was proclaimed as one who could not meet his engagements'. He lost all that belonged to him 'the house in Kensington Palace Gardens, with its costly furniture, its carriages, plate, library and pictures'. He now lived as an invalid in Brighton on the £15,000 settled on his wife. The other casualty was his wife, and she had to look after him, which was her punishment for marrying for money and then pursuing another man. 'Ruined! The thought of such disaster had never crossed her brains. Ruined! That Colossus of wealth – the man whom she had married for his money, while secretly she despised his power of accumulating money'. In contrast to Cassilis, his confidential clerk, Mr Mowl, who had pretended to be much more important that he was, simply got a job with another firm in the City: 'he was a clerk, and had always been a clerk: but he was a clerk who knew a few things which might have been awkward if told generally. He had a fair salary, but no confidence, no advice, and not much real knowledge of what his chief was doing than any outsider'. Even Cassilis's clients, who had been ruined along with himself, went on to better lives. Gilead Beck returned to the USA, accompanied by Lawrence Colquhoun, Phillis Fleming and others, and they settled in Virginia where they purchased land and lived happily ever after.[15] Certainly the impression is generated that by the late 1870s those in the City were not, in themselves, seen as evil people. That did not mean that the City had now redeemed itself within British culture, for it remained too much associated with company promotion, stock exchange speculation and foreign investment for that.

Evidence of the perception of the City by the late 1870s can be found in contemporary paintings, as this was one of the few periods when it attracted significant interest from artists. The City was not an easy topic for artists to paint, especially when what they were trying to convey its activities in money and finance rather than its buildings and streets or particular events. Nevertheless, such a feat was attempted at this time for the City of London by William Powell Frith in a series of paintings begun in 1877 and entitled 'The Race for Wealth'. These were meant to capture the career of the promoter of the Emma Silver Mine, Baron Grant, indicating what an impact that single scandal had upon public consciousness both at the time and for years afterwards. [16] What he chose to depict in the five paintings, according to Frith in his autobiography published in 1888, was '...the career of a fraudulent financier, or promoter of bubble companies; a character not uncommon in 1877, or, perhaps, even at the present time. I wished to illustrate also the common passion for speculation, and the destruction that so often attends the indulgence of it, to the lives and fortunes of the financier's dupes'. What 'The Race for Wealth' conveyed, in a sequence of paintings, was the fate of all who were seduced by the apparent ease by which money could be made in the City of London, and the consequences for those who succumbed to its temptations. The first picture showed the financier at the height of power with a scene from his office in the City, crowded with prospective investors being persuaded to buy shares.

> I planned my first scene in the office of the financier – eventually called the spider – the principal flies being an innocent-looking clergyman, who with his wife and daughters are examining samples of ore supposed to be the product of a mine – a map of which is conspicuous on the wall – containing untold wealth. The office is filled with other believers: a pretty widow with her little son, a rough country gentleman in overcoat and riding-boots, a foreigner who bows obsequiously to the great projector as he enters from an inner office – in which clerks are seen writing.

The next picture served two functions being located in the financier's own home. On the one hand it showed the personal rewards he had gained from his success in the City, as he lived in a fine house resplendent with good furniture and works of art and enjoyed the best of food and wine while waited upon by numerous servants. On the other hand, it revealed how the public were persuaded to invest by being wined and dined by the financier and flattered by the attentions of his socially well-connected associates, who profited from the business they introduced. In contrast, the financier himself was seen as 'an uncouth and vulgar figure' only acceptable in 'high society' because of his wealth and those who hoped to share in the riches created by his 'successful speculation'. The same applied to his wife, who was '...a vulgar type...' What is conjured up is a situation where the financier and his confederates made themselves wealthy by inducing naïve investors to buy shares in worthless enterprises.

The next three pictures then proceeded to show the fate awaiting those who indulged in this kind of activity. In the third scene, set in the home of an investor, the news of the collapse of the mining company had just been announced in the morning newspaper, causing dismay.

> The foolish clergyman sits at his breakfast-table, with his head bent to the blow. His wife, with terrified face, reads the confirmation of her worst fears in the newspaper, which a retreating footman has brought. Two daughters have risen terror-stricken from their chairs, and a little midshipman son looks at the scene with a puzzled expression, in which fear predominates. The catastrophe is complete: the little fortune has been invested in the mine, and the whole of it lost.

Though accepting that a highly probable outcome would be the financier escaping the consequences of his fraudulent company promotions Frith preferred to have him punished for his crimes. A fellow artist, J. F. Sullivan, painted a different ending to Frith's story, in a series of five cartoons in 1880, which appeared in the comic paper, *Fun*; entitled, *Odds on 'The Spider'*, the financier escaped punishment and retained his ill-gotten gains while the poor clergyman ended up as a road sweeper. As Frith had already used suicide as the last scene in his previous series of paintings, *The Road to Ruin*, which was about the evils of gambling, he had little choice left if the purpose of his morality tale was to show that corrupt City financiers could not escape the consequences of their actions. Thus, the financier was prosecuted for fraud as it could be proved that the ore used to entice investors had not come from the mine. The result was that he stood trial at the Old Bailey, and this was the next scene. 'See the financier there standing with blanched face listening to the evidence given by the clergyman, which, if proved, will consign him to penal servitude. His victims – recognizable as those in his office in the opening of my story – stand ready to add their testimony. The widow, the foreigner, the country gentleman, are there; and so also are some of his aristocratic guests'. The financier is then found guilty and sentenced to prison, and that is the subject of the last painting: 'in prison-garb the luckless adventurer takes his dismal exercise with his fellow-convicts in the great quadrangle of Millbank Gaol'.[17] These series of paintings present a powerful image of the City of London as a corrupting influence, and indicate that its place within British culture was increasingly dependent upon its association with specific financial activities rather than as a place or even a business community. The City was now a concept rather than a reality in the minds of many contemporaries and such a position was reinforced by the images produced by Frith and adapted by Sullivan.

However, these images of the City were not entirely negative in the late 1870s for there was a growing recognition of the investment opportunities it made available, at a time of low and falling yields on both the National Debt and British railway debentures. This can be seen in Wilkie Collins's 1878 short story, *The Haunted Hotel*. When Henry's old nanny discovered she has been left £400 she sought his advice on how to invest it.

> 'If you put your hundred pounds into the Funds, you will get between three and four pounds a year. The nurse shook her head. 'Three or four pounds a year? That won't do. I want more than that. Look here master Henry. I don't care about this bit of money – I never did like the man who has left it to me, though he was your brother. If I lost it all to-morrow, I shouldn't break my heart; I'm well enough off, as it is, for the rest of my days. They say you're a speculator. Put me in for a good thing, there's a dear. Neck-or-nothing-and that for the Funds!' She snapped her fingers to express her contempt for security of investment at three per cent. Henry produced the prospectus of the Venetian Hotel Company ... The nurse took out her spectacles'. Six per cent guaranteed she read, and the Directors have every reason to believe that ten per cent, or more, will be ultimately realized to the shareholders by the hotel. Put me into that, Master Henry'.[18]

To others the company promoter and the shares he sold to the investing public continued to stigmatize the whole City. In *The Great Tontine* by Hawley Smart, published in 1881, one of the minor characters was the company promoter, Anthony Lyme Wregis. He had made millions through promoting bogus mines and phantom railways or '...every description of bubble speculation that filled the pockets of those that started them at the expense of the unfortunate dupes that took shares in them'. When his schemes finally fell apart and he was bankrupted, Lyme Wregis took the usual way out and committed suicide.[19]

Increasingly, the City was associated in the public mind with this single activity of company promotion and the subsequent trading in shares on the Stock Exchange, even though there was an awareness that other activities continued to be of major importance. It was recognized, for example, that the City remained a place of trade. In the *Golden Butterfly* reference was made to the picture dealers who still operated from premises there, such as Bartholomew Burls and Company, Church Street, City. 'The shop was rather dark, though the sun of May was pouring a flood of light even upon the narrow City streets'. Though many of the pictures they sold were fake they conducted a successful business. Similarly, Collins, in the short novel, *Who Killed Zebedee*, published in 1881, one of the characters 'mentioned the names of a well-known firm of cigar merchants in the City'.[20] By the mid-1880s the importance, wealth and respectability of the successful City merchant had become embedded in British culture as can be seen from Anstey's humorous novel, *Vice Versa*, which appeared in 1882. The story revolved around Paul Bultitude, a Colonial Produce agent with offices in Mincing Lane and an agent in Canton. He was painted as complacent, conventional and rather old fashioned but very respectable. 'Mr Bultitude was a tall and portly person, of a somewhat pompous and overbearing demeanour; not much over fifty, but looking considerably older ... His general expression suggested a conviction of his own extreme importance'. He lived in a substantial house in Westbourne Terrace in London, from which he travelled to the City by bus. Anstey himself notes that the very mention of a City person would lead the reader to expect some kind of financial reverse, at the very least, or, more probably, revelations regarding financial irregularities.

> Habitual novel readers on reading thus far will, I am afraid, prepare themselves for the arrival of a faithful cashier with news of irretrievable ruin, or a mysterious and cynical stranger threatening disclosures of a disgraceful kind. But all anticipations must at once be ruthlessly dispelled. Mr. Bultitude, although he was certainly a merchant, was a fairly successful one – in direct defiance of the laws of fiction, where any connection with commerce seems to lead naturally to failure in one of the three volumes. He was an elderly gentleman, too, of irreproachable character and antecedents; no Damocles' sword of exposure was swinging over his bald but blameless head; he had no disasters to fear and no indiscretions to conceal.

The commercial City had become respectable whereas the financial City had not. Bultitude's brother in law, Marmaduke Paradine, had been involved in a series of dubious transactions while acting as an agent for a Manchester firm in Bombay. On his return to Britain he had become involved 'with the promotion of a series of companies of the kind affected by the widow and curate, and exposed in money articles and law courts'.

The continuing diversity to be found in the City as a place confused the image it projected to the public, though its functions were more and more identified with finance. The City had established itself as distinct from the rest of London. It was a place where men worked and made money, or lost it, while the rest of London was occupied by women and children as that was where homes were to be found and families lived. Besant had noted that already in *The Golden Butterfly*. 'They drove through the crowded City, where the roll of the vehicles thundered on the girl's astonished ears and the hard-faced crowd sped swiftly past her'.[21] The City was sandwiched between the East End and West End, characterized only by what it did and not by those who lived there. This comes across strongly in Besant's 1882 novel, *All Sorts and Condition of Men* where there is seen to be a sharp division between the West and the East of London as the residents of the City moved out. The rich went west and the poor went east, creating distinct and separate communities with few links between them. This left the City empty on Sunday, being filled during the week with people who arrived in the morning and then vanished in the evening. It was also a place of foreigners, like Germans, who became rich and then anglicized their names. The West End was a place of pleasure and entertainment with clubs, shops and theatres. '[T]he rich London merchants go north and south and west; but they go not east. Nobody goes east, no one wants to see the place; no one is curious about the way of life in the east'. The East End was seen as a place populated by small manufacturers producing all kinds of different articles, such as cardboard boxes to be filled by the wholesale merchants of the City. Though some may have worked in the City, the people of the East End were separate from the 'quill-driving clerk in the City' who was entitled to a fortnight's holiday every year on full pay.[22] The communities to the East and to the West were seen to possess their own distinctive culture, as depicted in such works as in George Gissing's 1889 novel, *The Nether World* (Clerkenwell) or in the 1896 novel by Arthur Morrison, *A Child of the Jago* (Shoreditch)[23] In contrast the City was no longer a residential community but a business one, and so lacked the diversity and human interest that attracted readers to novels of those kind.

This change in the way the City was perceived, as well as the recognition that it continued to be seen as both a commercial and a financial district, is evident in another of Walter Besant's novel, *All in a Garden Fair,* which appeared in 1883. It simultaneously praised the commercial side of the City while criticizing the financial, in a story of three young men competing for the hand of their tutor's daughter. Tommy became a City financier and failed, exposing himself as a crook and a fool and thus not fitted for marriage. Allen became a poet and acquired a wife who moved in literary circles. Will became a silk merchant in the City and it was he who married the girl on his return from China, having proved that he was safe and steady. None lived in the City but in a village in Essex, and that, along with the West End, was where the social life was centred. All began their City careers with commercial firms, having acquired a good education at the hands of their tutor. '...young men who know foreign languages are not so plentiful in the City, they command a price'. At the age of fifteen two of the boys, Allen Engledew and Will Massey, got positions as clerks with Brimage and Waring, where Allen's father had begun, before setting up for himself. 'the two boys, who had so long trudged to school, now went to the City and back by the same train, sat beside each other at the same desk, and took their dinners together for ninepence[24] at the same luncheon-bar'. Brimage and Waring was a firm of silk merchants with offices in the City and at the London and St. Katherine's Docks. The firm

> employs an immense quantity of clerks, workmen, porters, carters, and people of all kinds and it has branches and agencies in the Far East, and in France. The grey-headed men who draw large salaries, or have a share in the profits, have been at the House since they were boys. They entered as clerks, ambitious rising clerks. There are, also,

grey-headed men who entered with them as clerks, without ambition, hopeless clerks, who began to copy letters and add up, and are doing the same thing still, and draw, some of them, as much as two hundred pounds a year, and live at Stepney, or Penton-ville, or, it may be, happy Hoxton.

In contrast, the senior partner 'has got a town house at a place called Lancaster Gate, and a country house in Hampshire, and he's a Member of Parliament too'. For young men who wanted to rise in the world, both financially and socially, a firm of City merchants offered an obvious route if they were clever and worked hard. However, even within the commercial City there remained a hierarchy with wholesale trade being ranked above the retail trade, no matter the money made.

Will took to his work firmly believing that 'to make money one must be in the City'. He wanted to become rich, as that would make him both respected and powerful. The means to achieving that was 'a partnership in Brimage and Waring with ten thousand a year'. When the opportunity to go out to Shanghai on behalf of the firm arose he seized it, even though it meant an absence of years. This position was one of major responsibility leading to a possible partnership, if the person handled it well. The previous incumbent had become a drunk and his actions had endangered the reputation of the firm forcing his replacement. In contrast to Will, Allen came to hate the City, where he went 'every morning at half-past eight, and returns every evening at half-past six ... During this long time he sits upon a stool, he copies letters, he enters figures in a book, he adds up, he makes notes, he carries messages, he goes here, he goes there'. To Allen it was 'The same work every day; the same letters to be written; the same papers to be copied; the same figures to be entered and added up, the same chatter of the clerks'. He saw the work of a City clerk as mechanical, only suited to those from East End of London who lived in ignorance of the civilizing influences of the West End, with its theatres and clubs. What he wanted was to become a famous author, seeing writing as a much more worthwhile and honourable calling than making money in the City or even earning one's living there as a clerk. 'If you are a merchant, you live out your life for the sake of making money. Can that be compared with the life of an author – a poet – who shows the better life, who interprets the thoughts of the people?' Allen did not want to be in the City and had no ambition to become a wealthy merchant. 'the irksomeness of the work became everyday more intolerable to him, and the drudgery more aimless'. His mother wanted him to succeed in the City. 'Young men become known, they are promoted, they become heads of departments, or they go away and set up for themselves, as your father did when he saved some money, and was known to all his friends of the House'. Despite this parental pressure he resigned his position and started to write poems and stories, making ends meet by editing a trade journal. Even when he had established himself as a successful author, his mother continued to regret the fact that he had given up a promising career in the City. She came from a business background and could not see beyond it. 'He should have become one of the leading merchants in London, a grave and serious man, with a character. Not a play actor, to make people laugh and cry'. Those in the City could consider themselves superior because of their material success compared to others, such as writers. 'Literature is but a poor trade, a poor trade'. In contrast, the cultured classes felt themselves superior to those in the City because they could see beyond the world of money. 'Would any girl take a City man? Think of it – a money-making man, a man who buys and sells, when she might have a poet'.[25]

The third boy, Tommy Gallaway, started work in the City at the same age as the others, but joined his uncle's oil broking business, where he quickly became a partner. He was discontented '...with the slow business and small returns of the oil trade', having discovered the delights and expenses of West End living. That led him to explore the financial side of the City.

> There lies, not far from Capel Court, a mysterious world, the world of Finance. It is a world inhabited by a race resembling men, who spend their lives in whispering, chattering in corners, winking at each other, making signs, buying nothing at all without money, and making great profit thereat; selling for nothing what they have not got and going bankrupt over the transaction; building up great edifices for other people out of rotten eggs; knocking these down again and with the profits buying marble palaces; stealing the slender fortunes of widows. Orphans, clergymen, and all who are poor and defenceless; promising what they will never perform, stating what they know to be false, and prophesying things which will never happen. Their language among themselves is barbarous and impossible to understand. Outside, however, they can talk English.

This was a world where 'The atmosphere everywhere is filled with the perfume of bank-notes, shares, bonds, and coupons'. At the heart of this world was the company promoter who invited any person who inherited a fortune to 'drop his money in steamship companies, to throw it away in mines, to give it to the Americans for bogus railway shares, to bestow it upon needy directors in trams, flams, and shams of all kinds, to take shares in the stock of companies formed to prevent a tradesman from becoming bankrupt'. Those in the City who pursued a mercantile career, like Will, considered this financial business 'to be pure plundering and robbery' but acknowledged that it is 'a thing which wants a quicker brain and wider knowledge than any other trade in the world'.

Tommy did not possess these attributes, unlike a friend of his father's. This was Colliber, a man with a 'hooked nose, and sharp eyes and quick savage manner'.[26] He had begun in the City as a clerk to a wine merchant. From that he had moved into company promotion and made himself millions by the time he was fifty. 'From a clerk's desk to a great house in Palace Gardens; from a miserable shilling City dining room to all the best clubs in London'. He then lost most of it by the time he was sixty though he did salvage £20,000. His failure to the tune of half a million destroyed his livelihood as he was no longer trusted by others in the City.

Seeing a way to re-enter the City using Tommy as a front he introduced him to his broker, Gedge. He told Tommy to buy 10,000 Russian bonds at 4⅜ and sell them at the end of a fortnight, by which time they would have risen to 4⅞, making a profit of £50. This was the result and so Tommy started to study the market himself but could not understand why 'stocks went up and why they went down'. Having lost money he agreed to an offer from Colliber in which Tommy would do what he was told and take 25 per cent of the profits. Tommy resigned from his uncle's firm and opened his own office in the City. Within two years he had become a great success, being labelled 'A young Napoleon of finance'.

> He underwrote new companies, backed up old ones, strengthened the tottering, undermined the strong, was bull or bear and always right, and seemed to know beforehand the dividend that was going to be declared. ...companies for electric lights, for packet-boats, for tramways, for torpedoes, for telephones, for hotels, for newspapers, and a hundred other things. All these were started, promoted, shoved off by Mr. Gallaway; he underwrote them, he bought and sold their shares, he created a demand for them and got them quoted. One thing Mr. Gallaway never did; he did not become a director, nor did he buy anything, estate, business, or steamers; nor did he in any way at all associate his name publicly with the company, nor was he in the least degree responsible for the statements made in the prospectus.

On one scheme, the Sindbad Island Gold Mining Company, they made £45,000 through the issue of shares and then manipulating the market so that the insiders gained and the outsiders lost. To an extent the investing public had only themselves to blame. 'The British public is never tired of companies; sometimes there is a lull, but only for a short time, and then the game goes on again with undiminished vigour'. Most of the investors were men 'who had retired from business with their few thousands, the savings of a life's work, and thought four per cent a miserable return for their money, remembering the large profits they had made in trade'. Tommy felt no regret about 'defrauding and plundering widows and children and credulous persons'. Among them were women, who would invite financiers to dinner in the hope of getting an investment tip, 'they'll say anything to get round you'. One such was a Countess who persuaded Tommy into giving her inside information. 'I've been most cruelly deceived by the Countess. I thought she wanted my society; she only wanted my tips after all. I gave her one or two, and she plunged and made a little pile; and then she went on without me, and lost it all ... I knew her ladyship was a gambler, well enough'. Over a two-year period Colliber made £150,000 and Tommy £50,000 but it all came unstuck with the last company they promoted. The prospectus was 'a bundle of lies' and the shares quickly collapsed in price, leaving investors looking for someone to blame. Tommy was identified as responsible while Colliber fled. As Tommy would not repay the investors their money they took him to court so as to declare him bankrupt, and so get access to all his assets. 'There's one man, a clergyman, who ought to be a Christian, and because he's lost a paltry five thousand pounds he heads the lot – says I made false representations'. They were going to prove that Tommy 'the great promoter, wire-puller, financier, and operator could be made responsible for statements by which people had been robbed of thousands'. Tommy was convicted and made to buy back the shares issued, which bankrupted him. As with Colliber before him, Tommy had to give up business in the City, though he had hidden away £10,000, which allowed him to live comfortably.[27]

Even bankruptcy was not seen as the sin it once was because contemporaries were well aware of how easily it could occur to even the most respectable merchants because of the vagaries of trade. Those who made fortunes in the City retired to 'Buckhurst Hill, or to Sydenham, or go to Chiselhurst'. Those who were less successful ended up in Essex, such as Skantlebury, as did those who failed, like Sir Charles Withycomb, an ex-Lord Mayor, (owing £150,000) and Massey (owing £70,000), through ill-conceived speculations in trade such as 'shipping coals to Newcastle, sugar to Mauritius, rum to Jamaica, tea to China, or claret to Bordeaux'. There was also Mrs Engledew, whose husband, a silk merchant, had committed suicide when faced with failure and prosecution due to the actions of his partner, John Stephens, who had disappeared. Trust continued to be seen as the key to success in the City and when that was lost through failure there was no alternative but to depart. Though such people still

> talked about investments and consulted share lists ... There is no hurried rush to the City in the morning, nor is there the slow return in the evening; their feet tread no more the golden pavement; yet they have been there and still would go; and in their eyes it is the nearest approximation to heaven below.

It was recognized by the mid-1880s that the City delivered success and failure in equal measure, as those who worked there lived 'by buying cheap and selling dear'. Where this was accomplished through trade the results were considered acceptable whereas that was not the case with finance. There was always 'a deadly hatred of the City and all that belongs to money and money making'.[28] However, even in finance the public now appreciated the benefits that came from successful investments as well as the risks associated with the likes of speculation and company promotion. In Samuel Butler's novel *The Way of All Flesh,* which dates from the early 1880s, Edward Pontifex, observed that his friend Pryor 'knows several people who make quite a handsome income out of very little or, indeed, I may say, nothing at all, by buying things at a place they call the Stock Exchange; I don't know much about it yet, but Pryor says I should soon learn'. The result of this learning process was that Pontifex lost £2,685 out of the £5,000 he had invested, while Pryor absconded with the rest. After that Pontifex entrusted his remaining inheritance to his godfather who placed it first in the stock of the Midland Railway and then the London and Northwestern, with the result that it grew from £15,000 in 1850 to over £140,000 by 1882.[29] Whereas railways were now considered a safe investment speculation on the Stock Exchange remained very hazardous, as Robert Louis Stevenson observed in his 1885 novel, *The Dynamiter*. 'A hundred pounds will with difficulty support you for a year; with somewhat more difficulty you may spend it in a night; and without any difficulty at all you may lose it in five minutes on the Stock Exchange.'[30]

From the evidence available it does appear that more and more aspects of the City of London had made the transition from social pariah to semi-respectability over the course of the period from 1870 to 1885. This had been accomplished through a mixture of an absence of major frauds, collapses and speculative manias and a growing recognition among the public of the contribution it made through well-managed banking and investment facilities. The journey to respectability had been travelled furthest by the merchant and the banker, as they became increasingly trusted and respected. A similar process had taken place with insurance, as the creation of large and stable companies providing cheap life, fire and accident cover had removed this activity from contention within Britain. Like banks, insurance companies now conducted a dull and routine business and were staffed by professional though boring people. Even the Stock Exchange had undergone something of a change as it now housed markets for a wide range of securities valued by the British public, such as home and foreign railways. These produced unspectacular but steady returns which could be relied upon by those seeking a regular income. However, the Stock Exchange also housed markets for highly speculative securities, especially those issued by the numerous mining companies that enjoyed a somewhat transitory existence. These shares were more like lottery tickets or gambling chips, having little in common with consols or railway debentures, with their fixed rate of return. In addition, prices of securities did rise and fall constantly, causing those who lost to complain vociferously and accuse those in the City of cheating them. This meant that the Stock Exchange occupied a rather ambiguous position in terms of public regard. It catered for those looking for a reasonable return on their money, at a time when this was difficult to obtain because of the falling yield on the National Debt and the generally low rates of interest. It also catered for those willing to gamble on an unproven technology, such as electricity, or a potential mineral discovery, whether it was coal, copper, gold, lead or tin. Finally, there was to be no redemption for the company promoter no matter the success of earlier schemes. Such people were always associated with the latest investment fashion and were blamed by those who had followed it and then lost. The prominence given to these company promoters and the fate of the companies they created, blighted the whole image of the City in the eyes of the public from time to time. Compounding this was the fact that a number of these promoters were foreign, Jewish or both, which helped fuel criticisms of the City through the usual appeals to racial and religious intolerance.

By the mid-1880s the place of the City within British culture was a now a product of function not location. People commuted to the City, worked there and then came home again. It was what happened in these offices and on the trading floor of the Stock Exchange that determined how it was viewed. This suggests that British culture had taken on board the transition of the City from commercial community to financial centre and was now judging it accordingly. However, that judgement was strongly tinged with nostalgia for a City that was easier to understand because it involved people who both lived and worked there and were engaged in tasks that could be easily understood. In contrast, to many, the City's growing involvement with international finance made its operations both remote and obscure, so distancing it from the country within which these activities took place. A consequence of this was that the place of the City in British culture was not firmly rooted in the public mind but was dependent upon those aspects that came to the fore at any one time. Most prominent was speculation on the London Stock Exchange as this was widely and regularly reported in the main national newspapers. The other area that the public was very aware of was the field of operation of the company promoter through the appeals they made to investors for subscriptions to every new issue. As a result the public received a highly distorted impression of the City of London but used this as the basis of its overall judgement. The consequence was a continuing distrust of the City of London, because of its association with both speculation and investor losses, which was only partially balanced by an awareness of the important contribution it made to the normal conduct of commercial and financial business.

4 AVARICE AND HONESTY, 1885–1895

By the late 1880s the City was no longer seen as a place where swindlers could operate without redress, where violent fluctuations in the stock market could ruin investors overnight, or where sudden banking collapses could wipe out a person's entire savings. Though the City remained a place viewed with suspicion by many because of its connection with speculation and the world of money dealing, it did appear to have assumed an air of respectability and reliability among the population at large. However, that reputation was to be severely tested in the early 1890s in a series of financial and banking collapses at home and abroad. The most notable event that originated domestically was the collapse of the Liberator Building Society. This was a bank that had expanded rapidly through the strategy of continuously revaluing its portfolio of mortgaged property so as to justify ever more ambitious lending, and by paying generous rates of interest to small savers. Eventually the whole edifice collapsed in 1892 exposing massive fraud undertaken by its chairman, Jabez Balfour, who then fled abroad so as to escape prosecution. Important as the case of the Liberator Building Society was, in terms of the adverse publicity it created for the City, much more significant were events that took place abroad, such was the global reach of the City of London and the worldwide interests of British investors. Numbered among the most spectacular of these was the Baring Crisis of 1890. This crisis centred on the inability of borrowers in Argentina to service their debts, after a period of rapid expansion financed by selling securities in London to British investors through Barings, one of the City's largest and oldest merchant banks. Not only was Barings responsible for paying interest on these securities, as agent for the borrowers in Argentina, but it also had substantial holdings on its own account. The temporary suspension of interest payments on Argentinian debt and the near collapse of Barings bank helped to undermine confidence in all Latin American securities. British savers had also helped fuel the rapid growth of the Australian housing market by depositing large sums in banks there, having been attracted by the high rate of interest paid. When these banks experienced large losses, after a collapse in property prices and borrowers defaulting on their loans, British depositors found themselves unable to withdraw their money. This came to a head in 1893, shaking confidence in Australia as a field of investment. Finally, British investors had been increasingly attracted by the good returns available on the stocks and bonds of major US railroads, only to discover that much of this was based on over-optimistic earnings forecasts and financial deception, especially in the case of the Philadelphia and Reading Railroad. This also came to the fore in 1893 when the speculative bubble in the USA burst and many banks closed their doors. All these foreign financial events were well reported in Britain as they had major implications for British investors. What is unclear, though, is their effect on the reputation of the City of London. Judged from fundamentals the City's position as the foremost financial centre in the world remained unaffected by any of these events, being supported by its unrivalled connections and expertise, the depth and breadth of its markets, and the reputation of institutions like the Bank of England. The world needed a financial centre and London provided it, as witnessed by its importance at the centre of an increasingly extensive web of global banking connections. Conversely, the case of the Liberator Building Society reawakened dormant fears about banking collapses while the flight of Jabez Balfour turned the spotlight on the unsavoury side of finance. In addition, events abroad emphasized how the City exposed British investors and savers to volatile foreign markets and to the actions of foreign financiers. This leads to the question of whether it was fundamentals or events that were more important in determining the City's place within British culture. If it was events was it those taking place close to home that were more significant or those in far distant lands that made the greatest impact? Discovering what happened to the public perception of the City in the ten years between 1885 and 1895 will help provide answers.[1]

In the late 1880s a City banker was seen to be a person who went to work in the morning, undertook dull and routine tasks, and then returned home in the evening. In Jerome K. Jerome's *Three Men in a Boat*, which came out in 1889, it was remarked that 'George goes to sleep at a bank from ten to four each day, except Saturdays, when they wake him up and put him outside at two'. Hence his desire to escape the City through a boating trip on the Thames, if only briefly.[2] The collapse of the Liberator Building Society did not produce a backlash against City banking, suggesting that the public could distinguish between a specialized bank and those that were now at the heart of the financial system. This can be judged from one of Walter Besant's novels, written in collaboration with Rice. This was *Ready- Money Mortiboy,* which appeared in 1891. Though focusing on the risks inherent in banking it did not suggest that the City's banks were liable to collapse or that bankers were inherently dishonest people. Instead, the action was confined to a small local bank located the provincial town of Market Basing, in Holmshire, about an hour and half from London by train. In Market Basing there existed two banks, namely Melliship's bank and Mortiboy's bank. Whereas Richard Mortiboy was a hard and calculating banker, Francis Melliship was a kind and accommodating man, but both were honest. 'Mr Melliship advanced his customers at five per cent. Old Mortiboy at six or seven per cent;...Mr Melliship took the bad business; old Mortiboy the good-or none ... Mr Melliship never pressed a man, never turned a deaf ear to a tale of distress...' The inevitable result was the collapse of Melliship's bank as rumours about its solvency caused some depositors to withdraw their money, causing a run as others rushed to do the same. The ensuing panic nearly brought down Mortiboy's bank, even though it had been well managed and was completely solvent. Such a tale reflected an acceptance that banks needed to be well managed to survive, even though this meant charging high rates of interest and the refusal to lend when the risks were too great. If such caution was not observed then collapse was inevitable with unfortunate consequences for all, especially those who had trusted their savings to the bank. Knowing that his bank was on the verge of collapse, Francis Melliship committed suicide, even though he had done nothing wrong. He could not face the disgrace that would come from the failure of his bank, and the loss of status it would mean for him personally. His suicide left his widow and family to face the mob of depositors demanding their money. They lost their home and possessions, as well as their position in local society, and had no option but to move away, seeking refuge in the anonymity of London. Francis Melliship's son knew London having been sent there, aged nineteen, to be trained at his father's correspondent bank, indicating the position the City occupied as a centre of financial expertise.[3] Though the story was largely about events at some remove from London, the City does not escape entirely from criticism, both as a place of trade and finance. The City firm of picture restorers and art dealers, Barholmew Burls, not only conducted a legitimate business but also manufactured fake paintings in the style of whatever artist was popular at the time, which were then sold to the unsuspecting public. More significantly, the City remained a place where money was easily lost through speculation. Francis Melliship had tried to retrieve his financial position by using the bank's money to speculate on the London Stock Exchange 'he invested largely in foreign stocks, promising a high rate of interest; in Land and Credit Companies; in South American mining speculations. This was gambling; but he learnt the truth too late'.[4] The City continued to possess a reputation as a place where naïve investors could easily lose their money but not one where banking collapses took place.

Thus wealthy bankers remained acceptable members of society. 'Fancy the world presuming to laugh at a man with half a million and more of money!' was a comment made regarding Dick Mortiboy, when he acquired his father's business and wealth. However, the degree of respect that bankers commanded was conditional upon how they conducted their business and what they did with their money. When Ready Money Mortiboy died his funeral was attended only by his son, his bank clerk, and the family lawyer, despite the fact that he had led a blameless and successful life. Success as a banker did not make him liked or respected because he devoted his life to moneymaking. In contrast, when the son died his funeral was very well attended and the town erected a statue in his honour. Prior to inheriting the banking business of his father, and the accumulated fortune, this son had led a wasteful and even criminal life. However, unlike his father, he was not actively engaged in running the bank, leaving that to a clerk, whom he instructed to follow a much more considerate lending policy. In addition, he gave away much of his inherited fortune, with what remained being left to his poor but deserving relatives.⁵ Bankers had to behave in a certain way if they were to gain acceptance, and that involved generous lending at low rates of interest accompanied by considerable benefactions to the community and to relatives, in atonement for the fact that they had become wealthy through a business that was little more than moneylending. This reveals an inner contradiction in late Victorian culture between recognizing reality and wishing life to be different. The collapse of Melliship's bank showed what became of a banker, and those that relied upon him and trusted him, if the strict observance of conservative banking practices was not followed. That was suicide, disgrace and ruin. In contrast, Mortiboy's success as banker showed the fate awaiting a banker who did follow the banking code rigidly. That brought wealth but only at the expense of loneliness, failure as a husband and father, and universal dislike. Successful bankers could only achieve the position in society that they desired if they distanced themselves from the business from which their wealth came, and then gave away the money they had made. It was not that bankers were evil or corrupt people but rather that the pursuit of money set them apart from the rest of respectable society while they remained actively engaged in the business.

Thus, the reputation of the City appeared to have surmounted the effects of a brief though spectacular banking failure. A similar outcome was to be found for the impact made by fluctuations in the price of securities. The National Debt continued to be regarded as the safest investment, as in Collins's 1886 novel, *The Evil Genius*. When Captain Bennydeck inherited money on the death of his father he decided 'to invest it in the Funds, and to let it thrive at interest'.⁶ Similarly, in Oscar Wilde's 1895 play, *The Importance of Being Earnest*, Cecily Cardew's fortune was safely invested in UK government stock. Being in possession of 'about a hundred and thirty thousand pounds in the Funds' she was a very eligible young woman for any man seeking her hand in marriage.⁷ However, the low yield on such an investment drove those seeking an increased income to search for alternatives. When they did so there seemed to be an acceptance that this involved greater risks, as in Collins and Besant's 1890 novel, *Blind Love*, where it was stated that 'shares rise and fall – and companies sometimes fail'.⁸ Especially when these problems arose abroad, it could be blamed on the machinations of foreign financiers rather than the home grown variety. It was

Paris, in particular, that was seen to be the location of unscrupulous and corrupt bankers rather than London, reflecting the revelations associated with the attempt to finance the building of the Panama Canal. Following on from their success in building the Suez Canal the French embarked on an even more grandiose scheme, namely the creation of a waterway linking the Atlantic and Pacific through Central America. This proved to be grossly overambitious and investors placed the blame on the promoters in Paris when the scheme collapsed in 1889. In Oscar Wilde's play, *The Ideal Husband*, which was performed in 1895, it was a plot hatched abroad that was the principal feature not recent events in London. The setting was a house in Grosvenor Square, London, and the chief characters were both English, namely Sir Robert Chiltern, the undersecretary for foreign affairs, and Mrs Cheveley, an old school friend of his wife, but it was European financiers that were attempting to deceive the investing public. Mrs Cheveley had lived for many years in Vienna, where she had been befriended by a European financier called Baron Arnheim. It was on his behalf that she was using her social acquaintances in London to persuade Sir Robert to do something dishonest, as emerged from the conversation that took place between them.

'Mrs Cheveley. I want to talk to you about a great political and financial scheme, about this Argentine Canal Company, in fact.

Sir Robert Chiltern. What a tedious, practical subject for you to talk about, Mrs Cheveley.

Mrs Cheveley. Oh, I like tedious, practical subjects. What I don't like are tedious, practical people. There is a wide difference. Besides, you are interested, I know, in international canal schemes. You were Lord Radley's secretary, weren't you, when the Government bought the Suez Canal shares?

Sir Robert Chiltern. Yes. But the Suez Canal was a very great and splendid undertaking. It gave us our direct route to India. It had imperial value. It was necessary that we should have control. This Argentine scheme is a commonplace Stock Exchange swindle.

Mrs Cheveley. A speculation, Sir Robert! A brilliant, daring speculation.

Sir Robert Chiltern. Believe me, Mrs Cheveley, it is a swindle. Let us call things by their proper names. It makes matters simple. We have all the information about it at the Foreign Office. In fact, I sent out a special Commission to inquire into the matter privately, and they report that the works are hardly begun, and the money already subscribed, no one seems to know what has become of it. The whole thing is a second Panama, and with not a quarter of the chance of success that miserable affair ever had. I hope you have not invested in it. I am sure you are too clever to have done that.

Mrs Cheveley. I have invested very largely in it.

Sir Robert Chiltern. Who could have advised you to do such a foolish thing?

Mrs Cheveley. Your old friend – and mine

Sir Robert Chiltern. Who?

Mrs Cheveley. Baron Arnheim

Sir Robert Chiltern. [*Frowning*] Ah! Yes. I remember hearing, at the time of his death, that he had been mixed up in the whole affair.

Mrs Cheveley. It was his last romance. His last but one, to do him justice.'

At this stage the impression is given that Mrs Cheveley is a foolish woman who had believed the assurances of a foreign financier, with whom she was romantically involved, and so invested her fortune in a highly dubious company. However, Mrs Cheveley was no naïve investor. First she tried to bribe Sir Robert to change the statement he was going to make to Parliament. When he refused to be bribed she then tried to blackmail him. She had in her possession a letter from Sir Robert to Baron Arnheim which revealed that he had told him about the British government's intended purchase of the Suez Canal shares back in 1875, a few days before the announcement was made. The result was that the Baron had made a large fortune by speculating in the shares prior to the announcement, and had rewarded Sir Robert richly. Sir Robert was now on the verge of exposing the Argentine Canal scheme as a swindle. Mrs Chevely wanted him, instead, to praise its virtues knowing that such a statement, from a member of the government, would create a demand for the shares, so raising the price, and allow her to sell at a large profit. If he did not do this she would expose him, so ruining his political career. As she told Sir Robert, 'And now I am going to sell you that letter, and the price I ask for it is your public support of the Argentine scheme. You made your fortune out of one canal. You must help me and my friends to make our fortune out of another!' Initially, Sir Robert agreed to her demands, justifying to himself that he had committed no actual crime and that nobody had lost as a result. He blamed the Baron for persuading him to do it but he had accepted £110,000 from him after the deal was completed. With additional advice from the Baron he then trebled that amount in five years. In the end Sir Robert made a statement to Parliament exposing the scheme as a fraud but escaped exposure. A friend, Lord Goring, in whom he had confided, managed to obtain the letter from Mrs Cheveley by threatening to expose her as a thief. Rather than being a naïve investor who had invested in yet another joint stock swindle, Mrs Cheveley was playing a skilful game orchestrated by European financiers, and she nearly succeeded.[9]

Events that took place abroad, even if they affected British investors, were too remote to have sufficient impact so as to change public perceptions of the City, especially if the blame could be placed on foreigners not even resident in London. Nevertheless, it was always easy to revive popular antagonism towards the City based on previous events that were now given a contemporary outing because of events abroad. This can be seen in the work of the barrister, Montagu Williams. In his colourful description of people and places in London, published in 1892, it is difficult to separate fact from fiction and the present from the past, so creating a jumble of images. From these blurred images the City does not emerge with credit. Instead, it comes across as a place where standards had fallen as an older style of gentlemanly behaviour gave way to a more speculative age. Due to a combination of the agricultural depression and the aristocracy's own 'reckless extravagance, gambling', they were being displaced in London society by the 'nouveaux riches, Jews, and plutocrats'. These were buying up both the townhouses and country estates. 'ancient estates and old family properties have passed into new hands. Who have become possessed of them? Those who have made fortunes with great rapidity, by speculation or otherwise, in the City or in manufacturing districts, in England or the colonies'. However, it was not just that City people were pushing out the aristocracy; members of the aristocracy were being attracted by the opportunities in the City, in order to make money and repair damaged fortunes. A growing number of younger sons of aristocratic families were going into stockbroking, using family connections to get positions. In turn, these aristocratic stockbrokers used these connections to generate business, as they were paid a share of the commission on all sales and purchases. The result was that all their friends, family and acquaintances, including women, were being encouraged to speculate. 'Among the women of the beau monde, Stock Exchange gambling is rapidly becoming as dire a disease as baccarat and horse-racing'. 'At modern dinner-parties, if the conversation does not turn on racing, it is usually about the Stock Exchange ... instead of the usual society chat, which, Heaven knows, was usually as dull and stupid as it well could be, everybody discusses past City ventures, and the successes which the future may have in store'. There was a two-way fusion taking place between the City and the aristocracy but rather than making those in the City gentlemen it was making gentlemen into brokers.

William's greatest condemnation of the City was to be found in his description of the company promoter.

> There is no more remarkable being in the city of London, with its many curious trades and vocations, than the company promoter. He has existed there, and flourished like a green bay-tree, for many years past. Though everybody knows him, either personally or by reputation, there is in all quarters much uncertainty as to his origin and antecedents. The successful company promoters are enormously wealthy; they have palaces at Kensington or mansions in Grosvenor Square, besides charming places in the country, and are usually aspirants – and, it may be, not unsuccessful aspirants – for Parliamentary honours. They are, as a rule, Conservatives in politics, and have a large circle of titled acquaintances – impecunious lords, baronets, generals, admirals, and the like. The latter, who are termed 'guinea pigs', figure as directors of the companies launched by their City friends. The promoters drive to their business in well-appointed broughams, drawn by high-stepping horses. They are remarkably particular in their dress, and wear a good deal of jewellery, their massive rings being particularly conspicuous. Altogether their appearance, both in the City and in the West End, is calculated to impress the casual observer. Quick at figures, cool-headed, and gifted with a retentive memory, the company promoter is an excellent business man. There is a good deal of variety in his work. He transforms all manner of going concerns from private enterprises into share investments for the public. One day it is soap; the next, candles; then an hotel or a theatre, and so on. He also finds capital

for, and works – by syndicate, or as a company – mines, valuable and valueless. His ability in placing an undertaking before the public in an alluring form is marvellous. What prophetic visions of wealth for those who are wise enough to subscribe! What dividends await the investor – if he will only walk into the parlour! How eagerly the public rushes to secure shares in the Brobdingnagian Diamond Mine, The South African Auriferous Dust Company, and the Borneo Sea Salt Company! ... Many a company promoter, when he has amassed considerable riches, retires from business, and, as one of the moneyocracy, gives sumptuous dinners and splendid receptions, and, by these and other means, gradually elbows his way into fashionable society.

Williams then goes on to give an account of the rise and fall of a company pro-moter whom he had got to know over the years, as if he was an eyewitness to all that went on rather than a social commentator. This person was Leopold Stiff, who operated from large and opulent offices in the City, near the Old Jewry, and where he employed numerous clerks. 'On entering the building the visitor passed up a broad marble staircase, and his progress was likely to be impeded by the number of persons ascending and descending. In the throng were noblemen, officers in the Army, clergymen, fashionably-attired ladies, mothers and wives of the middle class, and, in fact, all sorts and conditions of men and women ... In one of the rooms there were gold ore specimens from the Gull Mine which prospective investors were coming to inspect from all over the country. It was crowded with men and women of all classes, including country gentlemen, wid-ows, City merchants, and clergymen. Everyone was closely inspecting the ore, which lay on tables placed about the apartment, or scrutinising the charts and maps that hung upon the walls. Standing in the middle of the throng, chatting very affably with those about him, was Mr. Stiff, whom I was surprised to see, as I fancied he had left me to return to the board-room. He was admirably dressed for office purposes, wearing a well-cut black velvet jacket and a double-breasted white waistcoat, across which hung a gold and turquoise watch-chain. He had a ruddy complexion and iron-grey hair, and I do not think I ever saw a man more calculated to inspire persons with confidence. He looked a philanthropist every inch of him. For my part, however, I confess that I had no consuming desire to take shares in the Gull Mine'. This description is remarkably similar to the first scene in Frith's series, *The Race for Wealth*, suggesting that this writer was passing off art and imagination from an earlier era as current reality. Williams had been one of those consulted by Frith in his quest for authenticity when undertaking his paintings in that series. What this illustrates is the power of invention to influence not only contemporary opinion but the beliefs of a later generation. The similarity with Frith's paintings continues as the author then described an evening at Stiff's house, to which he had been invited. This mirrors Frith's sec-ond painting with its description of the staff, the paintings, the food and wine, and the people there. 'In fact, I am bound to say that, could one have only forgotten how the money which procured the entertainment was acquired, it would have been possible to pass a most enjoyable evening'. There is then an interlude in Williams's account as Stiff establishes himself as one of the foremost financiers in the City of London, though his position is very precarious. Resulting from a financial crisis which began abroad, the speculative bubble burst, with Stiff believed to have fled in order to escape ruin, arrest or both. Jabez Balfour, of the Liberator Building Society had done just that, being eventually brought back from Argentina in 1895 to stand trial in London. In Williams's account the Gull Gold Mine turned out to be a complete swindle with no gold ever being found, despite the ore produced for display to potential investors. Numerous investors were thus ruined, having placed all their money in the scheme. This is the theme of Frith's third painting, which shows investors in despair on learning the news. Stiff was then arrested and put on trial at the Central Criminal Court in the Old Bailey, which, coincidentally, is what is represented in Frith's fourth painting. Stiff was found guilty and sentenced to five years' penal servitude in Millbank prison. 'From a West End mansion to Millbank is truly a curious transition'. The prison scene is the last of Frith's paintings.

Repetition as fact of Frith's powerful imagery of the rise and fall of a company promoter, based on events in the 1870s, suggests that actual events in the City in the early 1890s were much less important in forming public attitudes than deep-rooted prejudices. In the eyes of people such as Williams, the City was forever associated with Jewish moneylenders, preying on vulnerable individuals. This was despite the fact that he recognized that this activity now took place either in the East or West End and not the City. He was also aware that the City remained a major commercial City where roads were frequently 'choked with vans, either lumbering along with Smithfield or some City warehouse as their destination'. As a trained lawyer he also knew that the City was a centre of legal expertise. He even accepted that investors themselves had to accept some responsibility for their own actions.

> There is no one so gullible as an ordinary member of the British public. He will invest his last penny in an undertaking of which he knows absolutely nothing, although, if he reads his newspaper, he must be perfectly well aware that kindred enterprises have, times without number, been exposed as out-and-out swindles. This starting of bogus companies is very like the confidence trick, the ring dropping, and the painted sparrow. Of course, the 'fat' as it is termed, goes in a great measure to the promoter, and between him and the poor investor there are usually several individuals with their mouths very wide open.

Nevertheless, it was the City that was to blame when companies collapsed and investors lost money. Conversely, when a lawyer embezzled his clients' money the responsibility was not his alone because the act was caused by speculative losses in the City.[10] Increasingly it was the activities of the company promoter that dominated the public's perception of the City of London. They even became the subject of a Gilbert and Sullivan operetta with the production of *Utopia Ltd* opening in London in 1893. One of the highlights of this operetta was the song of the company promoter.

> *A Company Promoter this, with special education.*
> Which teaches what Contango means and also Backwardation
> To speculators he supplies a grand financial leaven,
> Time was when two were company
> But now it must be seven
> Yes – Yes – Yes
> Stupendous loans to foreign thrones
> I've largely advocated;
> In ginger-pops and peppermint-drops
> I've freely speculated;
> Then mines of gold, of wealth untold,
> Successfully I've floated,
> And sudden falls in apple-stalls
> Occasionally quoted:
> And soon or late I always call
> For Stock Exchange quotation
> No scheme too great and none to small
> For companification!

> *Some seven men form an Association*
> (If possible, all Peers and Baronets),
> They start of with a public declaration
> To what extent they mean to pay their debts,
> That's called their capital: if they are wary
> They will not quote it at a sum immense,
> The figure's immaterial – it may vary
> From eighteen million down to eighteen pence.
> I should put it rather low;
> The good sense of doing so
> Will be evident at once to any debtor,
> When it's left to you to say
> What amount you mean to pay,
> Why, the lower you can put it at, the better.
> They then proceed to trade with all who'll trust'em
> Quite irrespective of their capital
> (It's shady, but it's sanctified by custom);
> Bank, Railway, Loan, or Panama Canal.
> You can't embark on trading too tremendous
> It's strictly fair, and based on common sense
> If you succeed, your profits are stupendous
> And if you fail, pop goes your eighteen pence.
> Make the money-spinner spin!

For you only stand to win,
And you'll never with dishonesty be twitted,
For nobody can know,
To a million or so,
To what extent your capital's committed!
If you come to grief, and creditors are craving
(For nothing that is planned by mortal head
Is certain in this Vale of Sorrow
Saving that's one's Liability is Limited),
Do you suppose that signifies perdition?
If so you're but a monetary dunce
And start another Company at once!
Though a Rothschild you may be
In your own capacity,
As a company you've come to utter sorrow
But the Liquidators say,
Never mind – you needn't pay,
So you start another Company tomorrow! [11]

What the song reveals is a great familiarity with certain aspects of the City ranging from the terms in use on the Stock Exchange through the requirements of company law to the current investment fashions at home and abroad.[12] Throughout there was a recognition of the risks that investors ran in subscribing for shares in new joint stock companies, even if they were well-informed people in the City. In the story, *Cheating the Gallows*, by Israel Zangwill, which also appeared in 1893, Mr Newell, a respectable corn merchant, had lost most of his money by investing in 'bubble companies'.[13] Promoting joint-stock companies was widely seen as the easiest way to make money whereas buying the shares issued was the easiest way of losing it. In the 1895 novel by Max Pemberton, *The Impregnable City*, Adam Monk had 'lost his money upon the English Stock Exchange'and so had taken to wandering the world. He ended up in an island paradise in the Pacific as did Jacob Dyer, a disgraced company promoter from London, who had once made £40,000 in a week and had been chairman of sixteen companies. When Dyer's frauds were uncovered he fled from England, leaving behind his wife and child and 'two or three hundred widows and orphans penniless in London'. It was he alone, among numerous criminals from all over the world on the island, who betrayed the location community within which he had found refuge, in the expectation of rich payment from governments. He never collected, being killed by one of those whom he had betrayed. 'a trooper, bending over from the saddle, put a pistol to his ear and blew his brains out ... none died with more justice than this man, who had never known an honest thought nor done an unselfish action'. The City of London remained a byword for greed, corruption, and dishonourable conduct whenever the subject of company promotion surfaced, with the only fitting punishment for those who made their living by such means being a sudden and violent death.[14]

This distrust of company promotion and the manipulation of the market that followed was a unifying theme in the novel, *The Veiled Hand*, written by Frederick Wicks, which was published in 1892. It was subtitled *a Novel of the Sixties, the Seventies, and the Eighties*. Despite the attack on speculation and company promotion that the novel contained the City was recognized to be both multifunctional and multilayered. In 'the courts and alleys of the City' were to be found people such as Alfred Chippering, a wholesale haberdasher and warehouseman. He had become sufficiently wealthy to be in a position to buy a large house belonging to a landowning family, the Pottingers, after they had wasted all their money and were forced to sell. This process was viewed not with regret but as inevitable 'And so the wheel of fortune revolves upon its axis, and with inexorable justice illustrates the consequences of folly and the triumph of thrift'. Eventually Chippering became an MP and took a townhouse in Berkeley Square. Also in the City was Geoffrey Defoy. Geoffrey Defoy, whose aristocratic credentials dated back to the Norman Conquest, had gone into the City to restore the family fortune. 'Men go into the City with the expectation, or at least the desire, of taking something out of it ... Some simply dabbled and usually lost, some married daughters of City people exchanging a title for money, and some made a career of it'. Defoy married Chippering's daughter, Amy, despite the fact that he looked down on City people lacking his lineage, especially those who acquired titles. 'The peerage is now the reward of successful trades-people, contractors, financiers, salesmen, and, I suppose, commission agents'. He made an exception in the case of Amy as her father gave Defoy £250,000 in 3 per cent consols after the marriage took place. 'The motive of the Defoys and their kind was, and always will be, the necessity for replenishment: the motive on the other side was, and always will be, the discovery of a new ambition following the achievement of all the commoner social desires. The ingenuity of the spirit of envy is one of the most curious of the many extravagances of human ambition. When it has exhausted the resources of money, when its victim is possessed of everything that money can command, it frets for those things which no amount of money can buy, and chief among these is lineage'. Whenever the Defoys needed an infusion of wealth the eldest son was persuaded to marry the daughter of a City merchant or banker, though they considered such people beneath them. Such was the case with Geoffrey, while Amy was persuaded by her father to agree to the marriage, because of the position in society occupied by the Defoys.

The complication was that Geoffrey had secretly married Amy's cousin Muriel, possessor of a much smaller fortune, and had fathered two children. He kept this family hidden from the world and even used an assumed name, with Muriel not knowing his real identity, being known as Mrs Lucas. After his marriage to Amy, Geoffrey contrived to lead Muriel to believe he was dead, leaving her and her children to survive unsupported. This established him as disreputable and unscrupulous and would be in keeping with the standard view of City financiers. However, Defoy was not the only City financier whose character is examined. There was also Lord Freshfield, who was a highly respected and successful banker. He had accumulated a fortune of over a million pounds and been rewarded with a life peerage. Through a chance meeting Muriel and her son, Philip, were befriended by Morris Heritage, the nephew and heir of Lord Freshfield. Morris Heritage himself had become a person of stature in the City, following his uncle in the bank.

> My uncle, Mrs Lucas, was a banker of great wealth and high repute, the controller of great enterprises, and the monitor of the most prosperous merchants of the City. I am the son of his only sister. I inherited his wealth and his responsibilities, and although I have innumerable acquaintances I have not a single relation, and do not feel that I have a friend in the world. I am indeed absolutely alone. My wealth makes me suspicious, and I fear I am prone to suspect my fellows of unworthy motives, and sometimes unjustly.[15]

From these three characters there emerges a vision of the City as a home to all types of people whether defined by their business, their wealth, their character or their social standing. Nevertheless, the City continued to be distrusted as long it was associated with the Stock Exchange and the company promoter, as this was no better than gambling on cards, betting on horses or staking all on the throw of the dice in the casino at Monte Carlo.

> The object of the law being to protect the public, and particularly the public investor, the object of the promoter came to be the evasion of all provisions calculated to give that protection; and accordingly coaches and four by the dozen were devised to drive through all the Acts ever passed by Parliament in this connection, and toll bars were put up at every entrance into the City to make sure that nobody took advantage of the law without first paying the proprietors of these several coaches and four, what moral philosophers, unmollified by familiarity with City practices, would be disposed to call 'blackmail', so like were the practices referred to those of the freebooters and cattle raiders of earlier times.

The opportunities the City offered to those who wanted to make money quickly were seen to be increasingly attractive to members of the aristocracy.

> At first the ornaments of the gilded salons of fashion were a little shy of being associated with the City. They went about the business pretty much in the same way as a man pays his first visit to a pawnbroker. They secreted themselves in cabs in Pall Mall, whispered an address in Broad Street or Change Alley to the driver, and crouched in the corner of the cab till they got past Temple Bar, when they gradually emerged from seclusion and did their best to make a show of familiarity with the persons and places associated with their new ambitions. But one day it became current that the

son of a marquis had gone into the tea trade, and a year later the son of a Prime Minister became an export merchant and issued a circular from Downing Street. This was quite sufficient. The whole ruck of the aristocracy, not otherwise fully occupied, made a rush to the City. Helter-skelter and pell-mell they hustled one another to be first in the field, and proffered themselves to the highest bidder, regardless of everything so long as they were 'in the City'... In course of time the methods of the fraternity became so highly organised that vast establishments were created for the supply of titled directors on short notice, together with the most enticing baits to attract the unwary investor.

The offices of these company promoters were regarded as little better than gambling dens catering for those little interested in safe investments but willing to bet on the success of each new venture in the hope of making a large profit. 'As a rule there was not much of the widow and orphan associated with the business, but merely an aggregation of those thirsters after cent, per cent, who, in their pursuit of wealth, neglect the first principles of commerce, that high interest means bad security, and that in the City you should trust no one further than you can see him'. In the City the pursuit of money broke down normal social barriers as all were driven by the same motives, and so cooperated or competed as each new situation dictated. This can be seen in the composition of those involved in promoting a foreign mining company. In addition to the likes of Geoffrey Defoy, who was the sinister figure pulling the strings behind the scenes, there was Septimus Howler, of Howler and Smart, stockbrokers. He was very well dressed, in a rather flashy way but 'his voice was coarse and his manner vulgar'. There was also Mr Alister, of Bamberger and Alister, mining engineers, Marmaduke Bray, editor of the *City Tripod*; and John Huckle, of Huckle and Broil, City solicitors. These were the insiders though Huckle confined himself to the legal side of the business. Also involved, but on the outside, were Baron Geizer, the Marquis of Maladore, the Honourable James Faire, General Dowles and Walter Gowcher. These people formed the public face of any company because their status or connections would persuade investors to buy shares. Captain Sickle was to act as secretary to the company.

> They were a curious company – curiously dissimilar in social status, mental qualities, and vocation, but they had a common purpose somewhat akin to the vulgar ambition of making black appear white, and their proceedings were the more curious from the way the oddly assorted company hovered between keeping up an appearance of commercial probity and recklessly daring complete indifference to everything but the criminal law'.

They already owned a concession to mine copper in Obooboo in Cape Colony and Alister was to produce a favourable report about the mine's potential, based on a sample of ore. This would prove the value of the minerals located on the land and a company, the Great Coradell Copper Mine, would be floated. The money raised from the public would then be used to buy the mining concession from a man called Peter Shad, who was to pretend he had come from South Africa where he had bought the property. The capital of the company was fixed at £500,000 with the vendor to receive £350,000 of which half was in cash and half in shares. In reality Shad was going to be given £100 and the inner group would split the proceeds. Such deceit was only to be expected in the City, 'men of no birth, less wealth, and grosser tastes, emerged from the squalid processes of City muckraking and dazzled the populace by scattering tinsel gewgaws in their faces'. However, the public had only themselves to blame. 'These had for their reward the homage of the gaping millions, and in their train came trooping impecunious politicians, the dregs of the Court, and every phase of the later nineteenth century greed, which specially exhibited itself in an absorbing desire to reap without sowing, and to gather without even putting the hand to the sickle, to say nothing of the plough'.[16]

Even members of the government actively participated in the promotion of foreign mining companies, seeing it as a way of furthering the national interest and profiting themselves. One such was the Right Honourable Peter Finnessmore who told Heritage, 'Africa, my dear Heritage, is being developed, particularly South Africa, and I have been approached in the matter from the City ... South Africa needs developing in the interests of our growing population – I say populations, for some of our older colonies are getting crowded in parts, and South Africa is a marvellous country'. He became a director of the Great Coradell Copper Mine, and tried to persuade Heritage to become involved, stressing the importance of the national interest. Heritage was very reluctant as he regarded joint stock companies as 'legalised larceny' and believed that 'The Companies Acts have been perverted to the basest uses. They have in effect taken the place in the public mind of the forbidden lotteries and roulette tables, and are so far discreditable that every genuine enterprise is handicapped by the deceptions practised in company promoting'. As a result neither he nor his bank became involved in their promotion 'We have never identified ourselves with the management of companies'. Finnessmore replied, 'it's about time you made an exception to that rule, because joint-stock company enterprise is rapidly becoming the only outlet for capital'. He then stressed that, 'the development of the colonies. And especially South Africa, is part of the Government's policy, and I use my position as a private citizen to further an object approved by the Government to which I happen to belong'. Involvement with the Great Coradell Mine would assist imperial policy and make available an essential mineral resource. '...if we had more honourable men in joint-stock enterprises we should have less to complain of'. Faced with these arguments Heritage agreed to allow his stepson Phillip to become a director of the great Coradell Mine, believing that this company was actually sound and the experience would help him avoid pitfalls in the future. By this stage Phillip was a prospective MP, establishing himself in the City, and was courting an earl's daughter, Lady Alice.

Generally, the City was seen as a place where no quarter was asked or given and everyday business was a matter of rigid routine which had to be adhered to by those working there. Above all, trust and reputation were essential if any City man hoped to survive and prosper. 'There is a thick folio volume to be seen in the private rooms of bankers, bill discounters, and merchants of high standing which they prize highly. It is a record of the standing and commercial probity of all firms of any pretensions throughout the United Kingdom. To be recorded in that book at all is a distinction, and to be omitted is not to exist for any purpose, where confidence and good reputation are matters of concern to the inquirer'. However, every so often the City was consumed by a passion for a particular investment, such as mines, during which the careful judgements and conduct that normally applied were suspended. This was also the case in the panic that inevitably followed.

> We are accustomed in a general way to regard 'the City' as a hard place, where people make hard bargains and settle them in hard cash; where a man's word is supposed to be his bond, to be rigidly exacted, and if broken, never to be mended throughout all time. And so it is in a general way, and especially when the strong bargain with the weak, and where there is any individual wrenching and squeezing to be done; but every now and then a time comes upon the City when the frenzy of hysteria pervades everybody in it, and everything hard seems soft, invertebrate, and infantile.

It was during this frenzy that the Great Coradell Mine was promoted as a joint stock company, and so its newly issued shares proved very attractive to investors.

> On the morning of the issue the City was attacked by an epidemic. The bank that had the good fortune to receive the subscriptions – the Consolidated Bank of the Cape of Good Hope – was besieged by an eager crowd before its doors were opened; and all day long its ordinary business was reduced to the narrowest possible limits short of complete suspension, while the British investor poured his savings into the Great Coradell.

Wealthy investors had applied for their shares by post, paying by cheque, while it was 'the widow and the orphan' who besieged the bank with their applications. The result was the shares were oversubscribed, leading to much subsequent buying and selling as they rose in price. However, the promoters knew that the price would collapse and so they paid Shad, the nominal vendor of the mine, £1,000 and advised him to disappear so that he would not be around when the truth about the mine was revealed. What Defoy had done was to buy all the land around the mine so that it had no access to water. That put him in a position to blackmail the company once it began operations so increasing the amount he was likely to make from selling the mine in the first place. This was not known at the time the company was promoted.[17]

In addition both Defoy and Alister speculated heavily in the shares as they were in a position to control the news circulating about the mine and its prospects. Sometimes they were extensive holders of the shares, in the expectation of a rise due to the release of good news, while at other times they sold more shares than they owned, expecting to buy them back at a lower price when bad news was released. Both these operations involved a high degree of risk. When buying shares they borrowed heavily to finance their purchases while selling meant that they were exposed if the price rose rather than fell. Defoy got caught out in both operations. The money had been borrowed through the issue of short-term bills which had to be repaid in the near future but neither Defoy nor Alister had the money to do so, and new borrowing was difficult as money was getting tight in the City. Defoy then paid Alister £25,000 to accept responsibility for the bills. Alister agreed to this, fleeing to Madrid via Paris before the news came out in the City that Bamberger and Alister had failed owing £2 million. This left Defoy free to pursue the alternative plan of selling not only the shares he owned but far more, as he knew that the revelations about access to water would drive the price down. When the price of the shares in the Great Coradell collapsed there was a public scandal with small shareholders clamouring for something to be done. This was awkward for both Philip Heritage and his stepfather as they felt it was dishonourable for directors to speculate in the shares of their own company and profit from the inside knowledge they possessed. As a result Morris Heritage investigated the company and the mine, and discovered that the property had originally been bought by Defoy and then sold via Shad. The mine was a very valuable one though the promoters did not know that. What it required was a railway to get the ore out and that would cost more money. In order to extricate Philip from the bad press he was receiving, because of his association with the company, Heritage used his money to buy all the shares on offer. As Defoy and his associates were selling short, in the expectation of buying and delivering at a lower price, the result was that he was now the owner of more shares than were in existence. 'Having satisfied myself about the property, I ordered the purchase of the stock of the company, and as no one else would buy it, I hear this morning that I am possessed of the power to call up more than there is in existence, and I mean to have it delivered to my brokers. The price I have paid for it will make the property a cheap purchase for me'.

It was not just the prospect of buying a valuable property on the cheap that motivated Morris Heritage. He also wanted to extricate Philip from the bad publicity that had come from being associated with the company. Both Heritage and Philip had been duped by the likes of Finnessmore into believing the company was sound when in fact it was a scam. The promoters had used Philip's connection to Heritage to give the company a respectability it did not possess. As Heritage said to Philip,

> 'You have been associated with a parcel of swindlers and City blacklegs, and have been used by them to rob the investing public according to law ... these noble lords and right honourable gentleman ... do not think it unbecoming to lend their names to felonious transactions of this sort, under the protection of figments of law' ... He paused, and drew from the bundle of papers a formal looking draft of a letter that he said Philip must sign, and when signed, should issue. It was an announcement that Philip Heritage was prepared to buy at par all shares in the Great Coradell held at that date by shareholders who had subscribed to the original allotment on the faith of the prospectus, and who had not otherwise disposed of their shares.

As a result of this announcement the price of the shares would rise back up to par. This would force those who had sold shares short to pay that price in order to deliver the shares that Heritage had bought from them in the market, or pay the difference. 'I expect to sweep out of their greedy maws every penny they have gained. After this we must reconstruct the company, and put it on an honest footing'. When the announcement was made investor sentiment was transformed. If the house of Heritage was willing to buy then the mine must be a valuable property and so nobody was now willing to sell. Nobody in the City believed that the offer was made in good faith in order to preserve a reputation. The shares then went to a premium as those who had sold short tried to cover their positions. As a result a number were bankrupted. Finnessmore was saved by his sister but his reputation was in ruin and he had to resign from the government, which had been embarrassed by his involvement.[18]

Among those facing ruin as a result of Morris Heritage's actions was Defoy. In desperation, he then hatched another scheme to restore his fortune. This involved speculating in pig-iron warrants and then formenting a strike among those working in the iron industry by bribing a union leader. Defoy bought 100,000 tons of pig iron, for future delivery, through a firm of metal brokers, Lohman and Last.

> The firm of Lohman and Last was one of those international combinations which ensured a patriotic appearance for each in his competition, combined with an equal share of profit whether the transaction was consistent with a patriotic sentiment or not. If it were a case of English rails sent to Germany, then it was Last's doings, and if it were German girders put up in Great Britain, while destitute English furnacemen were being subscribed for by a benevolent public because they chose to strike, then it was Lohman's doing; but the balance sheet made no distinction with an eminently international conscience.

It was profit not patriotism that drove those in the City, even when conducting a legitimate business, such as supplying pig-iron. As it was, the strike collapsed leaving Defoy holding warrants that he could not pay for and that could not be sold. This ruined Lohman and Last as they could not pay for the iron that they had contracted to buy. Defoy was then left in a very exposed position at a time of panic in the City, when it was impossible to raise money or promote new companies.

> Day by day the uneasiness in the City increased, and the list of failures was added to, not only by those who could not help themselves but by others less involved, who thought it a convenient opportunity to free themselves from embarrassments that in less turbulent times would have been fought against with unvarying energy. The panic extended to every branch of trade, and was aggravated by a feeling of distrust and a refusal of all concessions that at other times would be the common incidents of trading.

The result was that Defoy was also declared bankrupt, and stripped of all his possessions to repay his debtors. 'Even when the blow actually fell on him Defoy was unable to construe the extremity to which he had come'. Instead he took to drink, consuming vast quantities of brandy as all his possessions were sold up around him to pay his debtors. He eventually became a homeless alcoholic, an outcast of society, and died. His wife then married Bray, the newspaperman, with whom she was already having an affair.[19]

Another theme that played its part in defining the place of the City in contemporary culture was the social acceptability of those who made their fortune there. City people continued to be seen as upstarts who had risen to prominence through the rapid acquisition of wealth and, as such, threatened the established order in society. This was especially marked by the 1880s as the landed gentry were being progressively impoverished by the collapse of rents during the prolonged agricultural depression, which had begun in the previous decade. The effect of that was to undermine the position of the rural aristocracy, once securely based on extensive land ownership, compared to urban business communities and their more volatile wealth derived from trade, industry and finance. Now such estates were being acquired by all manner of City people, such as Mr Henley who was a retired City merchant. In the 1890 novel *Blind Love*, by Collins and Besant, he was depicted as a ruthless but honest businessman, who invested the wealth he had amassed in the City in a portfolio of foreign securities and a large landed estate to the north of London.[20] This acquisition of landed estates by the nouveau riche of the City brought them into growing conflict with the upper echelons of the landed elite, as can be seen from the 1888 novel by Rider Haggard, *Colonel Quaritch V.C.* What emerges is a rural society under threat because of the erosion of 'the gulf which used to be fixed between the gentleman of family and the man of business who has grown rich by trading in money'. The point that is made time and again is that for all his wealth a City banker was not a gentleman, whereas an impoverished landowner and a retired military officer were. 'No education can make a gentleman of a man who is not a gentleman at heart', City people were forever excluded from respectable society because their behaviour was governed by their 'trading instincts'. A City banker was less well regarded than a crooked country lawyer who was also a bigamist! The actual story concerned Ida de la Molle whose family dated back to Norman times and occupied Honham Castle. The family now faced the loss of their estate because of the collapse in land prices and farm rents. Her father, a country squire, could not repay a mortgage of £30,000 held over their estate by Edward Cossey, and faced eviction. Edward Cossey was the heir to the firm of Cossey and Son, London private bankers. His father had made a fortune through successful speculation in the stock market, which he continued to conduct even on his deathbed. He had made £120,000 in one year, and was happy to boast about his triumphs. On the father's death Edward inherited not only the business but £600,000. While managing the bank's branch in Boisingham, Edward had fallen in love with Ida and wanted to marry her: 'he knew well enough that to marry a woman like Ida de la Molle would be the greatest blessing that could happen to him, for she would of necessity lift him up above himself. She had little money it was true, but that was a very minor matter to him, and she had birth and breeding and beauty, and a presence which commands homage'. Despite his money she hated and despised Edward and did not want to marry him. She wanted to marry Colonel Quaritch, a neighbour and a war hero, but Edward used the power that wealth from the City gave him to force her to agree to marry him in return for cancelling the mortgage. Her father persuaded her to do this as he wanted to remain on the estate. In the end, a lucky find of buried treasure allowed her to escape the clutches of Edward, save the estate and marry Colonel Quaritch. Edward then married the only daughter of an impecunious peer, so achieving the status he craved but not with the woman he wanted. A deep social gulf was seen to exist in the late 1880s between those in the City and the top layers of rural society, and this could not be easily bridged by money alone.[21]

This continuing antagonism between those in the City with money and no breeding and those in the countryside with breeding and no money is apparent in Gissing's 1892 novel, *Born in Exile*. The City was the 'triumph of the vulgar man' and 'represents the triumphant forces of our time ... the power which centres in the world's money markets – plutocracy'.[22] Similarly, in an 1892 story by Grant Allen, *The Great Ruby Robbery,* it was noted that Sir Everard and Lady Maclure, who lived in Hampstead, were too culturally superior '...to know such people as the Wilcoxes, who were something in the City, but didn't buy pictures; and Academicians, you know, don't care to cultivate City people – unless they're customers'.[23] Ingrained snobbery remained, making it difficult for those in the City to gain direct access to the upper echelons of British society even by the mid

1890s. This was evident from Marie Corelli's highly popular novel, *The Sorrows of Satan*, which was published in 1895. It warned against the power of money to corrupt all who came to possess it. According to Prince Lucio Rimanez, who was the devil in disguise, 'Any era that is dominated by the love of money only, has a rotten core within it and must perish'.[24] Furthermore, the power that came from money was a direct threat to the established social order. Prince Rimanez continued with his observations, 'We have come to a period of history when rank and lineage count as nothing at all, owing to the profoundly obtuse stupidity of those who happen to posses it. So it chances, that as no resistance is made, brewers are created peers of the realm, and ordinary tradesmen are knighted, and the very old families are so poor that they have to sell their estates and jewels to the highest bidder, who is frequently a vulgar 'railway king' or the introducer of some new manure'.

The City is singled out for attack, with the focus on Jewish financiers. Lord Elton had to sell his ancestral estate, Willowsmere, as a result of borrowing from and investing through Jewish bankers and brokers in the City. 'As a result of Lord Elton's unfortunate speculations, and the Jews' admirable shrewdness, Willowsmere, as I tell you is in the market, and fifty thousand pounds will make you the envied owner of a place worth a hundred thousand'. The estate was bought by Geoffrey Tempest, an impoverished writer, who had suddenly become immensely wealthy by inheriting over £5 million from a distant relative. He also married Lord Elton's daughter, Lady Sybil, and settled half his money on her. When Sybil committed suicide the estate and the money reverted to her father, who then completed the restoration of the family fortune by marrying Diana Chesney, the daughter of an American railway magnate.[25] In contrast, Geoffrey Tempest lost the remaining half of his fortune through the fraud and speculations of his lawyers, Bentham and Ellis, who had been entrusted with its safekeeping.

> The respectable pair of lawyers whom I had implicitly relied on for the management of all my business affairs in my absence had succumbed to the temptation of having so much cash in charge for investment – and had become a pair of practised swindlers. Dealing with the same bank as myself, they had forged my name so cleverly that the genuiness of the signature had never even been suspected – and, after drawing enormous sums in this way, and investing in various 'bubble' companies with which they personally were concerned, they had finally absconded, leaving me almost as poor as I was when I first heard of my inherited fortune.

The City was seen to possess the power to give and to take away in equal measure. Though the lawyers were clearly crooked they had been forced into that position because they had 'already lost large sums in bogus companies – and the man Bentham, whom I thought the very acme of shrewd caution, has sunk an enormous amount of capital in a worn-out gold mine'. [26] Tempest accepted his loss, would not prosecute Bentham and Ellis, and returned to his writing, relieved of the burden that the money had placed upon him.

Nevertheless, in comparison to the past, this antagonism towards the City was more subdued. It was recognized that City people covered a multitude of virtues and vices. In one of the classic novels of the age, *The Diary of a Nobody*, written by George and Weedon Grossmith in 1892, such a contrast emerged. It compared the career of a respectable clerk, working for a well-established City business, and that of his son, who had joined a firm of rather dubious stockbrokers. On the day that the father was made senior clerk 'as a result of twenty-one years of industry and strict attention to the interests of my superiors in office, I have been rewarded with promotion and a rise in salary of £100', his son, Lupin, 'Having been in the firm of Job Cleanands, stock and share brokers, a few weeks, and not having paid particular attention to the interests of my superiors in office, my Guv'nor, as a reward to me, allotted me £5 worth of shares in a really good thing. The result is today, I have made £200'. Inspired by this the father invested £20 through the son but lost all but £2 of it, as do the others that buy shares on the advice of the son. The firm of Job Cleanands then failed and the owner disappeared.[27] By then the City had become a career choice for many, including those from the upper echelons in society. In the short story entitled *The Model Millionaire*, published in 1891, Oscar Wilde quickly conjured up a picture of what a failure Hughie Erskine was as he could not find a successful opening in the City. This was despite the fact that he tried both finance in the shape of stockbroking and trade in the form of dealing in tea then wine. If even he, with his pleasant manners and good education, could not find a profitable career in the City, then there was no hope for him and he had no alternative but to exist on the £200 a year left to him by an aunt.[28] The City came across as a place where almost anyone of good breeding could find a profitable occupation, especially in those areas where contacts with the wealthy were of value, such as selling securities or expensive goods. With spreading literacy, and the circulation of London based newspapers, periodicals and books, there was a growing awareness of events in London, including the financial and commercial activities of the City. Combined with this was a greater understanding of the intricacies of market behaviour whether it involved the flotation of companies, transactions on the Stock Exchange or speculations in commodity contracts. These were accepted as a fact of life involving winners and losers because of the inherent risks involved. At the same time it was acknowledged that success in the City required special skills and the capacity for hard work, and that only a few possessed the necessary combination. In Conan Doyle's Sherlock Holmes story, *The Adventure of the Beryl Coronet*, dating from the 1890s, the City banker, Alexander Holder, was disappointed that his son was not to follow him into the business, having become involved with a free-spending aristocratic crowd. 'It was naturally my intention that he should succeed me in my business, but he was not of a business turn. He was wild, wayward, and, to speak the truth, I could not trust him in the handling of large sums of money. When he was young he became a member of an aristocratic club, and there, having charming manners, he was soon intimate of a number of men with long purses and expensive habits'.[29] In addition to the leading bankers there were also '...the ordinary run of bank clerks come gaily trooping into the Great City in shoals by the early trains', according to Headon Hill in the 1893 story, *The Sapient Monkey*.[30]

Those in the City were also seen as victims of crime, not just as being responsible for wrongdoing, as in a succession of crime stories emerging in the early 1890s. In *The Accusing Shadow* by H. Blyth, written in 1894, the story centres on the City firm of wholesale merchants, George Roath and Company. They dealt in Manchester goods and had a City warehouse located 'In that labyrinth of narrow streets, with towery buildings which lies between Fore Street and Cheapside, where railway vans forever block the road, and great bales of 'soft' goods monopolize the pavement'. It employed numerous travelling salesmen to sell its goods across Britain. The business was owned by George Roath 'a steady-going City merchant' who 'occupied furnished apartments in a good house in Highbury Park' but was moving to 'a large, old-fashioned house in Canonbury', as he was getting married. However, he was murdered by the cashier, Felix Sark, when he discovered that Sark was stealing from the firm.[31] In *Blind Love* Lord Harry Norland faked his own death so that his wife could claim against the life policy taken out with the City insurance company, The Royal Unicorn Life Insurance Company.[32] In *The Adventure of the Beryl Coronet* by Conan Doyle, the victim was the highly respected private banking firm of Holder and Stevenson. Sherlock Holmes was asked to solve the mystery of the theft of an expensive crown belonging to a member of the British aristocracy, but pledged to the bank as security for a loan of £50,000.[33] The 1895 story, *The Case of Laker, Absconded*, by Arthur Morrison, again featured a private bank in the City, Liddle, Neal and Liddle, as the victim of a clever criminal rather than one of the large joint-stock banks that were now dominant. This bank was robbed of £15,000 by a crook masquerading as its 'walk-clerk, who collected money and securities on its behalf from other banks'.[34] In the 1896 story by Herbert Keen, *The Tin Box*, the private bank in question was Drake, Crump and Company.

> The banking establishment of Messrs Drake, Crump & Co., was a small private concern which has long since been absorbed by one of the big joint-stock undertakings. In those days its affairs were conducted in a dingy old house with barred windows about halfway down Fleet Street, in a leisurely, sleepy kind of way. The cashier's office was in the front room, consisting of only three or four elderly clerks, and on presenting my card I was ushered into a gloomy little apartment at the back, where sat a

quaint white-headed old gentleman in knee-breeches, who was evidently one of the partners.

The impression given that this bank was very old-fashioned lacking the professionalism that was to be found in the branches of the large joint-stock banks. They could thus be duped by the wife of a convicted burglar trying to recover the proceeds of a theft of jewels from a safe deposit box they held. In order to cover her identity she persuaded a Mr Perkins to act for her. He worked for The Monarchy Insurance Office which made him trustworthy, allowing him to be taken in by a scheming woman while the story he told would be believed by a private banker.[35] If not being robbed by the criminal classes, the City was also robbed by its own staff. This was the case in two stories appearing in 1893. In *The Sapient Monkey* by Headon Hill, it is Trudways Bank that is robbed by one of its cashiers while in *Cheating the Gallows* by Israel Zangwill, the manager of The City and Suburban Bank, Everard G. Roxdal, steals a substantial sum of money and then disappears. Both were eventually caught and punished.[36]

Even stockbrokers got favourable treatment in contemporary crime novels, as can be seen from another Sherlock Holmes story. In *The Adventure of the Stockbroker's Clerk*, which appeared in 1891–2, Sherlock Holmes is called upon to solve a complex plot to rob a firm of City stockbrokers by a crook masquerading as one of their clerks. In this story those in the City appear as the very model of respectability. Hall Pycroft, a stockbroker's clerk, was a well-built, fresh-complexioned young fellow with a frank, honest face and a slight, crisp, yellow moustache. He wore a very shiny top-hat and a neat suit of sober black, which made him look what he was – a smart young city man, of the class who have been labelled Cockneys, but who give us our crack Volunteer regiments, and who turn out more fine athletes and sportsmen than any body of men in these islands.

Even the partners of stockbroking firms come across as caring employers who worked hard at their business in often uncertain circumstances, as can be seen when Pycroft gives a brief resume of his City career.

> I used to have a billet at Coxon and Woodhouse, of Draper's gardens, but they were let in early in the spring though the Venezuelan loan ..., and came a nasty cropper. I had been with them five years, and old Coxon gave me a ripping good testimonial when the smash came; but, of course, we clerks were all turned adrift, the twenty-seven of us. I tried here and there, but there were lots of other chaps on the same lay as myself, and it was a perfect frost for a long time. I had been taking three pounds a week at Coxon's and I had saved about seventy of them, but I soon worked my way through that and out the other end ... At last I saw a vacancy at Mawson and Williams, the great stockbroking firm in Lombard Street....this is about the richest house in London.

At any one time this firm had securities amounting to at least £1 million on its premises. He was offered the job at £4 per week. He was a hardworking and conscientious clerk who 'read the Stock Exchange List every morning' and was familiar with the current prices of all the main stocks. However, a criminal pretending to be Hall Pycroft managed to steal 'Nearly a hundred thousand pounds worth of American railway bonds, with a large amount of scrip in other mines and companies' before being apprehended by the police.[37] Those who worked in the City were simply ordinary people capable of either committing ordinary crimes, like a stockbroker killing his wife, or being subjected to them, whether robbery or murder.[38]

This did not mean that the City had lost its distinctive identity as it remained strongly associated with money making, especially through finance. However, even here another transition was taking place as the public increasingly recognized that the City was little associated with either personal moneylending or even retail banking. This can be seen in Besant's 1895 novel, *Beyond the Dreams of Avarice*. The story revolved around a doctor, Lucian Burley, who inherited a fortune. The Burley fortune had begun with Calvert Burley, who was a clerk to a City merchant, Mr Scudamore, at the time of the South Sea bubble in 1720. Scudamore was ruined speculating in South Sea shares whereas Calvert Burley made £22,500 using money stolen from the merchant. With that fortune Calvert Burley took over the merchant's business, which he had been increasingly managing. The merchant then died a bankrupt in prison with Calvert refusing to help. Extending help to those who had failed was never the custom in the City. Calvert Burley then became a successful City merchant worth £100,000 when he died. With this fortune Calvert married well and became respectable though misfortune followed him. His eldest son was hanged as a highway robber, his youngest son was kidnapped and his daughter died of smallpox. All this was regarded as a just punishment for the way he made his money. Lucian's grandfather, who was Calvert's grandson, converted his inheritance of half a million pounds into the huge amount of £12 million, producing a guaranteed income of £400,000 per annum as it was all safely invested in consols. He did this through a series of disreputable activities beginning with operating a gambling house, then a dancehall selling drink and finally moneylending, which had proved to be the most profitable. So disgusted was he by all this that Lucian's father had run away from home and started a new life. On inheriting the money Lucian's life began to change, with him becoming a miser and recluse like his grandfather. Only when a new will was discovered and he lost all the money did a normal life resume, including the return of his wife, Margaret, who had left him. What this represented was not an attack on the City but a general criticism of the materialistic aspects of contemporary society, 'this degenerate age', in which money could buy everything apart from a happy family life and spiritual peace.[39]

There remained an antagonism towards money combined with a recognition that it was essential, whether for everyday life or grand schemes for the good of the community. The same could be said of the City of London for it was seen to contain both good and bad people and to be pursuing both useful and wasteful ends. Such a balanced verdict emerges from the 1894 novel, *The Strait Gate*, by the prolific writer Annie Swan. The novel contained a strong moral element and was presented to Sunday school pupils, both as a reward for attendance and as an example of the standards that were required by contemporary society. The story concerned two brothers who shared accommodation in a boarding house in the vicinity of St Paul's Churchyard. The elder was Philip Heyward and the younger was Jack. Philip worked for a City merchant while the younger was training to be a doctor. Their father had been a vicar but was now dead. Their mother still lived in the small village in Sussex, Kingsmead, where his parish had been. At this stage they all lived comfortably as their father had come into a substantial inheritance before he had died. Unfortunately it had been largely invested in the Parquena silver mines, on the advice of one of his parishioners. When that company collapsed, which was seen as inevitable, his widow was left almost penniless. Philip, with his knowledge of the City, had warned her about the risks of a mining investment but she had taken no notice, as the company had appeared safe and paid a good dividend. As Philip told his mother, 'It is a common trick with rotten companies like the Parquena to return large dividends for a time to delude and ensnare new shareholders'. He referred to it as 'an infamous swindle'. which is suggestive of the Emma mine of an earlier generation, rather than current promotions.

Though clearly hardworking and successful, the son in the City, Philip, was seen to possess a 'narrow, grasping nature', being mean with money, clever at numbers, and good at writing. Even as a child he was 'making Mammon his god'. His own brother, Jack, referred to him as a 'money grubber', being 'next-of-kin to the miser who hoards his gold in a leathern bag hidden under the mattress of his bed'. Philip himself could not remember a time when he did not love money. 'I knew that money meant power, and that its possessor was a more important personage than he who lacked it'. On his father's death he had gone to London and entered the mercantile house of Gooderich Brothers, located in St Paul's churchyard. He had risen rapidly and was now the manager. He lived very economically and saved hard, for his ambition was to make himself a fortune. In contrast Jack, the trainee doctor, was the exact opposite. He was a warm hearted, impulsive and generous young man. Thus, without being regarded as corrupt or evil, and obviously pursuing an essential business successfully, the City man was seen to be driven by greed while the medical man wished to serve his fellow human beings. The fact that a life devoted to the pursuit of money in the City, no matter how respectable the work being undertaken, is further reinforced by the deathbed pronouncement of Christopher Gooderich, the sole owner of the mercantile house of Gooderich Brothers. As he lay dying he told Philip 'I have amassed a considerable fortune, the fruits of self-denial and frugal living, but

I question now if that is the best way to spend one's life'. The firm had been founded by his father but it was Christopher who had built it up into a large business, employing some unscrupulous business practices in the process. He had even lost contact with his only relative, a sister, but he now wanted to leave his fortune to her with £5,000 going to Philip. However, he died before the lawyer came to make a new will and an earlier one had left it all to Philip. Philip kept Christopher Gooderich's dying wishes to himself and so inherited £50,000 in cash plus the business.

With this fortune at his disposal, along with the business, Philip proposed to Mildred, the daughter of Lady Vere. She encouraged the match for no other reason than the fact that Philip was 'immensely rich' whereas they had very little money but continued to give the appearance that they had. This made her eager for her daughter to marry a wealthy man, even though the daughter did not love Philip.

> Of course, some of our friends may turn up their noses at Mr. Heyward's business connections, yet they need not, for trade is not to be despised in society as it used to be. The very peers dabble in commercial speculation, and isn't the son of a certain noble duke a banker? Yes, I am sure you ought to consider yourself a very fortunate girl, Mildred Vere, remembering your first youth is past.

Under the circumstances, and with continued pressure from her mother, Mildred agreed to the marriage. Gradually she learns to love Philip but tragedy strikes when the first child dies in infancy. At the same time the business does not prosper, despite the fact that Philip continued to manage it himself, working from 9 o'clock to 5 or 6 o'clock every day other than Sunday. The failure of a New York firm with whom they had dealings, cost the business a lot of money, revealing an understanding of the uncertainties that always plagued commercial life. Faced with these personal and business setbacks Philip realized that it all stemmed from his dishonourable action in not carrying out Christopher Gooderich's final request, and leading a life in which the sole object was the pursuit of money. He revealed all to his wife, which greatly strengthened their marriage, and they turn to Christianity for salvation. Philip then sought out Christopher Gooderich's heir, discovering that the sister had died but only after giving birth to a child. He gave this son £50,000 but is left with the business in gratitude for what he had done. He then determines to lead an honourable business life thereafter, which he did. 'His word is as good as his bond, and those who deal with him in business would trust him with untold gold'. The result was that he prospered commercially and enjoyed a happy family life, with his wife having more children.[40]

Despite all the events at home and abroad in the early 1890s the place of the City in British culture appears to have remained little altered. It was depicted as a relatively normal place of business populated by God-fearing and hardworking men with wives and families. City people made acceptable partners to the daughters of the impoverished landed gentry and happy marriages could result, suggesting a bonding between finance and land. The era of the gentleman capitalist had finally arrived. In turn, City financiers could be contrasted with the foreign variety, who appeared much more willing to engage in underhand practices. Those seeking to attach a similar label to City financiers were forced to hark back to an earlier period, masquerading as the present. The stability of British banks, with a sole and marginal exception, could also be compared to the position in Australia and the USA where collapses appeared commonplace. Even British companies appeared to have matured into reliable businesses paying interest on their debt and declaring dividends on their shares, whereas those to be found abroad were much more dubious, as revelations about false accounting and price manipulation emerged. Whatever lingering doubts remained about the City of London it appeared to be a much more respectable place than any other financial centre. Though British investors had lost out because of foreign defaults it was not the City that was held responsible, or even individual firms like Barings, but the foreigners who had received and misused the money. This suggests that events far from home had a rather limited effect on the place of the City in British culture. It also suggests that the problems of a single bank were insufficient to tarnish the reputation of the City as a whole. Instead, the City's overall reputation as a global centre for commerce and finance was sufficient for it to overcome occasional reverses. Similarly, the odd rogue like Jabez Balfour could not undermine the regard with which most City merchants, bankers and stockbrokers were held. It is evidence of this kind that has allowed the likes of Robinson to argue that the City became increasingly respectable and acceptable over the course of Queen Victoria's reign, contrasting some of the anti-financial rhetoric of the early years with its absence towards the end.[41] However, the picture is less clear-cut than that. The City's continued association with activities akin to moneylending and speculation condemned it in the eyes of many, whether their opinion was supported by evidence or not. Certain City people also remained beyond the pale, most notably the company promoter. It only took a minor incident and a flurry of publicity to revive the latent hostility to that species of person, and so condemn the City as a whole. Nevertheless, if the Victorian age had ended in 1895 it might have been possible to conclude that culture and economy had moved in tandem, with the power and prosperity of those in the City being reflected in its collective social standing, which then contributed to its success. Unfortunately for such a conclusion the next five years were to produce a fundamental revision in the place occupied by the City in British culture.

5 GOLD AND GREED, 1895–1900

A speculative bubble had been building up in London throughout the early 1890s. The dramatic reduction in external investment opportunities, with the crises in Australia, Argentina and the USA, had driven down British interest rates. This had fuelled a boom in house building and railway construction, as well as the conversion of established businesses into the joint stock form so that their shares could be sold to the public. Allied to the absence of borrowing by the British government the result was a period of low returns for investors and an increased willingness to look for new opportunities. Into this vacuum came the gold discoveries in South Africa and western Australia. Of all the metals in existence gold possessed a quality that no other had. This was its fixed price under the Gold Standard. Numerous currencies including the pound sterling had their value determined by a specific amount of gold for which they could be exchanged. Furthermore, the Bank of England was obliged to buy all gold offered to it at a fixed price. Thus, if gold could be found, mined, refined and then shipped to London it could be sold at a price known in advance. Given the discovery of new and large gold deposits in areas that were becoming accessible because of the railway, it appeared but a simple task of connecting supply and demand and profiting from the difference in price. Presented with such an opportunity investors quickly came to believe that every potential gold discovery offered a path to incalculable wealth. Gold mining appeared to possess the certainty of return that came with railways, because of their provision of a basic service, and the prospects of huge capital gain as the uncertainty of exploration gave way to the certainty of production. With gold there was no risk that the price would fall as output rose, as in the case of other metals and coal, for the demand was infinite and the price guaranteed. The 1890s was a decade when a succession of new countries were joining the Gold Standard, such as Russia and Japan, while its rival, silver, was losing its appeal as a monetary metal. All that was required was the application of capital to gold mining and the returns were secured, including the possibility of huge profits if the deposits proved particularly abundant and easy to access. As in the past the lure of gold seduced many to abandon logic and act on impulse.

Inevitably, the reality proved a disappointment when compared to the prospects. Even when gold was discovered the deposits could prove expensive to mine and process while transport was a major additional cost, considering their location. In addition, though geological science had advanced considerably over the Victorian period it still remained a matter of luck whether gold was found, and then in sufficient quantity and quality to justify production. Thus, even when every care had been taken to establish that there were reasonable prospects that gold might be found there remained a strong possibility that nothing of value might be produced after the expenditure of all the money raised from investors. The inevitable result was recriminations among those investors and a search for scapegoats, who were most easily found among those in the City who had brought these companies to the market. Among such people there were likely to be some who had made little effort to establish the worth of the mineral prospects they were selling or even deliberately produced false reports so as to persuade the public to purchase shares. However, that was only one dimension of the gold-mining boom. The other was speculation in the shares of the companies formed to explore for and then produce gold. Mining lent itself to speculation as there was never any certainty about the worth of a discovery until it had entered full and regular production. Thus, every rumour, whether true or false, stimulated sales and purchases as investors sought to capture the gains they had made or participate in future profits. Again, this created the opportunity for the unscrupulous to either profit from advance warning about the results from test exploration shafts or to circulate information that moved the share price in a direction from which they could profit. Again, it was inevitable that when the speculative fever collapsed those investors who had lost heavily would seek to accuse others of inducing them to participate. This then focused attention on that other prominent feature of the City, namely the London Stock Exchange and its members. Irrespective of whether investors were buying or selling and whether prices were rising or falling, brokers profited from the commission they charged their clients for every transaction they handled. Similarly, the jobbers who bought and sold on their own account in the Stock Exchange gained from the difference in price between the buying and the selling price, and thus did well as long as the market remained active. It was therefore these brokers and jobbers, and the Stock Exchange itself, who ended up being blamed when investors realized they had lost, not made, money through speculating in gold-mining company shares.

Further stimulating anti-City hostility in this brief period was the delayed effect of the Liberator Building Society collapse. Though that had taken place in 1892, it was not until 1895 that Jabez Balfour was returned to Britain to be tried for his part in the fraud that had taken place. He was sentenced to fourteen years in prison and the trial generated much publicity, as he had been a prominent public figure, including serving as mayor of Croydon and MP for

Burnley. Thus, though the City of London remained a financial centre of paramount importance over these years, its reputation was influenced not by that fundamental fact alone but a public perception that focused on fraud, frenzied speculation in shares that spilled onto the streets around the Stock Exchange, and the promotion of a huge number of companies whose prospects rested on nothing more substantial than the hope of finding gold in remote corners of the globe. Whether the reputation of the City could withstand this glare of publicity is the key question. Prior to 1895 the City's reputation had come through relatively unscathed, despite financial reverses at home and abroad, suggesting that fundamentals outweighed froth. However, the magnitude of the boom in shares of gold-mining companies, and then its subsequent collapse, was reminiscent of nothing seen since the railway mania of the mid-1840s. It was also conducted at time when far more people were able to participate because of the links between the members of the London Stock Exchange and their provincial counterparts through the telegraph and the telephone. Even those who did not directly participate were fully aware of the unfolding sequence of events through vivid accounts in nationally circulated newspapers and the work of the artists and photographers they employed.[1]

The virulence and depth of the anti-City hostility that followed the gold-mining boom can be gauged from Headon Hill's 1896 novel, *Guilty Gold*. It was published in 1896 and its subtitle, *A Romance of Financial Fraud and City Crime*, made explicit its attack on the City of London. In the course of the novel not one redeeming feature appeared relating either to the City of London as a whole, those who worked there or their families. All appeared so obsessed with the desire to make their fortune and spend money extravagantly that they would stop at nothing to achieve it. This included the impoverishment and suicide of investors and the murder of those who opposed them or threatened to expose their fraudulent ways. The main plot concerned a South African gold mine, the Golden Kloof Mining Company. In reality there was no gold, only a rather remote and unproductive farm. The promoters of the company were well aware of that. The owner of the farm, Guy Elwes, was the son of a country vicar from the village of Greenhurst in Sussex, who had gone out to South Africa to make his fortune so that he could marry his childhood sweetheart, Lucy Lethbridge. Having failed in farming he returned to England, where he fell in with a group of City people, as Lucy was the governess to the children of one of them, Theophilus Tiffany. These City people concluded that Guy was 'a woolly-brained young dolt, a gentleman by birth' and bought his farm for £800 despite being told by Guy that there were no gold deposits located on it. They then proceeded to float a company that intended to raise £150,000 to develop the non-existent gold. Of that a total of £95,000 in cash and shares was to be paid for the supposed gold-bearing land. Their intention was to unload their holdings before the lack of any gold emerged, as they had done several times before in various company promotions. At that stage the blame would fall on Guy, as the original owner of the farm. In a private conversation with Tiffany, Vardon made their intentions clear: 'we want a new combination of fools to squeeze, in the shape of a new company, and I am at my wit's end to find the material'. Tiffany did suggest 'a bankrupt American brewery or a nitrate field in Chili?' to which the more knowledgeable Vardon replied, 'All the rotten Yankee breweries are already owned by English investors, and the nitrate boom is played out ... No, I think the public are about ripe for a little flutter in gold mines, and that is where I am stuck. I haven't a gold mine, good, bad, or indifferent, to offer them'.[2]

In the absence of a gold discovery to convert into a company, and knowing the public's enthusiasm for such an investment, the promoters simply invented one, with Guy's farm constituting the bait for unwary investors. When threatened with exposure by Guy and the editor of a City newspaper, Barker Crabbe, the promoter of the company, Horace Vardon, killed the editor and made it appear that Guy was the culprit. Guy was then accused of murder and imprisoned awaiting trial. At one stroke Vardon had removed the threat to his scheme. However, Vardon had been seen murdering Crabbe by a young shoe black, Bennie Binks. His telephone conversation setting up the meeting with the City editor had also been caught on a self-recording phonograph that had been left in his office by an American inventor, Professor Drax, who was in London trying to interest the City in financing its development. Faced with his plan unravelling, Vardon attempted to kill not only the witness to the murder, but also Lucy and Professor Drax. He was caught in time by the police, convicted and hung. The others involved in the attempted fraud were also caught, convicted and imprisoned for terms ranging from one year to fourteen years penal servitude. Vardon's estate was confiscated, as were those of his co-conspirators, and used to compensate the investors, leaving their families penniless. Even the innocent associated with those who committed financial fraud could be shown no sympathy. Only the investors were blameless despite their obvious naivety. 'The British shareholder is the most good-natured animal under the sun when he thinks he is in a 'real good thing'. The thrust of the novel was the criminal greed of those in the City and the failure of government to take any action to prevent the duping of investors.[3]

Those involved in the promotion of the Golden Kloof covered a wide spectrum of City activities, but none were seen as anything other than crooks. The solicitor employed to defend Guy, George Davies, described them as 'a fair sample of the class of men who get up public companies in the City of London ... the men whom you good people in the country are so willing to take on trust, provided they come to you with a string of sponsors raked from the scum of the peerage, the off-scourings of the army, and the tag-rag and bobtail of Parliament'.[4] The chief character was Horace Vardon, 'a well built, physically handsome man of forty, having a sallow dark complexion that suggested a touch of southern blood'. He came from Camberwell in London where his father had run pirate buses and gambled on horse racing. Vardon had begun his City career as a stockbroker's clerk, but ended up in prison having defrauded the firm he worked for and then tried to murder his employer. After escaping from Dartmoor prison, by bribing a guard, he had assumed a new identity and became a successful company promoter in the City. By the time of the episode of the Golden Kloof he was described as 'at the very top of the tree in the City – occupies quite a unique position in the world of finance'. Acting as a financial agent, and never publicly involved in the companies he promoted, Horace Vardon was portrayed as one of those figures in the City who wielded power from behind the scenes and through others.

> Horace Vardon occupies a unique position in the City of London. Disliked, mistrusted – aye, even hated – by the solid, old fashioned magnates of the financial world, he was feared and bowed down to as well, because of the power he wielded and the number and magnitude of his undertakings. He was the Veiled Prophet of the City, sitting himself in the shade, and pulling the strings of infinite combinations that sometimes moved the uttermost ends of the earth.

He operated out of offices in Queen Victoria Street in the City, where he had a dozen well furnished rooms in Mansion House Chambers. He himself lived in bachelor chambers nearby in St James's Street but also had a country house, Backwater Lodge, on the outskirts of Henley. 'The house, nearly hidden among a cluster of beeches a hundred yards away, was of modern construction, and the grounds showed everywhere the signs of lavish wealth tastefully spent'.[5] Vardon's wealth and influence made him exceedingly popular within London society, though not with all, as was clear from his attendance at the Tiffanys' garden party.

> Everyone seemed to know, or be anxious to know, the great company promoter, whose wealth and resources were reputed to be without limit. It is true that the fashionable on Mrs Tiffany's visiting-list were of the smart rather than the exclusive division of society, but they numbered amongst them many titles, and any amount of talent of a kind, and both the titled and the talented were equally desirous of being civil to Horace Vardon. An acquaintance, who by the stroke of a pen can make you the possessor of a snug parcel of vendor's shares, which you may or may not be able to sell at a premium, or who can with equal ease appoint you to a well-fee'd seat on a directorate, is not to be despised, even if his name is not altogether untouched by rumours of sharp practice'.

It was only the most respectable members of society who shunned Horace Vardon.

Associated with him was Theophilus Tiffany who had trained as a barrister but was now an MP. He was known in the City as 'the King of the Guinea Pigs', indicating his presence as a paid director on the boards of numerous companies. 'Mr Tiffany's suave tones were more familiar to shareholders at company meetings in the City than to his colleagues of the legislative chamber. He was in Parliament because it paid, not because he liked it. The magic letters M.P. had a round, sterling value for a man who was a director of thirteen joint-stock companies, and chairman of ten'. He lived with his wife and children in a house in its own grounds in Surbiton, where he entertained on a grand scale. He was to be chairman of the company. Among the directors was Viscount Sligo, 'an impecunious Irish peer who owed his life to the bad shooting rather than to the goodwill of his tenants'. Another was Sir Howard Elymas, 'who had fitted himself for the direction of joint-stock companies by getting compulsorily retired from a cavalry regiment with a very bad record'. They were well aware of the fraud taking place, having been told by Lucy, when she met them at a party in the company's offices in the City, that 'All the gold there is ever likely to be in this company will come from the pockets of your deluded victims'. People such as these were the public face of the company as they gave it an air of respectability designed to appeal to investors. They attended the public meetings, met the shareholders and answered questions in return for their share options and fees. Though driven by greed and willing to countenance fraud they were marginal figures, and were not the real City criminals. Instead, they were more of a 'credulous dupe than a schemer'.[6]

The real villains were professional City people like Vardon. One of these was the broker to the company, Oswald Crawshay, who 'was an important personage, with a house in Park Lane, and a "place" in Surrey, of which county he was a J. P'. He 'thought himself honest so long as he did not infringe the rules of the Stock Exchange, which in his opinion covered all laws human and divine'. As broker to the company Crawshay was 'to arrange for purely imaginary dealings in Golden Kloof shares, by means of which they would be driven to a fictitious premium, and being so quoted in complacent financial journals, would lead investors to suppose that the 'securities' were being eagerly sought for'. As the London Stock Exchange did not outlaw such practices, and there was no law against them, Crawshay could escape punishment for his actions, even though he was to be responsible for creating a false market that would encourage investors to buy worthless shares. Crawshay represented that part of the City that kept within the law, and were thus considered respectable by society. Nevertheless, they too preyed upon the unsuspecting public. The other City people involved in the promotion of the Golden Kloof mine were breaking the law and could be prosecuted for their actions. Along with Vardon, who had foreign blood, the other main conspirators were both Jewish. One was Israel Levi, a City bullion dealer.

Levi is referred to as 'an oily little Jew of obsequious manners and an unwhole-
some appearance'. He supplied samples of gold-bearing ore that were meant to
have been found on the farm. From his conversation with Vardon it was made
clear that this was believed to be common practice in the City.

> The gold-studded lumps of glistening quartz were unpacked and closely inspected,
> amid protestations from Mr Levi that they had not, as Vardon suggested, been
> exploited at every gold-mining project during the last ten years. 'S'help me! But I
> faked 'em expreshly for the Golden Kloof', bleated the cringing Hebrew. 'You're too
> good a custhomer to play hanky with, Misther Vardon'.
>
>   'Yes, and I know a little too much about you, Levi, don't I, to admit to tricks',
> said Vardon'.

In the end Levi escaped prison by testifying against Vardon and his associates.[7]

The other Jew involved was Gus Eppstein who also used the name Sydney
Engledue, both to hide his true identity and to disguise the fact that he ran two
separate businesses in the City. He was Vardon's main associate in the City and
had worked closely with him in all his previous schemes. He was described as
'a fast-looking man, who wore a huge gardenia in his button-hole and brought
with him a flavour of strong cigars'. He 'spent most of his ill-gotten gains in music
halls and late restaurants'. His main business was as an outside broker in the City,
which meant that he operated an establishment where the public could bet on
the rise or fall of share prices as they clustered around the ticker tape machine
relaying prices from the Stock Exchange. These were known as 'bucket shops'
and it was one of these that Gus Eppstein ran, with Horace Vardon as a sleeping partner. Having an appointment with Gus Eppstein Lucy visited this bucket
shop and was shocked by what she saw.

> The air was thick with cigar smoke and spirituous fumes, the babel that arose from the
> twenty or thirty clients in the room was deafening, and every pause or break in the
> clatter of voices was accentuated by the whirr and click of the ceaseless 'tape'. There
> were three of these machines in the place, each being the centre of an excited group
> of gamblers ...Various and many were the types represented in this legalised 'hell', but
> two traits were common to all the flushed and eager faces of Mr. Engledue's clients
> – greed and credulity.

These clients ranged from retired military men, once-prosperous tradesmen and
City clerks 'with their hands fresh from their employers' tills'.

Planted in amongst them were a few of Vardon's associates who were there to
persuade customers to keep gambling until they had lost all their money, including any winnings that they may have briefly made.[8] Sir Howard Elymas, who sat
on the board of Vardon's companies, persuaded a young man to buy Mexican
Railway shares, even though he was aware that he had virtually no money left
and would be ruined if the shares fell in price. According to Sir Howard, 'My

dear boy, haven't I told you it's a certainty ... I had it straight from a quarter that never fails. Put every stiver you're worth into it, and make a thousand or so absolutely without risk of loss'. The young man did so but within minutes the price fell and he lost everything. Faced with the prospect of returning home and confessing that he has lost all his money, he left the 'bucket-shop' and tried to shoot himself in the street outside. Luckily Lucy and her father saw him, prevented it, and then took him to his parents' house in Park Lane. He turned out to be the Honourable Charles Burgon, and was the son of a Northamptonshire landowner and cabinet minister, Lord Tintagel. On hearing the story from his son and learning about the Golden Kloof Mining Company from Lucy and her father, Lord Tintagel offered to use all the power at his disposal to stop these frauds taking place in the City. The result was an investigation into Vardon and the Golden Kloof, leading to his fraudulent activities being exposed and those involved prosecuted.[9]

Eppstein was also directly involved in the company promotion business with Vardon. His main task was to persuade people living in the country to buy shares in the worthless companies being promoted by Vardon, as they were regarded as being much less knowledgeable with what was happening than those in London. For this operation he operated as Sydney Engledue, a respectable City broker. Such is Guy Elwes's innocence that he is even persuaded to buy shares in the Golden Kloof Mining Company as he did not realize until too late that it was proposing to develop a gold mine on the very farm he had sold. Believing that he is in receipt of confidential advice from a City insider, Guy also convinces his own father and Lucy's mother to put what little savings they had into the Golden Kloof mine. Eppstein had obtained through bribery various lists of those with savings to invest, such as those in receipt of government pensions, and circulated them extolling the wonderful prospects of the new mining company.[10] Vardon's own role was to write the prospectus for the Golden Kloof Mining Company in such a way that it would appeal to numerous investors while staying within the letter of the law. In this he had become very experienced. 'Every phase of that composition that read so trippingly had been thought out from every aspect, and its effect on friend and foe, on the public and on the legal mind, weighed and tested by the light of experience. That done, the outward form in which the document could be best dressed up to strike and catch the investor was made the subject of special study. Hours were spent in instructing the printers on matters of type and effective 'spacy', and on a judicious use of red ink and italics, then the whole was arranged and re-arranged till the great mantrap was ready for the final setting'. Once the prospectus was written, Vardon's other task was to persuade the City editors of the main newspapers to give it either extensive positive publicity or, at least, refrain from passing negative comment. This was mainly achieved through the simple device of paying for multiple advertisements in these newspapers. However, some editors had to be bribed if their support or silence was required. One such was Barker Crabbe, the editor of the *Financial Lynx*, who asked for fifty shares in the Golden Kloof if he was going to give it a favourable reception for, otherwise, he was going to expose it as a fraud.[11] Thus the newspaper press, and especially that associated with the City, was seen as fundamentally corrupt. The comment is made that 'It may even be that in one sense, by forming a precedent, Vardon was a benefactor, for if promoters habitually murdered financial editors, or vice versa, the loss would not be felt, while the gain to the community by getting the attendant circumstances threshed out would be incalculable'.[12]

This story ended with an attack on the City by Professor Drax, drawing upon his experience in the United States.

> You can't expect folk that are without guile themselves to see a serpent in every rose bush that's dressed up as sweet as most of these swindling companies are. It's the fault, I reckon, of your British Legislature for allowing them to rampage around unchecked. Why, it's the popular opinion in this country that in the States all men are cheats and boodle-mongers; but I tell you, sir, that such a thief as this man Vardon wouldn't be able to live amongst us – let alone making a living off us – for a single month. We've got thieves and rogues galore, but we don't allow systems of organised robbery.

In response Lord Tintagel promised government action to outlaw fraudulent company promotion in the City driven by the events surrounding the Golden Kloof mine and the corruption it had exposed.

> Thus, once for all, was broken up one of the most dangerous organizations for plunder that has ever disgraced the City, and, though many others disgrace it still, Vardon's detection and downfall will go far to check the abuses of company promotion by showing how little faith is to be placed in the most specious prospectus. The inception of the Golden Kloof was, after all, but a fair type of numberless kindred schemes reared on quite unsubstantial a foundation as Guy's few acres of farmland, but which, after making thousands of homes miserable, have sneaked quietly out of existence because they did not happen to be associated with a similar tragedy.

The City did not even redeem itself by financing Professor Drax's invention because he sold it to 'a private capitalist'.[13] In *Guilty Gold*, the impression conveyed was that the City was a place where no respectable person would wish to work, where innocent investors were defrauded by unscrupulous criminals, and where government controls were urgently needed. If *Guilty Gold* provides any reflection of prevailing culture one can only conclude that the late Victorians regarded the City of London not with pride but as a national disgrace that needed to be both shunned and curbed. It is no surprise that Guy does not choose a City career after all his experiences but becomes Lord Tintagel's bailiff and land agent at £800 a year. The reader is asked to contrast '...the worn, haggard, young man who had haunted the strange streets of the City in the vain attempt to escape from the meshes that held him' with his appearance on being able to marry Lucy and live in a house on Lord Tintagel's Northamptonshire estate. 'His honest, country-bred face shone with health, and in his eyes there was a sparkle of something more than hope'.[14]

Indicative of the fact that *Guilty Gold* was no isolated attack upon the City another novel appeared in the same year and covered much the same ground. This was Francis Gribble's *The Lower Life*. The significance of the title is made clear when two of the characters, Arnold Brabant and his fiancée, Helen Fanshawe, attended a sermon delivered by Seymour Dale, a fashionable preacher. He attacked speculation in general and the Stock Exchange in particular, contrasting the material path, or Lower Life, chosen by the speculator, with the spiritual path, or Higher Life, that should be the one chosen by all decent people. This greatly influenced Helen but had no affect on Arnold who relished all that he could now buy with the money he was making through company promotion and Stock Exchange speculation. He had become involved with Benjamin Cohen, a 'self-made man whose sudden fame had sprung up like a mushroom in the City of London, who touched no enterprise that he did not profit from, and whose marvellous Asbestos Companies were the financial topic of the hour'. By allotting Baldwin Blake shares in one of his companies, and then telling him when to sell at a profit, he had gained admittance to an exclusive London club, the Barbaric Club, which was mainly frequented by actors, painters, journalists, musicians and writers. Here he held court, impressing the small group of late-night drinkers by telling them that,

> If you look down on money, you're a pack of fools; and if you want to know the reason why, I tell you. But first of all, I'll ask you this: why isn't literature properly respected in this country? Why aren't the arts properly looked up to in this country? ... It's because the artist and the man of letters don't very often make a thousand a year. That's the one damning fact about them that the British public can't get over.

In contrast, his belief was that 'Never was such a time for making money in the City. As easy as shelling peas. As easy as picking up sovereigns out of the gutter'. Though 'Some of the Barbarians might despise him as a vulgar person and a money-grubber ... most of them were ambitious of his acquaintance'.

One such was Arnold Brabant, who at that time was a young barrister. He was very impressed by Cohen, noting that

> He was the one rich man in the room – living in Onslow Square, while the wealthiest of the others could only afford a house in Bedford Park – and it was inevitable that he should be known for a rich man wherever he was met. It was not merely the weight of his watch-chain, the glitter of his diamond studs, the gloss of his silk hat, and the fur lining of his overcoat, that proclaimed the fact aloud. Beyond all this, he had the inde-

finable air of the man who, provided that sufficient cause were shown, would be ready to sit down ostentatiously at any moment, and draw whatever cheque might be required. He had also the air of a man who is accustomed to dominate any assembly in which he finds himself – to dominate genially, if possible, but to dominate in any case.

At the same time Brabant considered Cohen to be an

ignorant, unmannerly vulgarian, who doubtless knew no better use for gold than to squander it on racehorses, and loose women, and champagne, and vainglorious display; while he, whose tastes were trained to delicate and refined enjoyment, who longed to travel, and to surround himself with beautiful things, who entertained ambitions, could not even earn enough to marry and keep a house together.

Though engaged to Helen, whose father was a doctor in Blackheath, Brabant was not yet earning enough to get married. Consequently, despite his personal dislike of Cohen he decided to go and seek his assistance, because 'man saw the reward of his labours sooner in the City than at the bar; and that was what he wanted'. This meant a visit to Cohen's office near the Stock Exchange, if he was to learn how to make money in the City: 'the ways of the City man are mysterious, suggesting to the uninitiated the black art, the diving-rod, or the philosopher's stone. He gives you the idea of making something out of nothing'. Brabant was willing to take his chance because success in the City would mean a rapid road to both wealth and marriage. 'It might be happiness and fortune; it might be rudeness and rebuff. There did not seem a third alternative. But time was flying, and he was off again, pushing his way along the crowded pavement of Cheapside, where the churches are hidden away among the houses, as though the overwhelming wordliness of the City of London cowed them, until he came to the confused confluence of six swollen streams of traffic in the front of the Royal Exchange ... Like so many a stranger before him, he thought it was the Stock Exchange'. Instead, the Stock Exchange went unnoticed.

He passed its mean and paltry entrance without even suspecting what it was. Specula-tors, with anxious faces, stood uncomfortably in its porch, like prisoners waiting for a verdict. Busy brokers, many of them hatless, with open note-books in their hands, passed in and out of the swing-doors. A gorgeous waiter, with gold braid upon his hat, bawled double-barrelled names continually through a speaking tube. Newspaper boys hung about the edge of the pavement, crying the contents of fifth-rate financial prints.

As a result of this meeting with Cohen, Brabant was advised to buy shares in the Rohilcund Mining Company, based on information that was not yet public. Brabant immediately contacted a broker, bought 500 shares, and then sold them next day for a profit of £112 after they had risen when the news broke. With this money and the connection to Cohen Brabant felt he could now afford to marry Helen. Though Helen felt speculation was morally wrong she now blessed the

Stock Exchange because the money that Arnold had made there allowed her to get married. 'What prejudice she had against gambling had been, at bottom, a prejudice against losing money'. By offering the possibilities of life-changing events through the making or losing of money the City could be loved by the former and hated by the latter.[15]

Brabant now abandoned the Bar and began working with Cohen as a company promoter. Cohen had moved on from asbestos mining to West Australian gold mines, where he was making even more money and spending it on giving lavish balls where the champagne alone cost £2,000. These balls were attended by those who were making money out of the promotion of these gold-mining companies and the subsequent speculation in their shares, such as brokers, jobbers, city editors and mining engineers. Most were corrupt, being paid by company promoters to produce favourable reports or encourage their clients to speculate in shares. Those that could not be bribed were a rare exception, such as Arthur Abraham, City editor of the Comet, as were those who did not dabble in shares, as with Austin Marillier, a mining engineer. Brabant took to this life and, over a period of eight years, became a power in the City in his own right.

> Cautious as well as bold, he never risked too much upon a single venture, so that he never made a loss that seriously checked his progress. When he could afford it, he bought a financial newspaper, and produced it to all appearance at a loss. It made him a man of influence, whom it was worth while to propitiate, and so brought him information that was useful in the markets. In this way he went on from strength, multiplied his interests, and increased his balance at the bank, moved from a bad address to a good, and from a good address to a better, until at last he could tell his wife that he was on the eve of a greater coup than ever.

He even employed Helen's brother, Basil, who, unlike Arthur, found the City's obsession with money distasteful. Eventually Basil confessed to his sister that work in the City was

> 'a confoundedly demoralizing life ... what I'm doing up in the City is gambling, and nothing else ...We sell things we haven't got, and we buy things we haven't the least intention of paying for. Do you suppose we deal in stocks and shares? Not a bit of it. The shares are only gambling counters, and what we do is to back our opinion that they'll go up or down. You wonder why I do it, perhaps. I do it because it's the only way I know of making enough money to marry Ida; and the horror is that, all the while I'm doing it, I feel that I'm being drawn further and further away from her'.

What Basil wanted to do was write poetry but that would not provide him with a living, and certainly one good enough to support a wife, as he wanted to marry his fiancée, Ida.

On the eve of Arnold's great financial triumph conditions in the City took a turn for the worse, when the downfall of the house of Baring shook the City ... In London the blows were raining thick upon the heads of the financiers. American rails fell, and Mexican rails followed them, and jobbers laughed in the faces of those who wanted them to buy their Argentine securities. The bottom was knocked out of all the markets in turn – out of the nitrate market, out of the Kaffir market, out of the miscellaneous market. Banks suspended payment, and industrial companies passed their dividends; on every settling-day there was awe and apprehension in the marble halls of the Stock Exchange, when the waiter, with his hammer in his hand, climbed up into his stand, and knocked three times, and in hard matter-of-fact tones announced that Mr So-and-so 'regrets to inform the House that he is unable to comply with his bargains'. It happened three times upon a single morning, and everyone wondered whose turn was coming next. The circle widened, and the country as well as London felt the shock. There was scarcely a spot in the United Kingdom where some trace of the calamity was not discernible. In wealthy Croydon whole rows of palatial houses stood tenantless, eloquent in their depressing desolation. Tradesmen bewailed bad debts, and debtors met them with talk of dividends that were overdue. Even in Ramsgate aged professional men were heard lamenting that they would have to 'die in harness', because the best part of their savings had gone down for ever in the Maelstrom. ... Arnold was not troubled ... because he had foreseen ... the smash soon enough to come out of it with ready money.

Nevertheless, the work involved in achieving that had made him ill so he decided that they should have a prolonged holiday in Ramsgate until a recovery took place. "It isn't the end of the world', he said.

It isn't even the end of the Stock Exchange. Trade is going on, and manufacture is going on. They may talk as they like about 'bad time', but the country as a whole is always saving money. Just now people are frightened, and put their money in the bank. Presently they'll be tired of getting one and a half percent on their deposits, and nothing at all on their current accounts. That's what we call 'a revival of confidence' and when it comes all the fun will begin once again. In the mean time, we've only got to sit tight, and live on the ready money'.

In Ramsgate there were

No more business worries now! No more piles of letters to attend to! No more telegraphing to Old Broad Street. His cunning schemes were locked up in the back of his brain, and his interest in the things out of which there was no money to be made returned to him. He could read poetry and feel its magic, not even throwing his book down when the Financial Telegraph arrived; he could wander away into Fairyland when Helen sang him Schubert's songs, instead of concocting a prospectus while he listened. It was almost the ideal life they had contemplated when they married, and had supposed their money was to buy.

However, this life was not to last, much to Helen's regret for, once the market started to revive he returned to his obsession with money.

His morning mail increased in bulk; he had to shut himself up for a long time every day to attend to it. He began to send telegrams to his brokers, to Benjy Cohen, to Barry McAlure; he wished to goodness there was a telephone in Ramsgate. He ran up to town two or three times, and spent the night at the Metropole. Instead of reading books, he read financial papers, turning into the station to buy them, and glancing over them while he walked with Helen on the pier. When she sang him Schubert's songs, he lay on the sofa, doing sums in his head. His talk grew sanguine and excited, but his face showed anxiety, and he ceased to enjoy the things which he had enjoyed during the past nine months. Prosperity, it seemed, had announced her advent, and was exacting payment in advance. The end came suddenly. A letter came of more pressing importance than his other letters, and determined him. 'I must go up by express', he said', and stop at the Metropole. You must follow me as soon as you can have the things packed. The time for making money is coming round again'.[16]

The result was that Arnold and Helen returned to London where they grew increasingly apart. Arnold's obsession with moneymaking was taking over his whole life. Intrigued by what was happening to Arnold and Basil Helen and Ida decided to visit the City.

On their right was the stiff solid façade of the Bank of England, with its wide gateways opening into silent courts – a building of solemn, stern, and almost of forbidding aspect; a building that seemed to say that here was the one fixed and solid rock set midst of the financial ocean, a rock against which the fiercest financial hurricanes must beat without avail. On their right was the Royal Exchange, whose bold front seems to speak the proud defiance of commercial England to the world, and whose sides are given over to such puny shops and offices. Between the two ran a crowded street, full of well-dressed men in a hurry – a street ignobly narrow, and with a vista of narrower and more ignoble streets beyond. There was nothing here, Helen felt, to claim or conquer her attention ... They turned the corner by the Threadneedle Street Post-Office, and the crowd changed its character. The centre of it was a certain insignificant swing-door, with opaque panels of glazed glass that never got a moment's rest from swinging. A constant stream of men, with little note-books in their hands, poured in and out in the direction of Threadneedle Street on the one side, and Old Broad Street on the other. A stationary row of men lined the pavement in front of it for a distance of twenty or thirty yards. They stood at the very edge of the kerb, with one foot in the gutter, so as not to block the traffic, and their eyes were fixed on the swing-door, watching the men who bustled in and out of it. Newspaper-boys tried to sell them the financial weeklies. A burly constable occasionally said, 'Move on, please! Keep the pavement clear!' but in a deferential tone of voice, as though he knew that he had moneyed men to deal with, and must not be peremptory.

When the women discovered this was the Stock Exchange they were shocked 'the building was hidden away, as though it were something to be ashamed of, behind the fronts of ugly modern houses, and ... the entrance through which men walked and trotted and ran, according to their temperaments, in the pur-

suit of wealth, was miserably low and narrow'. Ida, who had visited the City
before, told Helen,

> It's only the brokers, of course, whom you see passing in and out of the door. The
> people in the street are their clients. There is no waiting room. The man there in the
> gaudy livery calls the name of the broker who is wanted, through the speaking tube,
> and the broker comes out and consults with his clients in the porch or in the street,
> and then goes back into the House to do his business for him.

She then added that the scene in Throgmorton Street, outside the Stock
Exchange, got far worse after 4:30 in the afternoon when the outside market
took place as the Stock Exchange was closed. 'It's a mob, Helen – a howling,
savage mob that one can hardly pass through. Hundreds of well-dressed men, all
of them with their note-books, and half of them without their hats, pushing and
yelling and screaming like pandemonium let loose'. She wanted Helen to stay
and see it but Helen had had enough. She was disgusted. The women could not
believe that this is what happened and such was the source of the money which
brought them the jewellery and furs that they wore. They saw the people outside
the Stock Exchange as no better than gamblers at a gaming-table. Even worse
were the offices of outside brokers like Jacob Jacobson which they considered
nothing more than a casino.

It was not only investors that were carried away by the speculative fever for
it also took over the lives of the company promoters such as Arnold Brabant, to
the exclusion of all else. Absorbed with the details of finance he worked continuously, sustaining himself by drinking heavily during the day, with a particular
fondness for champagne, especially Roederer and Heidsieck's Dry Metropole.
His current project was a West Australian mining company called Armageddon, capitalized at £800,000, which he and Benjy Cohen had bought for only
£10,000. If this proved a success he expected to sell his shares at a large profit and
achieve his ambition of taking a house in Park Lane. In addition, he was using
the advance information that came to him, through the ownership of a newspaper, the *Mining Register*, to speculate successfully in mining shares. He would
buy shares in the morning and then sell in the afternoon, usually for a profit,
once the price had risen on the publication of favourable news.

> Arnold waited in the street while a clerk of the house of Marsden and Parkins did his
> business for him in the House. The two thousand shares which he had bought in the
> morning at 15.s he sold in the afternoon at 22s. 6d. – a profit of £750. It was tea-time,
> so he paused to drink a brandy-and-soda with his broker's clerk, who asked that, in
> due course, he might have the 'inside tip' concerning Armageddons. 'Certainly, 'said
> Arnold. 'It's a big thing, and I shall let all my friends stand in'.

Such was Arnold's obsession with making money in the City that he neglected
his wife and their marriage gradually fell apart. Helen had been shocked by

what she had seen in the City and the realization that her husband was actively involved. She found it difficult to resolve her inner conflict between her love for her husband and the material possessions bought by money made in the City on the one hand, and the realization how that money had been made and Arnold's role in it. It was not that Arnold had become an intrinsically evil person but rather the fact that the methods he employed in his 'money-grubbing' activities were vulgar, sordid and contemptible. '[T]hey dragged him down into a world of thought from which romance was crowded out; because they set their mark upon his soul, and made him impossible as a lover. He did sums in his head; he was worried and anxious and preoccupied; he had forgotten the language of sentiment'. She drew an unfavourable contrast between Arnold and the mining engineer, Austin Marillier 'A man who had eschewed the contaminating influence of Stock Markets'. She now saw Arnold as 'calculating, plotting, absorbed in figures, anxious about prices, scanning the tape, shouting into the telephone, now excited and now tired, but never really calm, his finer faculties rusting, his lower instincts in control!' while she pictured Marillier as 'the explorer in the forest, his iron nerves indifferent to danger, his eyes alert for every one of nature's changing charms, his mind at ease and free to roam, dwelling at leisure on sentimental memories – dwelling sometimes, it might be, when next he was alone in the wilderness, upon some memory of a sentimental talk with her!' The better the Armageddon shares did, the busier Arnold was but the more disenchanted Helen became, leading her towards an affair with Marillier, which went unnoticed by Arnold.[17] The message was clear. An excessive commitment to moneymaking in the City corrupted even those men who profited from their actions, driving their wives into the arms of others.

Arnold and Benjy were generating favourable reports about the prospects of the Armageddon mine while manipulating the share price by buying and selling simultaneously in both London and Paris, using their own money. This gave the impression that there was a large demand for the shares and drove the price of the shares to a premium. Once genuine investors had been attracted in by these devices they expected to unload their shares at a large profit. However, they were greedy and decided to wait for a final report from the mine, proving the presence of a large ore body. This would give the shares a final boost and allow them to unload at a huge profit, but a telegram arrived from Perth, Australia, saying that no ore had been discovered. On receipt of this information Arnold and Benjy sold not only the shares they owned themselves but far more. They were confident that, when the information was made public, they could buy in the market at a much lower price all that they needed to deliver to those to whom they had sold. When the news did break there was a panic as speculators tried to sell their shares. Arnold and Benjy made their way to Throgmorton Street, to watch.

The time was half-past four, and the market in the street was already in full progress. The noise was so great that they could hear the uproar long before they saw the crowds; and the crowd was so dense that when they reached it, they could only stand upon its outskirts. Cabs tried to get through, but turned back, abandoning the effort in despair. The police were powerless to force a track for them, to 'move on' any one, or to make the least pretence of keeping order. There was no business – only the fruitless effort to do business, in a market where every one wished to sell, and no one cared to buy.

When Arnold and Benjy were spotted the crowd turned on them but they escaped in a hansom cab. That evening Arnold and Benjy dined at the Savoy, followed by a round of the clubs to which they belonged. Though Arnold felt remorse for the ruined investors Benjy felt none. On his return home Arnold discovered a draft letter from Helen to Austin Marillier, which revealed to him that they had been having an affair. Such was the shock, coming after the excitement of the day, that he collapsed with brain fever, which left him incapacitated, forcing Helen to stay and look after him, rather than sailing to Africa with Marillier. In contrast, Ida, who had stayed true to Basil, despite his activities in the City, married him and they migrated to Australia, where he was going to practise at the Bar. Basil had lost most of his money in the Armageddon crash, not being one of the inner circle, and so had decided to abandon the City. As Ida said, 'it's better to be poor than to touch money made as that money was'. In contrast, Benjy Cohen was already planning a new company, the South-West Armageddon Exploration Company.[18] Clearly the City was no place for respectable people like Arnold and Basil for, if they did not forsake it, their health and happiness would be destroyed. In contrast, Jews like Benjy Cohen were able to thrive in the City because they possessed no moral scruples about the way they made money. Given the propensity of the public to speculate, the City was seen as an inescapable evil but not a place fitted for decent Englishmen.

Evidence of the deep impact made by the gold-mining craze on the place of the City within British society can also be found in the 1897 novel, *The Whirlpool*, by George Gissing. A conversation is reported between two of the main characters, Harvey Rolfe and his friend Cecil Morphew, which epitomized the divergence of views on Stock Exchange speculation in contemporary society.

> 'You don't speculate at all?' Morphew asked. 'Shouldn't know how to go about it, replied the other in his deeper note'. Morphew then explained, 'It seems to me to be the simplest thing in the world if one is content with moderate profits. I'm going in for it seriously – cautiously – as a matter of business. I've studied the thing – got it up as I used to work at an exam. And here, you see, I've made five pounds at a stroke – five pounds! Suppose I make that every now and then, it's worth the trouble, you know – it mounts up. And I shall never stand to lose much. You see, it's Tripcony's interest that I should make profits'. Rolfe replied that 'I'm not quite sure of that'. To which Morphew responded 'Oh, but it is! Let me explain...'

Tripcony was Morphew's stockbroker but the rest of the conversation about the techniques he employed to speculate successfully is not recorded. Cecil Morphew had trained as a lawyer but was living on a private income of £300 per annum which he considered insufficient to get married on, so he hoped to increase it by speculating on the stock market. An overriding theme of the period was the low rate of interest, and the effect this was having on the income of those dependent upon investments, forcing them to seek alternatives to the likes of the National Debt and railway securities.

The conversation then turned to the subject of Bennet Frothingham, who was considered a great financier, having started a company called The Britannia Loan, Assurance, Investment and Banking Company.[19] Morphew expressed his views thus,

> 'I'm convinced', said the young man presently, 'that anyone who really gives his mind to it can speculate with moderate success. Look at the big men – the brokers and the company promoters, and so on; I've met some of them, and there's nothing in them – nothing! Now there's Bennet Frothingham. You know him, I think? 'Rolfe nodded. ' Well, what do you think of him? Isn't he a very ordinary fellow? How has he got such a position? I'm told he began just in a small way – by chance. No doubt he found it so easy to make money he was surprised at his success. Tripcony has told me a lot about him. Why the Britannia brings him fifteen thousand a year, and he must be in a score of other things'.
>
> 'I know nothing about the figures', said Rolfe, 'and I shouldn't put much faith in Tripcony; but Frothingham, you may be sure, isn't quite an ordinary man'.
>
> 'Ah, well, of course there's a certain knack – and then experience –' replied Morphew, who was worried by rumours that the Britannia was in trouble, as he had money invested in it. In contrast to Morphew, Rolfe was a cautious investor and so suggested that 'Wouldn't you be much more comfortable if you had your money in some other kind of security?' to which Morphew replied
>
> 'Ah, but dear sir, twelve and a half per cent – twelve and a half! I hold preference shares of the original issue'. Rolfe's parting comment to Morphew was that 'Then I'm afraid you must take your chance'.[20]

This has all the elements that must have occurred during every speculative boom. On the one hand were those who were enticed by the prospect of great gain or higher rates of return and, on the other, those worried about the risks involved.

Another friend of Rolfe, Hugh Carnaby, was investing in Australian gold mining through an acquaintance, but, again, this was considered too risky an investment for Rolfe.

> 'That man you saw here tonight', Carnaby went on, 'the short, thick fellow – his name is Dando – he's just come back from Queensland. I don't quite know what he's been doing, but he evidently knows a good deal about mining. He says he has invented a new process of getting gold out of ore – I don't know anything about it. In the early days of mining, he says, no end of valuable stuff was abandoned, because they

couldn't smelt it. Something about pyrites – I have a vague recollection of old chemistry lessons. Dando wants to start smelting works for his new process, somewhere in North Queensland'.

'And wants money, I dare say', remarked the listener (Rolfe), with a twinkle of the eye.

'I suppose so. It was Carton that brought him here for the first time, a week ago. Might be worth thinking about, you know'. To this Rolfe responded,

'I have no opinion. My profound ignorance of everything keeps me in a state of perpetual scepticism. It has its advantages I dare say'.

'You're very conservative, Rolfe, in your finance', was Carnaby's reply, to which Rolfe's answer was 'Very'.

As it was, Carnaby's Queensland investment turned out to be very profitable as was an investment in a bicycle factory started by another acquaintance, Mackintosh, who had returned to Britain after a business career in Iraq and Australia, where he had met Carnaby. Eventually the bicycle company was floated on the Stock Exchange with great success.[21]

Driving this obsession with investments was the fact that people such as Harvey Rolfe and his family were living on interest and dividends from quoted securities, and these were falling in the 1890s.

> The redemption of his debentures kept him still occupied with a furtive study of the money-market. He did not dare to face risk on a large scale; the mere thought of a great reduction of income made him tremble and perspire. So in the end he adopted the simple and straightforward expedient of seeking an interview with his banker, by whom he was genially counselled to purchase such-and-such stock, a sound security, but less productive than that he had previously held'.[22] He did try to make himself familiar with what was happening in the City by reading a financial newspaper and consulting members of his club, but discovered that 'To study the money-market gave him a headache.

To supplement his investment income Rolfe put £200 into a photographic business with his friend Morphew. Morphew had raised his share by persuading a friend of his, who was the City editor of a newspaper, to print a damaging rumour about a company, so depressing its share price. This was done on behalf of the stockbroker, Tripcony, who, in return gave him a tip on the stock market, allowing Morphew to buy at seventy-five and sell at one hundred. This was another example of the widely held view that those in the City profited from manipulating the market, making themselves wealthy as a result, and so achieving a greatly enhanced social status. The daughter of the Earl of Bournemouth, Lady Isobel Barker, had married a City stockbroker, who was reputed to be a millionaire, and they lived in great style with a country estate, where they entertained royalty. Sudden success achieved through such means would inevitably breed resentment.[23]

In *The Whirlpool*, there is also the reappearance of the public's other major concern about the City: the consequence of a banking crisis. This concern had faded away during the 1880s as such events had become rare, but the bankruptcy of the Liberator Building Society, and the flight of its chairman, Jabez Balfour, had reawakened these fears, as is clear from the description of the collapse of the fictional Britannia Loan given by Gissing. Bennet Frothingham had built up the Britannia Loan over a period of thirty years, starting in a small rented office at the top of a newspaper building. Over that period the Britannia Loan had become a major financial institution in the City and Bennet Frothingham an accepted figure in certain quarters of London society. There was a general belief, according to Mrs Frothingham, that 'everybody thinks my husband can make them rich if only he chooses'. However, the Britannia collapsed and Rolfe went to watch what was happening at its City offices, when the rumour started spreading that it had closed its doors.

> At the end of the street in which the building stood, signs of the unusual became observable – the outskirts of a crowd, hanging loose in animated talk, as after some exciting occurrence; and before the bank itself was gathered a throng of men ... respectability's silk hats mingling with the felts of the lower strata. Here and there a voice could be heard raised in anger, but the prevailing emotion seemed to be curiosity. The people who would suffer most from the collapse of the high-sounding enterprise could not reach the scene of calamity at half an hour's notice; they were dwellers in many parts of the British Isles, strangers most of them to London city, with but a vague mental picture of the local habitation of the Britannia Loan, Assurance, Investment, and Banking Company, Limited.[24]

The impression was conveyed that it was not those in the City who would suffer from the collapse but investors and depositors the length and breadth of the land. It was they who were to suffer from the 'knavery' practised by Bennet Frothingham, who had shot himself in order to escape disgrace and punishment. 'Bennet Frothingham, no doubt, had played a rascally game, foreseeing all along the issues of defeat'. With that prospect in mind he had settled money on his wife and daughter so as to ensure they continued to have a comfortable lifestyle, though others were ruined and some committed suicide. All that happened to his family was that their social standing was ruined through association with his failure. 'The name of Bennet Frothingham stood for criminal recklessness, for huge rascality; it would be so for years to come'. That this was no isolated example of what went on in the City is made plain. In the City 'every one of them would be dishonest on as great a scale if they dared, or had the chance'.[25]

The result of such a vivid portrayal of a bank collapse was to both enhance fears about the risks involved in investment and to create a strong suspicion about the City of London and what went on there. However, as the excesses of the gold-mining boom faded away there was a gradual willingness to recognize that investors themselves had allowed greed to overcome their judgement and that not all of the companies were fraudulent. In Olive Schreiner's 1899 novel, *Trooper Peter Halket of Mashonaland*, the motives that had underpinned the speculative mania were recognized, so dissipating part of the responsibility for what had taken place away from the City. Peter Halket was a British soldier employed by the British South Africa Company to protect its property. While on guard he reflected on why he was there.

> He resolved he would make a great deal of money, and she (his mother) should live with him. He would build a large house in the West End of London, the biggest that had ever been seen, and another in the country, and they should never work any more .... All men made money when they came to South Africa, – Barney Barnato, Rhodes – they all made money out of the country, eight millions, twelve millions, twenty-six millions, forty millions; why should not he! ... He considered his business prospects. When he had served his time as volunteer he would have a large piece of land given him, and the Mashonas and Matabeles would have all their land taken away from them in time, and the Chartered Company would pass a law that they had to work for the white men; and he, Peter Halket, would make them work for him. He would make money. Then he reflected what he should do with the land if it were no good and he could not make anything out of it. Then, he should have to start a syndicate; called the Peter Halket Gold-, or Peter Halket Iron-mining, or some such name, Syndicate. Peter Halket was not very clear as to how it ought to be started; but he felt certain that he and some other men would have to take shares. They would not have to pay for them. And then they would get some big man in London to take shares. He need not pay for them; they would give them to him; and then the company would be floated. No one would have to pay anything; it was just the name – 'The Peter Halket Gold Mining Company, Limited.
>
> It would float in London; and people there who didn't know the country would buy the shares; they would have to give ready money for them, of course; perhaps fifteen pounds a share ...And then, when the market was up, he Peter Halket, would sell out all his shares. If he gave himself only six thousand and sold them each for ten pounds, then he, Peter Halket, would have sixty thousand pounds! ... And then the other people, that bought the shares for cash! Well, they could sell out too; they could all sell out! Then Peter Halket's mind got a little hazy. The matter was getting too difficult for him ...Well, if they didn't like to sell out a the right time, it was their own faults. Why didn't they? He, Peter Halket, did not feel responsible for them. Everyone knew you had to sell out at the right time. If they didn't choose to sell out at the right time, well, they didn't. 'It's the shares that you sell, not the shares you keep, that make the money'. But if they couldn't sell them? Here Peter Halket hesitated. – well, the British Government would have to buy them, if they were so bad no one else would; and then no one would lose. 'The British Government can't let British shareholders suffer'. He'd heard that often enough. The British taxpayer would have to pay for the Chartered Company, for the soldiers, and all the other things, if it couldn't, and take over the shares if it went smash, because there were lords and dukes and princes connected with it. And why shouldn't they pay for his company? He would have a lord in it too!'

Halket had come to Africa 'to make money' so as to escape his humble origins and buy everything he ever wanted, including a house with a cook and a valet and as much champagne as he wanted to drink. He could become an MP, marry anyone he wanted, and receive invitations to Sandringham. None of this was to be realized as he was shot while on duty.[26] For most people such an opportunity only existed through the purchase of shares in a gold-mining company and hoping that the gamble paid of.

Given that within society there was always a significant minority who would gamble, as Arthur Morrison noted in 1897, if it was not shares in gold mines it would be something else:

> Cycle companies were in the market everywhere. Immense fortunes were being made in a few days and sometimes little fortunes were being lost to build them up. Mining shares were dull for a season, and any company with the word `cycle` or `tyre` in its title was certain to attract capital, no matter what its prospects were like in the eyes of the expert. All the old private cycle companies suddenly were offered to the public, and their proprietors, already rich men, built themselves houses on the Riviera, bought yachts, ran racehorses, and left business for ever. Sometimes the shareholders got their money's worth, sometimes more, sometimes less – sometimes they got nothing but total loss; but still the game went on. One could never open a newspaper without finding, displayed at large, the prospectus of yet another cycle company with capital expressed in six figures at least, often in seven.[27]

It was also recognized by the end of the 1890s that those who lost from speculative excesses included some in the City rather than only innocent outside investors duped by insiders. Such a circumstance was central to the 1899 novel by H. Frederic, *The Market-Place*. The individual who planned and executed the operation was Stormont Thorpe, whose father had been a London second-hand bookseller. He had travelled around the world for fifteen years looking for an opportunity that would make him rich, and was now returning home having accumulated £8,000. In addition, he owned a rubber plantation in Mexico which he hoped to float as a company.

The first group in the City who agreed to help him took his money and did nothing in return, leading him to describe them as 'a swarm of relentless and voracious harpies'. He then turned to 'a group of City men concerned in the South African market'. These were all Jewish and, after being entertained at his expense, agreed to float the company but only if they were given 90 per cent of the shares. Thorpe turned this offer down and decided to promote the company himself, which so annoyed them that they tried to block him. To assist him in the floatation, Thorpe enlisted the help of Lord Plowden, whom he had met on board the boat taking him home. Plowden was keen to make money as the £100,000 in bonds he had inherited from his father had turned out to have a market value of only £1,300, being mostly worthless issues by the US Confederacy. Lord Plowden joined the Board at a salary of £300 a year, plus the promise of free shares. In turn he brought in the Marquis of Chaldon, a retired ambassador, at £500 a year, as chairman. The broker, a Scotsman called Colin Semple, who was to handle the issue of the shares, charged £500 plus £2,000 in shares; the solicitor £200 and 2,000 shares; the auditors £100 and 1,000 shares; the advertising agent £1,000 and 5,000 shares; and the editor of a newspaper £100 and 2,000 shares. Only the bankers did not charge and the offices in Austin Friars were rented with payment in arrears. Thorpe had to pay all these costs himself receiving in return 400,000 out of the 500,000 £1 shares issued on behalf of the company, known as Rubber Consols. However, the subscriptions from the investing public, 'small holders – country clergymen, and old maids on an annuity, and so on – all over the country', amounted to only £5,000. In order to generate a demand for the shares Thorpe instructed Semple to offer to buy them in the market at a higher price than the issue price. In the expectation that they would be able to buy the shares at the issue price the Jewish financiers, who had turned on him, sold shares. Within a short period Semple had bought 26,200 for Thorpe. However, as Thorpe had control over the issue of the shares, other than the 5,000 issued to genuine investors, he refused to release any more. He then forced the Jewish brokers to pay the difference between the current market price and the price at which they had sold the shares each time there was an official settlement on the Stock Exchange, when all bargains had to be completed. This took place fortnightly and the Jewish brokers had no option but to pay his asking price or face being expelled from the Stock Exchange as defaulters.

Thorpe's sister thought what he was doing was cruel but he justified his actions by telling her that this was no different from what these Jewish brokers had done to others.

'Everything in the City is cruel ... All speculative business is cruel. Take our case, for example. I estimate in a rough way that these fourteen men will have to pay over to us, in differences and in final sales, say, £700,000 – may be £800,000. Well, now, not one of those fellows ever earned a single sovereign of that money. They've taken the whole from others, and these others took it from others still, and so almost indefinitely. There isn't a sovereign of it that hasn't been through twenty hands, or fifty for that matter, since the last man who had done some honest work for it parted company with it. Well, money like that belongs to those who are in possession of it only so long as they are strong enough to hold on to it. When someone stronger still comes along, he takes it away from them. They don't complain; they don't cry and say it's cruel: they know it's the rule of the game. They accept it, and begin at once looking out for a new set of fools and weaklings to recoup themselves on. That's the way the City goes ... I used to watch those Jews' hands, a year ago, when I was dining and wining them. They're all thin and wiry and full of veins. Their fingers are never still: they twist around, and keep stirring like a lobster's feelers. But there isn't any real strength in 'em. They get hold of most of the things that are going, because they're eternally on the move. It's their hellish industry and activity that gives them such a pull, and makes most people afraid of them. But when a hand like that takes them by the throat' – and he held up his right hand as he spoke, with the thick, uncouth fingers and massive thumb arched menacingly in a powerful muscular tension – 'when that tightens round their neck, and they feel that the grip means business – my God! What good are they?'

After twelve fortnightly settlements the price of Rubber Consols reached £15 for each £1 share. By then Thorpe was being referred to as the Rubber King. 'City men, who hear more than they read, knew in a general way about this 'Rubber King'. He was an outsider, who had come in, and was obviously filling his pockets; but it was a comforting rule that outsiders who did this always got their pockets emptied for them again in the long-run'. The Stock Exchange would not intervene as the brokers who were being squeezed were not liked by the rest of the members. 'all the conspicuous ones belonged to the class of 'wreckers', a class which does not endear itself to Capel Court. Both Rostocker and Aronson, who it was said, were worst hit, were men of great wealth, but they had systematically amassed these fortunes by strangling in their cradles weak enterprises, and by undermining and toppling over other enterprises which would not have been weak if they had been given a legitimate chance to live. Their system was legal enough in the eyes alike of the law and of the Stock Exchange rules. They had an undoubted right to mark out their prey and pursue it, and bring it down, and feed to the bone upon it. But the exercise of this right did not make them beloved by their begetters and sponsors of their victims'. The others were Blaustein, Ganz, Rothfoere, Lewis, Ascher, Mendel, Harding, Carpenter, Vesey, Norfell and Pinney. They were mainly Jews though not all. One of those involved was called Fromentin, whom Thorpe believed to be Jewish because 'It was a foreign-looking name. I took it for granted'. Actually he was a Christian, but from the Middle East. Once he had finished squeezing the brokers and they had all paid up, Thorpe gave Lord Chaldron £30,000 and Lord Plowden £15,000 for their assistance, while Semple had made £65,000 from his part in the affair. It turned out that the rubber plantation did exist but was worthless. Thorpe's intention all along had been to make money out of manipulating the market in the shares, having seen how investors had followed the latest fashion during the recent gold mining boom. 'I'm told that the scum of the earth had only to own some Chartered shares, and pretend to be 'in the know' about them, and they could dine with as many duchesses as they liked. I knew one or two of the men who were in that deal – I wouldn't have them in my house'. Lady Cressage, a friend of Lord Plowden, admitted to Thorpe that 'It wasn't a nice exhibition that society made of itself – one admits that – but it was only one set that quite lost their heads. There are all kinds of sets, you know'. In addition, Thorpe was also driven by a desire for revenge over those in the City who had taken his money and not only failed to help him but tried to stop him. However, once it was all over he was happy to allow Semple to team up with one of the Jewish brokers, Rostocker, reconstitute the company with Lord Plowden chairman, float it in the City and either get lots of investors to buy the shares or repeat the squeeze on others. The City was a jungle in which there was a constant stream of companies from Britain and around the world being promoted, with some being genuine and others not. As Thorpe told an associate, 'you know what London is? You'd have had no more chance here than a naked nigger in a swamp full of alligators'.

Thorpe had cleared over half a million pounds from the affair, which he left with Semple to manage in the expectation that it would produce an annual income of £50,000 at the very least. That was after buying an 'extremely unremunerative' estate, Pellesey Court, in Hertfordshire, which contained a part Medieval and part Tudor mansion. Having made his fortune Thorpe intended to leave the City, and live on this estate. He was also sufficiently wealthy to marry into the aristocracy, especially as 'the good families have so very little money, and all the fortunes are in the hands of stock-jobbing people'. His wife was Lady Cressage, who was one of those 'beautiful women, trained from childhood for the conquest of a rich husband'. To him, what he had achieved was the natural progress of society, as he reflected that, 'Every generation sniffs at its nouveaux riches, but by the next they have become merged in the aristocracy. It isn't a new thing in England at all. It has always been that way. Two-thirds of the Peerage have their start from a wealthy merchant or some other person who made a fortune'. However, this was not the end for Thorpe. Once on his estate, he discovered that he did not want to cultivate country society. 'They were not his sort; their standards for the measurement of things were unintelligible to him' He became bored in the country, missing the excitement of the City and the power that people there wielded. As Semple, who was still active in the City and enjoying it, told him, 'You've set out to live the life of a rich country squire, and it hasn't come off'. Encouraged by his wife his solution was to devote himself to philanthropy in London.[28] The City emerges as a place of influence and excitement compared to the country, and even attracted a degree of sympathy for the Jewish brokers who had been made to disgorge some of the money they had made during the gold mining boom, out of those who were foolish enough to speculate and lose. None in the City were intrinsically evil as all played by the rules of the game and that meant they could emerge as either winners or losers.

It was also recognized by the end of the 1890s that many in the City had suffered from the prolonged collapse in financial activity that followed the end of the speculative boom. In John Oxenham's novel, *Rising Fortunes*, which appeared in 1899, sympathy was expressed for the plight of those in the City, though a career there continued to be regarded as far more 'lucrative' than others, and certainly those in art or literature. A City stockbroker called Dempster, who had provided the backing for a new paper called *The Point of View,* had run out of money. 'He's on the Stock Exchange you know, and this slump in South Americans is crippling him ... they're all having a sick time in the City, and every man I've spoken to vows he's on the verge of bankruptcy'.[29] This recovery of the City's reputation in the eyes of the public can also be observed in Conan Doyle's 1899 novel, *A Duet With An Occasional Chorus*. The book was an account of the courtship and early married life of Frank Crosse. Frank worked in the City as an accountant with an insurance company on £400 a year while his wife's father, a banker, provided his daughter, Maude, with an allowance of £50 per annum. Despite this strong City connection there is a clear separation between the world of the City, where Maude's father and husband both worked, and the home life they experienced elsewhere in London. As Maude said, rather irritably, 'I do hate the City of London! It is the only thing which ever comes between us', to which Frank replied, 'I suppose that it separates a good many loving couples every morning'. The City had become a place to which people went, earned a living, and then returned, with little remarkable happening there apart from speculation on the Stock Exchange. The one episode in the lives of Frank and Maude concerning the City that warranted a mention was the investment of a windfall of £50 in the El Dorado Proprietary Gold Mine on the advice of a stockbroker who was a friend of Frank's. The broker's advice turned out to be correct as the price rose but the couple became so worried that they would lose all their money that they got the broker to sell the shares and invest the £50 in consols, using the profit they had made to buy a piano.[30] Whatever the outcome, Stock Exchange speculation continued to bedevil the reputation of the City.[31]

This was in spite of the fact that other aspects of the City, especially those connected with commerce, were well regarded. Gissing had already described Basil Morton, a City corn merchant, in positive terms in the *Whirlpool*,[32] while in his 1899 novel, *The Crown of Life*, the central character was Piers Otway, a clerk in a firm of City merchants trading with Russia. Piers wanted to make his fortune but to do so honestly and relatively quickly. He achieved this by setting himself up as a Russian merchant in the City with a Swiss partner. Despite the fact that he was successful Piers was never happy in the City. A contrast was made between the City, where Piers was '...intent on holding his own amid the furious welter, seeing a delight in the computation of his chances; at once a fighter and a gambler, like those with whom he rubbed shoulders in the roaring ways', with a day he spent in the country where 'All about him lay the perfect loveliness of the rural landscape which is the Old England, the true England, the England dear to the best of her children'. Thus, when the opportunity allowed Piers to retire from an active role in the firm, he took it.[33] The City of London was seen as an urban jungle surrounded by rural tranquillity and so a means of escape was forever sought. The City was only to be experienced out of necessity, as it offered a means of rapid enrichment unrivalled by any other. Such a view also appeared in Henry Seton Merriman's novel, *Roden's Corner*, which was published in 1898.

> There are in the suburbs of London certain strata of men which lie in circles of diminishing density around the great city, like debris around a volcano. London indeed erupts every evening between the hours of five and six, and throws out showers of tired men, who lie where they fall – or rather where their season ticket drops them – until morning, when they arise and crowd back again to the seething crater. The deposits of small clerks and tradespeople fall near at hand in a dense shower, bounded on the north by Finchley, on the south by Streatham. An outer circle of head clerks, Government servants, junior partners, covers the land in a stratum reaching as far south as Surbiton, as far north as Alexandra Palace. And beyond these limits are cast the brighter lights of commerce, law and finance, who fall, a thin golden shower, in the favoured neighbourhoods of the far suburbs, where from eventide till morning, they play at being country gentlemen, talking stock and stable, with minds attuned to share and produce.

Among such people were also to be found the City banker who was now equated with the City merchant in the public's esteem. One such was Joseph Wade.

> Mr Joseph Wade, banker, was one of those who are thrown far afield by the facilities of a fine suburban train service. He wore a frock-coat. A very shiny hat, and he read the *Times* in the train. He lived in a staring red house, solid brick without and solid comfort within, in the favoured pine country of Weybridge. He was one of those pillars of the British Constitution who are laughed at behind their backs and eminently respected to their faces. His gardeners trembled before him, his coachman, as stout and respectable as himself, knew him to be a just and a good master, who grudged no man his perquisites, and behaved with a fine gentlemanly tact at those trying moments when the departing visitor is desirous of tipping and the coachman knows that it is blessed to receive. Mr. Wade rather scorned the amateur country-gentleman hobby which so many of his travelling companions affected. It led them to don rough tweed suits on Sunday, and walk about their paddocks and gardens as if these formed a great estate. 'I am a banker', he said, with that sound common sense which led him to avoid those cheap affectations of superiority that belong to the outer strata of the daily volcanic deposit – 'I am a banker, and I am content to be a banker in the evening and on Sundays, as well as during bank-hours. What should I know about horses or Alderney or Dorking fowls? None of 'em yield a dividend'.

Wade was a matter-of-fact man who believed in investing and making money, and he saw this as being typical of those in the City. 'He was, it must be remembered, a mere banker – a person in the City, where honesty is esteemed above the finer qualities of charity and beneficence'.

Wade's 'greatest interest in life would be money-making – if one only knew what to do with the money afterwards'. He had entered banking, married the daughter of the bank's owner, an only child, and then been a great success, becoming very wealthy in the process. His wife was now dead and his only child, a daughter called Marguerite, could not find a suitable husband, as she was too clever and forceful, and so had decided not to marry. She would have accepted a proposal from one possible suitor, Tony Cornish, and her father had offered him £150,000, plus his fortune on his death, if he asked Marguerite to marry him. There was difference in class between the two families, as Wade himself observed, telling Cornish 'I am distinctly City; you are as distinctly West End'. Cornish was the nephew of Lord Ferriby and eventually inherited the title, but that was not the reason that he would not propose. A banker's daughter was seen as a highly suitable match, which was not the case with all. '[N]o woman likes to see her husband's name on a biscuit or a jam-pot'. The problem was that he was in love with another woman, Dorothy, who was the sister of a City financier, Percy Roden. This left Marguerite with an unfulfilled life as she could not find a husband and, as woman, a career in the City was closed to her, despite her evident ability and connections. A woman was seen to be able to bridge class divisions through marriage but not business, as the City remained closed to her.

The actual story involved an attempt to corner the market in a chemical, Malgamite, which was essential for the paper-making industry. This involved financial activities in London and the operation of a chemical plant near the Hague, using a secret formula that was known only to a German chemist, Professor von Holzen. Once the monopoly was achieved the initial venture was turned into a joint stock company. The financial organization was in the hands of Holzen's partner, an English financier called Percy Roden. The company was to be registered in Holland to avoid paying income tax and because of the 'interference of the English Law in the management of a limited liability company'. This is suggestive of the fact that lower standards of corporate behaviour operated in Continental Europe than in Britain, but that the money and expertise to be found in the City was essential for any major enterprise. As Wade told those who were involved in the scheme, 'we in the City are plain-going men, who have no handles to our names and no time for the fashionable fads. We are only respectable, and we cannot afford to be mixed up in such a scheme as your malgamite business'. However, he did become involved as he was assured that the aim was to improve the working conditions of those in the chemical industry. When he realized that the purpose was to gain a monopoly of the supply of malgamite, force up the price, and make a fortune for Roden and von Holzen, he intervened to prevent it happening. 'For there was in this British banker a vast spirit of honest, open antagonism by which he and his likes have built up a scattered empire on this planet'. The result was that von Holzen was killed, the chemical works was destroyed and Roden fled Europe and disappeared, having placed the money he had made with banks not in London but in Hamburg and Antwerp. It turned out that the whole scheme had been Roden's idea based on what he had seen taking place in the USA, where such corners had been successful in the past. Again, the impression is conveyed that the worst practices and the lowest standards in finance were to be found abroad not in London. Roden himself is viewed sympathetically, admired for his knowledge and ability in financial matters, though pitied because of his obsession with money. As Wade commented, he 'had dealt with money-makers all his life, and knew that to many men money is god, and the mere possession of it dearer to them than life itself'. What Roden wanted was to make as much money as possible because then any woman would marry him, believing that, 'It is only a question of money. It always is with women. And not one in a hundred cares how the money is made'.

What emerges is that a City banker, such as Wade, could be ranked alongside Tony Cornish, an aristocrat, and Major White, who had won the Victoria Cross fighting in the colonies, as the very people who could be relied upon to thwart a plot to hold the paper industry to ransom. Though another City financier was involved in the plot, the real criminal was the German chemist, who had stolen the formula in the first place, combined with the use of American practices and lax standards in Continental Europe. By the late 1890s, the City had clearly recovered from the outright hostility and condemnation it had received in the wake of the gold-mining mania. In the absence of high profile events, such as a speculative mania, it steadily dropped from the public's horizons, though there were continued references to speculation. 'We grow wild with excitement over South African mines, and never recognize the old South Sea bubble trimmed anew to suit the taste of the day'. Company promotion also commanded a poor reputation, as in the comment about 'the thousand bogus companies that exist today'.[34] In *The Awkward Age* by Henry James, which was published in 1899, the City was largely invisible, apart from the observation that those men who had become wealthy through finance would make suitable husbands for the daughters of impoverished aristocrats.[35] The City banker and the City merchant were now perceived to be both wealthy and powerful as was the City solicitor. In the description of a City law office in Arnold Bennett's 1898 story, *A Man from the North,* it was observed that 'The pile of letters gradually disappeared into a basket. Before half a dozen letters were done Richard comprehended that he had become part of a business machine of far greater magnitude than anything to which he had been accustomed in Bursley. This little man with the round face dealt impassively with tens of thousands of pounds, he mortgaged whole streets, bullied railway companies, and wrote familiarly to lords'.[36]

Nevertheless, there remained an underlying antagonism towards the City, as evidenced by the brief mentions in Hornung's Raffles stories, which appeared around 1900. This was because of the whiff of speculation and fraud surrounding certain of its activities.[37] The problem was that the City was now seen as a world apart from the rest of society, as in a story by Guy Boothby, *The Duchess of Wiltshire's Diamonds*, published in 1897.[38] The City was a male world that

employed its own code of morality and was unduly subject to the influence of
Jews and foreigners. The real England remained either the rural south or the
industrial north. Even in London itself real people inhabited the East End, if the
working class was being discussed, or the West End, if it was the aristocracy, but
not the City in between. The City touched few directly, as what took place there
was of an increasingly complex and wholesale nature. The City was where merchants traded with other merchants, where bankers traded with bankers, where
brokers traded with brokers. What they did was beyond the comprehension of
the public, appearing to consist of constant buying and selling for no obvious
purpose. No longer was the City associated in the minds of the public with the
tasks of meeting their everyday commercial and financial requirements. Most
of the wealthy rarely visited the City for the conduct of business, as the local
accountant, banker, broker, retailer, solicitor or insurance agent met their everyday need. In turn it was those trusted agents that acted as the intermediary
between those in the City and their domestic clientele. A barrier had grown up
between the City and rest of Britain consisting not of the Roman Wall that had
once surrounded it but the remoteness of what it did. Behind the barrier the
City was seen to be an increasingly alien place whose focus had switched away
from Britain and towards the rest of the world. There was no appreciation of the
role that the City played in the economic life of Britain because that appeared
to lie with the local branch of the bank or the local stock exchange. This left
the City vulnerable to renewed criticism because it appeared to be irrelevant
to anyone who did not work there, and even those who did only understood
the particular business that employed them. Thus, in the wake of the collapse of
the gold-mining boom an antagonism towards the City developed that was difficult to counter. It transcended what actually took place there as these activities
were either discounted by the public because they did not understand them or
attributed to local representatives as no credit was given for the direction and
management that came from the City. This meant that the place of the City
within British culture was now heavily dependent upon those few aspects of the
business that took place there that did make a public impact. In particular, these
were Stock Exchange speculation and company promotion as these did project
themselves nationally through the newspapers. This meant that the reputation of
the City did not rest on a public appreciation of its manifold activities but was
at the mercy of fickle mood swings driven by newspaper headlines. These drove a
wave of anti-City hysteria in the aftermath of the gold-mining boom which then
faded in the late 1890s, but very slowly. The consequence of that hysteria was to
reverse the growing acceptance of the City, and those who worked there, within
British culture. Instead, it was once again viewed with a great deal of suspicion,
being seen as something rather alien and remote. The question is whether this
was only a temporary reaction to the excesses of the gold mining boom or a per-

manent switch in opinion. If it was temporary then the conclusion can be drawn that culture was a product of fundamental forces as they once again came to the fore. Conversely, if the shift proved to be permanent then the inference can be drawn that culture and economy were driven by separate impulses. Whatever the result it is clear that a temporary event of sufficient magnitude had the capacity to change public attitudes, at least temporarily.

6 MONEY AND MANSIONS, 1900–1910

After the speculative boom of the mid-1890s, which had focused the public's attention on the City, the early twentieth century brought in a less eventful period. Though the stock market continued to rise and fall and companies continued to be promoted and to fail, there was nothing akin to the craze for gold that had gripped the nation in 1895. Instead, the City of London continued to build up its position as the most important financial and commercial centre in the world. Turner, writing in 1902, claimed that

> London is the chief abode of the great god Money, whose throne, visible to all men, is in the heart of the City. From Queen Street and Guildhall to Gracechurch Street and Bishopsgate, from London Bridge to London Wall, lies a region in which the temples of the god cluster together in thick profusion. From here the greatest and the most numerous of his activities are conducted; for London, in spite of the rivalry of New York and the growing importance of Paris and Berlin as money centres, is still paramount as a headquarters of exchange and banking.[1]

On the commercial front, Beavan, writing in 1901, saw the City as '...the Mart of Nations', with Mincing Lane at its heart. This very range and extent of the City's activities defied easy generalization, beyond such statements about its role as a money market or a commodity market. Similarly, the complexity of the functions performed on behalf of global trade and finance made it difficult for the non-specialist to understand what the City actually did. Many of the familiar landmarks of the past, such as the private banks, had virtually disappeared, leaving the City inhabited by a vast mass of people and businesses carrying out tasks unintelligible to the lay person. Also, there was now little reason to visit the City, beyond St Paul's Cathedral, unless on business, for it had ceased to possess any retail activities apart from those meeting the needs of those who worked there. Beavan claimed that,

> To many thousands of born Londoners, the City is a terra incognita, and will remain so. They are essentially west-enders, and although the luxury that surrounds them is derived from commerce, and the head of the family is either banker, merchant, or stockbroker, with an office in some Court or Lane off easily accessible thoroughfares like Broad Street, Cornhill, or Lombard street, the probability is that neither his wife

nor his daughters could ever find their way thither, but would wander about hopelessly lost, so ignorant are most people of the intricate geography of that square mile called the City of London, whose resident population hardly equals that of Dover, but whose precincts over a million persons enter daily, Sunday excepted, on business bent.[2]

As a result the place of the City in contemporary culture was now wholly dependent upon the view taken of the business conducted there, and not even all business. The successful conduct of trade was taken as routine, as was the everyday operation of the commercial banks and insurance companies.[3]

Occasional notice of the more mundane and routine City activities did surface from time to time. In the Sherlock Holmes story, *The Adventure of the Norwood Builder*, published in 1903–4, it was observed that the City was the place where the wealthy still went to consult their legal advisers, as in the case of drawing up a will.[4] However, it was the occasional crises in the money market, the issuing of foreign loans, the promotion of joint stock companies and Stock Exchange speculation that was now the almost exclusive focus of public interest in the City.[5] In the absence of major stories regarding these, the City slipped from public gaze only to re-emerge when one broke. This can be seen from the later work of Headon Hill, for he rather ignored the City after 1900, apart from an occasional passing reference. In his 1905 novel, *Millions of Mischief*, despite the title, the only reference to the City of London, was a mention of 'smart young stockbrokers and pursy businessmen from London'.[6] Similarly, in *The One Who Saw*, also published in 1905, there was a brief aside mentioning 'an absconding company promoter' who had been found guilty at the Central Criminal Court and sent to prison.[7] There were others, though, who saw opportunities in what was happening in the City at this time to include it in their work. William Le Queux introduced a City theme into his novels, having ignored the subject earlier. Despite its suggestive title, his 1891 novel, *Guilty Bonds*, contained only one oblique reference to financial matters.[8] In contrast the City featured prominently in his 1904 novel, *The Crooked Way*, as it included both a stockbroker and a City merchant in a murder mystery. Neither were the guilty party, and the City escaped criticism. The merchant, Arthur Inwood, was 'prosperous and wealthy' through selling Welsh coal to foreign navies from a City office. Roy Royston was a young stockbroker who had experienced the fluctuations of the market.

> Roy was careless, easy-going, and rather extravagant, and one of the leaders of that practical-joking band who now and then caused such fun on the Stock Exchange ... For a time things went well with him, and he made money fast and at the same time spent it ... And then came the gradual change in his fortunes. Difficulties crowded upon him. Creditors pressed, bills were returned dishonoured, and ruin stared him in the face.

Luckily he was saved by receiving an inheritance of £30,000, from an uncle who had migrated to New Zealand. This allowed him to pay all his debts and re-establish himself as a successful stockbroker.[9]

It was even possible to begin to view most of those who worked in the City sympathetically, because of the business uncertainties they faced, but the '...confounded company promoter' remained an exception. Such was the case with Wilfrid Scarborough Jackson's novel, *Nine Points of the Law.* This was published in 1903 and was a lighthearted tale about how an attempted robbery of an English country house, belonging to a City banker, was foiled by one of his clerks who then married his daughter. The clerk was Mr. Wayzgoose. He had begun his City career aged sixteen, working for his father, as his parents could no longer afford his school fees due to a reverse in fortune. Eventually, his father's business collapsed. 'Mr. Wayzgoose, senior, after a stormy and adventurous career in the City, had finally suffered shipwreck there; and such odds and ends of his fortune as he had been enabled to retain he had taken on the turf, under the unhappy delusion that money was to be made there without strict attention to business principles'. All that was left to his son when he died was £50, and enough money for a black suit. A friend of his father's got him a job as a clerk with the City banking firm of Wayland and Mavors

> His plank was a wooden stool in the banking-house of Messrs. Wayland and Mavors, of Poultry, and his outlook as easily defined. Ten paces from him was the glass-enclosed sanctuary of Mr. Bigland, the chief cashier, grey, spectacled and bent, who, by dint of sticking to it, as he told young Wayzgoose, with a kind enough intention when he joined, had travelled thither in the course of thirty-five years from the stool now occupied by him. Thirty-five years to get across the floor of a counting-house!

However, he did get twenty-one days holiday a year. City life for a clerk was seen as dull and repetitive, involving commuting daily from Waltham Forrest, where he lived, to the Bank's office in the City. In contrast, that of a banker was regarded as both more interesting and rewarding, as Mr Mavors lived in mansion in the country. For both clerk and banker there was a distinct separation between the City and home and between work and leisure. This was made clear by Mavors's daughter. 'I tell him he can do what he likes at the bank, but when he is at home he must do what I like'. She was being courted by Lord Stonycrop's son, though, according to Wayzgoose's uncle, Mr. Bompas, who was also in the City, 'she ought to do better than that. Those fellows are no good on boards now, or won't be for a time'. As it was she preferred Wayzgoose and so married him, while his uncle helped him to set up his own business in the City. This suggests that an aristocratic match, when on offer, was no longer the preferred choice for the sons and daughters of City financiers. For many it was marriage with another from a City family that was the safe and preferred choice.[10]

By the beginning of the twentieth century mining companies could also be seen in a more favourable light, as the memory of the craze for gold faded. Nevertheless, there remained the suspicion that many mining companies turned out to be worthless, as this comment about a copper mine in a 1903 novel suggested. 'It isn't always necessary that there should be copper for one to sell a copper mine'. In this case there was, and the owners made a great deal of money as a result.[11] Another successful mine was the subject of John Oxenham's 1906 novel, *Profit and Loss*, though tin not gold was the mineral in this case. This story painted a rounded picture of the City of London in the Edwardian period. It centred round George Barty, cashier in Fraser, Rae and Burney's bank in Lombard Street, where his father had risen to the position of chief cashier after arriving in London from Cheshire. George was earning £300 a year, lived in Highbury, had married Margaret Irvine, from Largs, and they had two children. This happy and respectable life was not enough for him, and he started to speculate in shares.

Next door to him at Highbury lived for a time one James Craven, a young stockbroker, just begun business on his own account, after the usual bareheaded servitude with a big firm in Throgmorton Street, where he had learned many things, and among others to look after himself. He was a very decent fellow, however, and he did his best to keep Barty out of it. They travelled to the City together every morning, and sometimes smoked a pipe together of an evening. 'Take my advice, old man, and keep clear of it all. You outsiders are no use except to be gobbled up'. If he said it once he said it a dozen times. But Barty, living in an atmosphere of money, could no more keep clear of it than a cat in a dairy could keep clear of cream. Within six months of starting business on his own account, Craven had done the immense disservice to his fellows of making for himself a fortune by a series of audaciously flukes – strokes, he called them – in stocks. Six months before, he was running bare-headed about Throgmorton Street with the rest, and was curtly ordered about by his employers by his surname. Now he drove down occasionally in his brougham, just to take a look at the old place, and to see how the other bare-headed young men were getting along, and to afford them the opportunity of seeing for themselves how he had got on. The rest of the time he spent yachting and travelling and generally enjoying himself. And if the old firm met him and suggested an investment, he invariably replied with a laugh that he was 'not on'. If there was one thing he had learned it was when not to be on. Having picked his chestnuts out of the fire he had no slightest intention of throwing them back there. But then, you see, he had been on the Stock Exchange himself. Along with a great many others, George Barty believed he had as much brains as Jim Craven. It would pay the gentlemen of the Stock Exchange to permit a young man like that to make a snug little fortune every few years, out of the outsiders of course, just as ground-bait for the rest. That fortunate youth's good fortune ruined hundreds who believed, like Barty, that they had as much brains as he had. I know nothing about their brains or his. What I do know is that the Stock Exchange men were a great deal the better off for their belief, and they themselves a great deal worse off. They had the experience and the others had their money – in some cases. In others, Barty's to wit among many more, the Stock Exchange men had their money only in the sense of having won it. When it came to the gathering in of the fleeces, the lambs – curious offspring of bulls and bears – had nothing to offer beyond a few straggly hairs, which went but a very small way towards satisfying the demands of the ravening ones.

The outcome was that Barty lost heavily from his speculations, which he blamed on crooked dealings on the Stock Exchange. He faced bankruptcy as he still owed £900 after using up all his savings. '...facts are facts, and figures are brutal things when they are against you – especially on the Stock Exchange, which is an institution based on prompt settlements, quick returns, each man for himself, and death to the defaulter'. There was to be no rehabilitation for the Stock Exchange in the minds of the public as the constant rise and fall of prices created both winners and losers, and George Barty was one of the latter. George was offered a way out of his financial difficulties by his employer, Sir John Burney. Sir John lived in Kensington Palace Gardens and there met a constant stream of messengers travelling to and fro between his home and his bank in the City. This was a private bank handling the affairs of wealthy individuals, reflecting an earlier view of the City rather one in keeping with the dominant position occupied by the large joint stock banks. From one of these messages he learnt that his son, who worked in the bank, had forged a cheque and faced exposure. To cover up this crime, he persuaded Barty to take the blame and, in return, he would pay his debts and give him £5,000 for his family. Barty was then transported to Australia where he was reported to have died. This left his wife to look after his children alone. George had not died but, instead, had assumed the identity of a fellow prisoner, Charles Lindsay, and taken up farming in Australia. Drought had ruined his farming but he hoped to restore his fortunes, having discovered tin on his property. This took him to London with the idea of persuading someone in the City to float a tin-mining company.

> Mr Lindsay had come to Europe with one sole end in view, and that was the flotation of his tin mine on the London market. It was an exceedingly rich find. Skilfully exploited it would more than repair the fortunes which had drooped and died with his thousands of tortured sheep on the parched ranges. He had tried in the first place to float the property in the colony. But wool was bad, and everything was bad. The sheep had died by hundreds of thousands, and the spirit of enterprise had died with them. So he turned everything he had left, which was not very much beyond the land on which the tin deposits lay, into money, to pay for the best obtainable surveys, assays, and reports. And armed with these, and a few letters of introduction, he came to London, anticipating no great difficulty in getting the matter taken up there. But he found matters in London very little better than he had left them in Sydney. The public having suffered punishment from long-falling prices was, with sulky virtue, abstaining from speculation and even from investment, and Lindsay could not have chosen a worse time for bringing his wares to market any time these five years.

He decided to persevere as the City was beginning to pick up. 'The worst was past at last. The advertising columns of the daily newspapers began to swell somewhat with prospectuses of new companies, and it seemed to him that he might venture to approach some of his financial friends once more'. Using his past connections with Burney's bank he persuaded them to support the flotation of the tin-mining company even though they were not company promoters. The result was the successful flotation of The Glen Ingalls Tin Company, which brought him £150,000 and made him and his family wealthy. Compared to the accounts of the gold mining scams of the mid-1890s there was now a much more positive view of such enterprises though investors still needed to be wary of certain company promoters. One of them, James Felston, had 'ruined himself and everybody he came in contact with by his big financial schemes. He blew his brains out in the end'. Even his family suffered as, after his estate was straightened out, his only son Neil was left with investments sufficient to produce an income of only £300 per annum. He became an artist to supplement his income.[12] This association of the City with company promotion continually undermined its reputation in the eyes of the Edwardian public. In *The Four Just Men* by Edgar Wallace, which appeared in 1905, the criminal gang formed a company as 'the easiest way to conceal one's identity was to disguise oneself as a public company. There's a wealth of respectability behind the word "limited", and the pomp and circumstance of a company directorship diverts suspicion, even if it attracts attention'.[13] Such companies then attracted people who would join the board in return for a fee, as their presence would suggest to the public that it was a legitimate enterprise. In the E. Phillips Oppenheim novel, *A Prince of Sinners*, dating from 1903, Mr Henslow only became the Member of Parliament for Medchester because it would make him more attractive as a company director. According to Kingston Brooks, his election agent, 'I am afraid what I heard in the City the other day must have some truth in it. They say he only wanted to be able to write M.P. after his name for this last session to get on the board of two new companies. He will never sit for Medchester again'. The prospectuses issued by these companies were also regarded as works of fiction. When Lady Caroom's eloquence was admired because she 'has such a delightfully easy way of romancing', her daughter Sybil suggested that 'She ought to write the prospectuses for gold mines and things'.[14] In Kuppord's fanciful tale, *A Fortune from the Sky*, which came out in 1903, Fred Gurleigh was employed as a clerk at the salary of £3 per week by Mr Wallaby-Jones, a company promoter in the City. 'It was a clear case of swindling. All manner of bogus companies had been worked from that office'. Not only were innocent investors defrauded but Fred also lost his unpaid salary, and was left both penniless and unemployable, given the bad reputation of Wallaby-Jones. 'All Fred's overtime had been given to carrying out those swindles: and now, by an irony of fate, he was left to face the victims, and was himself accused as being an accomplice of the man who had robbed him of a month's wages ... He now understood that his main fitness for Wallaby-Jones's post was his ignorance of the world'.[15]

Similarly, the association of the City with speculation continued to fuel suspicion and even extreme hostility, far outweighing its role as a commercial centre. In *Will Warburton*, which was published in 1905, Gissing was aware that the City contained West India sugar merchants, but chose to focus on the effects on one of these when his partner bankrupts the firm through speculating in shares. Rather than blame his partner, Will Warburton turned his wrath on those 'City brutes' who had led him astray. 'A firm of brokers; unfortunate speculations; failure of another house – all the old story. As likely as not, the financial trick of a cluster of thieves ... He had always scorned the Stock Exchange, now he thought of it with fiery hatred'.[16] The Stock Exchange continued to be a place that fostered gambling as in a 1909 story from J. S. Fletcher's, *The Contents of the Coffin*. 'I mean that they've got the money. It hasn't gone on the Stock Exchange. Its not gone on the Turf. Its not gone over the card table'.[17] Mitigating this view, to an extent, was the recognition that the investing public had themselves partially to blame. It appeared that any type of joint stock company could be floated in the City. The subtitle of the novel *Sharks*, jointly written by Guy Thorne and Leo Custance and published in 1904, was *A Fantastic Novel for Business Men and their Families*. The principal character was Percy Thawne, employed by Slynge and Company as secretary to a number of the companies they had promoted, including The Mount Pisa Gold Mine and The Wild West Oil Corporation. Percy Thawne fitted into one of the three categories used to describe City clerks. The first category was the rather shabbily dressed clerk who frequented tea shops. They were 'the vast army of men-machines who can be hired for about thirty shillings a week' and were 'obviously unprosperous'. The second were more successful, being expensively but rakishly dressed, and they frequented the West-End music halls. They were also 'Bounders' and not to be trusted. The third group, to which Percy belonged, was expensively but conservatively dressed and were not to be found in either tea shops or music halls but in Piccadilly or Pall Mall, having been educated at 'public-school and university' before entering the family firm in the City. Percy worked for Slynge and Company, having got a position there through his widowed mother. This firm was located in Burdett Street, which was that part of the City that company promoters had made their own.

> The street was not occupied by commercial houses. Not a single merchant of repute had his offices there; no established business had chosen it for its headquarters, yet every floor in the tall buildings was tenanted; a plate with a more or less important-sounding name was fixed to every door. Burdett Street, in short, was the home of the company promoter. The great financiers who dealt in millions did not conduct their operations there, but the smaller fry found it congenial and convenient. Here might be found a score of astute individuals, quite well known in the City, all of whom

managed to extract two or three thousands a year from the public pockets, any one
of whom might succeed in pulling off a coup which would take him to Park Lane
– though frequently only en route to Dartmoor.

It was also noted that 'the great cloud of "Limited Liability" which hung over
Burdett Street ... gave such a comforting and friendly obscurity to the financiers
who practised there'.

Slynge and Company consisted of nobody other than Horatio Slynge, and
was '...merely the machinery by which Mr Slynge raked in money for his own
personal use and comfort. It was the web of a single spider, and none other had
part nor lot in it'. Horatio Slynge had promoted three joint stock companies. One
was a gold mine, The Mount Pisa Gold Mine, while another was involved in oil
exploration, The Wild West Oil Corporation. Both of these had been heavily
publicized in the press while their prospects had each been lauded in a glowing
prospectus, but neither had, as yet, discovered or produced any gold or oil. In
contrast, the other company, The Young Companies' Propagation Syndicate, was
privately held and produced a steady income for Horatio Slynge through '...buy-
ing up plots of land in obscure parts of the globe at cheap rates'. These plots were
then sold to others so as to give credibility to the claims made when new companies were promoted to develop minerals, rubber or anything else. In the City
such practices were both commonplace and acceptable because a different morality operated there. Whereas, 'To pick a pocket with one's fingers was of course
a blackguard thing....to pick a thousand pockets with a prospectus...' was not.
Company promoters, such as Horatio Slynge, were the 'Sharks' who preyed on
innocent investors. These were often female, such as Mrs O'Mea and Mrs Cragge,
who had been persuaded to buy shares in the Mount Pisa Gold Mine after reading the prospectus. As Slynge observed, '...every lady believes what she hears in
the City, especially if it is wrong'. No dividends had been paid, the shares were
worthless, and the company was on the verge of liquidation. Despite the failure
of his companies to produce dividends Percy Slynge was well regarded in the City.
According to the solicitor Mr Barlow, who acted for Percy's mother, '...he is a man
who is going to make a fortune in the near future. It's sharp practice, but he takes
no risks and does not speculate with his own money'. He then gave Percy's mother
the following advice. 'Tell your son from me to keep in with Slynge for a time,
get as much as he possibly can out of him without being identified with any of
his schemes too closely. Then let him bring his money to me to invest in sound
securities, leave Mr Slynge and look out for something less rapid but more steady'.
Unlike Mrs Crabbe, Percy's mother had her money in railway shares.

Percy Thawne quickly adapted to the morality of the City despite a highly
respectable background, being the son of a General, educated at Oxford, a keen

sportsman, and having a respectable widowed mother living in West Kensington.

> There is a curious infection about the air of the City. You may go down from the West End filled with high-minded ideals and lofty ambitions, yet, if you stay in the East long enough, the atmosphere of this place must affect you. It will creep over your spirit, crumble your ideals, and finally fill your soul with a fierce desire which nothing can assuage but the magic touch of gold. Percy had only been in his present situation for a short time, but the fever was upon him,

Percy soon aspired to become one of these City Sharks himself, observing that 'Really, company promoting is the only gentlemanly thing left to do in the City'. With no expectation of an inheritance other than an income of £200 per annum when his mother died, and no desire to 'toil away the best years of his life as a doctor or barrister' he saw the City as a means of becoming rich quickly. He realized 'that for a man who is generally clever a fortune large or small can be more quickly picked up in the City than anywhere else, provided he has once secured the entrée to Tom Tidler's ground. This Percy had done already, though as yet he was but inside the gate where the shekels had been already gathered'.

An associate of Slynge was Professor Pentique whose scientific inventions, such as an electric loom and an aerial ship, were behind 'a good many flotations which, if they did not attract very much attention in London, caused many eyes to open and mouths to water in the provinces'. He was an American 'of continental Jewish extraction, plump and with an intelligent, hairless face', who maintained a small office in Lime Street in the City, so that he could maintain regular contact with company promoters. His latest invention was an electrical device that was capable of raising sunken land from the seabed so that it formed new islands or even continents. Teaming up with Horatio Slynge they floated a company that would raise Atlantis, believed to be located off the west coast of Ireland. This was called 'The Lost Continent Recovery Company', and it sought to raise £2 million from investors. Such was the persuasive power of the prospectus, the enormous publicity generated by the scheme, and the idea of extending the British Empire by the acquisition of a vast new continent in the Atlantic, that the investing public rushed to buy shares in the new company. Mr Blaber, who was employed to write the prospectus, had no scruples about what he was doing.

> It amuses me to think, as I sit in some obscure tavern up a dingy court, that the words written by my pen are charming the gold from the pockets of greedy people all over England, that my words can sway and move the huge crowd of people who are dying to get rich without working! The fools – the grasping fools deserve to be cheated! Most of them do at any rate! And how lovingly I bait the hook for them. Your ordinary prospectus is either too dry and uninteresting to attract a speculator or it is so glowing and flowery that it frightens him. The secret of my success is that I know how to combine both methods. Point out the advantages of what you are putting on the

market, but do it without adjectives! That is one of my secrets ... The result is that an impression of solidity and sincerity is conveyed and a certain freshness and newness is found which the reader can't analyse but nevertheless feels. In a day, when thinking it over, the prospective investor imagines his first impressions to be entirely his own and entirely justified. I tell you, Mr Thawne, that one can hypnotise your ordinary greedy prospectus reader with decent English.

Helping in this task were journalists like Mr T. Grady, the editor of the *Investor's Ferret*, who were happy to either turn a blind eye to swindles or give them their support, if a suitable financial arrangement was made. Conversely, if they were not suitably bribed they would write unfavourable articles.

Driven by favourable reports regarding the progress in raising Atlantis, the £10 shares in the Lost Continent Recovery Company rapidly rose in price, reaching £100 each at one stage. This gave Slynge, Thawne, Prentigue and the others involved in the promotion the opportunity to sell, at a large profit, the shares they had allocated to themselves. As news arrived daily in the City that Atlantis was getting nearer the surface of sea, so the price fluctuated wildly in anticipation of the huge profits to be made as well as patriotic fervour for such an increase in the size of the Empire. When the report was received that Atlantis was once more visible the crowds outside the company's offices rejoiced. 'They ran about the City, intoxicated with delight, shouting, chaffing, capering. Such enthusiasm had never been witnessed before in the City of London'. The whole affair was a hoax but before this became apparent, Slynge, Thawne, Pentique and all their family and associates had fled with the money they had made. In the City there was riot outside the company's offices in Old Broad Street when the truth emerged, 'the people proceeded to wreck the Lost Continent offices, smashing every bit of furniture which they could lay hands on, and seriously mal-treating such of the staff as they were able to intercept'. Only the intervention of the police saved further destruction in the City but Slynge's private residence in Park Lane was ransacked by the irate investors, though 'absolutely nothing of any value...' had been left behind. Finally, there was a huge fight between the inves-tors themselves outside St Paul's Churchyard. By this time the shares had fallen to three shillings, while Slynge and Thawne were safely on their way, by private yacht, to an unknown island in the Pacific. Thawne married Slynge's daughter, and all lived happily ever after.[18]

Another far-fetched joint stock company promotion was the subject of the novel *The Yellow God* by H. Rider Haggard, which appeared in 1909. This began with a group of men meeting in a country house to plan the flotation of a company called Sahara Ltd. The intention was to develop the Sahara desert by flooding it but the whole scheme was completely fraudulent. Before it was wound up, though, the promoters expected to make themselves rich by gradually unloading shares on an unsuspecting public, duped into believing the feasibility of the project through heavy advertising and persuaded that the shares had value by the creation of a false market. When Alan Vernon, who had conceived the scheme and believed in it, discovered what was intended by the City financiers, he wanted to back out of the whole affair. This was despite the fact that he desperately needed money to keep the family estate going, because of the decline in farm rents and land values. However, he was informed by one of the City financiers, Champers-Haswell, that 'Promoters should not bother themselves with long views, Alan. These may be left to the investing public, the speculative parson and the maiden lady who likes a flutter – those props of modern enterprise'. Alan Vernon had principles, coming from a long-established country family, but the City financiers involved had not. They were portrayed as either vulgar upstarts, foreign or Jewish, possessed of money and nothing else. Champers-Haswell's country house was condemned as having been '... built in the most atrocious taste, and looked like a suburban villa seen through a magnifying glass'. These City financiers had used their wealth to buy up the estates of the impoverished gentry and then build large but hideous mansions on them. 'To describe them is unnecessary, for they have no part in our story, being only financiers of a certain class, remarkable for the riches they had acquired by means that for the most part would not bear examination'. These means involved fleecing the public of its money for their personal benefit as Barbara Champers, who was the niece of Champers-Haswell, made clear when she spoke to them.

> Finance, as I have heard of it, means floating companies and companies are floated to earn money for those who invest in them. Now this afternoon, as I was dull, I got hold of a book called 'The Directory of Directors', and looked up all your names in it, except those of the gentlemen from Paris, and the companies that you direct – I found about those in another book. Well, I could not make out that any of these companies have ever earned any money, a dividend don't you call it? Therefore how do you all grow so rich, and why do people invest in them?

She wanted nothing to do with those involved in such a business, turning down an offer of marriage from Sir Robert Aylward, who was Champers-Haswell's partner, and warning him as she did so that he faced eventual damnation for what he was doing.

> 'You men who have made money,' she went on with swelling indignation, 'who have made money somehow, and have bought honours with the money somehow, think yourselves great, and in your little day, your little little day that will end with ten lines of small type in the *Times*, you are great in this vulgar land. You can buy what you want, and people creep round you and ask for doules and favours, and railway porters call you 'my Lord' at every other step. But you forget your limitations in this world, and that which lies above you.'[19]

Even if a City financier escaped disgrace, failure or bankruptcy in the living world retribution clearly waited in the next!

H. G. Wells went a step further by suggesting that what took place in the City was the manifestation of the worst excesses of capitalism, rather than being the sole responsibility of the speculators and company promoters. In *Kipps*, which appeared in 1905, speculation was used to explain the loss of an inheritance of £24,000. The young solicitor to whom it had been entrusted had 'Speckylated every penny – lorst it all – and gorn'.[20] To Wells, the City of London was a place 'without plan or intention, dark and sinister' with his severest condemnation reserved for company promotion and those that carried it out. At least in speculation the investor had to share some of the blame for their losses, though it was those who handled the buying and selling who were primarily responsible because of their advice, encouragement and the profits they made handling the transactions. With companies that turned out to be worthless, compared to the prospects presented to the public when they were floated, it was much easier to see the innocent investor as being duped by a band of cunning rogues. In his 1909 novel *Tono-Bungay* Wells launched a vitriolic attack on the whole practice of company promotion in the City of London. Edward Ponderevo, a small town chemist, and his nephew George, created a patent medicine called Tono-Bungay. They then floated a company to produce and sell it, raising £150,000 from investors. George was astonished at the gullibility of the public, remarking, '£150,000 – think of it! – for the goodwill in a string of lies and a trade in bottles of mitigated water! Do you realise the madness of the world that sanctions such a thing!' Following this success they then promoted a string of similar companies all engaged in the manufacture and distribution of basic household items. The impression was given that little skill or effort was required to promote these companies because the public was so eager to buy the shares on the promise of regular and high dividends. Through George's eyes,

> It was a period of expansion and confidence; much money was seeking investment and 'Industrials' were the fashion. Prices were rising all round. There remained little more for my uncle to do, therefore, in his climb to the high, unstable crest of Financial Greatness but, as he said, to 'grasp the cosmic oyster, George, while it gaped' which being translated meant for him to buy respectable businesses confidently and courageously at the vendor's estimate, add thirty or forty thousand to the price and sell them again. His sole difficulty indeed was the tactful management of the load of shares that each of these transactions left upon his hands.

Whereas the running of the factory, where the medicines were produced, was seen as honest and worthwhile toil, the financial activities of the City involved 'a great deal of bluffing and gambling, of taking chances and concealing material facts'. Company promotion produced great gains in the short run as Edward Ponderevo became 'a great financier'. According to his nephew, George, 'At the climax of his boom, my uncle at the most sparing estimate must have possessed in substance and credit about two million pounds' worth of property to set off against his vague colossal liabilities, and from first to last he must have had a controlling influence in the direction of nearly thirty millions'. Inevitably the boom collapsed and the companies were exposed as grossly overvalued with Edward Ponderevo being labelled a criminal. Facing bankruptcy and worse he contemplated suicide but, instead, he and his nephew escaped to France in a hot air balloon, where he died a broken man. George did not blame his uncle for what he had done, but the financial system for making it all possible.

> This irrational muddle of a community in which we live gave him that, paid him at that rate for sitting in a room and scheming and telling it lies. For he created nothing, he invented nothing, he economised nothing. I cannot claim that a single one of the great businesses we organised added any real value to human life at all. Several like Tono-Bungay were unmitigated frauds by any honest standard, the giving of nothing coated in advertisements for money'.[21]

Increasingly the City was seen either as a proxy for capitalism or a place where fortunes could be speedily made and lost out of nothing.[22] In Bram Stoker's 1909 novel, *The Lady and the Shroud*, the accumulation of a vast fortune of 'well over a hundred million...' by Roger Melton, was attributed to his skill in 'commerce and finance' as he 'so kept abreast of all public and national movements that he knew the critical moment to advance money required'.[23]

Evidence of the growing recognition of the City as the leading source of wealth in Edwardian England is provided by the sequence of novels by E. Phillips Oppenheim. In *A Prince of Sinners,* dating from 1903, when a career in the City was proposed for Lord Arranmore, he turned it down as he had 'Too much money already' and he was well able to exert influence through sitting in the House of Lords. Similarly, Peter Bullsom became an MP, and to further his family's social ambitions by renting a house in London and the country, through the large fortune he had made in business and property speculation in the Midlands.[24] In a novel from 1904, *Anna, the Adventuress*, it was the ability of the City to make people wealthy and powerful that was being highlighted. The declining value of agricultural land and the National Debt undermined traditional forms of holding wealth. Mr Carter who 'lived on an annuity of one hundred and fifty pounds ... was constantly studying the *Financial Times*. A drop in consols depressed him for the whole evening. He was always au fait with the latest Stock Exchange rumours'. In contrast, there was Sir John Ferringhall, who had made his money as a merchant in the City. 'He was a business man, pure and simple, his eyes were fastened always upon the practical side of life. Such ambitions as he had were stereotyped and material'. He was 'steeped in traditions of the City and money-making, very ill-skilled in all the lighter graces of life' His grandfather had driven a van but Sir

John had become a knight and an MP, Lady Angela, who gave a dinner attended by Sir John and Lady Ferringhall, expressed the opinion that 'I am beginning to believe that we only exist nowadays by the tolerance of these millionaire tradesmen. Our land brings us nothing. We have to get them to let us in for the profits of their business, and in return we ask them to – dinner'.[25]

Oppenheim was fully aware that fortunes made in the City could disappear as quickly as they were made, as in the 1909 novel, *Jeanne of the Marshes*. Jeanne Le Mesurier was reputed to be a great heiress having been left a vast fortune by her father, a Parisian banker. As a result she became the toast of London society, pursued by young men because of her money, especially those from the gentry with a need to restore family fortunes devastated by the collapse of land values and rental income. However, the fortune had been reduced to a mere £14,000 because of numerous bequests and the depreciation of the securities in which it had been invested.[26] The volatility of share prices was one of the major themes in an earlier novel, *Mr Wingrave, Millionaire,* which appeared in 1906. Sir Wingrave Seton was a rich man with estates in Cornwall and a fortune in securities, carefully managed for him by a firm of London solicitors. He then used his wealth not only to develop a gold mine in the United States but also to speculate successfully in both Wall Street and the City of London. Those who lost by his actions were not other investors but professional speculators and Stock Exchange brokers who became caught by his sudden buying and selling operations. 'In the City, he was more hated and dreaded than ever. His transactions huge and carefully thought out, were for his own aggrandizement only, and left always in their wake ruin and disaster for the less fortunate and weaker speculators'. The successful barrister and Member of Parliament, Barrington Lumley, lost heavily as a result of Wingrave's actions and was only saved from bankruptcy by a loan from Wingrave himself. Wingrave had being going to marry the woman who became Lumley's wife and used his financial activities to obtain revenge, which he achieved as the loan gave him power over both of them. The Stock Exchange was a place where the clever and ruthless could make money at the expense of the naïve and weak, who were ruined or enslaved as a result. However, there was no attack on either the City as a whole or the Stock Exchange in particular but rather an acceptance that this was the way the system operated, and it was up to the individual what they used it for.[27]

In turn this wealth gave City people 'enormous power', according to Edgar Wallace, in his 1905 novel, *Four Just Men,* whether it was that of 'a capitalist controlling the markets of the world, a speculator cornering cotton or wheat whilst mills stand idle and people starve' or the 'tyrants and despots with destinies of nations between their thumb and finger'.[28] In the 1904 novel, *The Last Hope,* by H. S. Merriman, it was a British banker, John Turner, who foiled a plot to place a Bourbon on the French throne, having become aware of mysterious movements of money through his bank. 'it is always safe to ignore the conspirator who has no money, and always dangerous to treat with contempt him who jingles a purse. There is only a certain amount of money in the world ... and we bankers usually know where it is ... if one of the Great Reserves, or even one of the smaller reserves, moves, we wonder why it is being moved and we nearly always find out'. His motivation in blocking the coup by depriving it of funds was the belief that political instability was bad for business, for he did not care whether France was a republic, empire or monarchy.[29] This power of those in the City was seen to manifest itself in the titles they acquired, the town houses they built and the country estates they bought. Galsworthy's novel, *A Man of Property*, published in 1906, provides evidence that contemporaries were conscious of the growing penetration of society by those whom the City had enriched, but only those seen as safe and respectable were fully accepted. The basis of the Forsyte family's fortune lay with Jolyon Forsyte, who had come to London from Dorset and became a successful builder. Of his six sons two went into the City. One, also called Jolyon, became a tea merchant.

> About the house of Forsyte and Treffry in the City had clung an air of enterprise and mystery, of special dealings in special ships, at special ports, with special Orientals. He had worked at that business! Men did work in those days! These young pups hardly knew the meaning of the word. He had gone into every detail, known everything that went on, sometimes sat up all night over it. And he had always chosen his agents himself, prided himself on it ... Even now, when the business had been turned into a Limited Liability company, and was declining (he had got out of his shares a long time ago), he felt a sharp chagrin in thinking of that time.

Another, James, became a City solicitor while three of the others were involved with property in one way or another, related to the building work of their father, while one became a publisher. Of the next generation none entered the tea trade, reflecting the growing identification of the City with finance and services related to it. In contrast, the son of the City solicitor, Soames, became one himself, and two others entered insurance, including one becoming an underwriter at Lloyds.

By the Edwardian era the Forsytes, as a family, enjoyed the wealth generated in the City through trade, shipping and finance, but did not conduct it themselves. They lived in large houses in the West End of London, commuting to the City. The City solicitor, James Forsyte, was involved 'in arranging mortgages, preserving investments at a dead level of high and safe interest, conducting negotiations on the principle of securing the utmost possible out of other people compatible with safety to his clients and himself'. His son, Soames, acted as solicitor to the New Colliery Company whose chairman was the retired tea merchant Jolyon Forsyte. Above all, the main connection between the Forsytes and the City was the fact that they had, over the years, accumulated wealth that was invested in property of all kind, especially the securities issued by companies promoted and run from City offices. 'They had all done so well for themselves, these Forsytes, that they were all what is called "of a certain position". They had shares in all sorts of things, not as yet – with the exception of Timothy – in consols, for they had no dread in life like that of 3 per cent for their money'. To many in Edwardian society, the importance of the City lay in the financial and legal services that were to be found there. This was reflected in the changed status of stockbroking, as in this reference to Swithin Forsyte. 'Coming upon London twenty years later, he could not have failed to become a stockbroker, but at the time when he was obliged to select, this great profession had not as yet become the chief glory of the upper-middle class. He had literally been forced into auctioneering'.[30] Some of these City people had also made sufficient money to purchase one or more country estates for themselves. Galsworthy's 1907 novel, *The Country House,* makes reference to Thomas Brandwhite, of Brown and Brandwhite. He occupied a prominent 'position in the financial world' and, though retired, 'sat on the boards of several companies'. He had two places in the country and a yacht. In contrast, the sons of the gentry idled away most of their time in London clubs, blaming the Stock Exchange when they lost money speculating on shares and complaining about the extortionate rates of the interest charged by Jews, when they were forced to borrow money.[31]

Hilaire Belloc traced the whole process leading from City wealth to political influence and social acceptability in two connected novels written at this time. These are very suggestive that entering the topmost reaches was dependent upon whether the money had been made in commerce or finance or honestly or dishonestly while nationality and religion also played its part. In the 1904 novel, *Emmanuel Burden*, Belloc introduced the reader to the City through the merchant, Emmanuel Burden, and the financier, I. Z. Barnett. Burden had inherited his business from his father and, through hard work and reinvested profits, had built it up into a great success selling British manufactures throughout the world. He left a fortune of £257,000 on his death. In contrast, I. Z. Barnett's father had been a Jewish banker in Frankfurt, where his elder brother remained after he had come to London. In London, Barnett had anglicized his name and then built up a financial business. His first venture was the Haymarket Bank, which attracted depositors by offering to pay a very high annual rate of interest, namely 8 per cent per annum, which it could afford as long as the funds kept increasing. Once the deposits stopped growing, which happened when the fraudulent basis of the scheme was exposed in the press, the bank collapsed and the depositors lost all their money. Here again was a continuing resonance of Jabez Balfour and the Liberator Building Society, though now a fictional German Jew had been transposed for an English nonconformist. Also, unlike Balfour, Barnett escaped prosecution and censure, becoming a successful promoter of foreign companies in the City, such as the Anatolian Railway, This made him a rich man. His latest venture was the M'Korio Delta Development Company. He had come across the tiny British colony of M'Korio when cruising of the coast of West Africa. It consisted mainly of fever-ridden swamps but he saw the possibility of combining profit and imperial expansion if it could be converted into an economically successful corner of the British Empire. If he succeeded it would also promote his social and political advancement. What he wanted was 'true political power, a thing to him worth all the effort of life'.

To achieve this end Barnett needed the support of those with a commercial interest in the colony and a prominent establishment figure who would give the scheme respectability. Barnett's choice fell on Lord Benthorpe, a Wiltshire landowner, with strong military, political and colonial connections. Lord Benthorpe's grandfather had established the dynasty a century before when, as an Irish MP, he had sold his vote in favour of Irish unification and then married the only child of a London banker. By the 1890s a combination of excessive expenditure and low farm rents had rendered the family technically insolvent, existing only on the sufferance of the Anglo-Saxon Loan and Investment Company, to which their entire mansion and estate was mortgaged. As Barnett controlled this company Lord Benthorpe had little choice but to agree to become chairman of the new venture, while the promised allocation of shares offered the prospect of restoring family fortunes. Engaging the interest of the commercial men in the City proved more difficult. Charles Abbott was a City shipowner whose vessels – the Abbott Line – called at the colony on their way to and from South America. They only did so because they received a government subsidy. Having visited the M'Korio Delta, Abbott had a very low view of the area's economic prospects, and so refused to participate. Barnett could do very little about that because, as a shipowner, Abbott was 'a prosperous member of the most prosperous trade in England'. The other commercial person involved was Emmanuel Burden, as his trade in hardware, combined with a longstanding friendship with Charles Abbot, had led his firm into handling the imports and exports of the M'Korio Delta, though the business was marginal to the firm.

> In Mr. Burden's considerable affairs, the total of this petty offshoot did not amount to one-twentieth at the most; it rarely represented a profit of £400 – more commonly less than £300 in a year; and, to his natural compliance in Charles Abbot's judgement, therefore, was added a business experience which made of the Delta something mean and paltry in his conception.

He was thus not interested in the project.

However, Burden had a son, Cosmo, who, during his student days, had borrowed money from Barnett in order to escape from a breach-of-promise case. This put Cosmo under an obligation to Barnett, and it was through the influence that the son had with the father that Emmanuel Burden came to participate in the scheme. He put £25,000 into a syndicate, which then organized the flotation of the company. Burden increasingly disliked what was happening as he became aware of the influence that Barnett exerted over the Press, the lies that were told about the prospects of the M'Korio Delta, and the way the issue of shares was handled. Gradually, he came to appreciate Abbott's opinion, which was that the whole scheme was the product of cosmopolitan finance orchestrated by Barnett, whom Abbott referred to as 'a greasy German Jew'. By then, though, Burden had become too ill and dispirited to take effective action, and died shortly afterwards. The Company was successfully promoted with Cosmo quickly selling out at great profit. Overall, Burden appeared to be the only honourable person, as he was an 'honest Englishman and a good man'. All the others appeared flawed in different ways whether by greed, as in the case of Cosmo and Lord Benthorpe; prejudice and lack of vision, as in the case of Abbott; or the pursuit of power, as with Barnett. Only Burden subscribed to any kind of imperial mission for the Company while the others saw it merely in terms of their own self-interest, whether they supported or opposed it. If the story of the M'Korio Delta Development Company tells us anything about the contemporary perception of the connection between the City and Empire, it is to suggest that most in the City had a healthy scepticism towards colonial expansion and that the few who supported such schemes were seen to do so because of their own personal motives, rather than because of any collective imperial ideal.[32]

I. Z. Barnett and the M'Korio Delta Development Company next featured in Belloc's 1908 novel, *Mr Clutterbuck's Election*. By then Barnett had an established reputation in the City as the founder of the Anglo-Moravian Bank, while the M'Korio Delta Development Company had been sold to the British government, though it had never paid a dividend in seventeen years. The result was that Barnett had become both very wealthy and very well connected politically, being rewarded with the title Lord Lambeth. Eventually he became the Duke of Battersea with a house in London, Barnett House, and an estate in Scotland, Kendale. In the meantime he had been made Lieutenant Governor of the Indian State of Anapootra, which he used to make another fortune for himself. He had secretly transferred the ruby-mining concession in that state to a company, which he himself controlled. He then resigned his post of Lieutenant Governor and became director of the Anapootra Ruby Mines, which proved very profitable for all concerned. With his wealth and political connections the Duke of Battersea was now a very powerful figure in British society. The impression is given that by 1908 a City fortune could buy the possessor any position he wanted. The smaller the City fortune, the lesser the honour, as can be seen from the progress of Percy Clutterbuck in his pursuit of a knighthood. Percy Clutterbuck was depicted as the very best kind of Englishman. Though naïve he was completely honest and had made his money more by luck than by skill. He commuted daily to the City from Croydon, and was a merchant having '...a small agency concerned with the Baltic trade'. Most of his annual income of £700–1,000 a year was actually generated by speculating in securities, rather than in the business he had inherited from his father:

> This business had declined; for Mr Clutterbuck's father had failed to follow the rapid concentration of commercial effort which is the mark of our time. But Mr Clutterbuck had inherited, besides the business, a sum of close upon ten thousand pounds in various securities; it was upon the manipulation of this that he principally depended, and though he maintained the sign of the old agency at the office, it was the cautious buying and selling of stocks which he carefully watched, various opportunities of promotion in a small way, commissions and occasional speculations in kind, that procured his constant though somewhat irregular income.

Belloc paints a picture of an intimate City world in which people like Mr Clutterbuck thrived through deals done in the course of constant business and social interaction. It was one of these small deals that proved the beginning of Mr Clutterbuck's fortune. He lent £500 to a friend, Mr Boyle, who was also a City merchant living in Croydon. In contrast to Clutterbuck's business Boyle was a partner in a thriving firm of commodity merchants, Boyle and Czernwitz, which had a large office in the City, in Mark Lane, and a warehouse in walking distance at the docks. Boyle was not the dominant force in the firm, as it was now owned and run by a European financier, Baron de Czernwitz. He was described as a 'ponderous and well-clad form of a gentleman past middle age, with such magnificent white whiskers as adorn the faces of too many Continental bankers, and wearing a simple bowler hat of exquisite shape and workmanship. He was smoking a cigar of considerable size and of delicious flavour'. Baron de Czernwitz was a successful financier with experience across Europe and the United States who was now applying his flair, skills and money in various commercial activities in the City in contrast to the 'hard, dry, unimaginative temper of our English houses'. The upshot of the deal was that Mr Clutterbuck acquired a contract to supply the British army in South Africa with eggs at the time of the Boer War. These eggs were packed in brine in the warehouse belonging to Boyle and Czernwitz. However, no sooner had Mr Clutterbuck got involved but the war came to an end leaving Mr Clutterbuck with one million eggs and no purchaser, as the army's contract was only for the duration of the war. The impression was given that those who had sold Mr Clutterbuck the eggs were aware of the possible termination of hostilities and thus the risks involved. However, the British government agreed to honour the deal and Mr Clutterbuck received £45,000 in 3.5 per cent bonds in return for his eggs, which had only cost him a total outlay of £750.

On the advice of a friend, who despaired of ever selling his holding, Mr Clutterbuck then used the money to buy 72,000 shares of the Curicanti Docks. The shares then rose rapidly in value because the British government decided to develop the docks for strategic reasons. Mr Clutterbuck now had £70,000 to invest. Nevertheless, he remained a cautious investor. '[H]e retained his old offices. He invested, sold and re-invested upon a larger scale indeed than he had originally been accustomed to, but much in the same manner'. Similarly, his life-style was largely unaltered. 'He lived in the same house, with the same staff of servants; he entertained no more at home, for he was shy of meeting new friends, and but little more in the City, where also his acquaintance was restricted'. As a result his fortune gradually built up. 'This wise demeanour resulted in a con-tinual accumulation, for it is not difficult in a man of this substance to buy and sell with prudence upon the smaller scale'. After careful study of the stock market he bought 'What was obviously cheap, selling what even the mentally deficient could perceive to be dear', as in the case of the Siberian Copper Company. 'Mr Clutterbuck, having heard upon the best authority that the copper was entirely exhausted, had determined to convey to some other gentleman before the gen-eral public should acquire through the press, information which he had obtained at no small expense in advance of the correspondents'. The transformation of this modest fortune into a very large one was the result of chance, once again, not careful investment over many years. Upon the advice of Barnett's Bank, who had the responsibility for selling them, Mr Clutterbuck agreed to buy some rather risky 4.5 per cent bonds for the Municipal Council of Monte Zarro in Italy, believing them to be a good investment. 'It was not until he had twice dined, and generously, with a junior partner of the bank that he was finally persuaded to support the scheme with his capital, nor did his loyal nature suspect the bias that others were too ready to impute to the banker's recommendation'. Before completing the purchase he was taken ill, and so it was left to his clerk to carry it out. Instead of buying these bonds, the clerk, mistaking the instructions, bought shares in the Manatasara Syndicate, which had a concession to develop an area in the Upper Congo. This was a highly speculative venture being shunned by most investors, but Mr Clutterbuck's clerk bought 60,000 shares at a cost of £7,500. On the back of a sudden boom in the demand for wild rubber, which was found on its concession in the Congo, these shares quickly rose in price and Mr Clut-terbuck sold out for half a million pounds. Mr Clutterbuck was now a very wealthy man and so he retired from the City, left Croydon, and built a mansion for himself and his wife on seven acres of land in the Vale of Caterham in Surrey. This house was very expensive but totally tasteless, as befitted a City man. He then decided to run for parliament and was elected for a north London constitu-ency. This was in spite of the fact that he was totally uninterested in politics and was only concerned about the falling price of government stock and the need for a large gold reserve. Once elected, and believing that a substantial contribution to party funds had got other City people like Sir Jules Mosher a knighthood, he gave them a donation of £3,000.

As he did not get his knighthood immediately, he became bitter and disappointed, and sought the advice of a friend, William Bailey, about what to do next. Bailey was a rather eccentric man of independent means with an income of £4,000 per annum who was very well connected in society, being related to the Prime Minister. He had briefly been an underwriter at Lloyds as well as an MP but was now devoting his life to unearthing a Jewish conspiracy in Britain. His advice to Mr Clutterbuck was to publicize the affair of the Anapootra ruby mines, about which nothing was known but which was a scandal waiting to erupt. Mr Clutterbuck was completely bewildered by all this but did what he was told. This then brought the Duke of Battersea onto the scene. Bailey regarded the Duke as both Jewish and a foreigner, referring to him as the 'Peabody Yid'. This conjures up a combination of a philanthropist, because of the charitable housing provided by the Peabody Trust, and an avaricious Jewish financier. As Bailey put it, 'D'you suppose old Battersea can't make 'em dance? Why, the Peabody Yid's only got to wink and it's like a red-hot poker to the politicians'. Though Battersea did have influence with the Prime Minister he was not able to persuade him to give Mr Clutterbuck a knighthood. Instead, it was Bailey who managed to do that by going to see the Prime Minister and suggesting that Mr Clutterbuck would make a good friend but a bad enemy.[33] From this emerges a view of the City populated by two types of people. It was through the prism of these two extremes that the City was seen by the public, greatly complicating the position it occupied in contemporary culture. Above all, City people were seen as being focused on money to the exclusion of almost everything else, and this greatly restricted the role they played in social and political affairs. In one of his Father Brown stories, published in 1910–11, G. K. Chesterton referred to Sir Leopold Fisher, 'a wealthy City magnate', as a man to whom money mattered more than anything else.[34] A similar verdict appeared in the 1910 novel, *The Osbornes* by E. F. Benson, where Alfred Osborne is contrasted unfavourably with his younger brother Ernest. Ernest had become wealthy through success in manufacturing whereas Alfred had become even wealthier by speculation. Alfred was described as 'a queer wizened little figure', who had entered a stockbroker's office at the age of fifteen and by seventy had 'by means of careful and studied speculation, amassed a fortune'. Though a clever and cultured man, who would have easily passed as a Duke, Alfred had never married and had shown no interest in politics or society. Instead, he had devoted his life to making money. Even his interest in art was purely mercenary. He bought and sold rather than collected as he 'united to an unrivalled habit of being right with regard to the future movements of the stock market an equally unrivalled eye for the merits of pictures'. He was now living in a house in Richmond. In contrast, his brother had made less money but was happily married with two sons, had become an MP, and was accepted in society. It was Ernest and not his brother Alfred who became Lord Osborne. 'It showed that money was not everything, for Alfred was the richest of them all'.[35]

The City's perceived obsession with moneymaking was seen to differentiate those who worked there from the rest of society. This can be seen in *Howards End* by E. M. Forster, published in 1910. City people like Mr Wilcox were seen as hard and uncultured. He had made a fortune approaching a £1 million in the City, being involved with a number of companies. In contrast, there were the 'gentlefolk', such as Margaret and Helen Schlegel and their social circle. They were generous and cultured people but their existence was dependent upon the success of those in the City. The sisters lived comfortably on an inheritance which had been invested for them in high-yielding but safe foreign securities rather than the British railway stocks or government consols that their aunt, Mrs Munt, had suggested.

> Margaret, out of politeness, invested a few hundreds in the Nottingham and Derby Railway, and, though the Foreign Things did admirably and the Nottingham and Derby declined with the steady dignity of which only Home Rails are capable, Mrs Munt never ceased to rejoice, and to say 'I did manage that, at all events. When the smash comes poor Margaret will have a nest-egg to fall back upon'.

There was always the hint that anything connected with the City was somehow transitory. The Porphyrion Fire Insurance Company would 'be in the Receiver's hands before Christmas. It'll smash'. In the end Margaret Schlegel married Mr. Wilcox, for the financial security he could bring, while she provided a civilising influence in return. She neither loved nor respected him. It was Margaret Schlegel who was doing Mr Wilcox a favour by marrying him rather than the reverse.[36]

This social divide between the City and the rest of the upper echelons of British society is also evident in P. G. Wodehouse's novel, *Psmith in the City*, published in 1910. Wodehouse had worked briefly in the City office of the Hongkong and Shanghai Bank and used his knowledge of that for a story about two clerks in the London office of the New Asiatic Bank.

> Most of the men in the bank, with the exception of certain hard-head Scotch youths drafted in from other establishments in the City, were old public school men. Mike found two old Wrykinians in the first week. Neither was well known to him. They had left in his second year in the team. But it was pleasant to have them about, and to feel that they had been educated at the right place.

Both Mike Thompson and the other principal character, Rupert Psmith, had attended public school and regarded themselves as socially superior to other people in the City who had not. This superiority extended as far as Mr Bickersdyke, who was the chairman of the bank. 'A very able man. A very able man indeed', according to Mr Waller, who was senior cashier in the bank. Bickersdyke had worked his way up to the position of Chairman having started as a clerk in the bank many years before. Typifying the City financier he was totally devoid of social graces or cultural and sporting accomplishments, having concentrated on making money through business. As a result he was regarded as inferior, even a 'blighter', by Psmith and Thompson. 'As far as I can say without searching the Newgate Calendar, the man Bickersdyke's career seems to have been as follows. He was at school with my pater, went into the City, raked in a certain amount of doubloons – probably dishonestly – and is now a sort of Captain of Industry, manager of some bank or other, and about to stand for Parliament'.

The City that emerges from Wodehouse's novel was a place that combined mystery with boredom, and where human feelings were absent.

> Nobody can be proud of the achievements of a bank. When the business of arranging a new Japanese loan was given to the New Asiatic Bank, its employees did not stand on stools, and cheer. On the contrary, they thought of the extra work it would involve; and they cursed a good deal, though there was no denying that it was a big thing for the bank ... There is a cold impersonality about a bank.

The work of the bank was always beyond the comprehension of Mike Jackson.

> On his side, it must be admitted that Mike was something out of the common run of bank clerks. The whole system of banking was a horrid mystery to him. He did not understand why things were done, or how the various departments depended on and dove-tailed into one another. Each department seemed to him something separate and distinct. Why they were all in the same building at all he never really gathered. He knew that it could not be purely from motives of sociability, in order that the clerks might have each other's company during slack spells. That much he suspected, but beyond that he was vague.

Mike did not want to be there but had no alternative if he was to earn a living for himself, as his ability as a cricketer did not provide him with an income.

> You go and sweat all day at a desk, day after day, for about twopence a year. And when you're about eighty-five, you retire. It isn't living at all ... Mike did not like being in the bank, considered in the light of a career. But he bore no grudge against his inmates of the bank ... His fellow workers in the bank he regarded as companions in misfortune...They were a pleasant set of fellows in the New Asiatic Bank, and but for the dreary outlook which the future held – for Mike, unlike most of his fellow workers, was not attracted by the idea of a life in the East – he would have been fairly content ... The truth of the matter was that the New Asiatic Bank was over-staffed. There were too many men for the work. The London branch was really a nursery. New men were constantly wanted in the Eastern branches, so they had to be put into the London branch to learn the business, whether there was any work for them to do or not.[37]

Whereas the City was no place for the likes of Mike and Psmith, and so they left for sporting and outdoor pursuits, so the country could be a hostile place for those from the City who chose to settle there by buying an estate, if Joseph Hocking's 1906 novel, *The Man Who Rose Again*, is at all representative. Apart from the occasional disparaging references to Jews, as in Lord Telsize being described 'as rich as a money-lending Jew', it was those who were non-conformists that were discriminated against. The story involved Radford Leicester, a brilliant politician but a cynic, heavy drinker and atheist, who took a bet that he could persuade Olive Castlemaine to marry him. She was the most sought after heiress in London as well as being beautiful, cultured and clever. Her father was the 'managing director of, and chief shareholder in, one of the most prosperous and respectable firms in London'. They lived in the Beeches, a 'a fine old mansion' in its own extensive grounds in outer London.

> Being the only child of John Castlemaine, who occupied not only a high position in the City of London, but owned more than one fine estate in England, she had all that money could buy, while her father's integrity and honourable reputation made her the envy of those who, socially, would regard her as an inferior. For John Castlemaine, while bearing a name known in English history, and possessed of great wealth, was still a member of what is called 'middle classes'. He simply stood high up in his own class. He was not one of those who mingled freely with the men who guide the destinies of the nation. Rich men came to his house, men great in the world of finance; but men great in the world of politics and science and letters were unknown to him. Perhaps this was his own fault, or perhaps it was because his tastes were simple and because he did not possess the qualities which would attract men of influence and power to his house. For John Castlemaine was a plain man. He belonged to the merchant class, and he prided himself on the position he held.

Among the newly wealthy in Britain a City merchant like Castlemaine was seen as financially and culturally superior to a provincial businessman, such as Mr Lowry from Taviton in Devon, 'a commonplace man who had succeeded in becoming rich ... As a rule they looked at everything through the medium of money. To them passing events were of interest because of the effect they might have upon the financial market. And even here their outlook was narrow and superficial'.

Becoming tired of the daily commute into the City and the endless demands of business Castlemaine decided to retire and so bought an estate in Devon.

> I'm tired of London. The eternal fogs and grey skies of winter oppress me. For years I've longed to live in the country. Even at the Beeches we are more and more invaded by London fogs. Besides there is no necessity for me to live near London any longer. I have quite as much money as I need, and, added to this, I have been able to trust more and more in the heads of the various departments of my business. An occasional visit will be quite enough for me.

As London itself expanded, with the speculative builder buying up land and putting houses on it, those who made themselves wealthy in the City sought property ever further afield. Castlemaine sought space and fresh air which he could not get in London, not social status as he was content with the position he had already reached. However, this brought Castlemaine into contact with those long established in Devon, and he found himself ostracized. The farmers thought he was too grand while the County set avoided him because he was a Nonconformist, dissenter , and regarded him as 'of the nouveau riche order, because you have made your wealth by commerce'. It was easier to gain acceptance and rise in society in the relatively open world of London than the closed world of the countryside. This did not trouble Castlemaine. 'I do not imagine we shall be much poorer because of their lack of courtesy' as they could make their own society by inviting down friends from London. His daughter also observed, rather cynically, that 'it may be that in time the minor county families will overlook our other failings on account of your being a wealthy man', though she then wondered if such people were worth cultivating. After many twists and turns, she married Radford Leicester, after he had forsaken drink, discovered god, become wealthy in his own right and fallen in love with her![38]

If such was the reception that was seen to await a respectable nonconformist in the country the barriers to be overcome by Jewish financiers could be expected to be that much greater, given how they were viewed. In Oppenheim's *Anna, The Adventuress*, dating from 1904, whereas two non-Jewish bank clerks were pitied because of the 'deadly grind' of working in the City, two Jewish clerks were seen as completely at home in this environment: 'a couple of pronounced young Jews, who were talking loudly together in some unintelligible jargon of the City'. When Walter Brendon inherited a million dollars from a relative in New York, a Jewish acquaintance called Gudden immediately tried to interest him in a moneymaking scheme being organized in the City.

> Look here, he whispered. You're fond of the theatre, and that sort of thing, aren't you? If you care for a little flutter in a new production – there's a gold mine in the piece, s'help me. I believe I could get you a fifth share. It's a comic opera, with some ripping songs and dances, bound to take like wild fire. Of course it means going behind whenever you like, and you stand o.k. with all the girls. Friend of mine in the city's running the syndicate. What do you say? Will you come down and see him.

Walter turned him down.[39] What this reflected was the separation between the City from the rest of British society. In a Baroness Orczy story that appeared in 1901–2, *The Mysterious Death on the Underground Railway*, the City stockbroker, Andrew Campbell, was described as 'A tall, dark-haired man, with the word "City" written metaphorically all over him'. When travelling by underground he 'buried himself in the Stock Exchange quotations of his evening paper ... very much engrossed in some calculations'.[40] Thus the events going on around him, including murder, simply passed him by. The City was even felt to be impervious to the threat of a coming European war between Britain and Germany, which was the theme of a novel by E. Phillips Oppenheim, *The Mysterious Mr Sabin*, published in 1911. 'The Stock Exchange remained firm – there was no enthusiasm, but no panic'.[41] The global financial activities of the City, conducted by those with a cosmopolitan outlook, can be contrasted with the intimate nature of provincial finance, judging from the novels of Arnold Bennett. In the Midlands' pottery towns financial activities were handled by local people whom everybody knew and largely involved investments in local housing, local businesses, local hotels, local football clubs and local newspapers.[42]

The City of London escaped vitriolic condemnation between 1900 and 1910, as that period lacked the speculative outburst that had been such a feature of the previous decade. That did not mean that it resumed the place within British culture that it had achieved before 1895. Instead, the legacy of the speculative excesses of the 1890s remained a potent influence, greatly distorting the City's position within Edwardian culture. Though there was a general recognition of the City as a commercial and financial centre without peer, it was now primarily associated with fraud and speculation, despite a tightening of company legislation in 1900. It was the activities of these company promoters and the rise and fall of prices on the Stock Exchange that brought the City to the attention of the public, and the results were usually negative. The companies that failed and whose shares became worthless were the City stories that gained wide circulation, not those that paid steady dividends. Similarly, the movements in prices that were widely reported were those exhibiting the greatest gains or falls leaving the London Stock Exchange open to the accusation that it pandered to the gambling instincts of the population. The fact that the Stock Exchange remained a closed market continued to foster the belief that it allowed insiders to profit at the expense of outsiders. This was despite the fact that it was widely admired for its ability to police the activities of its own members, it being acknowledged that 'on the rare occasions when dishonourable conduct is proved against a member, expulsion, or a sentence of suspension equivalent to it, is swiftly meted out to the offender'. To the public the street market for South African and American shares was what they were aware of and that was nothing more than 'a yelling, pushing crowd of raving maniacs'.[43] Generally, the City remained closely associated with foreign or Jewish financiers, who could not be trusted, even though the most notorious of this period was the nonconformist Englishman, Whitaker Wright, who had been prosecuted by the Jewish barrister Rufus Isaacs. There was no recognition that these Jews and foreigners came to London because it was such an important commercial and financial centre, making a presence there essential for those involved in the international flows of money and commodities. The more the City succeeded as a global financial centre the more it was seen as alien by the British population because of the nature of the activities conducted there and the type of people it attracted. Once identified as a place of international finance in the 1890s the City failed to recapture its image as a British financial centre after 1900, and this coloured its place within British culture.

The other development that affected the position of the City within British culture after 1900 is that it came to be seen as a proxy for the battle between right and left or between capital and labour. The City was condemned by writers from the left, because it was seen to be the embodiment of capitalism, contributing to its survival through the fusion of money and land. Conversely, it was condemned by those from the right, who saw it as a threat to the established social order whether in London or in the country. Even a London property developer could be held in higher regard than someone who made his money in the City, as can be seen in Anthony Hope's 1901 novel, *Tristram of Blent*.[44] What cannot be denied is that by the Edwardian period the City of London had become a potent force within British culture, though one detached from either the people who worked there or the place it occupied. There were those in the City who had achieved success and wealth through ability, hard work and perseverance. Conversely there were also others who occupied prominent positions as bankers, brokers and merchants through family and other connections. Some in the City did integrate into landed society and were outspoken supporters of imperialism, celebrating British victories as in the Boer War with outbursts of patriotic feeling. Conversely, others did not integrate and were either indifferent to or hostile to Empire, recognizing that international peace and stability, not conflict, was what their business required. It was easy to generalize about the City from those to be found there because there were always people who fitted the profile. Conversely, such generalizations are highly dangerous as there were many that did not, for City people comprised so many different types, whether by class, religion, nationality or behaviour, though not gender. At the same time City people were complex individuals who held strong beliefs and expressed social, political, religious or intellectual views that were not necessarily driven by economic rationale, and could even be at variance to them. There was no single spokesman, or group, for the City, whose views could be taken as either authoritative or representative. The same applies to the City if judged in economic terms for it continued to be a very mixed community. The City encompassed both commercial and financial activities as well as a growing number of business and professional services such as the accountants and lawyers. Some of these were focused on the City's global role but others met the needs of the domestic economy. Again, this makes it difficult to generalize about the City because it fulfilled so many different functions simultaneously.[45]

What can be concluded is that in the Edwardian era the City failed to recover the more favourable position it had established for itself by the early 1890s. Partly this was due to the enduring impact of the gold mining boom, and the damage that had inflicted on the City's reputation. However, it had more to do with a change in the way the City was judged. Increasingly, the City was being drawn into diverse but linked arguments over capitalism and socialism and between those who wished to preserve an English way of life against foreign influences and those who took a more cosmopolitan stance. This represented something new for the City. In the middle of the nineteenth century judgements about the City had ceased to be based on place and been replaced by function. At the beginning of the twentieth century the City ceased to be judged by function but rather as the physical embodiment of the concept of cosmopolitan capitalism. As the home of the London Stock Exchange the City was seen to lie at the centre of wasteful speculation conducted in securities drawn from around the world. The City was also the base from which promoters converted existing businesses into joint stock companies whose shares then became new gambling counters. To many people neither this speculation nor company promotion made any positive contribution to material well-being, while it was easy to point to the losses experienced by investors who bought shares that fell in value or subscribed to new issues made on behalf of companies that subsequently failed. In contrast, it was more difficult to describe the importance of the City in the intricate web through which flowed credit, capital and commerce, and the contribution that made to both economic progress and the functioning of the world economy. In the wake of the speculative excesses of the mid 1890s and the attack upon cosmopolitan capitalism, the City of London experienced something of a credibility gap in the Edwardian age that made it impossible for it to re-establish a positive image.[46] Whether that was to endure in the years before the First World War or be reversed through recognising the actual role played by the City in international finance is a question that needs to be answered.

7 WEALTH AND POWER, 1910–1914

In the years before the First World War the City of London reached its peak of global influence. Located in this one small district of the metropolis of London were some of the most important commercial markets in the world, with the most influential financial institutions in the shape of the Bank of England, Lloyds and the London Stock Exchange, and many of the world's largest banking and insurance companies. In addition, it was from the City of London that international trade, finance and shipping was organized, facilitating the global distribution of money and merchandise.[1] However, most of these varied activities, though widely recognized and admired, only dimly impinged upon the public imagination, being conducted in a dull and routine manner and of a highly technical nature. In contrast, it was events on the Stock Exchange that continued to absorb most public interest, with the rise and fall of prices being attributed to the manipulation of insiders, especially in mining and oil companies. The fortunes of individual companies also attracted attention, especially newly promoted ones, as any sudden bankruptcy, bringing ruin to investors, could be laid at the feet of a financial genius or scheming fraudster. Thus, along with the brokers and jobbers who daily bought and sold shares, it was company promoters and their constant stream of offerings that helped identify the City of London in the public mind. The period also witnessed both a speculative mania, centring on rubber plantation companies, and a run on the Birkbeck Bank in 1910 followed by its collapse in 1911. There was even a scandal in 1912 over accusations of insider trading, involving prominent members of the Liberal government, Sir Herbert Samuel and Sir Rufus Isaacs, and the chairman of the Marconi Company, Godfrey Isaacs, who was the brother of Sir Rufus. Above all, the public were especially fascinated by the personification of the City in the shape of certain flamboyant and newsworthy financiers that appeared to thrive in its precincts, with again many of the most prominent being Jewish or foreign or both, such as Barney Barnato, Ernest Cassel, and Saemy Japhet.[2] This raises the question of which was more important in determining the place of the City in British culture. Was it the position it occupied in global finance and commerce and the efficient management of the country's banking system? If so then it might be expected that the City would find itself at the heart of British culture with those who worked there being at the pinnacle of social acceptability, whether they were a humble clerk or grandiose financier. Conversely, an impression that the City had become the preserve of foreigners or Jews could provoke deep-rooted anti-Semitic and xenophobic sentiments, helping to fuel anti-City feeling among those who might consider themselves to be patriotic Englishmen. The position occupied by the City in the global financial system, through its banks and markets, also made it a target for those opposed to capitalism and desirous of replacing it with a more equitable system such as socialism. Finally, the City attracted criticism because of the conspicuous wealth possessed by some of the most prominent financiers, such as the Rothschilds, and their opulent country mansions. The very success of the City and those who profited from its ascendancy inevitably provoked a reaction from those who did not share in the wealth it created, and saw their lands, houses and accumulated possessions bought up. On the eve of the First World War the City was such a large, diverse and cosmopolitan financial and commercial centre that it was capable of being all things to all men. What needs to be determined is whether there was a widely held view of the City in British culture and what that view was.

To many the City of London remained forever cursed because of its association with moneylending, and that remained unchanged in this period. Such continuity can be seen from one of Walter Besant's later novels, namely *The Alabaster Box*. This was the story of a man who had been well-educated and brought up to mix with the best in society, only to discover it was all paid for from the proceeds of moneylending. His father had begun life as a builder and undertaker, who used his money to buy houses, for which high rents were charged, evicting those who could not pay. He also lent to those who could not borrow from banks, charging very high rates of interest to the very poorest. Eventually he opened a bank himself, though not in the City but in the West End, in Golden Square. He then married the daughter of a General and they had one son, Gerald Moorsom. Eventually, he closed the bank and retired with a large fortune, cutting himself off from those who knew him in the past. He even created a false history with portraits of fictitious ancestors and changed his name from Rosenberg to Moorsom, though he had no regrets about the way he had made his money. 'I have never been able to understand why money-lending is not considered as honourable a profession as any other'. His son, who had been brought up a Christian, was profoundly shocked by the revelation regarding his origins and that he was not a wealthy gentleman of three or four generations standing. 'One thing his father did not fully understand, how his son had been taught in a thousand ways, by his mother, by his school, by his companions and friends, to regard certain forms of money-getting as base and dishonourable to the last degree...'. After his father died, and he inherited a large fortune, Gerald tried to come to terms with the position he found himself in. The only way he could do this was to return to the part of London where his father had begun. There he discovered long-lost relatives, and started to make restitution to them and the others in the locality for all the wrongs that he believed his father had done through his moneylending. The implication was obvious. The only repentance for the son of a usurer was to make good the evil done by giving the money back. In that sense nothing had changed, though in another sense the change was profound as the City was no longer the source or even location for the evil that was moneylending. That now took place elsewhere in London, depending upon whether the borrowers were the poor in the East End or the supposed rich keeping up appearances in the West End.[3]

The City was still recognized as a commercial centre, as can be seen from Annie Swan's *The Bondage of Riches*, which was published in 1912. John Wycherly 'was the ordinary type of City man, tall yet firmly built, with a good square head and a shrewd, yet not unkindly eye. Wycherly had risen from the ranks of the very poor. His father had driven a market cart on the country roads of Evesham, selling there from the produce he had on the acre of garden ground surrounding his little cottage'. Wycherly had been 'A plodder at school, without vices or any temptation in that direction'. He married the daughter of a local farmer and had five children. He worked in the City, in Bishopsgate.

> None knew better than Wycherly himself that his success in the City – where he was head of a department in a great industrial store – was neither lucrative nor conspicuously honourable. He was merely part of a great machine, only acceptable to his employers so long as he did his work efficiently and made his department pay. The increasing competition, the introduction of new and sometimes doubtful methods into business life, had made Wycherly's position for a few years back one of extreme difficulty, even of peril.

He was in danger of replacement by a younger, more dynamic and less scrupulous man and that led him to worry about how he would provide for his wife and family in the future. They lived in a rented house in Brixton, near the Crystal Palace. All this conjured up how relentless, hard and uncertain was City life for those performing essential but mundane tasks for limited reward.

One day Wycherly received an envelope. 'But what was in the envelope? It looked important, but then stockbrokers and others were in the habit of sending their touting circulars in such envelopes nowadays'. The letter was from a firm of solicitors in London – Yardley, Ransom and Chard in Lincoln's Inn – telling him that he had inherited a fortune from a casual acquaintance in the City, a man called Halliwell Drage. The estate comprised the Manor House and lands of Mitchelham in Hertfordshire, and property in London, including in the City. The estate alone produced an income of £2,000 per annum and the rents and other property brought the total up to £7,000–8,000. Mitchelham had long been in the Drage family but was not the source of his wealth, for he had made his money in the City. The fact that Drage was unmarried, without close relatives or friends, and had devoted himself to moneymaking is indicative of what contemporaries believed was required to succeed in the City. Wycherly was a happy family man and had not enjoyed success.[4] This ability of the City to generate large fortunes for the lucky few, as well as destroy them for others, was a prominent feature of the way it was viewed by the public on the eve of the First World War. This can be seen from Grace Pettman's novel, *A Study in Gold*, which also dated from 1912. Again, it concerned a man whose life was transformed through inheriting a fortune. Mark St Leonard was an unemployed journalist contemplating suicide while standing at the Blackfriars end of the Embankment and watching the Thames flow by below him.

> Around him the still greater tide of the City was setting towards home, and rest, and recreation; after another day of toil the great stream of human life was sweeping back across the bridge: humble toilers on foot, others in tram or bus, while a few – pitifully few – were borne luxuriously to station or home reclining at ease among the cushions of a motor-car or well-appointed carriage.

The human tide was seen to consist of both the 'weary work-girl' and 'prosperous City magnate' with many buoyed up by the fact that 'Friday night meant the prospect of a long week-end away from the grime and grind of the City'.

Mark had come to London to work on a newspaper twenty years before but had never succeeded in getting a permanent job and was now unemployed. He had a wife, two children, a boy and girl, and an aged mother to support. His 'only son Geoffrey was earning a pittance as clerk in a mercantile house in the City ... What little of his salary was left after tram fares, lunches, and clothes were paid for, went in cigarettes and tickets for places of amusement in South London'. Geoffrey regarded the job as drudgery and had little expectation of advancement. Along with him in the counting house in Mincing Lane was another youth, Watkins, who was being trained to take over the business as his uncle was the owner: 'Watkins had been compelled to work his way through the various departments, and learn every branch in detail'. Mark's daughter, Margaret, also worked in the City and, again, despite being clever and hardworking, had no prospects. 'In spite of a good knowledge of modern languages, she was only able to secure a small wage as a typist in a City office' The family lived in a small flat in Camberwell. Even in the City, where fabulous fortunes could be made by a few, life was a continuous struggle for the many. As it was, Mark inherited £100,000 through the will of a deceased relative. This allowed him to buy a country estate, Heathermoor Hall, and give up looking for work. The estate he bought, located on the border between Sussex and Surrey, was being sold because 'The owner had met with financial losses'. Again, the uncertainties of life were emphasized with only land being seen as secure, though generating a poor return.[5]

The purchase of the country estate brought Mark St Leonard and his family into contact with their neighbour, 'Caleb Otto-Smith – the financier ... rumour has it that he doesn't know the extent of his own wealth – whatever he touches turns to gold'. He was 'the most successful company promoter and financier of the day'. In personal appearance he was 'A stout florid man, past middle age'. Mark's son Geoffrey felt that a friendship with this man would open up society for them. 'To be received at Castle Royal would be a passport to the best society in the county – at least, so Mark St Leonard fondly imagined' Coming as he did from a gentry background in Somerset, but after years of impoverishment, Mark was keen to establish himself in society, and so leaped at the opportunity to cultivate Otto-Smith. He told his daughter:

> it is common knowledge in the City that Otto-Smith financed the Great Mountain Mines Scheme, and cleared a cool half million over the Chinese Railway deal! He is a man worth knowing – when one has money to invest. 'But I thought Cousin Horace's fortune was all carefully invested?' said Margaret quickly.
>
> 'So it is – too carefully for my fancy: why, some of the investments are bringing in little better than consols!'
>
> 'But they are safe investments, Father', protested Margaret, who had picked up a good deal of practical knowledge in the City office where she worked, and had learned to look askance at large dividends and gilt-edged securities.
>
> 'Pardon me, my dear', said Mark St. Leonard with lofty complaisance, 'you are a woman-and women know nothing about finance whatever! It is your place to make the world beautiful and charming for the men who transact business. You must remember that if Mr. Otto-Smith knew the amount of my fortune he would probably smile pityingly: such a sum would appear very small to a man who deals in millions every day. I have no doubt in his hands my fortune would soon increase tenfold!' Margaret gazed at her father in startled fashion. There was a new expression in his eye – was it the covetous gleam of one who longed to add gold to gold?

City financiers like Otto-Smith had the power to captivate naïve investors such as Mark, especially at a time when the returns he could promise were so much better than those to be obtained from safe investments. In contrast, even someone with limited financial knowledge could see that the higher the rate of return the greater the risk involved, but Margaret's views were discounted as she was only a woman.

The result was that a friendship developed between the occupants of the neighbouring houses. Otto-Smith had bought his estate from the Earl of Halesmere, who had to sell because of horse-racing debts. Otto-Smith then built a large new mansion, called Castle Royal, on the site of an old Norman fortress. This represented the triumph of the City over an impoverished English aristocracy, who had contributed to their own decline through gambling. The new house was neither ugly nor vulgar, as might be expected from a City financier, but regarded as a showpiece being described as 'a pile of magnificence and beauty not to be equalled in the county'. However, it was not due to Otto-Smith that the house and its furnishings were so admired but to his invalided half-sister, who lived with him. She had been injured in a railway accident when they fled from Russia as Polish Jewish refugees. Her mother had been killed in the accident. The house overawed Mrs St Leonard on her first visit, as she told Margaret.

> 'To be received here as guests, to drive in our own carriage, when a few weeks back we could not afford a penny for a London bus, and our home was on the edge of a slum – oh, Margaret, there exists no greater power than the power of gold!' Margaret was silent for a moment, then she said
>
> 'Yes, mother, I think, nay, I am sure, there is one power that is greater still. Gold may perish – or vanish: but the greatest of all remains – it is the power of the love of God!'

Margaret had taught in the Camberwell Mission and had hoped to marry the young man who ran it, Howard Farnborough, but her father had made it clear that, now that they were wealthy, that was no longer possible. The message was emerging that wealth could corrupt all unless they maintained a strong Christian faith.[6]

One reason for the friendship was that neither family was accepted within country society as both were regarded as incomers and upstarts. The St Leonards were known to have been poor until they had come into the inheritance, while Otto-Smith had not only made his money in the City but was also foreign and Jewish. Again, it was Margaret who was sufficiently attuned to the social nuances to know what this meant for their acceptability, as she explained to her mother. 'The county people here are most likely very exclusive, socially. Even such a home as Castle Royal, and the possession of boundless wealth, would not count with the more exclusive of the aristocracy, if pedigree were lacking'. Margaret's mother still did not understand why such rich, cultured and pleasant people like Caleb and Rachel Otto-Smith had no friends in the county and so Margaret had to be even more blunt in explaining

> 'Why, Caleb Otto-Smith is a Jew, a foreign Jew, who has anglicized his name. Didn't you notice what a real Jewess Miss Rachel appears?'
>
> 'A Jew?' Mrs St. Leonard, whose experience of her Semitic neighbours in South London had not predisposed her favourably towards the race, looked aghast.
>
> 'Why, mother', said Margaret, smiling, 'surely you are not prejudiced because of that? I think Miss Otto-Smith is one of the sweetest invalids I have ever met. I shall be only too glad to go and see her, as often as she cares for a visit. But it is possible that, as a Jewish financier, Mr Otto-Smith, with all his riches, is not received by the social world here, or in London; nor shall we be, you will find, in spite of father's anxiety on

the point'. Mrs. St. Leonard was silent, but Margaret's keen-sighted intuition speedily proved to be right.

Even by the early twentieth century, money could not buy entry into society and this was widely recognized. Entry was doubly difficult if the money was made as a financier and company promoter in the City and the person in question was foreign and Jewish. Even among Jewish circles Caleb and Rachel Otto-Smith were outsiders. 'She and her brother were not openly known as members of the rich Jewish community which is such a power in the financial circles in England'. They were Jewish but not practising and had anglicized their names on coming to England. Thus they were also ostracized by the wealthy and long-established Jewish financial community in Britain, among whom numbered the Rothschilds. None of this was sufficient to dissuade Margaret's father from cultivating them as friends. 'What if Margaret is right, and he comes of a family of Polish Jews – refugees from suffering and persecution at the hands of the Russians! I am proud of the acquaintance of a man who has become a wizard in the City where gold is concerned! It is more than likely he will do something for Geoffrey, if we play our cards well!' Greed and self-interest were now driving Mark. In contrast Margaret did not like Caleb Otto-Smith, 'From the very first, Margaret had not been able to conquer a secret feeling of aversion to Caleb Otto-Smith; to her, he seemed the embodiment of all that her City life had taught her to look upon with suspicion – greed of gold, speculation, and riches amassed by the toil and loss of others, and it might be even at the cost of their souls as well!' Though she did like his sister, Rachel, she tried to use her influence to convert her to Christianity.[7]

This did not mean that Otto-Smith was shunned by society as a whole for there were many like Mark St Leonard who saw something of the alchemist in him. 'Caleb Otto-Smith was a man flattered and fawned on by many, because of his gold, and the financial power behind his name in City circles: to a great extent, in the particular set of Society in which he moved, he could make friends with whom he would'. It was for that reason that Mark St Leonard consulted Caleb Otto-Smith, as a friendship developed on the golf-course, about investing the money he had inherited so as to obtain a better rate of return. As Mark complained, 'there is no chance of any increase in value, or dividends, while the money remains invested where it is!' Caleb's advice was 'sell out, and re-invest? I could put you in the way of a good thing or two – if you will promise not to pass the tip on to others. There are some shares to be had at a low figure now, but I am in the know that there is a boom expected, and you may double, treble, all you invest next week, or else leave it to bear a fabulous dividend later'. Attracted by the possibility of doubling or trebling the £100,000 he had inherited Mark entrusted his fortune for Otto-Smith to invest.

Following Caleb Otto-Smith's advice, Mark St. Leonard sold out several thousand pounds of his capital, and purchased shares in some inflated company of which the Jewish financier was promoter, chairman, and principal shareholder. As Otto-Smith had predicted, an altogether unaccountable boom took place the very next week in these particular shares: Mark St. Leonard sold out, doubling his capital, and speedily secured from the master of Castle Royal another tip which was sure to turn his small fortune into untold gold. Elated by success, the lust of the speculator fired Mark St. Leonard's blood. He sold out a still larger number of the sound investments his distant kinsman had left him, and plunged madly into the whirlpool of speculation, always seeking the advice of Caleb Otto-Smith, and following it carefully – always, too, finding this led to deciding upon some company in which the Jew held supreme interest. But Mark St. Leonard was only too glad of this; to him Caleb Otto-Smith was the embodiment of commercial sagacity and success, as well as the possessor of untold gold. To do as he did must be to do well: to follow his advice must of necessity spell success, since he had been of all men the most notoriously successful in recent years.

Mark was a weak man, led astray by Otto-Smith, who was catering to 'the gambler's greed and the miser's insatiable craving'.

Margaret discovered what her father was doing and became very worried, as her time working in the City had taught her to be very suspicious of the type of investments that he was making. She insisted on her father making a settlement on her and her mother. The fortune inherited had been invested in bank shares, and these were considered solid and safe investments by this period, though the dividends were low and no capital gain could be expected. Margaret advised her father against selling them, telling him that 'The bank is safe as a bank can be, the yearly interest is good, and it would be nice to know that, if misfortune and disaster did happen to come, there was at least a small yearly income that could not be touched'. Mark agreed to his daughter's request though recommending to her that she switched out of the bank shares and into Pandora Estate, which was paying 25 per cent. He said to Margaret,

> You have a careful business head, Margaret, – your caution must surely be derived from some unknown Scottish ancestor! You shall certainly have the money in your own name, if you like; your mother too, if she cares about it. At the same time, I think the interest the bank is paying is ridiculously low. Why, here the Pandora Estate – which is Mr. Otto-Smith's own affair, only he most generously accepted fifty thousand of mine to invest in it – is paying twenty-five per cent, and every week promises more!

Margaret refused his advice and kept her money in bank shares, believing that her father was gambling not investing.[8]

Not content with making a fortune in the City, where he had 'climbed the rungs of the financial ladder to almost fabulous success', Caleb Otto-Smith wanted to establish himself in society through marriage. What he craved was to complete his ascendancy through a suitable marriage. 'Men of his type who had accumulated wealth usually sought in marriage a girl of rank, who had the entrée of the very highest society, and was willing to exchange the prestige of her title and ancestry for a share of the millionaire's gold'. Among the possibilities was Lady Beatrix Urbeville, whose father, the Marquess of Limehouse, was close to bankruptcy.

> Most of these girls had been trained by ambitious mothers to believe that the chief end of their lives was to make a brilliant match; possibly not one among them would have refused to bestow her aristocratic hand upon the grey-haired unprepossessing financier who had come to England as an alien, a young Polish Jew, a well-nigh penniless exile.

Until then Otto-Smith had tended to shun society as it had shunned him, but now he decided to make a flamboyant entry, partly to dispel the rumours that were floating around that his schemes were coming unstuck and partly to attract a suitable bride. He thus took a 'a huge mansion in Park Lane' while Mark took a flat near Hyde Park in order to participate in the social activities that were planned. Though Otto-Smith 'could never hope to ride on the topmost wave of English society, and win his way into the circles of the highest rank, there were many well-known and titled families who were only too ready to receive the great company promoter to their homes, and accept the invitations he appeared willing to bestow upon anyone who was anything at all in London society, if only they would attend his lavish entertainments'. It was 'only the most select circles of society' who 'were proof against the charm of the financier's gold'. Otto-Smith's origins, religion and the source of his wealth made it difficult for him to obtain the type of wife he coveted.

Otto-Smith started to court Margaret, encouraged by her father who considered him '...a Napoleon of Finance'. Margaret was "'The only girl I ever wanted – just because she was different from the money-hunting crew who angle for my gold, and laugh at me for my lack of pedigree!'" Margaret would not agree to marry him, especially as she was still seeing Howard Farnborough, who thought of Otto-Smith as a 'Jewish company promoter ... A man as hard as the gold he coins so rapidly, though according to some accounts his finance has been on too high a plane to be sound of late. 'When she turned him down he threatened to expose her brother as an embezzler, if she did not change her mind. Geoffrey was now working in the City for Otto-Smith and had taken money from the office to pay his gambling debts. Margaret still would not agree and Otto-Smith accepted defeat, knowing that if he exposed Geoffrey, Geoffrey would reveal all about the true state of his financial affairs and the means used to persuade investors to buy shares. Margaret regarded Otto-Smith as 'a grey-haired, pompous Jew' who, 'neither by birth nor breeding was he anything like a true gentleman'.

She also resented the fact that her father had tried to force the marriage upon her and invested all the family's money in Otto-Smith's companies.

> If my father has staked his daughter – and his fortune – in bidding for a millionaire husband, he has lost – that is all. I am glad beyond words that I refused Caleb Otto-Smith, refused him firmly and finally, before I knew that he is living in a glass house, and his millions are probably a myth! Mother, if what I heard to-night was true, the fortune that father inherited will vanish as suddenly as it came; in a few short months at most, he is likely to be a ruined man!

What she had overheard at the party Otto-Smith gave at his Park Lane House was a conversation between two ladies, who had been informed about the true state of his financial affairs by a relative.

> 'I begin to wish I had never come. I hate to be mixed up with anything of the kind. But my cousin, Lord Bobby Egremont, told me just now that he is quite sure. The end is only a few months off, at most'. The other lady spoke in puzzled ones, as if doubtful about something. 'But the display to-night – the cost must be fabulous; look at the decorations, and the supper! Why, the man must be rolling in riches!'
>
> 'Once, perhaps, but not now. This town house, and extravagant display, are all bids for regaining the fortune that has melted away in rubbishing companies. Some of the shareholders are clamouring for their money, and the money subscribed for the new companies that he is floating is being used to pay big dividends on the old shares. It is even said he intends to get married. Some people fancy he has been smitten by a little nobody in the country, whose father has confided all his fortune to Otto-Smith for re-investment'. The other lady gave a subdued sigh.
>
> 'Some green goose he has plucked – not the first by many a hundred! Why, the man's schemes are a legion – a myriad stars would fall if his companies came to grief!'
>
> 'Well, I can assure you he is playing his last cards; it is but a question of time. Whatever you do, don't let yourself be drawn into these South Sea Bubble investments. Lord Bobby told me Otto-Smith tried hard to get him to put a huge sum into a new venture, but my cousin has cut his wisdom teeth; he stands to lose a good deal as it is'.

All this turned out to be true with Mark St Leonard losing most of the fortune he had inherited. Otto-Smith tried to salvage something by staging a fire at Castle Royal, having already sold some of his most prized possessions privately, including a Velasquez to an American buyer. His intention was to collect on the insurance. Unfortunately his sister was accidentally caught up in the fire, having moved rooms because of repainting. Though she was rescued she died shortly afterwards. At the same time Margaret had spotted Otto-Smith at the house though he was meant to be in London, and informed the police. They then traced Otto-Smith's movements, took evidence from the servants about the disposal of the paintings, and started searching for him as he had disappeared. As a result the insurance company would not pay out.

Otto-Smith's disappearance, and the attempted insurance fraud, fuelled new rumours in the City about the state of his companies, creating a financial panic. 'Knots of people had gathered early in the morning outside the closed doors of the offices of Otto-Smith's companies, increasing to a crowd at midday. All sorts of rumours were rife concerning his financial position'. Then the news broke that the companies he was associated with had collapsed and that he had absconded.

> The bubble had burst. The companies floated by Otto-Smith were hopelessly bankrupt; his affairs had been placed in the hands of the official receiver, and a warrant was out for the great financier's arrest for conspiracy and fraud – and another that charged him with the fire at Castle Royal, which, resulting in his sister's death from shock, might possibly be altered to the more serious charge of manslaughter.

Geoffrey fled to the USA in case he was charged with embezzlement while Mark was left only with the small estate he had bought, but he could not afford the upkeep of the house. His wife and daughter had the small amounts settled upon them, and with that they could afford the rent of a small suburban villa in Frensham, to which they moved. Though travelling in disguise, Otto-Smith was traced to Europe, through the use of wireless-telegraphy, and apprehended aboard an American liner bound for New York. He was extradited to Britain, made to stand trial and then sent to prison. Margaret married Howard Farnborough who was to become the vicar of a large parish in Coventry, having been given the parish because he had saved Lord Blackdown's son from drowning in a heroic rescue. The message was clear. Speculation was gambling, company promotion was corrupt, and Christianity was the only true path. There was no sign here that the City was gaining a social acceptability within Britain that befitted its status as a global financial centre. Though the underlying antagonism towards anything to do with money was now greatly moderated, this did not extend to either speculation in shares or company promotion, especially when undertaken by foreign Jews.[9]

Some evidence of the fact that it was speculation and company promotion that lay at the heart of public antipathy towards the City on the eve of the First World War, rather than racism and anti-Semitism, is to be found in a novel by Joseph Hocking, entitled *God and Mammon*, which also appeared in 1912. Money made in the City was forever tainted and so could not produce a fulfilled and contented life, as Sir William Pilken discovered, despite being a highly successful and respected City financier. He had come to London to run the office of a provincial solicitor.

> He was not content to do the ordinary work of a lawyer. He wanted to deal in millions. And he did it, too. He gained the confidence of capitalists. He advanced schemes which these capitalists laughed at first, but supported afterwards. He became the leader in matters of international importance ... he was soon making £50,000

a year, and controlled a tremendous amount of London finance. But that did not satisfy him. He was invited to stand as a candidate for a constituency in the Conservative interest, and he got elected. After that he obtained a baronetcy, and married the daughter of old Lord Lessing, the Secretary for Foreign Affairs ... twenty years ago he was an office boy in a small country town, and now he lives in a fine house in Berkeley Square, with a peerage at his feet whenever he is disposed to pick it up.

Pilken was referred to as 'the Colossus of the financial world' and a man with his 'finger on the pulse of the whole thing'. He had palatial offices in the City, which cost £3,000 per annum in rent. All this encouraged both admiration and emulation, especially as Pilken was regarded as an honest financier.

'As far as I know, there has never been a breath of scandal about him. His money is clean, as far as money can be clean. He has done it all by brains, push, pluck, perseverance. That's what I always say. London gives a cold welcome to the mediocre man, but it opens its arms to the man of real ability – the man who means to succeed and never gives up trying. And when London opens its arms, nothing is impossible'.

However, Pilken was a deeply unhappy man, especially when he reflected on the sacrifices he had had to make in order to achieve it.

I work harder than a galley slave. Why do I not give it up? I have more than enough for all my needs; I have reached the summit of my ambition. But I can't give it up. One thing has led to another, and I dare not retire until I see my schemes through. Besides, should I be content if I gave it up? I am tired of the whole thing, and yet it chains me fast. I have become a money-making machine, and the machine must not stop. Besides, so much depends on my keeping at it ... I remember, when I first came to London, I was full of schemes ... I was eager, restless, ambitious ... and I determined to forge ahead ...But was it worth while? Does it bring a man happiness? And yet I don't know. If I had failed, I should have been utterly miserable; I think I should have gone mad.

Pilken was a Nonconformist, had taught in a Sunday school in his home town of Braytown, and had intended to marry a fellow Nonconformist Sunday school teacher. On coming to London and achieving success he had dropped his Nonconformity, as it 'was not the fashion' and had found a wife from among the aristocracy. The marriage was not a success and there were no children.

I determined to be among what was called the aristocracy, and so I married my wife. I thought it would sound well to be able to say that Lord Lessing was my father-in-law, and he was glad to have me for a son-in-law – at a price. And I paid that price. My wife consented to be the wife of a rich man, but of course she never loved me. It is so bourgeoise for the daughter of a peer to be in love with her husband. And now where am I? Yes, I have my house in Berkeley Square and my country places, but I'm loveless and childless – and that is success!

Pilken's wealth and power had brought him nothing but unhappiness among the trappings of success, but that was not evident to the outside world. This appeared to be the general verdict of the City itself at this time, as the rest of the novel reveals.

One of those so impressed by the career of Sir William Pilken that he decided to emulate him was George Tremain, a young country solicitor in St Tidy in Cornwall. He felt there was nothing for someone of his talents and ability in Cornwall, even though his family, who were Quakers, had lived there for generations. This was all inspired by a chance meeting one evening with some men from London, who spoke about the opportunities that were open there to someone with his talents. The next morning he told his father, for whom he worked, that, 'After dinner at Mr. Terefry's, those London men were speaking of the fortunes which had been made in London. They told of poor lads who came there a few years ago, who are now leaders in finance, and law, and politics. They could never have done anything in the country. What happens here?' His father advised him to think carefully about such a move as numerous people went to London and failed. Nevertheless, George's father agreed that he could go to London as the representative of their firm. In London George soon realized how difficult it was to generate any business as he was both unknown and without connections. He complained that London 'is a great octopus, stretching out its tentacles everywhere. It has no pity, no mercy. It paralyses weak men; it takes hope out of the strongest'. Unable to establish a successful legal practice in London, George switched to finance, with the deliberate intention of emulating Sir William Pilken, having read a recent biography of him. Again he met with exactly the same problems until he called upon old Quaker friends of his father, John and William Caske, with a proposal for a new property development. They had an office near Austin Friars, in the City, from which they conducted a safe and respectable financial business, as John told George 'Neither my nor I are men who engage in risky speculations. For that reason – and I say with pride – our names have weight in this great city. Our money, such as it is, is clean money ...we do not speculate'. George was of a different view. 'Everything would stagnate but for speculation ... Every new newspaper, every new hotel, every new enterprise whatsoever, is in the nature of speculation'. They did not deny that but considered there were different types of speculation and they considered the scheme that George wanted them to become involved with as highly speculative. They advised George to stick to law and safe business, and promised to help him if he did, adding that he should start attending the Friends meeting house, if he wanted to make further contacts.

Despite the setback George was determined to persevere in London as he did not want to return home a failure, even though he had left behind in Cornwall a girlfriend, Mary Trefry. He went to explore the City so as to get a sense of what it offered.

> Presently he stood in front of the Royal Exchange and watched the great throng of men and women. He knew that he stood at the financial centre of the great British Empire. Within a few yards from where he stood, fortunes were made and lost in a day. Here, too, many of the great projects of the world were determined, and men, who a few years ago as were poor and unknown as he, could, by a stroke of the pen, make or mar the fortunes of thousands. Close to him was the Bank of England, a few yards away was the Stock Exchange, just across the way was the Mansion House, while within the circle of a few hundreds of yards the business of the world was influenced if not largely controlled. He realized it all, and his heart throbbed madly at the thought of it. But he took no part in it all. He was outside the charmed circle.

Gradually his business as a solicitor picked up as clients consulted him. One of those clients led to a contact with Quill and Steel, 'one of the best-known firms of solicitors in London'. They acted for members of the Stock Exchange and joint stock companies. 'There were some who said that their business was not of the kind which old-fashioned lawyers boast about'. George decided to approach them with his scheme. 'Those old Quakers would not touch it because they are old-fashioned and do their business in an old-fashioned way, but I believe there are possibilities in it. I believe it is sound, too. It only wants capital and enterprise and brains'. The scheme that George had in mind was a property development on the outskirts of London. It was on a piece of land near the sea and involved housing, a hotel, a golf-course, and a fifteen-mile stretch of railway. Quill and Steel also turned it down as too risky. 'Even with the most skilful advertisements, and the most rosy prospectus, it would take at least ten years to make the thing pay'. In their opinion it was the type of development that a railway company undertook, not private investors, as they looked for excitement and the promise of large gains rather than a solid business.[10]

The turning point in George's City career came with a chance encounter with Arthur Ackroyd. He had recently arrived from South Africa, where his parents, originally from Yorkshire, had settled before he was born. What took him to London were the very rich gold deposits on the land he farmed. He told George, 'we feel, even out in South Africa, that London is the centre of everything... South African mines are worked from London. There's wealth in Africa, wealth untold, but English money has to be put into Africa in order to get it'. He was worried that he would be swindled by London financiers because that had happened to others, and so was looking for someone he could trust. George befriended Arthur and agreed to try and get the mine floated as a company in return for a quarter of any money that they got. He explained to Arthur that many in the City were equally suspicious of those who arrived claiming to have discovered a valuable gold deposit.

London financiers are very chary. More than one has been bitten by people who have come claiming to have discovered gold mines. Either the mines have been 'salted', or the 'pockets' have turned out to be next to worthless. As a consequence, they will hardly give a hearing to the men who come with tales of discovery.

What Arthur offered to do was to use the connections he had developed in the year he had been in London to get a hearing for Arthur and his mine:

> if I convince them that the thing is worth while, and they cable to a mining expert, he will immediately proceed to the spot, and after examination he will send his report. If that report is satisfactory, we can make our terms'. Arthur wanted to know where the money to develop the mine was coming from, so George explained. 'When the people I have in my mind are convinced that the thing is genuine – and, of course, I am assuming that it is genuine – they will set to work to form a company. Having secured a number of suitable people, we draw up a prospectus, which we shall send out to the people who invest. Then we must get hold of the financial papers and advertise with them. In return for this they will write up the venture.

This reflected a considerable maturity in the way that the City was now viewed in comparison with how it was viewed in the mid-1890s.

George used his connections with John and Michael Caske to approach Sir William Pilken about taking up the mining project. As the Caske Brothers were respected merchants in the City Pilken listened to them and granted George an interview. They were not happy about being used in this way but did it because George was a fellow Quaker and they knew and respected his father. Pilken agreed to consider the scheme that George and Arthur put in front of him. Sir William immediately cabled a reputable mining expert, a Mr Trevose, to undertake a survey of the mine. Trevose was a reputable man unlike many others in South Africa 'whose report could have been bought'. When the report came it was a positive one and so a company was formed, the Bilberry Creek Gold Mine. One of the directors was the Marquis of Dresden, a penniless peer with heavily mortgaged estates. Though 'he had no capital to invest and was utterly ignorant of business matters ... he was the owner of a good old name, and he had a seat in the House of Lords'. Even in the case of an entirely reputable South African gold mine, resort was made to the use of figureheads in order to persuade investors to buy the shares being issued. When his mining company proved a success George returned home for a visit. By then he had become so impressed by London, compared to Cornwall, telling Mary Trefry. 'Down here one has no idea of the great surging life of London and of the other great cities. You see, it is from London that the empire, yes, and, in spite of what other countries say, the world is ruled'.[11] On his return to London George found himself in demand as a company promoter because of the way he had handled the South African mining business.

> The rapid success of George Tremain in the world of finance is the talk of City men even to this day. His was one of those phenomenal flights, which happen only rarely, but which always arouse the wonder, the admiration, and the envy of those who stand and watch. Within a few months ... George was a prominent figure in the heart of the financial world. He was associated with many of the great money schemes of the time, and everything he touched succeeded'. This success came through a combination of ability and hard work. 'He found that the claims of his many enterprises were constant and exacting, and he determined that nothing should fail to succeed for want of personal attention on his part. From early morning to late at night he toiled, taking little or no interest in anything save business.

As a result he became immensely rich and established himself as a highly successful financier in the City of London, though many considered him 'a mere company promoter – a mere speculator'. Even he had moments of self doubt, thinking of himself as 'a clever juggler with finance'. Beyond that he was aware that 'The men with whom he had become daily associated were mere money-making machines. They lived for money. Everything was seen through the eyes of the financier'. Though his wealth and success brought him many admirers and invitations to social events, he socialized little, recognizing that the way he had made his money denied him access to the highest social circles. 'He realized that, in spite of his success, he was regarded in certain circles as an outsider. The magic doors of the world's elite were closed to him, and he could only open them by marrying a woman of high position. Money might do a great deal, but it could not do everything'. He thus decided to abandon his courtship of Mary Trefry and cultivate Winifred Dresden instead.

> Old Dresden may be practically a pauper, but he has influences in circles which are closed to me. He has political influence, social influence. Unless I marry – in the right quarters, no matter how wealthy I may become, I shall be regarded as a parvenu, an upstart – a – a somewhat of a bounder. On the other hand, if I went into Parliament as the son-in-law of the Marquis of Dresden, nothing would be impossible to me.

Such a match also appealed to Winifred as she was the daughter of 'A penniless peer' and had 'been in the marriage market for years'. She said of herself, 'I can't afford to marry for love, and those who could afford to buy me – well, they don't feel inclined'. Winifred exhibited no affection towards George and 'was constantly galled with the thought that she was looked upon by her acquaintances as one who was marrying a parvenu because of his money, that she was the price which her father was paying in order to have his debts paid. This thought had kept her from consenting to an early marriage, and it made her somewhat ungracious to George himself'. She therefore entered into the arrangement in a rather detached way. Lady Clare Maurice, who had befriended George when he first came to London, told him that he was making a mistake when the engagement was announced.

You don't love the woman you have asked to marry you. You are not marrying a wife; you are marrying a name, a position, you are marrying at the bidding of miserable ambition. She would tell her footman to show you the door but for your money, and you would as think of marrying an iceberg but for her name and position. You are buying an entrance into a poor, miserable, empty world by paying a spendthrift's debts; you are making a mock of all the most beautiful things in the world, you are throwing away the crown of life.

The Marquis of Dresden only gave permission for the marriage because George offered to pay his debts and switch his political allegiance. He looked down upon George because he 'was not of his own class, he was a parvenu, and although he received him into his house as a social equal, he could not help recollecting that he would not have done so from choice. It was only necessity which had compelled him to admit this commoner into the bosom of his family'. The Marquis was determined that Winifred would marry for money, so as to save the family name and estate, and if not to George then to an American called Skinner, whose father was immensely rich. All that mattered was that George would settle a large fortune on his daughter and pay off the family's debts, and this was well understood by Pilken, who had gone through the same process in the past with disastrous personal consequences. 'While Tremain is making money, they toady to him; but let him lose it – then he may become a beggar for all they care'. Pilken told Dresden exactly what he thought of him.

> Men of your class are friendly to such as I while it pays you. You come to me now with flattering words, because you think I can help you. If by chance I lost my money, it would be no more "My dear Pilken" this, and "My dear Pilken" that. You wouldn't know me. It's the same with Tremain. While he was spoken of as the young Napoleon of finance, you went around saying that his engagement with your daughter was purely a love-match, and now that there is talk about the young Napoleon being sent to St. Helena, you –'
> 'But what can I do?' said the other. 'Don't you see my position? I daren't allow Winifred to marry a poor man. Think of my financial position. I-I tell you I've been building a good deal on this, and my case is serious .

A marriage of this kind was a complex bargain involving both sacrifice and gain for both parties rather than a simple conquest of the new men of finance by the old landed families or the reverse. Each side brought something to the arrangement, each expected to profit from it, and each expected to lose by it.[12]

This marriage never took place, being postponed for various reasons, one being a lack of interest on Winifred's part. More important was the Marquis's concern that the fortune possessed by George, 'the Napoleon of finance', was not well secured. Rumours started to circulate that George's schemes were proving less successful than in the past and the Marquis of Dresden had picked up on these.

Although he professed to have no knowledge of business himself, he spent a great deal of time studying financial questions. Moreover, he made a special point of being friendly with well-known financiers, and it was immediately after a long conversation with a German Jew, Klein by name, that he spoke of a possible delay to the wedding. After this he was often seen in the City of London, wearing an anxious look. Presently there were hints in financial circles that 'Young Napoleon's schemes were not doing very well, and men watched George Tremain's face with a great deal of curiosity. After this it was rumoured that 'young Midas was not invulnerable, after all'.

Dresden was worried that George would suffer the same fate as Blacketer-Whitten who had risen almost as quickly and owned a number of estates, but then failed and shot himself. Here was a clear reference to the real case of Whitaker Wright, which still resonated a decade later. As it was, George had lost £30,000 in an Argentine scheme and was now trying to recover his position in another that was not entirely legitimate.

Enticing prospectuses had been issued concerning it, and many influential names had been printed on those same prospectuses, but in order to carry the scheme through he had to consent to things which he had no desire for the world to know. There was nothing absolutely dishonest about it, nothing that could be called a violation of British law, although even his co-directors smiled meaningly, and hinted that they were sailing close to the wind.

Dresden was aware of this having been told by an elderly Jewish financier, Aaron Zimmerman, that George had

a pig thing on now ... It is vun of the piggest and cleverest things I ever heard of. If he pulls it through, he will make a mint of moneys. And he have done it so cleverly, too. I tink he stands to gain, whoever loses ... he is a speculator, and speculators haf always a bad name. but what then? it is pizzness, and people forget and forgif if he make a million ... He is clever enough for anything. Besides, he haf need to make this thing a success. He haf been badly hit, and he must make a big haul, or he go under. But he haf done well. He haf got some of the best names in England to back him, and I think he go through.

George was staking everything on this one scheme in the hope that it would restore his fortune. 'It was a gambler's chance, and he staked everything upon it ... if he succeeds he will be another Rothschild' was Dresden's opinion, but until the success was assured he would not allow the marriage to proceed. If he failed they would abandon him. When rumours about problems with this new scheme started to surface George was approached by Felix Lazarus.

a short dark man ... It was evident to the most casual observer that Mr. Lazarus' name did not belie his race. He was a Jew of the most pronounced order. He was expensively dressed. His fur-lined coat was very costly. His hat had evidently been newly ironed. He wore a heavy gold chain, while several costly diamond rings bedecked his thick chubby fingers.

He edited an influential newspaper, which was 'financed by the less respectable portion of the Semitic community' and privately circulated among City people. In return for £2,000 he would produce an article enthusiastically supporting the proposed scheme. If not he would produce one damning it. With considerable misgivings George agreed to pay. What emerges from this is a continuing anti-Semitic undertone to the prevailing prejudices against the City of London. The City was seen to be a place where Jews were a large and powerful group and used their knowledge and influence for their own advantage, whatever the cost to others. It was also recognized that differences between individual Jews existed. As George told Pilken,

> Personally I have no prejudice against Jews ... I know several who are among the straightest men in London. It has become the thing to malign them, but speaking as I find, they are quite as honourable as – other people. Of course, there are two classes among them; the desirable ones and, and the other sort.

Pilken's reply was less magnanimous. 'You may be right about Jews; there are doubtless many straight, honourable men among them; but there's nothing under heaven worse than the shady members of the Semite race'.[13]

This payment for favourable reports about the scheme backfired.

> It was believed that he [George] had paid a huge sum for certain articles that had appeared, and it had not added to his reputation as an honourable financier. Besides, as the things which had been lauded to the skies had not turned out successfully, a good many unpleasant remarks had been made. Of course, George had become pretty well hardened to the gossip in the City, and was, therefore, less influenced by it than he had been in the earlier stages of his career, but he was still sensitive to sneers, especially when those same sneers contained an element of truth.
>
> On the surface all still appeared to be going well for George, as any visitor to his office in the City could observe. 'Whatever might be the gossip in business circles, there was no appearance of failure or distress here. Prosperity seemed to abound everywhere. The fittings of the offices were rich and solid, clerks were busily engaged at their various desks, the click of typewriters was constantly heard, and everything suggested prosperity ... The young man who had come to London only a few years before, unknown and poor, was now a tremendous power ... One man after another sought audience with him, gave their reports and asked for his guidance, but in no instance did he seem flurried or dismayed. He seemed to see into the heart of a situation in an instant, and his judgements were quick and far-reaching. Everything appeared to be governed with the regularity and precision of clockwork. Nothing seemed to disturb him. More than once, while in the midst of dictating important letters, the telephone bell at his side would ring, but his conversation on the telephone, no matter how important, never seemed to break the thread of his thoughts; he would return to the letter as though he were undisturbed.

Beneath the surface the situation was different. The very people who had profited from his earlier schemes were now avoiding him, while his rivals in the City
were trying to destroy him. He was now vulnerable because of his financial losses
and the undermining of his reputation as a man who could be trusted. 'What
financier in London can afford to have all his affairs brought before a court of
law?' Though Lazarus liked George and wanted to help him, he could not as
he was being paid by a rival to print unfavourable reports about George and his
latest scheme. Unless George would help him financially, so as to free himself
from his rival, Lazarus would have to continue to print such stories, whether
true or false. What this indicated was the cut-throat nature of business in the
City, with a financier in trouble being deserted by associates and undermined by
rivals using all means available, whether fair or foul. This was hardly an arena for
gentleman capitalists. Faced with such a situation George

> was utterly disillusioned now about the sweets of riches. Of course, he still longed to
> be rich, still longed for all that money could buy – but what was it all worth when he
> had to buy the silence and buy the praise of men like Mr. Lazarus. For that was what
> it meant. His life as a speculator, a company promoter, had laid him open to all sorts
> of terrors, of which blackmail was not the worst.

He concluded success in the City left no room for either moral scruples or Christian ethics.

Tormented by these thoughts George refused to give in to blackmail this time
and allowed the damaging article to appear in Lazarus's newspaper. The effect
was immediate as people's attitude towards him changed, including his own staff.
'Clerks looked at him in a questioning, frightened way; his secretary was anxious
and flurried'. The article also made George reflect upon what he had been doing.
'I've boasted that I've been an honest financier, and I've never put myself within
the power of the law. But is any speculator honest? Have I not been trading on
credulity and ignorance ... I have lost my soul'. When the rumours about him
reached Cornwall his parents immediately came up to London to question him
about the truth of the newspaper stories that described him as 'a cruel, pitiless,
self-seeking Midas, robbing orphans, cheating widows, and thinking only of
your own gain'. In the wake of these rumours the scheme he was mastermind-
ing collapsed, ruining a number of its most prominent backers, including Lord
Densdale, though leaving George a rich man. 'I was clever enough to get out of
the thing before the crash came'. However, he decided to use his wealth to save
these people though it left him with nothing. He told Winifred and his father
of his intentions and they could not believe it. It ended his engagement with
Winifred as he no longer had the fortune that alone made the marriage possible.
When it emerged what he had done all London was amazed. 'Some called him
a fool, with a very strong adjective attached to it; others laughed scornfully, and

wondered what other schemes he had in his mind; while many more spoke of it as the most Quixotic and yet the most honourable act that London had witnessed for many years'. Though Pilken offered George a partnership, he decided he had had enough of London and finance. He had rediscovered his Quaker faith and realized that it was incompatible with the life he had been leading in London. This made him glad that he had lost all the money he had made there and could leave without a stain on his character. He returned to Cornwall, took over his father's legal practice, and married Mary Trefry.[14] Whatever success might be found in the City, even by respectable people, it was forever tainted by being associated with speculation and company promotion. This was despite the fact that success in the City brought great rewards that were not simply material but could include a knighthood or better, as Arnold Bennett suggested in a novel published in 1913, *The Regent*.[15] Nevertheless, to many Christianity and the City were incompatible, leaving the field clear for either the unscrupulous or the Jews. There were openings in the City for Christians, but only as long as they confined themselves to particular types of business, such as trade, and conducted it according to honest principles.

Reflecting the fact that the City was now such an established feature of British life E. Phillips Oppenheim produced not one but two novels in 1912 that featured it prominently. One was *Havoc*, which combined the City with a tale of international espionage. Stephen Laverick and Alfred Morrison were partners in a small firm of City stockbrokers, Laverick and Morrison, with an office in Old Broad Street. Laverick was 'wholly British' whereas Morrison was 'a Jew to his finger-tips, notwithstanding his altered name'. The firm was facing ruin having lost £40,000 in a month, due to speculation undertaken by Morrison. Laverick was bearing up but Morrison was a broken man. The firm had to find £25,000 by the following morning but had less than £1,000 to hand, nothing left in the bank, and no more credit to call upon. Laverick refused to borrow from friends in case he could not pay it back, though under pressure from Morrison to do so.

> 'Have you ever thought what it will be like, Laverick, to be hammered?'
> 'I have', Laverick admitted wearily, 'God knows it seems as terrible a thing to me as it can to you! But if we go down, we must go down with clean hands. I've no faith in your infernal market, and not one penny will I borrow from a friend'. The Jew's face was almost piteous. He stretched himself across the table. There were genuine tears in his eyes. 'Laverick', he said, 'old man, you're wrong. I know you think I've been led away. I've taken you out of our depth, but the only trouble has been that we haven't had enough capital, and no backing. Those who stand up will win. They will make money'.

The bank had refused to extend them further credit and none of Morrison's friends in the Stock Exchange were the type to lend each other money. Laverick had friends on the Stock Exchange who would lend him money but he would not ask.

> Laverick said nothing. Words were useless things, wasted upon such a creature. He eyed his partner with a contempt which he took no pains to conceal. This, then, was the smart young fellow recommended to him on all sides a few years ago, as one of the shrewdest young men in his own particular department, a person bound to succeed, a money-maker if ever there was one! Laverick thought of him as he appeared at the office day by day, glossy and immaculately dressed, with a flower in his buttonhole, boots that were a trifle too shiny, hat and coat, gloves and manner, all imitation but all very near the real thing. What a collapse! 'You're going to stay and see it through?' he whined across the table. 'Certainly', Laverick replied. The young man buried his face in his hands. 'I can't! I can't!' he moaned. 'I couldn't bear seeing all the fellows, hearing them whisper things – oh, Lord! Oh Lord! ... Laverick, we've a few hundreds left. Give me something and let me out of it. You're a stronger sort of man than I am. You can face it – I can't! Give me enough to get abroad with, and if ever I do any good I'll remember it, I will indeed'.

Laverick gave Morrison £250 and told him to go, suggesting South Africa as a good choice, but he was determined to stay and face the consequences of financial ruin and social disgrace.

After he had finished putting the firm's affairs in order Laverick went out into the City. 'There is no place in London so strangely quiet as the narrow thoroughfares of the City proper as the hour grows toward midnight'. As he walked between Crooked Friars and Royal Street he came across 'a passage, almost a tunnel for a few yards, leading to an open space, on one side of which was a churchyard – strange survival in such a part – and on the other the offices of several firms of stockbrokers, a Russian banker and an actuary'. This was 'a region of great banks and the offices of merchant princes' and not a 'quarter ... frequented by the criminal classes'. Nevertheless, in that dark passage Laverick came across the body of a man. In looking for identification he discovered a package containing documents and £20,000 in cash. Faced with the failure of his firm he took the money and returned to his office. Even a person as honourable as Laverick could be tempted to rob a dead man in order to save himself from ruin.

> He told himself that the thing which he had done was for the best. He owed it to himself. He owed it to those who had trusted him. After all, it was the chief part of his life – his City career. It was here that his friends lived. It was here that his ambitions flourished. Disgrace here was eternal disgrace. His father and his grandfather before him had been men honoured and respected in this same circle. Disgrace to him, such disgrace as that with which he had stood face to face a few hours ago, would have been, in a certain sense, a reflection upon their memories. The names upon the brass plates to right and to left of him were the names of men he knew, men with whom he desired to stand well, whose friendship or whose contempt made life worth living or the reverse. It was worth a great risk – this effort of his to keep his place. His one

mistake – this association with Morrison – had been such an unparalleled stroke of bad luck. He was rid of the fellow now. For the future there would be no more partners. He had his life to live. It was not reasonable that he should allow himself to be dragged down into the mire by such a creature.

Such were his thoughts as he walked from his office to Queen Victoria Street to hail a cab to take him home.

Failure to honour his bargains, even to a man such as Laverick, with a family name unsullied by scandal, meant the end of his business in the City for those were the rules he operated under. He revealed this to a friend David Bellamy, who operated as a British spy.

> 'My grandfather lived and died a member of the Stock Exchange, honoured and well thought of. My father followed in his footsteps. I, too, was there. Without becoming wealthy, the name I bear has become known and respected. Failure, whatever one may say, means a broken life and a broken honour. I sat in my office, and I knew that the use of those notes for a few days might save me from disgrace, might keep the name which my father and grandfather had guarded so jealously free from shame. I would have paid any price for the use of them. I would have paid with my life, if that had been possible'.

Laverick had to provide £20,000 to take up the shares that Morrison had agreed to purchase but had expected to sell when the price rose. Unfortunately, the price had fallen steadily forcing them to find extra money to make good the difference between what they could borrow on the shares from the bank and the price they had agreed to pay. By depositing in the bank the £20,000 he had got from the dead man Laverick was able to make good the difference between what he had to pay and what he could borrow. Shortly after meeting his engagements the shares that Morrison had speculated in, 'Unions', started to rise. Morrison's instinct was right but his timing wrong. By the end of the day there would have been no need for Laverick to borrow to cover his position, such had been the rise in price. Laverick, unlike Morrison, did not speculate on his own account, confining himself to the safe business of advising clients about their investments, as in the case of the international opera singer, Mademoiselle Louise Idaile. She came to see him in his office in the City.

> 'I know that here in the city you are very busy making money all the time, so I must not stay long. Will you buy me some stocks, some good safe stocks, which will bring me in at least four per cent.?'
>
> 'I can promise to do that,' Laverick answered. 'Have you any choice?'
>
> 'No, I have no choice', Louise told him. 'I bring with me a cheque – see I give it to you – it is for six thousand pounds. I would like to buy some stocks with this and to know the names so that I may watch them in the paper. I like to see whether they go up or down, but I do not wish to risk their going down too much. It is something like gambling but it is no trouble'.

Due to a wise choice of stocks the portfolio was showing a profit of nearly £1,600 within a few weeks. This revealed both sides of stockbroking as it covered both speculating on the rise and fall of individual shares for a quick profit and the need for investors to achieve a reasonable and relatively safe return, which could only be achieved through holding a well-selected portfolio of securities chosen with professional advice.[16] From this tale emerges a side of the City that was safe, necessary and respectable as well as another that was risky, unnecessary and disreputable. The former was undertaken by English people with a good pedigree and a strict code of conduct whereas the former was the preserve of Jews who had changed their name to hide their identity and who would stoop at nothing to make money or escape retribution.

The fact that strongly divergent views on the City were held by contemporaries is also represented in E. Phillips Oppenheim's other 1912 novel, *A Millionaire of Yesterday*. This charted the rise of Scarlet Trent.

> My father was a carpenter who drank himself to death, and my mother was a factory girl. I was in the workhouse when I was a boy. I have never been to school. I don't know how to talk properly, and I should be worse even than I am, if I had not to mix up with a lot of men in the City who had been properly educated. I am utterly and miserably ignorant. I've got low tastes and lots of 'em.

In order to make his fortune he went to Africa where he lived a rough and dangerous life but returned to England with a concession to mine gold, which he had obtained from a native chief. He sold a share in this concession to a City mining syndicate, who were to finance the development of the gold mine and then float a company called the Beckwando Land and Mining Company. This was no instant success but he profited due to his skill and perseverance.

> For years the narrow alleys, the thronged streets, the great buildings of the City had known him day by day, almost hour by hour. Its roar and clamour, the strife of tongues and keen measuring of wits had been the salt of his life. Steadily, sturdily, almost insolently, he had thrust his way through to the front ranks.

He also had to survive problems in Africa as the mine was developed, as well as an attempt by an estranged partner, Hiram Da Souza, to destroy him by throwing all the shares he owned on the market. 'Trent, with his back against the wall and not a friend to help him, faced for twenty-four hours the most powerful bull syndicate which had ever been formed against a single company'. Trent was forced to borrow money to buy the shares in order to maintain the confidence of his backers, using a loan from the bank. Then Da Souza, who was a Jewish financier in the City, persuaded the bank to call in its loan of £119,000 despite being secured on shares worth £150,000. Trent managed to replace that loan but only by using all the money at his disposal, while he had also agreed to buy a large number of shares on account, which could have bankrupted him as he had no means of paying for them. Salvation came in the shape of a cable from West Africa which announced 'a great find of gold before ever a shaft had been sunk'. The result was that the shares shot up in value allowing Trent to sell out at a profit of £100,000 instead of facing bankruptcy. He emerged as the great saviour of the company both in the City and in Africa, being hailed by the newspapers as an 'empire-maker and a millionaire'.

With the wealth that his fortune from mining brought, Trent became a great social success with invitations to numerous country houses, though he was only too aware that this acceptance was dependent upon his money. 'He knew very well that it was his wealth, and his wealth only, which had brought him as an equal amongst these people, all, so far as education and social breeding was concerned, of so entirely a different sphere'. He had only acquired 'the veneer of a City speculator' for beneath it all he remained 'a Gold Coast buccaneer'. He was also aware how fickle was City wealth and thus the status it brought. 'A Company like the Beckwando Company is very much like a woman's reputation, drop a hint or two, start just a bit of talk, and I'll tell you the flames'll soon do the work'. His wealth allowed him to purchase a country estate, build a palace in Park Lane, own racehorses, and marry the granddaughter of an earl. What came across was the power of the City of London to make and unmake those from a humble background through the rapid accumulation of enormous wealth. 'A few years ago he [Trent] had landed in England friendless and unknown, to-day he had stepped out from even amongst the chosen few and had planted his feet in the higher lands whither the faces of all men are turned'. The City of London was a place where those with drive, determination and ability could succeed despite the opposition of the established order. Conversely, it was also the location of the 'courts and alleys of the money-changers' market'. Scarlet Trent could be admired as the man who got his woman and made his fortune, but he was the exception within the City. In contrast to the rest of those in the City, Trent remained a decent and honourable man, despite all he had done in his life.

> His had not been the victory of honied falsehoods, of suave deceit, of gentle but legalised robbery. He had been a hard worker, a daring speculator with nerves of iron, and courage which would have glorified a nobler cause. Nor had his been the methods of good fellowship, the sharing of 'good turns', the camaraderie of finance. The men with whom he had large dealings he had treated as enemies rather than friends, ever watching them covertly with close but unslackening vigilance.

Though Trent had been successful in the City he despised both the methods he had used and the people he had dealings with. He described his activities in the City as 'a life of lies and gambling and deceit ... You're never quite dishonest, and you're never quite honest. You come out on top, and afterwards you hate yourself. It's a dirty little life'.

For all the power the City possessed to make people wealthy it also corrupted them in the process. 'With the handling of great sums of money and the acquisition of wealth, had grown something of the financier's fever'. In contrast to other financiers, Trent was aware of how the City was changing him.

> He had started life as a workman, with a few ambitions all of a material nature – he had lived the life of a cold, scheming money getter, absolutely selfish, negatively moral, doing little evil perhaps, but less good ... All the wealth of Africa could never make him anything different from what he was ... Already he was weary of financial warfare – the City life palled upon him.

He wanted out but also wanted the wealth that only the City could bring him. 'I would shut up my office to-morrow, sell out, and live upon a farm. But I've got to keep what I've made. The more you succeed the more involved you become. It's a sort of slavery'. Once his fortune was secured through the success of the Beckwando Land and Mining Company, Scarlet Trent left the City. In the words of his wife-to-be, Ernestine Wendermott, 'You can't enjoy money alone! You want to race, hunt, entertain, shoot, join in the revels of country houses!' To emphasize how different Trent was the contrast was made with another City financier, Hiram Da Souza, who was 'coarse and large', being both foreign and Jewish. He had been 'a City man all my life, and I know a thing or two'. He was a man who would stop at nothing to achieve success in the City, including lies, blackmail and deception. Fitting his character was the office he had in the City, which was located near Lothbury. 'It was in a back street off an alley ... A blank wall faced it, a greengrocer's shop shared with a wonderful, cellar-like public house the honour of its more immediate environment'. Within was Da Souza's own office which 'was barely furnished, and a window, thick with dust, looked out on the dingy back-door of a bank or some public building. The floor was uncovered, the walls were hung with the yellow maps of gold-mines all in the West African district'. This was the authentic face of a company promoter and mining financier in the City of London, not that of Scarlet Trent.[17] As such it suggests a continuing suspicion of everything connected to the City along with an acceptance that exceptions did exist, though they did not extend to Jews or foreigners.

Certainly the influence of Jews and foreigners on the City's financial operations was widely recognized at this time, as in Gilbert Parker's 1913 novel, *The Judgement House*. It was City-based financiers who ran the mining operations in South Africa, and had made themselves rich by doing so. In turn they exerted influence upon the British government so that it adopted policies in South Africa favourable to them, despite the risks that a war with the Boer republics would lead to one with Germany. Among them was Wallstein, who was described as the fairest, ablest, and richest financier of them all, with a marvellous head for figures; and invaluable and commanding at the council-board, by virtue of his clear brain and his power to co-ordinate all the elements of the most confusing financial problems. Others had by luck and persistence made money - the basis of their fortunes; but Wallstein had showed them how to save those fortunes and make them grow; had enabled them to compete successfully with the games of other great financiers in the world's stock markets ... Wallstein knew little and cared less about politics; yet he saw the use of politics in finance, and he did not stick his head into the sand as some of his colleagues did when political activities hampered their operations.

The fact that Wallstein was German led him to be vilified by the press as 'the Jew Mining magnate, who didn't care a damn what happened to England so long as his own nest was well lined'. Though 'He was spoken of as a cruel, tyrannical, greedy German Jew, whose soul was in his own pocket and his hand in the pockets of the world. In truth he was none of these things, save he was of German birth'. In addition to Wallstein was Fleming, 'a dour but financially able Scot', and De Lancy Scovel who acted for Rhodes but had built up a personal fortune of £1 million in the process, which allowed him to buy an estate in Leicestershire. Another was Barry Whalen, an Irishman who had trained as a doctor and Clifford Melville, whose name was originally Joseph Sobieski, from Poland. Finally there was Rudyard Byng, who had amassed a fortune of £4 million from promoting South African gold-mining companies in London. This had allowed him to build a grand but rather vulgar house in London and buy an estate in Wales, Glencader Castle. When he entertained on a lavish scale members of the aristocracy were glad to accept his invitation because of both the free food and drink available and the share tips they might pick up.

What united this disparate group of financiers was their common 'instinct for money-making'. This was resented by the likes of Ian Stafford, whose grandfather had been a Duke. He was unhappy that 'Wealth was more and more the master of England ... new- made wealth; and some of it was too ostentatious and too pretentious to condone, much less indulge'. These new men of money were compared to 'gold as yet not worn smooth by handling, the staring, brand-new sovereigns looking like impostors'. However, it was these nouveaux riche who were now dominant. 'Men who had made their money where copper or gold or oil or wool or silver or cattle or railways made commercial kings, ...'. In contrast there were the real people, such as 'the land-poor peer, with his sense of responsibility', the professional man, and the little merchant. Symbolizing the transformation was the fact that Stafford had lost his fiancée to Rudyard Byng. Nevertheless, both the City financiers and landed aristocrats, such as Stafford, found themselves on the same side at the time of the Boer war as they saw their interests and those of the British Empire in South Africa as being identical. In contrast, those who opposed them, like Adrian Fellowes, were driven by personal animosity. Fellowes hated Rudyard Byng because he had been ruined through speculating in the shares of one of the mining companies that Byng had promoted. It was he that eventually betrayed their plans to the Boers, leading to the outbreak of war. Both Ian Stafford and Rudyard Byng volunteered to fight in South Africa once war was declared. Stafford was killed but Byng survived.[18]

On the eve of the First World War the City was increasingly seen as at the centre of a web of international finance involving people from all over the world and investments on a global scale. That was definitely the case with South African mining finance but it also extended into other fields, as in the novel *Swirling Waters,* by Max Rittenberg, that came out in 1913. This described a cosmopolitan world of high finance including Paris and New York and involved both a Canadian and an American, which revolved around London. 'The clerk who lives out his life in the rabbit-warren of the City of London by day, and in a cheap, pretentious, red-brick suburb by night, believes firmly that outside London not much matters'. There were even contrasting personalities with one financier being more interested in science than money while the other was a ruthless man of business who cared little for people. The former was Clifford Matheson, who had been born in Canada and began as a stockbroker's clerk in Montreal but was now a successful financier operating in both Paris and London. Though regarded as an honest financier 'Matheson had been associated with other schemes which had a bad odour in the nostrils of City men'. One was the Saskatchewan Land Development Co. 'The company was a moderately successful one, but in its early days the shares had been "rigged" to an unreal figure'. As a result many speculators lost money when they sold out while long-term investors got a moderate return. It was considered that speculators had only themselves to blame. As a result of his financial success Matheson had married the daughter of Sir Francis Letchmere, a country landowner and company director, who was very pleased when his daughter married a City financier.

> Five years ago he had married into a well-known English family, and the doors of society had been opened wide to him. But this marriage had been a ghastly mistake. Olive, after marriage, had showed herself entirely out of sympathy with the idealism that formed so large a part of the complex character of her husband. She wanted money and power, and drove spurs into her husband that he might obtain for her more and more money. Any other ambition in Clifford she tried to sneer down with the ruthlessness of an utterly mercenary woman.

In a strange reversal, it was the wife from a landed background who lusted after money and power, whereas Matheson wanted to devote his life to medical research. The result was a loveless and childless marriage, in which Matheson became disenchanted with the world of finance despite his success.

The latter was Lars Larssen, who was obsessed with money. He was the son of Scandinavian immigrants to the USA and, having entered a shipbroker's office, he had made a fortune through shipping re-insurance and then as a shipowner. 'He would allow nothing to stand in his path. Scruples were to him the burden of fools'. He had a large and well-equipped office in Leadenhall Street, in the City, as well as another in Paris and New York. The London office dealt with shipping, keeping in touch with his fleet through the wireless. Both men were combining to promote a company, Hudson Bay Transport, Ltd., that would build a 5000-mile railway from the interior of Canada to Hudson Bay at a cost of £5 million. There a port would be built that would take wheat to Europe via Larssen's shipping line. The company would be controlled by Larssen, though most of the money required would come from the public, which was where Matheson came in. Matheson was to be chairman of the company with his father-in-law, Sir Francis Lechmere, on the board of the company along with Lord St Aubyn, a director of The London and United Kingdom Bank, and Gervase Lowndes Hawley Carleton-Wingate MP, both of whom were personal friends. Lars Larssen was to be managing director. Nevertheless, Matheson was worried the scheme would fail because of 'Stock Exchange "wreckers"'. In the end Matheson blocked the Hudson Bay scheme because he believed that Larssen was trying to dupe the public. He then abandoned his City career after his wife, who had become a morphine addict, died, and chose, instead, to devote himself to science assisted by a partially sighted new wife who had a background in art and design. In contrast, Larssen did not accept defeat and moved onto other financial projects.[19]

By this date even the company promoter in the City had become respectable, ranging from the ruthless tycoon to the well-meaning philanthropist. This can be seen in Algernon Blackwood's *A Prisoner in Fairyland,* which appeared in 1913. Henry Rogers, having been brought up in Bromley, in Kent, had made a fortune in the City by the time he was 40, through 'Twenty years of incessant and intelligent labour'. He had invented improved manufacturing processes and made large profits from the shares he held in the companies he had formed to develop his patents. One such company was The Patent Coal Dust Fuel Company, which had bought his invention for blowing fine coal dust into a furnace whereby an intense heat was obtainable in a few minutes. Though remaining a paid director of these companies, and concerned to ensure that they were successful, he had sold his patents to a new company and so relinquished direct responsibility. 'he was now a gentleman of leisure with a handsome fortune lying in his bank to await investment'. He had never married, living in rooms in St James's Street, near Piccadilly, from which he travelled to the City by taxi-cab, and that was the 'grinding daily machinery' of London life. He now wanted to do something meaningful having been exposed to 'the degrading influence of the lust for acquisition' over his years in the City. He travelled to Switzerland and drew a contrast between the 'scurrying busybodies in the City' and the relaxed pace of life there, with the Swiss countryside emerging as 'a bigger, richer life than all London had supplied to him in twenty years'. Though the City was a place where wealth was created for the benefit of all it was also a place of unremitting toil that was, ultimately, unfulfilling because it did not satisfy the imaginative and creative elements that existed within human beings. No matter how honourable and successful a City person might be, life there was essentially inferior to one that involved living in the country or following a cultural pursuit. The only solution was an escape into a world of make-believe for a person of intelligence and imagination, such as Henry Rogers. It was not just City tycoons who were worn down by a life in the City for the same was true for their clerks. His clerk, Herbert Minks 'was a slim, rather insignificant figure of a man, neatly dressed, the City clerk stamped plainly over all his person' but he wrote poetry while commuting daily from Sydenham 'in his third-class crowded carriage'[20] Only escape from the City could free the human soul, whether it took the form of the realms of fantasy or the Swiss countryside.

The City appeared to exert a magnetic fascination on the British public because of the power those in it could wield, as well as the constant fluctuations in individual fortune. This emerges in Bennett's 1913 novel, *Teresa of Watling Street*. Richard Redgrave, while standing opposite the head office of the British and Scottish Banking Company in the City and watching what was taking place around him mused that, 'Since money is the font of all modern romantic adventure, the City of London, which holds more money to the square yard than any other place in the world, is the most romantic of cities ... And if the City, as a whole, is romantic, its banks are doubly and trebly romantic. Nothing is more marvellous than the rapid growth of our banking system, which is twice as great now as it was twenty years ago – and it was great enough then'. On entering the bank he was further impressed when he realized that, 'Fifty millions of deposits were manoeuvred from day to day in that parlour, and the careers of eight hundred clerks depended on words spoken therein'. After this eulogy to the City the emphasis switched to its seamier side, namely an attempt to make money by manipulating the market in mining company shares. Heading the bank was Simon Lock, a self-made man, who was also chairman of a group of gold mining companies. He and a group of other financiers were trying to make money by agreeing to sell shares in the La Princesse mining company, even though they did not own any, in the expectation that they could deliver them by buying them in the market at the lower price that their selling would produce. However, someone else had bought up most of the available shares and so they were short of the number that they had agreed to sell, and the price was being forced up as they tried to make up the difference, leaving them with a huge potential loss. Sir

Arthur Custer, one of the financiers involved, did not understand the implications of what had happened.

> I don't understand the methods of the Stock Exchange – never did ... I only came into the City because a lot of fellows like yourself asked me to ... Tell all these people whom we have contracted to sell Princesse shares that we simply can't supply 'em, and tell 'em to do their worst. Their worst won't be worse than a dead loss of over two and a half millions.

But Simon Lock, with his long experience in the City, was only to well aware of the difficult position they were in.

> 'My dear Sir Arthur', said Simon Lock, 'there is no crying off in the City. We have contracted to deliver those shares, and we must deliver them, or pay the price – commercial ruin'.
> 'The Stock Exchange', Sir Arthur blustered, 'is one of the most infamous institutions – 'Yes' Simon Lock cut him short, 'we know all about that. The Stock Exchange is quite right as long as we are making money; but when we begin to lose it immediately becomes infamous'.

Unable to deliver the shares, Simon Lock committed suicide, even though he left an estate of £1 million. He realized that his career as a City financier was over as nobody would now trust him. Trust was vital to the operation of the City and those that broke that bond of trust found it very difficult, if not impossible, to regain it and so death or disappearance remained the only alternatives.[21] The City was seen as a place that operated according to its own moral code, and one that was at variance from that of society as a whole. Manipulating prices was considered perfectly acceptable though that led to innocent investors being cheated. However, failing to meet one's bargains on the Stock Exchange was not, even though many would regard these as little better than bets on the rise or fall of prices. The City emerged as a place where games of chance were played for extreme stakes, with failure being met with death and success richly rewarded.

Representative of the prevailing view of the City of London on the eve of the First World War was the 1914 novel by William Le Queux, suggestively entitled *Sins of the City: A Story of Craft, Crime and Capital*. This novel opened with a conversation between two old Eton school friends namely Wallace Vipan, an explorer recently returned from South America, and Gerald Mildmay, an electrical engineer with his own business in London. Wallace Vipan asked, 'There are surely other objects in this life than the mere making of money, aren't there?', to which Mildmay replied, 'You wouldn't think so, my dear fellow, if you had much to do with the City. There, it's money, money, nothing but money, and don't be too particular how you get it, so long as you do get it'. Vipan had tried the City briefly for a career but, preferring the outdoor life, he soon left it. He was a man of action who used his private income to undertake expeditions around the world. In contrast, Mildmay was proud of his engineering skills and despised those in the City and what they did there. This even extended to his own friends who had made a successful career in the City, such as Sir Charles Olcott, a financier. He was 'considered too clever, too hard hearted, too good a hand at a bargain'. Nevertheless, the vigour and dynamism of the City also came across in an early morning scene near the Bank of England, in the heart of the City. 'Here was all bustle and hurry, Clerks, typists and City men were passing and re-passing in their thousands to their daily tasks' And this was accompanied by 'crowding and pushing'. Another aspect of the City was also evident and that was its ability to generate wealth. Despite the City's reputation, and that of those who worked there, Vipan wanted to revive his City connections. He had a commission from an Italian prospector, Piero Balbi, whom he had met in Peru, to float a copper mine in London, as that was where investors in such projects were to be found. As the money to be made from selling the mine to the public would allow Vipan to marry and settle down he approached Olcott about the possibilities of floating it as a company in the City. This was despite the advice of his fiancée, Pauline Spencer, who was the daughter of Lord Oxendale. She had met Olcott because her father had business with him, and had formed the opinion that 'I don't like him. I don't trust him'. When asked his view on the mine Olcott enthused over the prospect, immediately calling the proposed company, 'The Queen of the Cordillera'. He then explained how easy it would be to promote, given the right backing

> a big capital, flaring prospectus, with big names on the directorate and a glowing report from a couple of good mining engineers, then the public would be after it like flies round a honey-pot. They love a mine; there are so many possibilities about it. In their eyes, the 'face' is always glittering with ore and diamonds which only require which only require digging out and selling. Oh! There's nothing like a mine to scoop the dollars in with. Country people go for it – parsons, widows, with their little all, and so on.

Olcott introduced Vipan to Henry Ellis, a member of the London Stock Exchange, who operated from a 'big, gorgeously-furnished room' in the City. Ellis was an expert at how to go about organizing mining companies, as he told Vipan. 'The first thing to be done is to form a small syndicate, then for one or two of us to go out to Peru, obtain absolute possession of the mine and such concessions as we find necessary from the Government, arrange for a good report from some sound mining engineer, and rake in the shekels'. In turn Ellis introduced Vipan to an even more important City figure, Giuseppe Guelfo, who, according to Lord Oxendale, 'certainly does possess a great name for making money in the City'. Guelfo was 'An Italian by birth, a cosmopolitan by education and upbringing ... a big man in the financial world of London and the Continent', though many regarded his operations as somewhat dubious. He was wealthy and success-ful, trusted by the likes of Lord Oxendale, who was on the boards of numerous companies in the City. Guelfo had offices in both London and Paris from which he conducted extensive and varied financial operations. One of his specialities was mining finance, especially that related to South Africa, and so he had the connections necessary to obtain the funding that was required for Vipan's pro-posed Peruvian mine. However, after his various meetings with Guelfo, Ellis and Olcott, Vipan was discovered dead in his rooms, having been strangled, and the papers relating to the mine had been stolen.

These papers then came into Guelfo's hands in Paris, through a German called Hans Reichardt. Once he had them in his possession Guelfo summoned Ellis to Paris so that they could make arrangements to go out to Peru and secure the mine. At this stage a distinction is made between Guelfo, who was 'a hard-ened, cold villain' and Ellis, who was 'a weak coward with some grains of a better nature still lying dormant within him'. Whereas Guelfo had risen from humble origins in Italy and would let nothing stand in his way, Ellis came from a privi-leged background and had been well educated at an English public school. He was 'a gentleman, well read and of a cultured mind' who had been corrupted by the City of London through those that he had met there and the nature of the business that they did.

> Henry Ellis was not a thoroughly hardened individual, and for a City man he was mod-erately honest. He would not rob a fellow-creature openly; his standards of morality forbade that. But the ways of the City, or, in other words, 'business', had told upon him, and if a good thing came the way, without being too particular as to the nature of that good thing, he was quick to snap at it. His association with Guelfo had not improved him, save financially. It had blunted his early ideals and had taught him that money was everything and that how it was obtained was the second consideration.

Thus Ellis was happy to accompany Guelfo to Peru so that they could make the arrangements necessary to bring it out as a company in London. That involved time, trouble and expenses, indicating an awareness that bringing out a mining company in the City was a complex and expensive procedure. One element of that was ensuring that a favourable report was obtained from the mining engi-neers, whatever the prospects of the mine; and this could be best achieved through bribery, as the more that was paid for the report the better it would be. Having achieved what they had set out to do, Guelfo and Ellis returned to London in order to bring out the mining company. However, the Italian pros-pector in Peru, Signor Balbi, had been crossed by Guelfo in the past and wanted revenge. Also, Ellis had an old Harrow schoolfriend, Roland Kendrick, who was a member of the Stock Exchange. In contrast to Ellis he was honest and straight-forward, avoiding anything 'shady or questionable'. What all this suggested was an awareness that not all those in the City were bad. Despite the obsession of those in the City with making money

> there are honest and dishonest ways of making it. As a result Kendrick gained the trust of Signor Balbi, who had discovered an even better mining prospect in Peru, and it was he, not Ellis and Guelfo, who were entrusted with floating this company. Kendrick explained to Guelfo, who was threatening to ruin him if he was not cut in for a slice of the deal, 'I'm going to run this show as I've run every one with which I've had anything to do – on the square. It will stand on its own merits, and as far as I am concerned, the public shall see that there is at least some honesty in the City.

This way of proceeding was regarded as 'something new in the way of mines'. In contrast to the mine promoted by Guelfo, where the ore body was soon exhausted, the one launched by Kendrick proved a great success and made everyone rich. Luckily for Lord Oxendale the £7,000 he had invested in the mining company promoted by Guelfo was returned to him intact even though the share price had collapsed. His daughter Pauline had threatened to expose Guelfo's crooked activities if her father did not get his money back, and to silence her Guelfo paid up. This prompted Lord Oxendale to say to himself that 'I really believe that if Providence had made a boy of her (Pauline) instead of a girl she would have had a better head for the City than her old father!' Considering the fact that Lord Oxendale had been so easily taken in by the speculative mining schemes promoted by Guelfo this may not be as high praise as it might otherwise appear! It does, though, indicate the continuing view that the City was no place for women.

Not only did the mine promoted by Guelfo fail to prosper, but another of his schemes, The Upper Belgravian Estate Company, was also in trouble. Up to this time Guelfo had earned himself a reputation in the City as a promoter of successful companies, and this had created a loyal following among investors and the stockbrokers who advised them. 'The great financial king of the City could always command attention at any meeting at which he was present; his words were hung on by many who regarded him almost as a god. He had learnt the secret of making money, and if he favoured a project, surely it must be well'. At public meetings 'such was his standing in the world of stocks and shares that there were some who imagined that they gained a kind of reflected glory merely being acquainted with him'. Similarly, in the case of the Peruvian mining company 'the name Guelfo at the head of the prospectus had induced many who could but ill afford it to invest all their savings in the mine, in the hopes of reaping a golden harvest'. This reputation had begun to come unstuck as the companies he had promoted produced poor results for their shareholders, leading to demands for explanations. At the annual general meeting of the Upper Belgravian Estate an enquiry into its affairs was ordered, despite the objections of Guelfo. This enquiry threatened to destroy his reputation and thus the trust of investors. 'Committees of inspection are dangerous things when books are not quite in order. Public meetings may be gulled and coaxed into believing many things, but in the calm and quiet of an office facts and figures assume their true proportions and cannot so easily be juggled with'. Guelfo continued to believe that this was but a passing crisis, telling Kendrick, when he met him outside the Royal Exchange in the City, 'we men in the City often find ourselves in tight corners and yet get out of them. This is not the first time I've been in the box. I'm only thankful that Nature makes more than half humanity fools. The City wouldn't thrive without that exceedingly useful provision, would it, eh?' However, the word in the City was about that he was in financial trouble. His situation was then made worse when Sir Charles Olcott, one of his fellow company promoters, disappeared so as to avoid bankruptcy and prison. Before Guelfo could likewise flee, he was killed by the associate who had strangled Vipan. Financial ruin, prison or death seemed to remain the only fates open to company promoters in the City of London on the eve of the First World War.

This tale ended with the rehabilitation of Ellis and the marriage of Pauline and Kendrick. Both men had become rivals for Pauline's hand in marriage, and though Kendrick recognized that she was 'above me in social position, and it may be in worldly wealth', that proved no barrier. Union between landed gentry and respectable elements in the City, such as an honest stockbroker, was deemed perfectly possible. Realizing the error of his ways Ellis vowed that 'for the future my hands shall be clean' though he recognized that 'In the City it will be a hard fight', Ellis himself blamed the City of London for corrupting him 'though I had been well brought up by a loving mother whose soul was a soul of honour, yet contact with the City and its ways had so dulled and warped my better nature that I had put aside all the good I had learnt at her knee and had given myself up, body and soul, to the lust for gold ... I saw others about all doing the same and, weak fool that I was, I followed in the crowd'. The City attracted the immoral and crooked in society and corrupted those who worked there, no matter how principled and well brought up they were. Though there were those in the City such as Kendrick, whose honesty was rewarded with both wealth and marriage to the daughter of a Lord, they were clearly exceptions for it took real strength of character to resist the financial immorality that was clearly rife there.[22]

In whatever light the City was held it had embedded itself into British culture by the eve of the First World War, as can be seen from Joseph Conrad's 1914 novel, *Chance*. By then, even the failure of a company promoter could be seen sympathetically when viewed through the effects it had upon his family. Conrad had made brief reference to the City of London in his 1902 novel, *Heart of Darkness*, where a company director captained the yacht, an accountant played dominoes and a lawyer lounged on a rug, suggestive of the public's views of each.[23] In *Chance* the City was much more central, indicating the rise of its importance within British culture. *Chance* was about what happened to the child of a financier when she found herself alone and penniless after his downfall and imprisonment. The father, de Barral, had begun as a bank clerk before embarking on his own account, accepting small deposits and promising returns of 10 per cent per annum. Success led him to establish the Orb Deposit Bank and the Sceptre Trust. Using money collected from thousands of small depositors, and driven by the need to pay high rates of interest, de Barral took greater and greater investment risks, such as 'a harbour and docks on the coast of Patagonia, quarries in Labrador'. Many turned out to be worthless, as 'He had been the prey of all sorts of swindlers, adventurers, visionaries, and even lunatics'. The City was seen as frequented by either those 'ready to cut your throat' or the gullible like de Barral. The bank and the trust company both collapsed, and his only defence was that the public had little knowledge of what took place in the City. 'Gentlemen don't understand anything about City affairs – finance'. He was sentenced to seven years penal servitude and stripped of all his assets by his creditors, leaving his daughter to fend for herself, in an unsympathetic world, being the daughter of a disgraced financier. When released from prison de Barral emerged as a bitter and troubled man, who eventually committed suicide, after a failed attempt to murder his daughter's husband.[24]

This hardly suggests that the City had gained general acceptance in British culture, as a mixture of past and current misdemeanours committed by a few, continued to exert a powerful influence on public perceptions. In the 1914 novel, *When William Came,* by Hector Munro (Saki), it was sarcastically observed that 'I didn't know that writing was much in his line ... beyond the occasional editing of a company prospectus'.[25] This was despite the fact that the City as a whole was recognized as being 'stable', 'respectable', 'honest', as in the words of Norman Angel writing in 1913. Such views also extended to key institutions in the City like the Bank of England, regarded as a byword for financial stability, while the London Stock Exchange was described in 1912 as 'the nerve-centre of the world, the hub of the financial universe'.[26] The public were certainly conscious of the financial power of the City, as in John Buchan's short story, *The Power-House,* that appeared in 1913. Though the City included such people as Julius Pavia, an East India merchant, stockbrokers handling the investments of wealthy clients or crooked trade union officials, and 'an oldish, drink-sodden clerk from a Cannon Street bucket shop', at its heart lay the likes of the international financier, Andrew Lumley. He was 'a money-lender of evil repute', with an apartment in London and a house in the country, but his activities made him central to a 'a great system of credit. Without our cheques and bills of exchange and currency the whole of our life would stop'.[27] To contemporaries on the eve of the First World War, the City was admired because it epitomized the power of Britain and its Empire. Conversely, it was feared because that power could be usurped by the unscrupulous for their own ends, so endangering Britain and its Empire. The City was admired because it had the power to change peoples' lives by enriching them through successful investment but it was also feared because it could also impoverish them through unsuccessful speculation and bank collapses. The City was admired as a place where individuals could advance with amazing rapidity, whatever their origins, allowing them to challenge the landed elite for social status. It was also feared for exactly the same reason, as it had the potential to upset the established social order by promoting the interests of religious minorities, foreigners and those without culture or breeding. Above all the City was a place where the normal rules of civilized behaviour did not apply as all that mattered was the expertise required to buy and sell at a profit time and again. For that alone it was simultaneously admired and feared by the general public.

Despite the fact that the City was the most important commercial and financial centre in the world in 1914 it was neither understood nor liked by most of the British public. The more it undertook a global role the more a gulf opened up between it and the British people, and this made it impossible for it to gain the cultural acceptance that its economic position warranted. Allied to that the company promoter had become the manifestation of financial corruption and greed, replacing the money lender of old, but sharing, in the eyes of the public, similar characteristics, such as being Jewish, or foreign, or both. Though the City of London had been transformed in the course of the Victorian and Edwardian eras it remained as far from public acceptability at the end as it was at the beginning, though the grounds upon which that antagonism was based had also been transformed. By the eve of the First World War the City had accumulated too many critics for it to gain acceptance. That had looked likely in the early 1890s after it had made the transition from being judged as a place to one where it was valued because of the functions it performed, and these became better understood. However, that regard was reversed by the effects of the gold mining speculation, as this produced a critical appraisal of the way the City operated, and the apparent ability of those who occupied positions of power and influence there to enrich themselves through fraudulent means and escape punishment for their crimes. That re-appraisal of the practices prevalent in the City then became a more generalized attack after 1900. Increasingly the City was seen as the embodiment of all that many in British society did not like about the direction it was heading. A number of these were of a longstanding nature such as the latent anti-Semitism that waxed and waned over time. As the City contained a number of prominent and successful Jewish bankers and brokers it was an obvious target for those who held such views. However, the City was also the recipient of criticisms that were driven by more recent events on the wider political, social and economic stage. There were those who did not like the fact that Britain no longer seemed master of its own destiny because of the rivalry of other nations, especially Germany, and this could be equated to the arrival of foreigners in the City, a number of whom were German. Others disliked the fact that Britain was being drawn into military conflicts abroad, and this could be attributed to those in the City who profited from the additional territory acquired and the stability imposed at public cost. For some there was nostalgia for the passing of an older social order as rural England was invaded by those who had made money in the City and could buy up country estates. Finally, there were the new breed of anti-capitalists and they found in the City an easy and popular target because of the constant buying and selling on the Stock Exchange, and the attendant rise and fall in prices, as that appeared to be nothing other than wasteful gambling rather than productive investment. When combined the forces lined up against the City represented a powerful lobby preventing its cultural acceptability, and that was the case on the eve of the First World War.

CONCLUSION: AN ANTI-FINANCIAL CULTURE?

The City of London grew, flourished and changed throughout the Victorian and Edwardian periods. It lost its residential population to other parts of London and the suburbs, and ceased to be a manufacturing centre as those activities relocated to areas where land and labour was cheaper. This did not mean that the City became an exclusively financial district by the First World War, for commercial and shipping business not only remained but experienced absolute growth, as did the vast range of ancillary services such as accountancy and law along with new ones like consulting engineers, loss adjusters and advertising agents. Though contemporaries were aware of the continuing presence of so many diverse groups and activities within the City of London, the nature of the work that most did, and the lack of contact, meant that they increasingly passed unnoticed. The result was to focus public attention on those aspects of the City that did make an impact on the public. Even here, change was taking place. Whereas in the mid-nineteenth century banking crises and insurance company collapses continued to occur, these had both become something of a rarity by the end. In each case both banking and insurance had become dominated by large and well-capitalized joint stock companies that delivered regular returns to their shareholders while safeguarding deposits and paying out on their policies. This had the effect of reducing their activities to ones that the public took for granted and so did not require comment. As a consequence, the public's awareness of the City became increasingly confined to a very narrow range of its overall activities. This awareness was continuously enhanced by growing literacy and ease of communication. It became possible to know, at a glance, the current state of the stock market or the latest speculative fad, rather than such information being confined to a small elite located in London. Anything associated with speculation on the Stock Exchange and the promotion of joint stock companies generated public interest because of the constant fluctuations in prices and the making and losing of fortunes. Inevitably, it was the most spectacular of these that attracted the greatest interest. The outcome was that the public saw the City of London through an increasingly narrow prism, and this excluded the great bulk of the daily routine of organizing domestic and international trade, finance and shipping. In contrast, great attention was paid to the spectacular rise of company promoters, as they emerged from obscurity, built opulent town houses, bought large country estates, gave lavish parties, married aristocratic ladies, and gained titles. Equally engrossing was their spectacular fall when their financial schemes collapsed leading to public outcry from those who had lost money, followed by extradition from whatever country to which they had fled, prosecution for fraud, conviction and sentencing. A few real-life examples fed this public appetite, so providing an enduring impression of the City based on a tiny handful of people. Similarly, the existence of a number of prominent Jews in the City, such as the long-established Rothschilds or more recent arrivals like Ernest Cassel, helped to create an impression that the City was dominated by an alien clique.[1]

Over time the public thus ceased to see the City for the place it was or even in terms of the business it did but, instead, it became identified with a small number of specific activities and particular people. As these involved speculation on the Stock Exchange and company promotion the result was rather negative. Speculation was seen as nothing more than betting on the rise or fall of prices, and was deprecated by most as a consequence. Company promotion occupied a similar position. It involved either the conversion of an existing business into a joint stock company, which was felt to offer no obvious benefit, or a gamble on a possible mineral discovery or unproven technology. Certain positive features of the City did come to the fore from time to time. While the railway mania was initially regarded as akin to the South Sea Bubble its legacy was a transport system that all could appreciate. That did produce a change in attitude among the public. Despite continuing negative comment in the 1850s, associated with speculation and company promoters, there was a general appreciation of what the City had made possible. Allied with the growing public confidence in London banks, especially the Bank of England, and London investments, particularly the National Debt, this led to a grudging acceptance that the City was important and deserved recognition for what it did. There was even an abatement of anti-Semitism as the likes of the Rothschilds became anglicized and the number of new arrivals from Continental Europe remained low. This acceptance of the City was most marked in the case of its commercial aspects. Criticism of City merchants, which had been evident before the nineteenth century, not only largely disappeared but was also reversed as they became seen as important and respectable, so fully deserving the wealth they possessed and the position in society they had attained. A similar process also began to take place with City bankers, as crisis and collapse were increasingly associated with the provincial variety. The merchant banker was seen as a powerful figure in the financial world, through his ability to raise loans and finance trade, while the deposit banker became the guardian of the nation's savings and the trusted provider of business credit, with the strength of the Bank of England lying behind it all. Countering this positive imagery in the mid-1860s was the damaging consequences of the speculative boom centring on joint stock companies and the subsequent collapse of the discount house, Overend and Gurney, shortly after converting to limited liability. The excesses of speculation and the aroma of fraud that surrounded certain of the activities that took place in the City continued to undermine any improvement in its reputation for stability and honesty. Given that Britain was still in the early stages of creating the world's first modern economy, a lingering suspicion of the City and what took place there was perhaps inevitable. However, growing familiarity combined with a recognition of the important role played by the City in commercial and financial life, could be expected to improve the way it was regarded from 1870 onwards.

After 1870 the nature of the City was transformed. Increasingly the City ceased to be a place of residence and became, instead, a place of business. This steady decline in the human dimension of the City was accompanied by a growing perception that the City was solely a place of finance. Though the City merchant received growing respect, indicating that their role was now fully recognized, it was not they that characterized the City any longer. A similar fate overtook the City banker. As the business of everyday banking became an anonymous process conducted in a routine manner through branch networks directed from head offices staffed by highly-trained workers, so the banker became a trusted and respected figure in society. However, this did little for the reputation of the City, as the people who sat on the boards of these banking companies did not attract the public's interest in the same way as the more colourful private bankers of the past. A similar process took place with insurance as it became a matter of calculation and certainty conducted by well-managed companies rather than a gamble on lives, fires and wrecks. The consequence was that a vast array of City business passed from public notice being conducted by people who commuted there every morning and left every evening, having made their individual contribution to the functioning of the world's largest and most important financial centre, without much understanding of how it fitted into the whole. Nevertheless, this left a few features that did resonate with the public. Some were longstanding ones such as the merchant bankers who owned and ran their own businesses. They gained increasing prominence after 1870 as it was they who were responsible for managing the vast outpouring of British wealth that was invested across the world in this period. As a number of these merchant bankers were either foreign or Jewish or both, their presence served to emphasize the City's alien nature. In addition to the merchant bankers, who did command a degree of respect, was the new profession of company promoter. The promotion of companies that were either the conversion of existing businesses or formed to develop a new technology, explore the world for minerals and oil, or produce exotic crops in far away lands, required a new breed of financiers who could convert the ideas and hopes of adventurers and entrepreneurs into the type of business entity that would attract the interest of investors. Such people then became a prominent feature of the City in the eyes of the public, being akin to the alchemists of old as they appeared to possess the power to turn base metal into gold. When some failed to do so either because of fraud, bad timing or unrealistic expectations, the public were, naturally, quick to condemn them as a group. Finally, the Stock Exchange continued to possess a somewhat unsavoury image even though both the National Debt and railway securities came to be seen as sound investments. The problem was that it was also the place where the shares of these new joint stock companies were traded. It seemed impossible for the City to shed the negative image of the past even though certain of those activities that had fostered it had become routine and respectable, because others that were novel and volatile took their place.

Nevertheless, the period from the late 1870s to the early 1890s did appear to be one in which the City came to project a more acceptable image, as the Overend Gurney collapse receded from view and the revelations regarding market manipulation and foreign loans faded. This did not mean that the City was, by any means, well regarded as it continued to be perceived negatively because of its association with gambling and fraud. However, that grudging acceptance bordering on admiration was abruptly reversed in the mid-1890s, due to a series of problems associated with overseas investment followed by the spectacular rise and fall of speculation in the shares of gold-mining companies. These events emphasized the negative aspects of the City in the eyes of the public, such as the influx of foreigners, the outflow of money and the instability caused by periodic financial crises. These countered the positive images associated with stable banking, remunerative investment opportunities and global importance. The strong negative reaction that followed the collapse of the gold-mining boom did abate somewhat after 1900 but it did leave a lasting legacy. By then the imagery of the City as a place populated by foreign and Jewish financiers had taken its hold over the public's imagination, fuelled by the evident wealth of a few, such as the Rothschilds, as well as their strong connections to the British aristocracy and even royalty. The impression given was that a cosmopolitan elite had taken control of Britain through the wealth that the City allowed them to amass. With that wealth they could either buy up the estates of impoverished British landowners or marry their offspring to the sons and daughters of bankrupt aristocrats. Furthermore, through the influence that their wealth and connections gave them these City people were placed in a position to determine policy for Britain and its Empire. Despite recognizing that in the City Britain possessed the dominant financial centre in the world, the response it produced was not so much one of admiration but rather a mixture of fear and envy. The fear arose because the influence of those in the City was seen to be a threat to the established social order in Britain, and even to a British way of life as represented by the manor houses and villages of rural England. This envy arose because of the ostentatious wealth of these City financiers which appeared to be obtained without effort as nothing was produced in the process. In the background there also continued to lurk the age old suspicion of anything connected to money and the anti-Semitism found in any Christian country. In addition, the years between 1900 and 1914 saw the increasing identification of the City with capitalism. As the location of the institutions and the markets that lay at the heart of capitalism it was, perhaps, inevitable that those who preferred a different system would eventually focus their attention on what was taking place in the City of London. It was much easier to convince people that capitalism was evil by pointing to its excesses in the City than argue in the abstract. By likening the City and its activities to a casino, in which not only shares but entire businesses were bought and sold for no obvious purpose, it was possible to emphasize the wasteful and unproductive nature of capitalism itself.

The effect of these changes in the way the City was perceived was to make it impossible for it to gain general acceptance and thus establish for itself a positive and consistent position within British culture. When it was being judged as a place at the beginning of the Victorian era it was seen to exist apart from the rest of society. In the City was to be found a dense mass of humanity packed together pursuing activities that were not fully intelligible to most. This generated awe among those who visited it as they had problems comprehending its vastness and diversity. They also observed that many in the City lived in squalor while a few enjoyed enormous riches and that generated both pity and envy. Conversely, as a place, the City did generate some positive impressions. It was where hard work and perseverance could overcome class and gender barriers. Those enriched by the City could achieve social status and power as long as their money came from such legitimate pursuits as commerce and even banking but not speculation and company promotion. The negative images might outweigh the positive but the City possessed certain redeeming features in the early Victorian years. However, as the City came to be judged on the basis of function not community in the mid-Victorian years it lost a number of these positive images, such as being associated with trade, while a number of the negative ones were emphasized, especially Stock Exchange speculation and company promotion. However, as the benefits to be derived from improved banking and expanded investment opportunities came to be more appreciated, the City did appear to overcome these negative images in the later Victorian period. That was then reversed towards the very end of Queen Victoria's reign, when the City became engulfed by a brief but spectacular speculation in the shares of foreign gold-mining companies. That might have proved only a temporary setback if it were not for the fact that the City was being used as proxy for cosmopolitan capitalism in the Edwardian era. As such, it generated a degree of antagonism driven by the critics of both capitalism itself and those who resented the presence in Britain of wealthy foreigners and Jews. The combination of these was to produce a very negative image of the City in the years leading up to the First World War.

It can be concluded that Britain did not develop a pro-City culture in the course of the Victorian and Edwardian years. There were times when it did move in that direction but there were others when the reverse took place. This suggests that there was neither a consistent nor a direct relationship between economy and culture from either direction. Instead, the relationship between the two was much more complex and subject to numerous influences. The fact that the grounds used to judge the City were not constant but subject to major shifts made it especially difficult for it to achieve and then command a stable image in the eyes of the British public. Added to that was its immense diversity which threw up different images as one element supplanted another in the eyes of the public. As a pro-City culture did not emerge in the course of the Victorian and Edwardian eras it can be suggested that culture was not a simple product of economic forces though they may have been one of the influences at work. Certainly there is no evidence to suggest that British culture embraced the City in these years, possibly because deep-seated prejudices against money, speculation, Jews and foreigners could not be overcome in the space of even a century. Conversely, as the City was able to grow and flourish throughout it can be argued than its prevailing negative image among the British public was no impediment to its success. Jewish and foreign financiers, for example, were subjected to generalized anti-Semitic abuse throughout the Victorian and Edwardian eras, that was possibly even more extreme at the end than at the beginning, but that did not prevent them from both being very successful in the City and gaining entry to the very highest echelons of British society. This did not mean that the public were indifferent to the City, for it occupied a prominent place within British culture. The City financier had become something of a stereotype by the Edwardian era, for example. The cultural world and the financial world did not exist in completely separate spheres and City people were great patrons of art and architecture. What appeared to be possible was a divorce between the world of finance, which occupied the working day, and the world of culture, as that was to be found in the home during the leisure hours. Those who worked in the City were no different from their peers. They could appreciate and enjoy all types of cultural pursuits while also recognizing the necessity of generating the income and wealth that enabled them to do so. To the City clerk that might extend to no more than a visit to a music hall, a cheap novel and a holiday at the seaside. For the City banker it might include an evening at the opera, a country house and an expensive collection of art and furniture. For both, the means came from the constant buying and selling, borrowing and lending, inquiring and advising that was the business of the City.

This failure of the City to gain a positive image within British culture can be contrasted with the steady improvement in the status of manufacturing industry and the British industrialist over the same time period.[2] Even by the middle of the nineteenth century manufacturing industry was beginning to shake off its negative image. Instead, there was a growing appreciation of the manufacturer in British culture, as such people produced and sold products that were real and could be bought by ordinary people. Mrs Craik's novel, *John Halifax, Gentleman,* which appeared in 1856, was a eulogy to the life of a Cotswolds woollen textile manufacturer.[3] Similarly, in *Commercial Tales and Sketches*, dating from 1864, it was Percy the Plodder that won praise, because he became a successful provincial manufacturer and a happily married man, whereas Geoffrey the Genius chose the City, where he enjoyed a spectacular but brief career that ended in bankruptcy and emigration.[4] The late Victorian and Edwardian eras also produced fictional examples that reinforced the view that manufacturing industry provided a clear path to wealth and respectability as in the description of Sir William Vane-Shorrocks, in Oxenham's 1899 novel, *Rising Fortunes.*

> Bill Shorrocks had entered the factory of which he afterwards became owner, as a small, tow-headed boy of eleven. He had worked steadily up till he became foreman, manager, then, through a fortunate invention, part owner. Presently he bought out his partners, captured another invention that practically made him a monopolist in his own special line, and at sixty was as hard-headed a millionaire as Lancashire ever cared to be proud of.[5]

Whereas the Edwardian stereotype of the City man was of someone who was probably foreign, probably Jewish, and probably crooked, that of a manufacturer was the reverse. This can be seen in a series of Yorkshire novels that appeared in the Edwardian era as they all trace the rise to fame and fortune of native individuals and families. In the 1903 novel, *Thompson's Progress*, by C. J. Cutcliffe Hyne, the hero is a woollen textile manufacturer,[6] whereas in R. H. Bretherton's, *An Honest Man,* which was published in 1909, it is a manufacturer of packaging machinery.[7] In the case of *The Osbornes*, by E. F. Benson, which was published in 1910, the scene shifts to the success of a family of hardware manufacturers in Sheffield.[8] Even the City merchant could not compete with the northern manufacturer in public regard, as is apparent in George Du Maurier's novel, *The Martian*, which was published in 1898. Robert Maurice was a successful and respected City wine merchant but considered his business career of little value. 'Bring me up to invent, or make something useful, if it is only pickles or soap, but not to buy and sell them' He saw the only achievement of a City merchant being 'To amass wealth'.[9]

As an industrial nation Britain was in relative decline before the First World War though actual output and exports continued to grow strongly. The problem was that modern methods of manufacturing were spreading rapidly and British production was being challenged strongly by the likes of Germany and the USA as well as a host of other nations. Nevertheless, the manufacturer and the northern industrialist had become revered figures in contemporary British culture. The public could understand and appreciate industry because it involved the production and sale of items with which they were familiar. In turn, this was undertaken within Britain and by British people, whether it was the workers or the factory owners. Finally, the collective achievements of these mills and factories were seen to lie at the foundation of Britain's economic success and the building up of an immense Empire. In the eyes of the public the successes of industry could be contrasted with agriculture which had declined to a position where it no longer fed the British population or employed the bulk of the workforce. Industry could also be compared favourably with the City of London, which was associated with activities that appeared to have no tangible output, such as banking and broking. It was also seen to contain numerous foreigners and Jews. This suggests that, compared to industry, what took place in the City was too much at variance with what society considered respectable for it to gain acceptance in the same way. No sooner had one component of the City managed to achieve that acceptance than it was replaced by one that did not. Whereas manufacturing enjoyed the onward march of progress with the triumph of textiles being followed by steel and shipbuilding, the City was forever associated with speculation and fraud. Industry was associated with production, in the same way as agriculture and mining, while the City suffered from the primeval antagonism towards the middleman in business combined with the perennial suspicion attached to those who dealt in money. Whereas manufacturing made the transition from a world of constant toil among grime and exploitation to become the workshop of the world, the City remained immersed in greed and fraud.

The best that could be expected for the City was an abatement of an anti-financial culture rather than its replacement by a pro-financial one. The Victorian period opened with the negative legacy of the mid-1820s speculative boom while the Edwardian era closed with the negative legacy of the 1890s gold-mining mania. In between there were positive repercussions arising from the railway mania and negative ones from foreign loans scandals as well as high-profile court cases or suicides of prominent financiers. From this it can be concluded that the mood of the public was a fickle one, for the City lacked the means of firmly establishing itself in a positive light within British culture in the way that more tangible economic pursuits could, such as agriculture, mining, manufacturing or transport. This then poses the question of what happened to the place of the

City within British culture after 1914. London continued to be a financial centre of major international importance, though challenged and even displaced by New York, while the stock market continued to rise and fall and fraudulent financiers continued to exist, be prosecuted and commit suicide.[10] Nevertheless, for much of the period between 1914 and 1945 the British public had far more important concerns than what was happening in the City, such as two wars, a worldwide economic depression and mass unemployment. Also, events in London were greatly overshadowed by those in New York where the Wall Street Crash of 1929 far outweighed anything London could produce, being ranked alongside the South Sea Bubble as one of the speculative booms and collapses of modern times. Even after the Second World War the City was rather sidelined, as the focus for public attention was largely the activities of the government. The Bank of England was now in state ownership and most of the other activities of the City were subject to government controls and market regulation whether operating domestically or internationally. It was only slowly from the 1970s onwards that the volatile markets and rampant capitalism returned to London, especially after the ending of exchange controls in 1979 and the liberalization of the Stock Exchange in 1986. Out of this re-emerged the City of London as a financial centre of major importance in the world, and capable of providing a serious challenge to New York.[11]

Possibly reflecting the fact that the public's attention had strayed away from an interest in the City, evidence for its position within British culture after 1914 is rather sparse. Virginia Woolf's novel, *The Voyage Out*, though appearing in 1915, was very much a pre-war creation, and reflected the views current then, such as the clear resentment that 'the management of the world' was given to those with money rather than breeding.[12] In contrast, those whose views were influenced by the First World War do reflect a somewhat changed stance towards the City. In George Birmingham's novel, *Gossamer*, which also appeared in 1915, there was a sense that contemporaries saw the City's financial power ebbing away to New York, and viewed that with disappointment. British culture had not appreciated the City at the pinnacle of its power but regretted its passing. Sir James Digby was travelling by boat across the Atlantic 'to look into the affairs of certain Canadian companies in which I had invested money'. On board he met Carl Ascher. Ascher had been born in Hamburg but came to England as a young man to pursue a career in banking. 'my particular kind of banking, international banking, can best be carried on in England. That is why I am here, why my business is centered in London, though I myself am not an Englishman. I am a German'. He was also married to an American, so emphasizing the cosmopolitan nature of the pre-war City banker. It was noted that 'Ascher is a banker, one of those international financiers who manage, chiefly from London offices, the complicated kind of foreign business which no ordinary man understands anything about, a kind of business which, for some reason, very few Englishmen undertake'. Ascher was on his way to New York to work on the finances of Mexican railways. He told Digby over dinner, 'As a firm we don't lose directly whatever happens in Mexico. What we have to consider is the interests of our customers, the people, some of them quite small people, who went into Mexican railways on our advice. Banking-houses don't put their money into investments. That's not our business. But banking is a very dull subject. Let's talk of something else'. Ascher came across as a very cultured man who tried to explain international finance to Digby.

> I listened, and learned several things which interested me very much. I got to understand, for instance, why a sovereign is sometimes worth more, sometimes less, when you try to exchange it for dollars or francs; a thing which had always puzzled me before. I learned why gold has to be shipped in large quantities from one country to another by bankers, whereas I, a private individual, need only send a cheque to pay my modest debts. I learned what is meant by a bill drawn on London. It took me nearly half an hour to grasp that.

As a result Digby realized the importance of international finance and was very impressed. In contrast to Digby, a fellow passenger, an Irish MP called Gorman, was of the view that 'No qualities are required for success as a financier except a low kind of cunning and a totally unscrupulous selfishness'. What he resented was the power wielded by these financiers. Ascher 'and his brother financiers are the unseen rulers, the mysteriously shrouded tyrants of the world'.

What Digby saw was that at the heart of the international financial system lay the bonds of trust between bankers across the world, and that if this trust disappeared there would be a worldwide crisis with devastating consequences. According to Ascher, 'If the bankers in any country doubt the solvency of bankers in another country, if there's the smallest hesitation, an instant's pause of distrust or fear, then international credit collapses'. All this took place unseen by the public, leading financiers to be viewed with suspicion. 'Gorman holds the theory that financial men, Ascher and the rest, are bloated spiders who spend their time and energy in trapping the world's workers, poor flies, in gummy webs'. Ascher had an office in New York as well as London and it was the one in New York that was now seen to be the nerve-centre for international trade and finance.

> These men were in touch with the furthest ends of the earth. Coded telegrams fluttered from their hands and went vibrating across thousands of miles of land or through the still depths of the oceans, over unlighted tracts of ooze on the sea-bottom. In London the words were read and men set free pent-up, dammed streams of money. In Hong Kong the words were read and some steamer went out, laden, from her harbour. Gold was poured into the hands of tea-planters in Ceylon. Scanty wages in strange coins dribbled out to factory workers in Russian cotton-mills. Gangs of navvies went to work laying railway lines across the veldt in Bechuana Land. There

was no end of the energy controlled, directed by these cable messages, nor any bounds to their field of interest ... Perhaps hardly one of all the busy men I watched quite knew what he was doing. They juggled with figures, made précis of the reports of money markets, dissected and analysed the balance-sheets of railway companies, decoded messages from London or from Paris, transcribed formulae as abstract, as remote from tangible things as the x and y of algebraic equations ... Ascher and men like him have spun fine threads, covering every civilized land with a web of credit, infinitely complex, so delicate that a child's hand could tear it.

The successful operation of the world economy was 'dependent on the smooth working of the system of world-wide credit'. The contrary view was expressed by Gorman, who felt that. 'The slime of the financier lies pretty thick over the world'. Whatever the view the impression conveyed was that New York rather than London was now in control.

With the outbreak of the War this network of international finance fell apart.

In a very few months, before the end of the summer which followed my home-coming, I was to see the whole machine stop working suddenly. The war god stalked across the world and brushed aside, broke, tore, tangled up, the gossamer threads. Then, long before his march was done, while awestruck men and weeping women still listened to the strident clamour of his arms, the spinners of the webs were at work again, patiently joining broken threads, flinging fresh filaments across unbridged gulfs, refastening to their points of attachment the gossamer which seemed so frail, which yet the storm of violence failed to destroy utterly.

Ascher had a nephew in the German high command, who warned him that a war was coming. This worried Ascher as he knew how it would upset the delicate balance of international finance. 'The declaration of war will not simply mean the ruin of a few speculators here and there. You know enough about the modern system of credit to realize something of what we have to face. There will be a sudden paralysis of the nerves and muscles of the whole world-wide body of commercial and industrial life. The heart will stop beating for a short time – only for a short time, I hope – and no blood will go through the veins and arteries'. With the outbreak of war Ascher faced financial ruin while his loyalty to Britain was also tested. He had built up a successful life and a successful bank in London and could not simply abandon both because of war between Britain and Germany. Instead, he advised the British government and became a naturalized British subject, so saving his business from ruin, though many people turned against him because he was German.[13] Whereas before the First World War City financiers could be portrayed as alien, either because of religion or race, those who remained, once hostilities broke out, could not be criticized in this way as they had shown their commitment to Britain, especially those of German Jewish origin. This made it possible for them to be identified as British patriots rather than foreign financiers. There were also many in the City who fought and died for their country or made a valuable and public contribution to the war effort either through donations of money or their management expertise. Again, this altered public perceptions and helped establish the City financier as a respected and valuable member of the community. This comes across in Arnold Bennett's 1926 novel, *Lord Raingo*, modelled on the company promoter, Max Aitken (Lord Beaverbrook). There were some anti-City sentiments expressed, such as the comment, 'My belief is the devil was born somewhere in the City, near the Bank of England', or the observation about his pre-war dealings that 'although he had bought and sold vast undertakings, he had learnt little about any of them beyond what might emerge from a ruthless, critical examination of their books of account'. Overall, though, what is conveyed is the positive contribution that even a company promoter could make at a time of national emergency, which was suggestive that the City and the Country were really all on the same side.[14]

John Buchan was another novelist who expressed positive views on the City between the wars. These ranged from a brief mention in his 1919 novel, *Mr Standfast*, with the City being portrayed as the place where respectable people went to consult their stockbroker, to a positive account of a company promoter in one of the short stories in the 1932 book, *The Gap in the Curtain*. Arnold Tavanger, originally from Geneva, is described as a completely anglicized City financier who specialized in buying failing companies and turning them round, which had brought him a large following among investors. In his own words, 'I'm not the man who makes things, but the man who provides the money for other people to make them with'. This was regarded as perfectly acceptable. 'He had done bold things, too, and more than once defied City opinion and won'. In the City 'His name stood high for integrity as well as for acumen and courage, but he was not regarded as companionable'. He was currently speculating in the shares of a Rhodesian mining company called Daphne Concessions, producing a mineral called michelite, used in the steel industry. It had never paid a dividend after five years of operations and was now considered very speculative. Tavanger travelled around the world tracking down the investors and buying their shares as the company was not quoted. At the same time agents of a US mining company, American Anatilla, were also tracking down the shareholders and trying to buy the shares. The US company mined michelite in Nicaragua and was controlled by the Glaubsteins, immensely rich New York financiers. In the end Tavanger lost out to the Glaubsteins as one of their scientific staff had developed a new smelting process that gave them the edge. Tavanger sold out to them at a loss of £20,000.[15] Not only was the City financier now respectable, including a foreign born company promoter, but financial power had moved from London to New York.

This did not mean that the crooked financier trying to dupe naïve investors had departed from the scene. That was a theme covered in the rather surreal novel by Basil D. Nicholson, *Business is Business*, which appeared in 1933. It was a story of an unscrupulous rogue who tried one moneymaking ploy after another, each being more far fetched than the previous. The final scheme was, 'Interplanetary Communications, Inc', which intended to construct a rocket in Willesden capable of interplanetary travel. What is absent, though, is any attempt to locate these activities in the City of London of the day, as would have been the case before 1914. Unlike pre-war tales of human cupidity and greed, this book made no direct attack on the activities of City financiers.[16] This suggests that the place of the City in British culture had changed as a result of the First World War. On the surface the City looked the same after the First World War as before, from this description of it on a Saturday afternoon in the 1930 novel, *Angel Pavement*, by J. B. Priestley.

> Very soon the City itself would be standing over until Monday: the crowds of brokers and cashiers and clerks and typists and hawkers would have vanished from its pavements, the bars would be forlorn, the teashops nearly empty or closed; its trams and buses no longer clamouring for a few more yards of space, would come gliding easily through misty blue vacancies like ships going down London River; and the whole place, populated by caretakers and policemen among the living, would sink slowly into quietness; the very bank rate would be forgotten; and it would be left to drown itself in reverie, with a drift of smoke and light fog across its old stones like the return of an army of ghosts. Until – with a clatter, a clang, a sudden raw awakening – Monday.

However, beneath the surface the City was now devoid of part of that dynamic spirit that had both attracted and repelled those who had observed it before 1914. In *Angel Payment*, the City firm in question imported wood veneers from the Baltic which were then sold throughout Britain by a team of travelling salesmen. The owner of the business, Dersingham, 'thinks he's gentleman amusing himself', and that was the problem as there were 'Too many of his sort in the City ... That's how the Jews get on, and the Americans. None of that nonsense about them'. The novel ended with the most dynamic member of the firm, Golspie, though also the one with the most dubious business practices, leaving by ship.

> 'Better take a look at London', said Mr Golspie to his daughter, as they walked round the deck. 'There it is, see?'
>
> 'There's nothing to see', said Lena, looking back at the glistening streaky water and the haze and shadows beyond. 'Not worth looking at'. 'All gone in smoke, eh? I mean the proper London'.[17]

There was a palpable sense that something had been lost as a result of the First World War.

That sense of loss was also evident in Vincent Seligman's novel, *Bank Holiday*, which came out in 1934. International finance now revolved around New York leaving the City as a rather quiet but honourable backwater. The novel was centred around the City merchant bank of Tulloch and Conway, where little happened until the partners arrived at 10 o'clock or after. These partners were all family members and had been educated at Eton, with Sir Alexander Tulloch being the senior partner. Like the pre-war years the City remained a place of mystery and chance.

> Like the wife and mother of many a financier, Lady Tulloch entertained only the haziest notion of how her men-folk spent their days. There was for her the proverbial terror of the unknown about 'the City'. A dark, mysterious, unwholesome place where things went fairly well for a time, and then all of a sudden a crisis arose from nowhere, and you had to prepare yourself at a moment's notice to give up your house, sell your jewels and furs and retire to a tiny semi-detached cottage in the suburbs to end your days in semi-shameful obscurity. Then the crisis was somehow or other surmounted, or just disappeared as mysteriously as it had arisen, and you remained where you were, or even moved to a bigger house, and everything in the City was rosy – until the next blow fell.

Unlike the pre-war years the City had now become rather boring, with the war being a defining experience, both personally and for the business that the firm did. As one of the partners noted, 'I find that England is too hard up from the War to be able to finance Foreign Governments on any reasonable scale'. That business was now done in New York, leaving the City merchant bank to provide credit to small and somewhat dubious European businesses, such as a Norwegian timber company. Sir Alexander Tulloch admitted that 'our function is just the humble one of greasing the wheels of international trade and helping people to buy each other's goods' and the result was 'pretty dull'. In his view, 'As far as Europe was concerned ... the heyday of International Finance had passed, probably for ever ...With a mighty stir, Wall Street aroused itself to secure the financial leadership of the world which England in her poverty had been forced to relinquish'. There was an associated firm in New York, run by cousins, and it was now dominant, with the one in London being the junior partner in any joint business. With continuing financial turmoil in Europe, Tulloch and Conway had turned their attention to domestic business opportunities in Birmingham and Leeds, which was seen as 'a change which, most of us will admit, is for the better'.[18] By the 1930s the City merchant bank was well on the way to acquiring the image of a rather conservative family-run British institution, which was to lead to its condemnation in the 1950s and 1960s, in the face of aggressive US competitors. This was certainly not the picture that the public had in mind when they thought about City financiers before 1914.

Generally, the existence of something of a vacuum in British novels covering money and finance between 1914 and 1970 suggests that the place of the City within British culture was very much a product of incidents and characters that attracted public attention. The everyday affairs of the City were considered remote, routine and technical by most of the population and so did not stimulate interest. Especially after the Second World War the strict control exercised by the state owned Bank of England over the banking system, and the rigorous policing of the securities market by the Stock Exchange, eliminated most of the crises and scandals with which the City had been associated with in the past. One consequence of this was to make the City unattractive to foreigners while penal taxation and heavy regulation made it difficult for financiers to amass the wealth which had attracted such envy before 1914. Finally, an awareness of what had happened to Jews in Germany in the 1930s made it unacceptable to voice anti-Semitic sentiments openly. Without these stimuli the City lapsed into a position where it was viewed as something of a backwater, criticized because of its complacency, its resistance to change and the social networks that led to the exclusion of outsiders. This was a very different City from that of the Edwardian era and so it dropped from view. That was to change from the early 1970s onwards with the greater volatility in financial markets, events such as Big Bang in 1986, investor enthusiasm for company shares traded on the Stock Exchange, and a re-emergence of global capitalism as exchange and capital controls disappeared. These supplied the raw material which fuelled a revived interest in the City among the British public. The film, *The Wild Geese,* which was released in 1978, harkened back to an earlier era by casting the villain as a City banker, willing to betray anybody in his search for mining concessions. Typifying the City in the 1980s was Caryl Churchill's rather unflattering play, *Serious Money.* What saved the City was the even worse reputation of Wall Street, as it was that financial centre which had become the focus of global media interest. The way it was portrayed in the film *Wall Street,* released in 1987, was reminiscent of the way the City of London was seen before 1914. Wall Street was a place where 'Greed was Good', and the normal moral code of society did not operate.[19] The appearance of the financial thriller in the 1990s was very much fuelled by the actions of rogue traders such as Baring's Nick Leeson, whose speculations brought down that bank in 1995. The fact that the actions of a single individual could destroy the bank he worked for proved highly attractive to those looking for a story that was both believable and cataclysmic about the risks inherent in global capitalism, even though the actions took place in Singapore not London. Similarly, the appearance of a small number of high profile women in the City encouraged others to include the female banker in novels, so adding sex to the thrill of financial speculation and collapse.[20]

What all this suggests is that the place of the City of London in British culture was never a positive one for it either had no place at all or a negative one. To some it was the unacceptable face of capitalism while to others it was the embodiment of capitalism itself. It seemed to matter little how much or how little the City changed for there was always something about it that caused offence to a significant portion of the British population. As the merchant stopped being viewed as the middleman cheating both buyer and seller, the banker appeared as the person who charged exorbitant rates of interest and lost savers their money. As the banker became increasingly respectable there emerged the company promoter who sold worthless securities to a trusting public. Throughout, there were the members of the Stock Exchange, conducting secret dealings behind closed doors, with the result that investors never bought or sold at the best price. Also, as the City was always home to a significant foreign community, because that was where Britain's international trade and finance was conducted, its loyalty to the country in which it was located was always in question. Money made in the City was forever Guilty Money because its origins did not lie in what was real but in money itself. This verdict leads to a number of conclusions regarding the place occupied by the City of London in Victorian and Edwardian culture. One is the absence of a causal link between economic and cultural change. Certainly, the City merchant followed by the City banker and then, after the First World War, the City stockbroker rose in public esteem, being seen as conservative, respectable and admired. Their wealth was no barrier to social acceptance having been acquired through legitimate means, though there were always reservations attached to newly acquired riches. That did not mean that the public ignored the financial world. There was an abiding interest in the fortunes made or lost in the City, especially if the process was quick and spectacular. This grew over the Victorian and Edwardian eras, fuelled by a London based media that fed the public's appetite for lurid stories, and the regular occurrence of speculative booms and crashes and their human consequences. A product of this interest was the waxing and waning of an anti-financial culture, driven by the public's response to headline-grabbing stories. In periods when little that was newsworthy took place the public's mood swung towards an appreciation of the City's benefits, especially in terms of the organization of trade and the conduct of routine financial business. When events in the City attracted widespread public attention, as during a speculative boom, the response was generally negative. In the upswing there were those who criticized the City as nothing more than a casino, whereas in the downswing there were the complaints from those who had lost money. That then continued for some time afterwards if fraudulent wrongdoings were detected and prosecutions ensued. As the City always contained a number who were Jewish or foreign, because of its operations as a financial centre, such people were readymade scapegoats to explain the losses experienced by investors. Only slowly did a more balanced judgement re-emerge, until reversed during the next bubble. The froth of fraud was forever associated with the City of London for, if there were no current examples to support such a view, there were always earlier ones, such as the South Sea Bubble and then the Railway Mania, or events elsewhere as with the Mississippi Bubble in Paris or the Wall Street Crash in New York. Like the rise and fall of individual company promoters they could be referred to time and again as evidence of intrinsic truths about the City of London. Above all there was the association of the City with capitalism which underpinned an underlying antipathy.

Culture is a rather complex and diffuse concept, making generalizations difficult. What can be concluded is that the existence of an anti-financial culture in Victorian and Edwardian Britain was of varying strength, but ever present. It was certainly much more visible and strong than any anti-industrial culture. From this it can be concluded that the relationship between economy and culture was neither a direct nor an inverse one. Culture was not a simple product of economic developments, with or without some kind of lag, as Britain did not acquire a pro-City culture despite its global success before 1914. Conversely, economic progress was not itself a product of culture as the absence of that pro-City culture testifies. This may appear a short conclusion for a long book but it is a significant one, given the claims that have been made for the existence of such a relationship. It is almost as if the economic and the cultural inhabit separate worlds as, indeed, they increasingly did in the case of the City of London. However, strong connections existed between these worlds though actions in each did not necessarily impinge on the other, apart from during major speculative surges or criminal revelations. In response to each the City improved its mechanisms for self regulation and the public became temporarily wary of certain aspects of the City, such as Stock Exchange speculation and company promotion. Eventually, though, normal business resumed. What changed after 1914 was the intervention of government, as this provided a strong link between the two worlds. Through the agency of government, culture could influence economy because policies were introduced in response to perceptions. For the City of London this meant a prolonged period during which the conduct of its affairs was subject to external rules and regulations while its functions and operation were determined by government control and influence. The results of such a change were both positive, such as in terms of investor protection, and negative, in reducing the dynamism of the City. It was only towards the end of the twentieth century that a partial return to the previous situation was made. What remains to be seen is whether the global financial crisis of 2007–8, including the collapse of a British bank after a classic run in which depositors rushed to withdraw their savings, will result in a return to excessive government intervention. Judging from the comments of prominent politicians and those in the media this does appear likely as those in the City, along with Wall Street, were seen to be primarily responsible for what took place because of their greed and irresponsible behaviour. The only differences between the pre-1914 era and today was the absence of obvious anti-Semitism and the replacement of the company promoter by the hedge fund manager as the evil perpetrator of financial ruin. As in the past, it continued to be far easier for the public to identify a small group, who could then be blamed for what had taken place, than to attribute responsibility to, for example, democratically elected but overspending governments, lax central bankers seemingly unaware of the consequences of their inaction, or their own collective greed in expecting to profit from easy credit and rising property prices. It is only to be hoped that governments respond to this financial crisis with measured restraint and recognize their own complicity in the events that have unfolded. What may appear obvious at the time, especially to the public at large, may not necessarily be true, as the detailed investigation of the interaction between the culture and the City of London before 1914 reveals. Unfortunately, popular perception lends itself to manipulation by politicians seeking to deflect criticism in order to achieve re-election. However, the resulting legislation can have major and unforeseen consequences because the real underlying causes are left untouched.

NOTES

Introduction

1. *F. T. Wealth*, 1 (Spring 2008), p. 6.
2. J. Humphreys, *BBC Radio 4*, 26 April 2008.
3. H. Withers, *International Finance* (London: Smith, Elder & Co., 1916), p. 111.
4. W. D. Rubinstein, *Capitalism, Culture and Decline in Britain, 1750–1990* (London: Routledge, 1993), p. 52.
5. E. Rosenberg, *From Shylock to Svengali: Jewish Stereotypes in English Fiction* (London: Owen, 1961), pp. 14, 27, 33–5, 140, 168–9, 297, 344.
6. J. A .Hobson, *Imperialism: A Study*, revised edn (London: Allen & Unwin, 1938), pp. 56–7.
7. A. Robinson, *Imagining London, 1770–1900* (London: Macmillan, 2004), pp. 114–23, 162.
8. See M. J. Weiner, *English Culture and the Decline of the Industrial Spirit, 1850–1980* (Cambridge: Cambridge University Pres, 1981). This thesis is then examined from a number of perspectives by other historians in B. Collins and K. Robbins (eds), *British Culture and Economic Decline* (London: Weidenfeld and Nicolson, 1990).
9. P. Johnson, 'Civilizing Mammon: Laws, morals and the City in Nineteenth Century England' in P. Burke, B. Harrison and P. Slack (eds.), *Civil Histories: Essays Presented to Sir Keith Thomas* (Oxford: Oxford University Press, 2000), pp. 302–3, 319.
10. P. J. Cain and A. G. Hopkins, *British Imperialism: Innovation and Expansion, 1688–1914* (London: Longman, 1993), p. 127; P. J. Cain and A. G. Hopkins, *British Imperialism: Crisis and Reconstruction, 1914–1990* (London: Longman, 1993), p. 267; T. L. Alborn, *Conceiving Companies: Joint-Stock Politics in Victorian England* (London: Routledge, 1998), p. 10. For a recent examination of the assimilation of successful businessmen into the British elite between 1870 and 1914 see J. F. Peck and J. A. Smith, 'Business and Social Mobility into the British Elite, 1870–1914', *Journal of European Economic History*, 33 (2004), pp. 485–518. For the continued importance of London as a dominant centre of income and wealth in Britain see N. Crafts, 'Regional G. D. P. in Britain, 1871–1911: Some Estimates', *Scottish Journal of Political Economy*, 52 (2005), pp. 54–64 and W. D. Rubinstein, 'The Role of London in Britain's Wealth Structure, 1808–99: Further Evidence' in J. Stobart and A. Owen (eds), *Urban Fortunes: Property and Inheritance in the Town* (Aldershot: Burlington, 2000), pp. 131–49.
11. I. Stone, *The Global Export of Capital from Great Britain, 1865–1914: A Statistical Survey* (London: Macmillan, 1999), pp. 6, 28: Tables 56 and 61; D. C. M. Platt, *Britain's*

Investment Overseas on the Eve of the First World War: The Use and Abuse of Numbers (London: Macmillan, 1986), pp. 45–7; R. C. Michie, *The London Stock Exchange; A History* (Oxford: Oxford University Press, 1999), p. 88; R. C. Michie, *The City of London: Continuity and Change since 1850* (London: Macmillan, 1992), pp. 72–5, 78, 151, 159–60.

12. R. C. Michie, 'One World or Many Worlds?: Markets, Banks, and Communications, 1850s–1990s' in T. de Graaf, J. Jonker and J. J. Mabron (eds), *European Banking Overseas, 19th–20th Centuries* (Amsterdam: ABN AMRO Historical Archives, 2002), p. 244.

13. *London Corporation, City of London Day Census, 1911: Report* (London: Simpkins, Marshall, Hamilton, Kent & Co. Ltd., 1911).

14. G. Jones, *British Multinational Banking, 1830–1990* (Oxford: Clarendon Press, 1993), pp. 414–15.

15. *The Banking Almanac* (London: Thomas Skinner and Co., 1913), pp. 38–57, A. S. J. Baster, *The International Banks* (London: P. S. King & Son, Ltd., 1935), p. 4.

16. See R. C. Michie, 'The City of London and British Banking, 1900–1939' in C. Wrigley (ed.), *A Companion to Early Twentieth Century Britain* (Oxford: Blackwell, 2003), pp. 249–69; R. C. Michie, 'Friend or Foe: Information Technology and the London Stock Exchange since 1700' *Journal of Historical Geography*, 23 (1997), pp. 304–26; R. C. Michie, ' The Invisible Stabilizer: Asset Arbitrage and the International Monetary System since 1700' *Financial History Review*, 15 (1998), pp. 5–26; R. C. Michie, 'Insiders, Outsiders and the Dynamics of Change in the City of London since 1900', *Journal of Contemporary History*, 33 (1998), pp. 547–71.

17. For a recent debate on this subject see L. Guiso, P. Sapienza and L. Zingales, 'Does Culture Affect Economic Outcomes?' *Journal of Economic Perspectives*, 20 (2006), pp. 23–48.

18. Lord Macauley, *The History of England*, 5 vols (London: Longman, 1848), vol. 1, p. 272.

19. F. M. L. Thompson (ed.), *The Cambridge Social History of Britain, 1750–1950*, 3 vols (Cambridge 1990), vol. 1, pp. 16–17, (Garside), pp. 481, 496, 508; Robinson, *Imagining London*, p. 47, 114–23; J. Innes, 'Managing the Metropolis: London's Social Problems and their Control, *c.* 1600-1830', pp. 53–80, on. p. 63 and L. Schwarz, 'Hanoverian London: The Making of a Service Town', pp. 93–110, on. pp. 107, 170, 179, 182; both in P. Clark and R. Gillespie (eds), *Two Capitals: London and Dublin, 1500–1840* (Oxford: Oxford University Press, 2001); D. M. Abramson, *Building the Bank of England: Money, Architecture, Society, 1694–1942* (New Haven, CT and London: Yale University Press, 2005), pp. 21–2, 160; P. Gauci, *Emporium of the World: The Merchants of London, 1660–1800* (London: Continuum, 2007), p. 74, 94.

20. See T. Nicholas, 'Enterprise and Management' in R. Floud and P. Johnson (eds), *The Cambridge Economic History of Modern Britain*, 3 vols. (Cambridge: Cambridge University Press, 2004), vol. 2, pp. 228–32.

21. A poll conducted in 2007 in the UK found an overwhelming majority antagonistic towards both globalization and business leaders, with a desire for government intervention to limit the economic effects of the former and to cap and tax the earnings of the latter. In contrast, most economists considered that dismantling of controls and the lowering of taxation contributed to global economic growth. *Financial Times* (23 July 2007).

22. For an exploration of the complex and changing relationship between the City of London and the British Government over the twentieth century see the various chapters in R. C. Michie and P. A Williamson (eds), *The British Government and The City of London in the Twentieth Century* (Cambridge: Cambridge University Press, 2004).

23. H. D. Wynne-Bennett, *Investment and Speculation* (London: Shaw Publishing, 1924), p. 322; A. E. Davies, *What to look for in a Prospectus* (London: Allen & Unwin 1926), p. 10. See L. W. Hein, *The British Companies Acts and the Practice of Accountancy, 1844–1962* (New York: Arno Press, 1978), pp. 129–32.

24. F. M. L. Thompson, *Gentrification and the Enterprise Culture: Britain 1780–1980* (Oxford: Oxford University Press, 2001), p. 155.

25. For one historian who has successfully used novels as a means of identifying contemporary culture see J. Taylor, *Creating Capitalism: Joint-Stock Enterprise in British Politics and Culture, 1800–1870* (Woodbridge: Royal Historical Society/Boydell Press, 2006).

26. F. Wicks, *The Veiled Hand: A Novel of the Sixties, the Seventies, and the Eighties* (London 1892), 'Preface'.

27. See J. Taylor, 'Business in Pictures: Representations of Railway Enterprise in the Satirical Press in Britain, 1845–1870', *Past and Present*, 189 (2005), pp. 111–45; B. Weiss, *The Hell of the English: Bankruptcy and the Victorian Novel* (Lewisburg, PA: Bucknell University Press, 1986), p. 56; Robinson, *Imagining London*, p. 164.

28. T. W. Craik (ed.), *The Revels: History of Drama in English*, 7 vols (London: Methuen & Co.) vol. 6 (1975), pp. 33–5; vol. 7 (1978), pp. 7–9, 14–18; J. Moody, 'The Drama of Capital: Risk, Belief, and Liability on the Victorian Stage' in F. O'Gorman (ed.), *Victorian Literature and Finance* (Oxford: Oxford University Press, 2007), pp. 96–9.

29. K. Grahame, *Pagan Papers* (London: John Lane, 1898), pp. 65, 188–9.

30. For the world of novelists, novels, publishers and booksellers in this period see the encyclopedic P. Waller, *Writers, Readers and Reputations: Literary Life in Britain, 1870–1918* (Oxford: Oxford University Press, 2006).

31. For a few examples of those who take this approach see P. Bratlinger, *Fictions of the State: Culture and Credit in Britain, 1694–1994* (Ithaca, NY and London: Cornell University Press, 1996); C. Gallagher, *The Industrial Reformation of English Fiction: Discourse and Narrative Form, 1832–1867* (Chicago, IL: University of Chicago Press, 1985); B. Knezevic, *Figures of Finance Capitalism: Writing, Class and Capital in the Age of Dickens* (New York and London: Routledge, 2003); Weiss, *The Hell of the English*.

32. Both Weiner and Finn have fallen into this trap, for example. See M. C. Finn, *The Character of Credit: Personal Debt in English Culture, 1740–1914* (Cambridge: Cambridge University Press, 2003).

33. See the entries in M. C. Rintoul, *Dictionary of Real People and Places in Fiction* (London: Routledge, 1993).

34. For a recent introduction to the subject of finance and literature see the introduction and chapters in O'Gorman (ed.), *Victorian Literature and Finance*.

35. S. Petch, 'Law, Literature, and Victorian Studies' *Victorian Literature and Culture* 35 (2007), pp. 361-384, on p. 374; H. F. Tucker, *A Companion to Victorian Literature and Culture* (Oxford: Blackwell, 1999), p. 225 (C. Crosby); Knezevic, *Figures of Finance Capitalism*, p. 43; Weiss, *The Hell of the English*, p. 15. More generally see the special issue of Victorian Studies devoted to Victorian investors. *Victorian Studies*, 45 (2002).

36. See X. Barron (ed.), *London 1066–1914: Literary Sources and Documents*, 3 vols (Mountfield 1997), vols 2 and 3.

37. Finn's discussion of finance is largely confined to personal lending and borrowing before 1850, for example. See Finn, *The Character of Credit*.

38. See N. Russell, *The Novelist and Mammon: Literary Responses to the World of Commerce in the Nineteenth Century* (Oxford: Clarendon Press, 1986), and J. R. Reed, 'A Friend to Mammon: Speculation in Victorian literature' *Victorian Studies* 27 (1983–4), pp. 179-202.

1 Capitalism and Culture: 1800–1856

1. Russell, *Novelist and Mammon*, pp. 24, 26, 29; P. Slack, 'Perceptions of the Metropolis in Seventeenth Century England', pp 161–180, on p. 162 and L. Hannah, 'The Moral Economy of Business: A Historical Perspective on Ethics and Efficiency', pp. 285–300, on p. 286, both in Burke et al (eds), *Civil Histories*; A. Pollard (ed.), *The Representation of Business in English Literature* (London: Institute of Economic Affairs, 2000), Speck, pp. 19–24. For general attitudes towards finance see S. Banner, *Anglo-American Securities Regulation: Cultural and Political Roots, 1690–1860* (Cambridge: Cambridge University Press 1998),and R. E. Wright, *One Nation Under Debt: Hamilton, Jefferson, and the History of what we Owe* (New York and London: McGraw-Hill, 2008).

2. W. H. Ainsworth, *John Law: The Projector* (London: Chapman and Hall, 1864).

3. Gauci, *Emporium of the World*, pp. 2, 4, 14–15, 8, 104, 125–7, 135, 151, 208.

4. J. Austen, *Pride and Prejudice* (London: T. Egerton, 1813), pp. 75, 82, 177, 228, 269, 318, 336, 366, 374, 386, 395–6.

5. Sir W. Scott, *Rob Roy* (London: Longman, Hurst, Rees, Orme, & Brown 1818), pp. 67–8, 70–3, 82–3, 94, 114, 166–7, 222–35, 262, 266, 417–8, 420, 423, 426–7, 452.

6. W. H. Ainsworth, *Old St. Paul's: A Tale of the Plague and the Fire* (London: Collins, 1841), pp. 15, 194, 605, 637.

7. For the positive view of bankers in the works of Sir Walter Scott, see C. Munn, 'The Positive Depiction of Entrepreneurs and Entrepreneurship in the Novels of Sir Walter Scott' (Unpublished paper), pp. 11–13.

8. For these events see R. C. Michie, *The London Stock Exchange*, ch. 2.

9. T. L .Peacock, *Crotchet Castle* (London: T. Hookham, 1831), pp. 127–8, 130–1, 145, 148, 164–5, 200, 248.

10. H. Martineau, *Berkeley the Banker*, 2 parts (London: Charles Fox, 1833) part 1, pp. 2, 8, 13–24, 38–9, 65–7, 82, 132–141, 156–7; part 2, pp. 24–5, 131, 138–9.

11. Pollard (ed.), *Representation of Business*, Carnall pp 36, 48.

12. Ainsworth, *Old St. Paul's*, p. 15.

13. Russell, *Novelist and Mammon* pp. 99, 191–2, 195–6.

14. C. Dickens, *Dealings with the Firm of Dombey and son, wholesale, Retail, and for Exportation* (London: Bradbury & Evans 1846–8), pp. 20, 57, 64, 105, 110, 149, 193, 213–17, 355, 732–4, 743, 863–4, 935–9, 954.

15. W. M. Thackeray, *The History of Samuel Titmarsh and the Great Hoggarty Diamond* (London 1841), pp. 9, 32–3, 46, 50–1, 66, 74–5, 78–82, 91–4.

16. W. M. Thackeray, *The Book of Snobs: Sketches of Life and Character* (London 1846), pp. 28–31

17. That is to be found in *Rob Roy*, for example. See pp. 222–5.

18. W. M. Thackeray, *Vanity Fair* (London 1847–8), pp. 54–6, 140–1, 145, 157, 202, 206–7, 213–4, 217, 253, 538–42, 713.

19. B. Disraeli, *Coningsby or The New Generation* (London: Henry Colburn, 1844), pp. 230–2, 235–8, 242, 278, 357–8.

20. B. Disraeli, *Tancred or The New Crusade* (London: Henry Colburn, 1847), pp. 112, 114–5, 124–6, 165, 212, 254, 282.

21. F. E. Smedley, *Frank Fairleigh or Scenes from the Life of a Private Pupil* (London: A. Hall, 1850), pp. 48, 84.

22. In the pre-decimal British coinage there were twelve pennies to the shilling and 240 to the pound. Thus one-and-nine was one shilling and nine pence, or twenty-one pennies.

23. G. M Reynolds, *The Mysteries of London* (1844–56), ed. T Thomas (Keele: Keele University, 1996), pp. 26–9, 46, 66–7, 75, 132–3, 197, 234–7, 304–8, 323.

24. C. Brontë, *Vilette* (London: Smith, Elder & Co., 1853), pp. 95, 109.

25. W. M. Thackeray, *The Newcomes: Memories of a Most Respectable Family*, 2 vols (London: Bradbury and Evans, 1853–5), vol. 1, pp. 14–18, 41, 52, 55, 57, 106, 279, 314; vol. 2, pp. 92, 124–5, 128–9, 165–6, 287–9, 295, 299, 301, 344–5, 358–363, 379, 399, 434.

26. For an idea of the impression it made in Scotland see W. E. Aytoun, *How we got up the Glenmutchkin Railway and how we got out of it* (1845), in W. L. Renwick (ed.), *W. E. Aytoun: Stories and Verse* (Edinburgh: Edinburgh University Press, 1964), pp. 1–39.

27. W. M. Thackeray, *The Diary of C. Jeames De La Pluche, Esq.* (1854), in *The Works of William Makepeace Thackeray* (London: Smith, Elder & Co., 1872), vol. 8, pp. 311–12.

28. C. Kingsley, *Yeast: A Problem* (London, 1851), pp. 113–14, 155–6, 158, 170–1, 180, 197, 211.

29. R. Bell, *The Ladder of Gold: An English Story* (London: Richard Bentley, 1850), pp. 52, 87, 98–100, 167.

30. Ibid., pp. 104, 107, 118

31. Ibid., pp. 129–31, 160–3, 171, 188, 195,199, 224–30, 256–7

32. Ibid., pp. 201, 302–3, 306–11, 315, 366–7, 398, 437

33. Mrs Gore, *The Money Lender* (London: Geo. Routledge & Co., 1854), pp. 16–17, 23, 31, 38, 46, 95, 98,113, 134–9, 167–8.

34. Ibid, pp. 153, 162–3, 167, 181–90, 208–9, 226–7, 242.

35. Ibid., p. 152.

36. E. Robinson, *The City Banker or Love and Money* (London: C.J. Skeet, 1856), pp. 3, 8–9, 22–5.

37. Ibid., pp. 22–25, 203.

38. Ibid., pp. 22, 52, 336–7, 346–7, 420–4.

39. W. Collins, *A Rogue's Life* (London: Household Worlds, 1856).

2 Financiers and Merchants: 1856–1870

1. For the development of the City in the nineteenth century see R. C. Michie, 'The City of London: Functional and Spatial Unity in the Nineteenth Century' in H. A. Diederiks and D. Reeder (eds), *Cities of Finance* (Amsterdam: Proceedings of the Colloquium, 1991), pp. 189–206. For London as a financial centre in comparative perspective see Y. Cassis, *Capitals of Capital: A History of International Financial Centres, 1780–2005*, trans. J. Collier (Cambridge: Cambridge University Press, 2006).

2. C. Dickens, *Our Mutual Friend* (London: Chapman & Hall 1864–5), p. 174.

3. C. Dickens, *Little Dorrit* (London: Bradbury & Evans 1857), pp. 445, 628, 772, 777. See Pollard (ed.), *Representation of Business*, pp. 72, 75, 82.

4. For details of financial misdemeanours in the City at this time see G. Robb, *White-Collar Crime in Modern England: Financial Fraud and Business Morality, 1845–1929* (Cambridge: Cambridge University Press, 1992).

5. C. Lever, *Davenport Dunn or The Man and the Day*, 3 vols, (Leipzig: Bernhard Tauchnitz 1859), vol. 1, pp 22, 26, 41–3, 108, 130–2; vol. 3, p. 25.

6. Ibid., vol. 2, pp. 16–19, 101, 127, 166–7, 175–7, 181–3 ; vol. 3, pp. 29–30, 34–5, 39–40, 152–3.
7. Ibid., vol. 3, pp. 104–5, 118–20.
8. Ibid., vol. 1, pp. 55, 61, 243 ; vol. 2, p. 128–31, 152–5; vol. 3, pp. 30, 131, 361.
9. Ibid., vol. 2, pp. 169, 190–216 ; vol. 2, p. 195 ; vol. 3, 150–1, 160–1, 174–5.
10. Ibid., vol. 2, pp. 195, 238; vol. 3, pp. 52–3, 84–6,130, 336.
11. Ibid., vol. 3, pp. 122, 161, 328–334, 336–340, 361–2.
12. Ibid., vol. 3, pp. 352–3, 358–62.
13. C. Lever, *That Boy of Norcott's* (London: Smith, Elder & Co., 1869), pp. 172, 192, 196–7, 222, 313–17.
14. A. Trollope, *The Three Clerks: A Novel* (London: Bentley, 1858), pp. 73, 81, 85–8, 98, 110–12, 156, 165–6, 229, 247–8, 304–5, 311–2, 379, 399, 418–21, 472.
15. Mrs H. Wood, *East Lynne* (London: Richard Bentley, 1861), pp. 2–3
16. Mrs H. Wood, *Oswald Cray: A Novel* (London: Richard Bentley, 1864), pp. 150–1, 161, 214–15.
17. Ibid., pp. 250–2, 282–7, 294–5, 330–340, 343–8, 416, 444–8, 450–4.
18. Ainsworth, *John Law*, pp. 42, 192, 280, 408.
19. *Commercial Tales and Sketches* (London 1864), pp. 16–17, 36, 72–3, 96–7, 136–41, 151, 160–1, 166–8, 217, 272, 276.
20. C. Reade, *Hard Cash; A Matter-of-fact Romance* (London: Sampson Low, Son, & Marston, 1863), pp. 8–9, 93, 105, 126–32, 167, 213–28, 249–53, 358, 415–7, 549, 563, 569, 604–5, 610–13.
21. C. Reade and D. Boucicault, *Foul Play* (London: Bradbury, Evans & Co., 1868), pp. 1–3, 36–7, 53, 106–13, 310–11, 408–12.
22. C. Dickens and W. Collins, *No Thoroughfare* (London: Chapman & Hall 1867), pp. 7–10, 26, 36, 43, 65–6, 68–9.
23. B. Disraeli, *Lothair* (London: Longmans, Green, and Co, 1870), pp. 119, 206, 366–7.
24. M. E. Braddon, 'Levison's Victim' (1870), in *Victorian Tales of Mystery and Detection: An Oxford Anthology* (Oxford: Oxford University Press, 1992), pp. 69–82.
25. F. G. Trafford [C. Riddell], *George Geith of Fen Court* (London: Tinsley Brothers, 1864), pp. 8, 12–13, 17, 21–2, 25, 55, 88, 106, 114–5, 139, 161.
26. Ibid., pp. 247–8, 255, 339, 349, 361.
27. Ibid., pp. 183, 194–7, 202–3, 246,251, 307, 380, 450.
28. Ibid., pp. 388. 393–4, 397, 468–9.
29. F. G. Trafford [C. Riddell], *The Race for Wealth*, 2 vols (Leipzig: Bernhard Tauchnitz, 1866), vol. 1, pp 8–11, 14–15, 17–19, 22, 56–7, 77, 109, 121, 196, 224–7, 236–7, 242–3, 258–9, 308–9, 317.
30. Ibid., vol. 2, pp 55, 58–60, 62, 172–180, 257, 287, 308–13.
31. Ibid., vol. 2, pp 82–3, 87,125–6.
32. Mrs J. H. Riddell, *Austin Friars* (London: Tinsley Brothers, 1870), pp. 2, 7, 27, 44–5, 63–4, 73, 121,150–3,194, 204–5.
33. Ibid., pp. 234–6, 243, 380–6.
34. Ibid., pp. 70–3, 151–3, 242–3, 300, 312–13.
35. Ibid., pp. 73, 167–9.
36. W. Collins, *The Moonstone* (London: Tinsley Brothers, 1868), pp. 54, 300, 507.
37. C. Dickens, 'Hunted Down' in M. Cox (ed.), *Victorian Tales of Mystery and Detection* (Oxford: Oxford University Press, 1992), pp. 48–65, on p. 48.

38. For an attempt to arrive at a generalization see G. R. Searle, *Morality and the Market in Victorian Britain* (Oxford: Clarendon Press, 1998), pp. 78, 84–5.

3 Damnation and Forgiveness: 1870–1885

1. For the development of the City in this period see R. C. Michie, 'The City of London: Functional and Spatial Unity'. For a comparative perspective, especially the position of Paris and Berlin, see Cassis, *Capitals of Capital*.

2. J. S. Le Fanu, *Checkmate* (London: Hurst and Blackett, 1871), pp. 4, 33, 80, 107, 113, 121, 126, 158, 184–5, 194, 204–5, 207, 216, 222–3, 242, 310, 336–7, 310.

3. A. Trollope, *The Last Chronicle of Barset* (London: Smith, Elder & Co., 1867), p. 259 (I would like to thank Philip Williamson for this reference).

4. A. Trollope, *The Way We Live Now*, 2 vols (London: Chapman and Hall, 1874–5), vol. 1, pp. 30–4, 48–9, 84, 268–9, 349; vol. 2, 26–7, 89, 91–2, 99, 140, 294, 304, 307, 319, 361.

5. A. Trollope, *The Prime Minister*, 4 vols (London: Chapman and Hall, 1876), vol. 1, pp. 1–15, 21, 26–7, 222, 228, 230–6; vol. 2, p. 173, 194.

6. The Spectre, *Ye Vampyres: A Legend or The National Betting-Ring, Showing What Became of It* (London: Samuel Tinsley, 1875), pp. 9–10, 17–18, 24.

7. For more on Baron Grant and the Emma Silver Mine see Robb, *White-Collar Crime in Modern England*, pp. 99–101.

8. Spectre, *Ye Vampyres*, pp. 22–4, 44–5, 50–1, 53, 62–3, 70–1, 75, 81, 133–4, 157, 176–7, 192–3.

9. Ibid., pp. 190, 196, 205, 207–8, 230, 264, 274–9, 280–1.

10. See H. Roy, *The Stock Exchange* (London: Houlston and Wright, 1860), p. 13; E. McDermott, *The London Stock Exchange: Its Constitution and Modes of Business* (London: Railway News and Joint-Stock Journal, 1877), p. 35; A. Crump, *The Theory of Stock Exchange Speculation* (London: Longmans, Green & Co., 1874), p. 10; H. May, 'The London Stock Exchange' *Fortnightly Review* (1885), pp. 566–80.

11. E. Pinto, *Ye Outside Fools! Glimpses inside the Stock Exchange*, new edn (London: Samuel Tinsley, 1877), pp. 34, 370.

12. W. Besant and J. Rice, *The Golden Butterfly* (London: Chatto and Windus, 1877), pp. 47, 86–90, 498, 509.

13. Ibid., pp. 47, 130–2, 141,165, 175, 228–9, 285, 490

14. Ibid., pp. 333–9, 431, 443, 486, 519–22

15. Ibid, pp. 532–6, 560–73

16. C. Wood, *Victorian Panorama: Paintings of Victorian Life* (London: Faber & Faber, 1976), pp. 11, 13, 16–17, 37–42; L. Lambourne, *Victorian Painting* (London: Phaidon, 1999), pp. 273–4; A. Noakes, *William Frith: Extraordinary Victorian Painter* (London: Jupiter Books, 1978), p. 126; Robinson, *Imagining London*, p. 164. More generally see C. Wood, *William Powell Frith: A Painter and his World* (Stroud: Sutton, 2006); M. Bills and V. Knight (eds), *William Powell Frith: Painting the Victorian Age* (New Haven, CT and London: Yale University Press, 2006).

17. W. P. Frith, *My Autobiography and Reminiscences* (London: Richard Bentley and Son, 1888), pp. 295, 343, 356–9, 354, 461, 469; *Fun*, 31 (23 June 1880), p. 250.

18. W. Collins, *The Haunted Hotel* (London 1878), p. 151

19. H. Smart, *The Great Tontine* (London: : Chapman & Hall 1881), pp 15, 38, 40–1, 145.

20. Besant and Rice, *Golden Butterfly*, p. 264; W. Collins, *Who Killed Zebedee?* (London 1881), p. 13.

21. Besant and Rice, *Golden Butterfly*, pp. 153–4, 187.

22. W. Besant, *All Sorts and Condition of Men* (London: Chatto & Windus, 1882), pp. 12–13, 28–9, 57, 133, 152, 166, 175, 261, 326, 384–6.

23. G. Gissing, *The Nether World* (London: Smith, Elder & Co., 1889); A. Morrison, *A Child of the Jago* (London: Methuen & Co., 1896).

24. i.e. nine old pennies out of the 240 in a pound.

25. W. Besant, *All in a Garden Fair: The Simple Story of Three Boys and a Girl* (London: Chatto & Windus, 1883), pp. 29–30, 34, 45, 57–8, 68–70, 86, 103–7, 226, 232–5, 257, 282, 308.

26. The reference to a 'hooked nose' suggests that he was Jewish but this is not stated.

27. Besant, *All in a Garden Fair*, pp. 8–13, 101, 125, 133–9, 147, 150–3, 156–7 196–7, 199–203, 238, 240–1, 26–5, 283–4, 295–6, 298–301.

28. Ibid., pp. 8–13, 29, 32,175,209, 220, 238, 240.

29. S. Butler, *The Way of all Flesh* (London: Grant Richards, 1903), pp. 264, 273–4, 316–7, 370–1, 381, 419 (Though the novel was published in 1903 the author stopped work on it in 1884).

30. R. L. Stevenson, *The Dynamiter* (London: Longmans, Green & Co., 1885), p. 2

4 Avarice and Honesty: 1885–1895

1. For an overview of the City in this period see R. C. Michie, 'The City of London as a Global Financial Centre, 1880–1939: Finance, Foreign Exchange and the First World War' in P. L. Cottrell, E. Lange and U. Olsson (eds.), *Centres and Peripheries in Banking: The Historical Development of Financial Markets* (Aldershot: Ashgate, 2007), pp. 41–80.

2. J. K. Jerome, *Three Men in a Boat* (London: Simpkin, Marshall, Hamilton, Kent & Co., 1889), pp. 11, 17.

3. All provincial banks had a London correspondent bank to which they sent idle funds and from whom they borrowed funds when required. By this date such arrangements were increasingly being replaced by branch banking directed from a London head office.

4. W. Besant and J. Rice, *Ready-Money Mortiboy: A Matter-of-fact Story* (London, 1891), pp. 1–2, 117–18, 121–4, 143, 192–3, 323.

5. Besant and Rice, *Ready-Money Mortiboy*, pp. 318, 394, 423, 444.

6. W. Collins, *The Evil Genius* (London: Chatto & Windus, 1886), p. 228.

7. O. Wilde, *The Importance of Being Earnest* (performed in 1895, printed 1899), in I. Murray (ed.), *Oscar Wilde, The Major Works* (Oxford: Oxford University Press, 1989), p. 529.

8. W. Collins and W. Besant, *Blind Love* (London: Chatto & Windus, 1890), pp. 127, 254, 295. The novel was completed by Besant at Collins's request.

9. O. Wilde, *An Ideal Husband* (performed in 1895, printed 1899), in *Wilde, Major Works*, pp. 404–9, 418–421, 456–7, 460.

10. M. Williams, *Round London: Down East and Up West* (London: Macmillan, 1892), pp. 181–2, 217–18, 221, 224, 228, 256–270, 299, 304–12, 331, 341.

11. W. S. Gilbert and A. S. Sullivan, *Utopia, Limited; or, the Flowers of Progress* (1893), in *The Complete Plays of Gilbert and Sullivan* (New York and London: W.W. Norton, 1976), pp. 535, 537–8.

12. Business on the London Stock Exchange was conducted on the basis of fortnightly settlement when all purchases had to be paid for and all securities sold had to be delivered. Contango was the term applied to a deal whereby payment was delayed until the next settlement date. Backwardation was the term used when it was the delivery of the securities that was delayed. In each case the cost of the delay was a payment representing the current price of the securities and the agreed price when the deal was struck. Under the Companies Acts a company had to have at least seven shareholders before it could be registered for Limited Liability. Once registered, a company was only liable for any losses it made to the extent of its capital. Those holding shares could lose the value of the fully paid up shares they held but nothing more, whereas in a partnership those owning the business were responsible for all its debts to the fullest extent of their wealth.

13. I. Zangwill, 'Cheating the Gallows' (1893) in Cox (ed.), *Victorian Tales of Mystery*, pp. 241–53, on p. 243.

14. M. Pemberton, *The Impregnable City* (London: Cassell & Co., 1895), pp. 86, 92–3, 246–7, 306.

15. F. Wicks, *The Veiled Hand: a Novel of the Sixties, the Seventies, and the Eighties*, (London: Eden & Co., 1892), pp. 10–11, 53–5, 67, 117–18, 166,170–3, 200, 220–1.

16. Ibid., pp 177–9, 181–6, 189–193, 202–5.

17. Ibid., pp., 237–240, 250–4, 256, 264–5.

18. Ibid., pp., 268–9, 275, 281–2, 291, 314, 316.

19. Ibid., pp., 306, 311, 393, 398–9, 416.

20. Collins and Besant, *Blind Love*, pp. 57, 91,114.

21. H. R. Haggard, *Colonel Quaritch V.C.* (London: Longmans, Green & Co., 1888), pp. 32–3, 46–7, 85–8, 90,104–5, 126–7, 160–3, 248–50.

22. G. Gissing, *Born in Exile* (London: A. & C. Black, 1892), pp. 3–5

23. G. Allen, 'The Great Ruby Robbery' in Cox (ed.), *Victorian Tales of Mystery*, pp. 214–232, on p. 214.

24. M. Corelli, *The Sorrows of Satan* (London: Methuen & Co, 1895), p. 63.

25. Ibid., pp. 12, 76, 98, 173, 386–7.

26. Ibid., pp. 264, 384–6.

27. G. and W. Grossmith, *The Diary of a Nobody* (London: Arrowsmith, 1892), pp. 19–20, 87, 93–4, 147–8, 163–5, 170, 203, 207.

28. O. Wilde, *The Model Millionaire* (1891), in V. B. Holland, (ed.), *The Complete Works of Oscar Wilde* (London: Collins 1948–66), p. 219.

29. A. C. Doyle, 'The Adventure of The Beryl Coronet' (1892) in *The Complete Illustrated Sherlock Holmes* (Ware: Omega Books, 1986), pp. 237–51, p. 240.

30. H. Hill, 'The Sapient Monkey' (1892) in Cox (ed.), *Victorian Tales of Mystery*, pp. 233–41.

31. H. Blyth, 'The Accusing Shadow' (1894), in Cox (ed.), *Victorian Tales of Mystery*, pp. 303–41, on pp. 310–4, 338.

32. Collins and Besant, *Blind Love*, pp. 127, 254, 295. The novel was completed by Besant at Collins's request.

33. Doyle, 'Beryl Coronet' in *Complete Illustrated Holmes*, pp. 312–21

34. A. Morrison, *The Case of Laker, Absconded* (1895), in H. Greene (ed.), *The Complete Rivals of Sherlock Holmes* (London: Bodley Head, 1973), pp. 5–73, pp. 45, 66.

35. H. Keen, 'The Tin Box' in Cox (ed.), *Victorian Tales of Mystery*, pp. 420–37, pp. 424–6.

36. Hill, 'The Sapient Monkey' pp. 233–4, 239–40 and I. Zangwill, 'Cheating the Gallows', p. 241–2, 245, 252. Both in Cox (ed.), *Victorian Tales of Mystery*.

37. Sir A. C. Doyle, 'The Adventure of the Stockbroker's Clerk' (1893) in *Complete Illustrated Holmes*, pp. 311–21.

38. F. Hume, 'The Greenstone God and the Stockbroker' (1894), in Cox (ed.), *Victorian Tales of Mystery*, pp. 274–89, on pp. 275, 286.

39. W. Besant, *Beyond the Dreams of Avarice* (London: Chatto & Windus 1895), pp. 10–11, 47, 58–9, 148–9, 156–161, 309, 324.

40. A. S. Swan, *The Strait Gate* (London: S.W. Partridge & Co., 1894), pp. 1–13, 16–18, 23–4, 74–5, 102, 154–7, 161, 204, 207, 232, 238–9.

41. See Robinson, *Imagining London*.

5 Gold and Greed 1895–1900

1. I have dealt with this brief period extensively in R. C. Michie, 'Gamblers, Fools, Victims or Wizards? The British Investor in the Public Mind, 1850–1930' (Paper delivered at a conference on investors, Milton Keynes, June 2008), More generally, see R. C. Michie, *The London Stock Exchange*, ch. 3.

2. H. Hill, *Guilty Gold: A Romance of Financial Fraud and City Crime* (London: C. Arthur Pearson Ltd., 1896), pp. 1–4, 16–17, 34–6, 66, 69, 78, 351–2.

3. Ibid., p. 78, 116.

4. Ibid., pp. 347–8.

5. Ibid., pp. 10–14, 134–5, 346–7

6. Ibid., pp. 2–6, 41–5, 66.

7. Ibid., pp. 40–1, 346–7.

8. Ibid., pp. 207–9.

9. Ibid., pp. 209–14.

10. Ibid., pp. 15–16, 27–33.

11. Ibid., pp. 35–9, 47–64.

12. Ibid., p. 352.

13. Ibid., pp. 351–3.

14. Ibid., p. 354.

15. F. Gribble, *The Lower Life* (London: A. D. Innes & Co., 1896), pp. 1–2, 6, 8, 10, 14, 16, 20–1, 25, 30–1, 61.

16. Ibid., pp. 32, 40–5, 53–5, 63–71, 73–4.

17. Ibid., pp 91–3, 100–1, 108–9, 118–120, 126–9, 137, 142, 149,192, 195–7, 236–7.

18. Ibid., pp 131–3, 149, 152, 176, 190–1, 238. 278–80, 285,288–9 294, 303, 307–11.

19. G. Gissing, *The Whirlpool* (London: Lawrence and Bullen, 1897), pp. 6–10, 14–15, 17, 38, 40, 42–4, 48, 52, 64, 85, 118, 129, 166, 194, 196–7, 204–5, 231, 259, 302, 377, 383, 416.

20. Ibid., pp. 6–10

21. Ibid., pp 17, 129, 166, 196–7, 259, 383, 418

22. Ibid., p. 231 cf 194, 416

23. Ibid., pp. 204–5, 377

24. Ibid., pp. 14–15, 38, 40, 42

25. Ibid., pp. 43–4, 48, 52, 64, 118

26. O. Schreiner, *Trooper Peter Halket of Mashonaland* (London 1897), pp. 27–36, 83.

27. A. Morrison, 'The Affair of the "Avalanche Bicycle and Tyre Co. Limited."'(1897), in Greene (ed.), *Complete Rivals of Sherlock Holmes*, pp. 103–130, pp. 103, 106–7.

28. H. Frederic, *The Market-Place* (London: William Heinemann, Ltd, 1899), pp. 6–11, 20–2, 26–7, 36, 44, 48–9, 81–2, 157, 181–4, 187, 197, 202–3, 205, 214, 217–19, 236, 240, 282–5, 293–4, 296, 306, 308–9, 312, 358–9.

29. J. Oxenham, *Rising Fortunes: The Story of a Man's Beginnings* (London: Hurst and Blackett, 1899), pp. 73, 164, 172–4, 221–3, 273–5.

30. A. C. Doyle, *A Duet With An Occasional Chorus* (London: G. Richards, 1899), pp. 11–12, 249–262.

31. For another brief example see G. Du Maurier, *The Martian: a Novel* (London: Harper, 1898), p. 302.

32. Gissing, *Whirlpool*, p. 302.

33. G. Gissing, *The Crown of Life* (London: Methuen & Co., 1899), pp. 61, 112, 159, 179, 297.

34. H. S. Merriman, *Roden's Corner* (London: Smith, Elder & Co 1898), pp. 94, 191–2, 121–42, 192–5, 220–1, 245, 269, 332, 341–2.

35. H. James, *The Awkward Age* (London: William Heinemann Ltd 1899), pp. 40, 64, 141–2, 172, 239, 271.

36. A. Bennett, *A Man from the North* (London: John Lane, 1898), p. 12.

37. E. W. Hornung, *The Black Mask* (London 1901), in *The Collected Raffles Stories* pp. 234, 324–5; E. W. Hornung, *Raffles: The Amateur Cracksman* (London 1899), p. 126.

38. G. Boothby, *The Duchess of Wiltshire's Diamonds* (1897), in Greene (ed.), *Complete Rivals of Sherlock Holmes*, p. 75.

6 Money and Mansions: 1900–1910

1. C. C. Turner, 'Money London' in G. R. Sims, *Living London* (London: Cassell & Co., 1902), reprinted in R. C. Michie (ed.), *The Development of London as a Financial Centre* (London: I. B. Tauris, 2000), pp. 33–57.

2. A. H. Beavan, *Imperial London* (London: J.M. Dent & Co., 1901), pp. 217–18, 227, 243, 314.

3. For the development of the City of London in this period see R. C. Michie, 'The City of London and British Banking, 1900–1939' in Wrigley (ed.), *Early Twentieth-Century Britain*, and R. C. Michie, 'A Financial Phoenix: The City of London in the Twentieth Century' in Y. Cassis and E. Bussierre (eds), *London and Paris as International Financial Centres* (Oxford: Oxford University Press, 2005).

4. A. C. Doyle, 'The Adventure of the Norwood Builder' (1903) in *Complete Illustrated Holmes*, pp. 555–68, pp. 557–8.

5. Pollard (ed.), *Representation of Business*, Simmons p. 99; Barron (ed.), *London*, vol. 3, pp. 137, 308.

6. H. Hill, *Millions of Mischief: The Story of a Great Secret* (London: Ward, Lock & Co., 1905), p. 56.

7. H. Hill, *The One Who Saw* (London: Cassell & Co., 1905), pp. 74, 79.

8. W. Le Queux, *Guilty Bonds* (London: G. Routledge & Sons, 1891), p. 103.

9. W. Le Queux, *The Crooked Way* (London: Methuen & Co., 1908), pp. 5, 159–60, 214.

10. W. S. Jackson, *Nine Points of the Law* (London: John Lane 1903), pp. 24–31, 36, 57, 159.

11. C. J. C. W. Hyne, *Thompson's Progress* (London 1903), pp. 245 cf. 249.

12. J. Oxenham, *Profit and Loss* (London Methuen & Co., 1906), pp. 5–8, 10–11, 48, 115, 262, 273–4, 295, 309–11.

13. E. Wallace, *The Four Just Men* (London: Tallis Press, 1905), p. 28.

14. E. P. Oppenheim, *A Prince of Sinners* (London: Ward, Lock & Co., 1903), pp. 81, 120, 136, 165–6, 168–9, 176–7.

15. S. Kuppord, *A Fortune from the Sky* (London: Thomas Nelson & Sons, 1903), pp. 16–17,20–1.

16. G. Gissing, *Will Warburton: A Romance of Real Life* (London: Archibald Constable 1905), pp. 18, 91, 96–100.

17. J. S. Fletcher, *The Contents of the Coffin* (1909), in Greene (ed.), *Complete Rivals of Sherlock Holmes*, p. 924.

18. G. Thorne and L. Custance, *Sharks: A Fantastic Novel for Business Men and their Families* (London: Greening & Co.,1904), pp. 2–15, 20–3, 30–3, 50–5, 144–5, 156–7, 180–1, 188–9, 226–9, 232–5, 278–9, 298–9, 340–5.

19. H. R. Haggard, *The Yellow God : An Idol of Africa* (London: Cassell & Co 1909), pp. 1–18, 20, 22, 33–4, 40, 42, 48, 51–2, 86, 89, 116.

20. H. G. Wells, *Kipps: The Story of a Simple Soul* (London: Macmillan & Co., 1905), pp. 219, 223, 296, 306.

21. H. G. Wells, *Tono-Bungay* (London 1909), pp. 81–2, 128–9, 180–3, 241, 289, 297, 304, 325–7.

22. Pollard (ed.), *Representation of Business*, pp. 139, 180–2.

23. B. Stoker, *The Lady and the Shroud* (London: William Heinemann, Ltd, 1909), pp. 32, 43. Conversion of this fortune to current values would make Roger Melton worth £5 billion.

24. E. P. Oppenheim, *A Prince of Sinners*, pp. 81, 120, 136, 165–6, 168–9, 176–7.

25. E. P. Oppenheim, *Anna, The Adventuress* (London: Ward, Lock & Co., 1904), pp. 8, 26–7, 56, 63–4, 72, 94, 110, 13.

26. E. P. Oppenheim, *Jeanne of the Marshes* (London: Ward, Lock & Co., 1909), pp. 22, 26, 46, 174, 193, 251.

27. E. P. Oppenheim, *Mr Wingrave, Millionaire* (London: Ward, Lock & Co., 1906), pp. 15, 40, 104–117, 161, 235–6.

28. Wallace, *Four Just Men*, p. 66.

29. H. S. Merriman, *The Last Hope* (London: Macmillan & Co., 1904), pp. 144–151, 211, 307–9, 330–1.

30. J. Galsworthy, *The Man of Property* (London: William Heinemann, 1906), pp. 12–13, 16, 19–20, 29, 36, 55,63, 67, 87, 145–6, 175, 178, 184, 186, 225.(The other volumes in the Forsyte Saga were written after the First World War and so have been excluded from consideration here).

31. J. Galsworthy, *The Country House* (London: William Heinemann, Ltd, 1907), pp. 10–11,183–4.

32. H. Belloc, *Emmanuel Burden, Merchant, of Thames St., in the City of London, Exporter of Hardware: A Record of his Lineage, Speculations, Last Days and Death* (London, 1904), pp. 54–61, 65–76, 82–91,104, 113, 119, 121–2, 158, 170–1,196–7,206–7, 212, 223.

33. H. Belloc, *Mr Clutterbuck's Election* (London: E. Nash, 1908), pp. 1–3, 11–13, 16–18, 20–4, 31–46, 52–62, 87–8, 120, 152, 180–1, 193–8, 216–220, 272–6.

34. G. K. Chesterton, *The Innocence of Father Brown* (London 1910/11), in *The Complete Father Brown* (Harmondsworth: Penguin, 1981), pp. 55, 61, 64.

35. Benson, *The Osbornes*, pp. 68–71, 263–4.

36. E. M. Forster, *Howards End* (London: Edward Arnold, 1910), pp. 28–9, 58, 139–140, 168–9.

37. P. G. Wodehouse, *Psmith in the City* (London: A. & C. Black, 1910), pp. 11, 19, 26–7, 30, 71–2, 77, 128, 131–2.

38. J. Hocking, *The Man Who Rose Again*, (London: Hodder & Stoughton, 1906), pp. 4, 11–14, 36–7, 69, 75–6, 238, 246–8.

39. Oppenheim, *Anna*, pp. 8, 26–7, 56, 63–4, 72, 94, 110, 139.

40. Baroness Orczy, *The Mysterious Death on the Underground Railway* (1901/2), in Greene (ed.), *Complete Rivals of Sherlock Holmes*, pp. 221–41, pp. 234–5.

41. E. P. Oppenheim, *The Mysterious Mr Sabin* (London, 1905), pp. 234, 296

42. The most relevant novels are Arnold Bennett, *Anna of the Five Towns* (London: Chatto and Windus, 1902); *Clayhanger* (London: Methuen & Co., 1910); *Hilda Lessways* (London: Methuen & Co., 1911); *These Twain* (London: Methuen & Co., 1916); *The Card* (London: Methuen & Co., 1911). See especially Bennett, *Anna* pp. 41–5, 64–6, 109, 111.

43. H. Norman and G. C. Ashton Jonson, 'The London Stock Exchange' *Century Illustrated Monthly Magazine* (June 1903), pp. 177–94, pp. 177, 189, 193. See Robb, *White-Collar Crime in Modern England,* pp. 156–7.

44. A. Hope, *Tristram of Blent: An Episode in the Story of an Ancient House* (London: John Murray, 1901), pp. 3, 12–15, 398–9, 463.

45. For the suggestion that the City was a close-knit community with strong links to southern landed society and possessed an imperial orientation see Cain and Hopkins, *British Imperialism: Innovation and Expansion*, pp. 127–9, 189. For the presence of Jews and foreigners in the City see J. Camplin, *The Rise of the Plutocrats: Wealth and Power in Edwardian England* (London: Constable, 1978), pp. 46, 49, 54.

46. For the functioning of the global financial system in these years see R. C. Michie, *The Global Securities Market: A History* (Oxford: Oxford University Press, 2006), chapter 4.

7 Wealth and Power: 1910–1914

1. For an overview of the City of London on the eve of the First World War see R. C. Michie, 'The City of London and British Banking, 1900–1939' in Wrigley (ed.), *Early Twentieth-Century Britain*; R. C. Michie, 'The City of London and the British Government: The Changing Relationship' in Michie and Williamson (eds), *British Government and the City of London*; and R. C. Michie, 'A Financial Phoenix: The City of London in the Twentieth Century' in Cassis and Bussierre (eds), *London and Paris as International Financial Centres*, pp. 15–41.

2. W. J. Baker, *A History of the Marconi Company* (London: Methuen & Co., 1970), p. 17, J. Camplin, *The Rise of the Plutocrats*, pp. 46, 49, 55, 156. Entries in the *ODNB*.

3. W. Besant, *The Alabaster Box* (London, 1911), pp. 4–11, 13, 66, 220, 230, 250.

4. A. S. Swan, *The Bondage of Riches* (London: S. W. Partridge & Co., 1912), pp. 7–9, 20–1, 36.

5. G. Pettman, *A Study in Gold* (London: S. W. Partridge & Co., 1912), pp. 9–10, 15, 55, 65, 70, 100.

6. Ibid., pp 101, 104, 115–17, 121–3, 126.

7. Ibid, pp 127–8, 130, 132, 137.

8. Ibid., pp 146–150, 157, 165, 171, 201, 204–5, 207–8.

9. Ibid., pp 165, 171, 201, 204–5, 207–8, 210–15, 219–222, 226–7, 276, 280, 284–6, 294.

10. J. Hocking, *God and Mammon* (London: Ward, Lock & Co., 1912), pp. 6–8, 25–8, 48–9, 58, 67–9, 71–2, 74–5, 79–81, 120–3, 265.

11. Ibid., pp. 90–4, 98–101, 107–9, 126–7, 143.

12. Ibid., pp. 152, 155–158, 164, 178–82, 185–6, 245, 267–8, 273–5.

13. Ibid., pp. 212, 214–16, 219, 232–3, 245, 257, 263–5, 267–8, 275.

14. Ibid., pp 270–6, 279–80, 285, 288–9, 291–2, 298–9, 301, 306, 313.

15. A. Bennett, *The Regent: A Five Towns Story of Adventure in London* (London: Methuen & Co., 1913), pp. 7, 28, 38–9, 49, 148–150, 252–3.

16. E. P. Oppenheim, *Havoc* (London: Hodder & Stoughton, 1912), pp. 62–8, 74, 98–9, 105, 116, 118, 236, 289–90, 314–5, 320–1, 329–330, 342–5.

17. E. P. Oppenheim, *A Millionaire of Yesterday* (London: Ward, Lock & Co., 1912), pp. 60–7, 72, 90–1, 102, 114–15, 121–3, 134, 146, 170–2, 261–4, 273, 278, 296–300, 302, 314.

18. G. Parker, *The Judgement House* (London: Methuen & Co., 1913), pp. 39–43, 52, 66, 86, 117, 259–60, 269, 310–11, 470–2.

19. M. Rittenberg, *Swirling Waters* (London: Methuen & Co., 1913), pp. 1–3. 7–11, 18, 29, 44–6, 54, 73–5, 92–3, 150, 186, 277, 292–3, 308–9.

20. A. Blackwood, *A Prisoner in Fairyland* (London: Macmillan & Co., 1913), pp. 1–6, 15–19, 55, 221, 227, 229, 318, 402, 432, 458–9.

21. A. Bennett, *Teresa of Watling Street: A Fantasia on Modern Themes* (London, Methuen & Co 1913), pp. 7–9, 12–13, 137, 140–1, 159–160, 207.cf Pollard (ed.), *Representation of Business*, Morris pp. 141–2.

22. W. Le Queux, *Sins of the City: A Story of Craft, Crime and Capital* (London: 1905), pp. 5, 7–10, 12–13, 21–8, 34, 38, 55–7, 71, 76–9, 83, 93, 95–9, 101, 108, 120, 122–4.

23. J. Conrad, *Heart of Darkness* (London: William Blackwood & Sons, 1902), pp. 5–7.

24. J. Conrad, *Chance* (London: Methuen & Co, 1914), pp. 6, 68–71, 78–81, 84–209, 228–9, 362, 377, 385, 433–4.

25. Saki [H .H. Munro], 'When William Came', in *The Penguin Complete Saki* (London: Penguin, 1982), pp. 705, 720–1.

26. N. Angell, *The Great Illusion: A Study of the Relation of Military Power to National Advantage*, Special Edition (London: William Heinemann, Ltd, 1913), pp. 71, 73; Abramson, *Building the Bank of England:* p. 205; W. Landells, 'The London Stock Exchange', *Quarterly Review* (1912), pp. 88–109, p. 106.

27. J. Buchan, *The Power-House* (1913; Edinburgh: Polygon, 2007) pp. 11, 13, 31, 45, 57, 60. It originally appeared in *Blackwood's* Magazine.

Conclusion

1. For a flavour of life in Victorian and Edwardian London for those whose wealth came from the City, see two books by Shirley Nicholson, *A Victorian Household* (Stroud: Sutton, 1994), and S. Nicholson, *An Edwardian Bachelor* (London: Victorian Society 1999).

2. For the argument that Britain developed an anti-industrial culture in this period see Weiner, *English Culture and the Decline of the Industrial Spirit*, pp. 128, 145. For a critique of that argument see Collins and Robbins (eds), *British Culture and Economic Decline*, Robbins, pp. 5, 21, Rubinstein, p. 61.

3. D. M. Mullock (Mrs Craik), *John Halifax, Gentleman* (London: Hurst and Blackett, 1856).

4. *Commercial Tales and Sketches* (London 1864), pp. 96–168.

5. Oxenham, *Rising Fortunes*, pp. 73, 164, 172–4, 221–3, 273–5.

6. C. J. C. W. Hyne, *Thompson's Progress* (London: George G. Harrap, 1903).

7. R. H. Bretherton, *An Honest Man* (London: Methuen & Co., 1909), pp. 1–3, 73, 338, 395

8. Benson, *The Osbornes*, pp. 4–7, 14–17, 37–8, 144–5, 154–5, 170–3, 210, 259, 263, 272, 378.

9. Du Maurier, *The Martian*, pp. 131, 315, 426–7.

10. For two interwar examples see two articles by P. S. Manley. 'Gerard Lee Bevan and the City Equitable Companies' *Abacus: A Journal of Accounting and Business Studies*, vol. 9 (1973), pp. 329-351; 'Clarence Hatry' *Abacus*, vol. 12 (1976), pp. 49-60.

11. For these years see the following R. C. Michie, 'The City of London and the British Government', in Michie and Williamson (eds), *The British Government and the City of London*, pp. 31-58, R. C. Michie, 'A Financial Phoenix' in Cassis and Bussierre (eds.), *London and Paris as International Financial*; R. C. Michie, 'The City of London as a European Financial Centre in the Twentieth Century' in *Europaische Finanzplatze im Wettbewerb* (Bankhistorisches Archiv-Beiheft 45, Franz Steiner Verlag, Stuttgart 2006), pp. 51–81.

12. V. Woolf, *The Voyage Out* (1915; Barnes and Noble: 2004), pp. 8–9, 18, 35, 43, 55,183, 300

13. G. A. Birmingham, *Gossamer* (London: Methuen & Co., 1915), pp. 9–10, 14, 22, 27, 30, 35, 45, 54, 76, 99, 101–3, 107, 114, 198–201, 220–1. For New York's transformation as a financial centre over this period see R. L. Bruner and S. D. Carr, *The Panic of 1907: Lessons Learned from the Market's Perfect Storm* (New York: New Jersey: John Wiley & Sons, Inc., 2007) and W. L. Silber, *When Washington Shut Down Wall Street: The Great Financial Crisis of 1914 and the Origins of America's Monetary Supremacy* (Princeton, NJ: Princeton University Press, 2007).

14. A. Bennett, *Lord Raingo* (London: Cassell & Co, 1926), pp. 24, 38–41, 38, 72, 124.

15. J. Buchan, *Mr Standfast* (London: Hodder & Stoughton, 1919), p. 48; *The Gap in the Curtain* (London: Hodder & Stoughton, 1932), pp. 57–93.

16. B. D. Nicholson, *Business is Business* (London: Martin Secker, 1933) pp. 13, 128–42, 152, 166–92.

17. J. B. Priestley, *Angel Pavement* (London: William Heinemann Ltd 1930), pp. 34, 52, 166–7, 174, 261, 277, 417, 481, 604, 608.

18. V. Seligman, *Bank Holiday* (London: Longmans, Green & Co., 1934), pp. 1–2, 9–13, 26–8, 41, 46–9, 64–7, 76, 92–3, 104, 216–18, 298–7, 300.

19. Entries in J. Walker (ed.), *Halliwell's Film and Video Guide 2000* (London: HarperCollins, 1999); C. Churchill, *Serious Money: A City Comedy* (Bristol: Proscenium, 1987).

20. This paragraph owes much to N. Marsh, *Money, Speculation and Finance in Contemporary British Fiction* (London: Continuum, 2007), pp. 1, 8, 12–16, 35, 45, 70–1, 96, 108–110, 115, 131, 143.

WORKS CITED

This book is largely based on a close reading of British fiction written between 1800 and 1914. The works that have proved most useful are listed under 'Novels'. These novels have not been chosen scientifically but through following up leads, browsing in secondhand bookshops, and discussing the subject with anyone who would listen over the past twenty-five years. I hope that I have identified every major novelist and their works that have covered the subject of the City of London and high finance. Other than that the book rests on the research and reading in financial history that I have conducted over a period of almost forty years. This has focused mainly on the history of the City of London as a financial and commercial centre, the London Stock Exchange and the global securities market. It has appeared in print in various forms and the most relevant are listed under 'Other Works'. My own work is a product of both the research that I have conducted and that of other financial historians, and this has been acknowledged in my publications. However, some of the more recent work by financial historians has been listed along with that of more general scholars and literary experts, and contemporary publications to which direct reference has been made.

Novels

Ainsworth, W. H., *Old St. Paul's: A Tale of the Plague and the Fire* (London: Collins, 1841).

Ainsworth, W. H., *John Law: The Projector* (London: Chapman and Hall, 1864).

Allen, G., 'The Great Ruby Robbery' in Cox (ed), *Victorian Tales of Mystery*, pp. 214–32.

Anon., *Commercial Tales and Sketches* (London: 1864).

Austen, J., *Pride and Prejudice* (London: T. Egerton, 1813).

Aytoun, W. E., 'How we got up the Glenmutchkin Railway and how we got out of it' (1845) in W. L. Renwick (ed.), *W. E. Aytoun: Stories and Verse* (Edinburgh: Edinburgh University Press, 1964), pp. 1–39.

Bell, R., *The Ladder of Gold: An English Story* (London: Richard Bentley, 1850).

Belloc, H., *Emmanuel Burden, Merchant, of Thames St., in the City of London, Exporter of Hardware: A Record of his Lineage, Speculations, Last Days and Death* (London, 1904).

—, *Mr Clutterbuck's Election* (London: E. Nash, 1908).

Bennett, A., *A Man from the North* (London: John Lane, 1898)·

—, *Anna of the Five Towns* (London: Chatto and Windus, 1902).

—, *Clayhanger* (London: Methuen & Co., 1910).

—, *Hilda Lessways* (London: Methuen & Co., 1911).

—, *The Card* (London: Methuen & Co., 1911).

—, *The Regent: A Five Towns Story of Adventure in London* (London: Methuen & Co., 1913).

—, *Teresa of Watling Street: A Fantasia on Modern Themes* (London: Methuen & Co., 1913).

—, *These Twain* (London: Methuen & Co., 1916).

—, *Lord Raingo* (London: Cassell & Co., 1926)

Benson, E. F., *The Osbornes* (London: Smith, Elder & Co., 1910)

Besant, W., *All Sorts and Condition of Men* (London: Chatto & Windus, 1882).

—, *All in a Garden Fair: The Simple Story of Three Boys and a Girl* (London: Chatto & Windus, 1883).

—, *Beyond the Dreams of Avarice* (London: Chatto & Windus, 1895).

—, *The Alabaster Box* (London, 1911).

—, and J. Rice, *The Golden Butterfly.* (London: Chatto and Windus, 1877).

—, and —, *Ready-Money Mortiboy: A Matter-of-fact Story* (London: Chatto & Windus 1891)

Birmingham, G. A., *Gossamer* (London: Methuen & Co., 1915)

Blackwood, A., *A Prisoner in Fairyland* (London: Macmillan & Co., 1913)

Blyth, H., 'The Accusing Shadow' in Cox (ed.), *Victorian Tales of Mystery*, pp. 303–41.

Boothby, G., 'The Duchess of Wiltshire's Diamonds' (1897) in. Greene (ed.), *Complete Rivals of Sherlock Holmes*, pp. 74–102.

Braddon, M. E., 'Levison's Victim' (1870) in Cox (ed.), *Victorian Tales of Mystery*, pp. 69–82

Bretherton, R. H., *An Honest Man* (London: Methuen & Co., 1909)

Brontë, C., *Villette* (London: Smith, Elder & Co., 1853).

Buchan, J., *The Power-House* (1913; Edinburgh, Polygon, 2007).

—, *Mr Standfast* (London: Hodder & Stoughton, 1919).

—, *The Gap in the Curtain* (London: Hodder & Stoughton, 1932)

Butler, S., *The Way of all Flesh* (London: Grant Richards, 1903).

Chesterton, G. K., 'The Innocence of Father Brown' (London 1910–11) in *The Penguin Complete Father Brown* (Harmondsworth: Penguin, 1981), pp. 9–168.

Churchill, C., *Serious Money: A City Comedy* (Bristol: Proscenium, 1987).

Collins, W., *A Rogue's Life* (London: Household Words, 1856).

—, *The Moonstone* (London: Tinsley Brothers, 1868).

—, *The Haunted Hotel* (London: Chatto & Windus, 1878).

—, *Who Killed Zebedee?* (London: The Seaside Library, 1881).

—, *The Evil Genius* (London: Chatto & Windus, 1886).

—, and Besant, W., *Blind Love* (London: Chatto & Windus, 1890).

Conrad, J., *Heart of Darkness* (London: William Blackwood & Sons, 1902)

—, *Chance* (London: Methuen & Co., 1914).

Corelli, M., *The Sorrows of Satan* (London: Methuen & Co, 1895).

Cox, M. (ed), *Victorian Tales of Mystery and Detection* (Oxford: Oxford University Press, 1992).

Dickens, C., *Dealings with the Firm of Dombey and son, Wholesale, Retail, and for Exportation* (London: Bradbury & Evans, 1846–8).

—, *Little Dorrit* (London: Bradbury & Evans, 1857)

—, *Our Mutual Friend* (London: Chapman & Hall, 1864/5).

—, 'Hunted Down' in. Cox (ed.), *Victorian Tales of Mystery*, pp. 48–65.

—, and Collins, W., *No Thoroughfare* (London: Chapman & Hall, 1867).

Disraeli, B., *Coningsby or The New Generation* (London: Henry Colburn, 1844).

—, *Tancred or The New Crusade* (London: Henry Colburn, 1847).

—, *Lothair* (London: Longmans, Green, and Co., 1870).

Doyle, A. C., *A Duet With An Occasional Chorus* (London: G. Richards, 1899).

—, 'The Adventure of the Beryl Coronet' (1892) in *Complete Illustrated Holmes*, pp. 237–51.

—, 'The Adventure of the Stockbroker's Clerk' (1893) in *Complete Illustrated Holmes*, pp. 311–21.

—, 'The Adventure of the Norwood Builder' (1903) in *Complete Illustrated Holmes*, pp. 555–68.

—, *The Complete Illustrated Sherlock Holmes* (Ware: Omega Books, 1986)

Du Maurier, G., *The Martian: a Novel* (London: Harper, 1898).

Fletcher, J. S., 'The Contents of the Coffin' (1909) in Greene (ed), *Complete Rivals of Sherlock Holmes*.

Forster, E. M., *Howards End* (London: Edward Arnold, 1910).

Frederic, H., *The Market-Place* (London: William Heinemann, Ltd, 1899).

Galsworthy, J., *The Man of Property* (London: William Heinemann, Ltd, 1906).

—, *The Country House* (London: William Heinemann, Ltd, 1907).

Gilbert, W. S. and Sullivan, A. S. *Utopia, Limited; or The Flowers of Progress* (London 1893), in *The Complete Plays of Gilbert and Sullivan* (New York and London: W. W. Norton, 1976), pp. 507–60.

Gissing, G., *Born in Exile* (London: A. & C. Black, 1892).

—, *The Whirlpool* (London: Lawrence and Bullen, 1897).

—, *The Crown of Life* (London: Methuen & Co., 1899).

—, *The Nether World* (London: Smith, Elder & Co., 1889).

—, *Will Warburton: A Romance of Real Life* (London: Archibald Constable, 1905).

Gore, Mrs, *The Money Lender* (London: Geo. Routledge & Co., 1854).

Gribble, F., *The Lower Life* (London: A. D. Innes & Co., 1896).

Greene, H., (ed.), *The Complete Rivals of Sherlock Holmes* (London: Bodley Head, 1973).

Grossmith, G. and W., *The Diary of a Nobody* (London: Arrowsmith, 1892).

Hill, H., *Guilty Gold: A Romance of Financial Fraud and City Crime* (London: C. Arthur Pearson Ltd., 1896).

—, *Millions of Mischief: The Story of a Great Secret* (London: Ward, Lock & Co., 1905).

—, *The One Who Saw* (London: Cassell & Co., 1905)

—, 'The Sapient Monkey' (1892) in M. Cox (ed.), *Victorian Tales of Mystery*, pp. 233–41.

Hocking, J. *The Man Who Rose Again*, (London: Hodder & Stoughton, 1906).

—, *God and Mammon* (London: Ward, Lock & Co., 1912).

Holland, V. B., (ed.) *The Complete Works of Oscar Wilde*, (London: Collins, 1948–66).

Hope, A., *Tristram of Blent: An Episode in the Story of an Ancient House* (London: John Murray, 1901).

Hornung, E. W., *Raffles: The Amateur Cracksman* (London: Methuen & Co., 1899).

—, *The Black Mask* (London: Grant Richards, 1901).

Hume, F., 'The Greenstone God and the Stockbroker' in. Cox (ed.), *Victorian Tales of Mystery*, pp. 274–89.

Hyne, C. J. C. W., *Thompson's Progress* (London: G. Harrap 1903).

Jackson, W. S., *Nine Points of the Law* (London: John Lane, 1903).

James, H., *The Awkward Age* (London: William Heinemann Ltd, 1899).

Jerome, J. K., *Three Men in a Boat* (London: Simpkin, Marshall, Hamilton, Kent & Co., 1889).

Keen, H., 'The Tin Box' in Cox (ed.), *Victorian Tales of Mystery*, pp. 420–37.

Kingsley, C., *Yeast: A Problem* (London, 1851).

Kuppord, S., *A Fortune from the Sky* (London: Thomas Nelson & Sons, 1903).

Le Fanu, J. S., *Checkmate* (London: Hurst and Blackett, 1871).

Le Queux, W., *Guilty Bonds* (London: G. Routledge & Sons, 1891).

—, *Sins of the City: A Story of Craft, Crime and Capital* (London F. V. White & Co, 1905).

—, *The Crooked Way* (London: Methuen & Co., 1908).

Lever, C., *Davenport Dunn or The Man and the Day,* 3 vols (Leipzig: Bernhard Tauchnitz, 1859).

—, *That Boy of Norcott's* (London: Smith, Elder & Co., 1869).

Martineau, H., *Berkeley the Banker* (London: Charles Fox, 1833).

Merriman, H. S., *Roden's Corner* (London: Smith, Elder & Co., 1898).

—, *The Last Hope* (London: Macmillan & Co., 1904).

Morrison, A., *A Child of the Jago* (London: Methuen & Co., 1896).

—, 'The Case of Laker, Absconded' in Greene (ed.), *Complete Rivals of Sherlock Holmes*, pp. 45–73.

—, 'The Affair of the 'Avalanche Bicycle and Tyre Co. Limited' in Greene (ed.), *Complete Rivals of Sherlock Holmes*, pp. 103–30.

Mullock. D. M., (Mrs Craik), *John Halifax, Gentleman* (London: Hurst and Blackett, 1856).

Saki [Munro, H. H.], 'When William Came', in *The Penguin Complete Saki* (London: Penguin, 1982).

Murray, I (ed.), *Oscar Wilde, The Major Works* (Oxford: Oxford University Press, 1989).

Nicholson, B. D., *Business is Business* (London: Martin Secker, 1933).

Oppenheim, E. P., *A Prince of Sinners* (London: Ward, Lock & Co., 1903).

—, *Anna, The Adventuress* (London: Ward, Lock & Co., 1904).

—, *The Mysterious Mr Sabin* (London, 1899).

—, *Mr. Wingrave, Millionaire* (London: Ward, Lock & Co., 1906).

—, *Jeanne of the Marshes* (London: Ward, Lock & Co., 1909).

—, *Havoc* (London: Hodder & Stoughton, 1912).

—, *A Millionaire of Yesterday* (London: Ward, Lock & Co., 1912).

Orczy, Baroness, 'The Mysterious Death on the Underground Railway' in Greene (ed.), *Complete Rivals of Sherlock Holmes*, pp. 221–41.

Oxenham, J., *Rising Fortunes: The Story of a Man's Beginnings* (London: Hurst and Blackett, 1899).

—, *Profit and Loss* (London: Methuen & Co., 1906).

Peacock, T. L., *Crotchet Castle* (London: T. Hookham, 1831).

Parker, G., *The Judgment House* (London: Methuen & Co., 1913).

Pemberton, M., *The Impregnable City* (London: Cassell & Co., 1895).

Pettman, G., *A Study in Gold* (London: S. W. Partridge & Co., 1912).

Pinto, E., *Ye Outside Fools! Glimpses inside the Stock Exchange,* new edn (London: Samuel Tinsley, 1877).

Priestley, J. B., *Angel Pavement* (London: William Heinemann Ltd, 1930).

Reade, C., *Hard Cash; A Matter-of-fact Romance* (London: Sampson Low, Son, & Marston, 1863).

—, and Boucicault, D., *Foul Play* (London: Bradbury, Evans & Co., 1868)

Reynolds, G. M., *The Mysteries of London* (1844–56), ed. T. Thomas (Keele: Keele University Press, 1996).

Robinson, E., *The City Banker or Love and Money* (London: C. J. Skeet, 1856).

Trafford, F. G. [Riddell, C.], *George Geith of Fen Court* (London: Tinsley Brothers, 1864).

—, *The Race for Wealth*, 2 vols (Leipzig: Bernhard Tauchnitz, 1866).

Mrs J. H. Riddell, *Austin Friars* (London: Tinsley Brothers, 1870)

Haggard, H. R., *Colonel Quaritch V. C.* (London: Longmans, Green & Co., 1888).

—, *The Yellow God: An Idol of Africa* (London: Cassell & Co., 1909).

Rittenberg, M., *Swirling Waters* (London: Methuen & Co., 1913).

Schreiner, O., *Trooper Peter Halket of Mashonaland* (London, 1897).

Scott, Sir W., *Rob Roy* (London: Longman, Hurst, Rees, Orme, & Brown 1818).

Seligman, V., *Bank Holiday* (London: Longmans, Green & Co., 1934).

Smart, H., *The Great Tontine* (London: Chapman & Hall 1881).

Smedley, F. E., *Frank Fairleigh or Scenes from the Life of a Private Pupil* (London: A. Hall, 1850).

The Spectre, *Ye Vampyres: A Legend or The National Betting-Ring, Showing What Became of It* (London: Samuel Tinsley, 1875).

Stevenson, R. L., *The Dynamiter* (London: Longmans, Green & Co., 1885).

Stoker, B., *The Lady of the Shroud* (London: William Heinemann, Ltd., 1909).

Swan, A. S., *The Strait Gate* (London: S. W. Partridge & Co., 1894).

—, *The Bondage of Riches* (London: S. W. Partridge & Co., 1912).

Thackeray, W. M., *The History of Samuel Titmarsh and the Great Hoggarty Diamond* (London, 1841).

—, *The Book of Snobs: Sketches of Life and Character* (London: Punch Office, 1848)

—, *Vanity Fair* (1848: London, Konemann, 1998).

—, *The Newcomes: Memories of a Most Respectable Family* (London: Bradbury and Evans, 1853–5).

—, 'The Diary of C. Jeames De La Pluche, Esq.' (London 1854), in *The Works of William Makepeace Thackeray*, 12 vols (London: Smith, Elder & Co., 1872).

Thorne, G. and Custance, L., *Sharks: A fantastic novel for business men and their families* (London: Greening & Co., 1904).

Trollope, A., *The Three Clerks: A Novel* (London: Bentley, 1858).

—, *The Last Chronicle of Barset* (London: Smith, Elder & Co., 1867).

—, *The Way We Live Now*, 2 vols (London: Chapman and Hall, 1874–5).

—, *The Prime Minister* (London: Chapman and Hall, 1876).

Wallace, E., *The Four Just Men* (London: Tallis Press, 1905).

Wells, H. G., *Kipps: The Story of a Simple Soul* (London: Macmillan & Co., 1905).

—, *Tono-Bungay* (London: Macmillan & Co., 1909).

Wicks, F., *The Veiled Hand: a Novel of the Sixties, the Seventies, and the Eighties* (London: Eden & Co., 1892).

Wilde, O., *The Model Millionaire* (1891) in *Complete Works of Wilde*.

—, *The Importance of Being Earnest* (performed in 1895, printed 1899) in *Wilde, Major Works*, pp. 480–538.

—, *An Ideal Husband* (performed in 1895, printed 1899) in *Wilde, Major Works*, pp. 392–475.

Wodehouse, P. G., *Psmith in the City* (London: A. & C. Black, 1910).

Woolf, V., *The Voyage Out* (1915; London: Barnes and Noble, 2004).

Wood, H., *East Lynne* (London: Richard Bentley, 1861).

—, *Oswald Cray: A Novel* (London: Richard Bentley, 1864).

Zangwill, I. 'Cheating the Gallows' (1893), in Cox (ed.), *Victorian Tales of Mystery*, pp. 241–53.

Other Works

Abramson, D. M., *Building the Bank of England: Money, Architecture, Society, 1694–1942* (New Haven, CT and London: Yale University Press, 2005)

Alborn, T. L., *Conceiving Companies: Joint-Stock Politics in Victorian England* (London: Routledge, 1998).

Angell, N., *The Great Illusion: A Study of the Relation of Military Power to National Advantage*, Special Edition (London: William Heinemann, Ltd, 1913)

Baker, W. J., *A History of the Marconi Company* (London: Methuen & Co., 1970)

The Banking Almanac (London: Thomas Skinner and Co., 1913).

Banner, S., *Anglo-American Securities Regulation: Cultural and Political Roots, 1690–1860* (Cambridge: Cambridge University Press, 1998).

Barron, X., (ed.), *London 1066–1914: Literary Sources and Documents*, 3 vols (Mountfield: Helm Information, 1997).

Baster, A. S. J., *The International Banks* (London: P. S. King & Son, Ltd., 1935).

Beavan, A. H., *Imperial London* (London: J. M. Dent & Co., 1901)

Bills, M. and Knight, V. (eds), *William Powell Frith: Painting the Victorian Age* (New Haven, CT and London: Yale University Press, 2006).

Bratlinger, P., *Fictions of the State: Culture and Credit in Britain, 1694–1994* (Ithaca, NY and London: Cornell University Press, 1996).

Bruner, R. L. and Carr, S. D., *The Panic of 1907: Lessons Learned from the Market's Perfect Storm* (New Jersey: John Wiley & Sons, Inc., 2007).

Burke, P., Harrison, B. and Slack, P. (eds.), *Civil Histories: Essays Presented to Sir Keith Thomas* (Oxford: Oxford University Press, 2000).

Cain, P. J. and Hopkins, A. G., *British Imperialism: Innovation and Expansion, 1688–1914* (London: Longman, 1993).

— and —, *British Imperialism: Crisis and Reconstruction, 1914–1990* (London: Longman, 1993).

Camplin, J., *The Rise of the Plutocrats: Wealth and Power in Edwardian England* (London: Constable, 1978)

Cassis, Y., *Capitals of Capital: A History of International Financial Centres, 1780–2005* trans. J. Collier, (Cambridge: Cambridge University Press, 2006).

Cassis, Y. and Bussierre, E. (eds.), *London and Paris as International Financial Centres* (Oxford: Oxford University Press, 2005).

Clark. P., and Gillespie, R. (eds), *Two Capitals: London and Dublin, 1500–1840* (Oxford: Oxford University Press, 2001).

Collins, B., and Robbins, K., (eds), *British Culture and Economic Decline* (London: Weidenfeld and Nicolson, 1990).

Crafts, N., 'Regional G. D. P. in Britain, 1871–1911: Some Estimates' *Scottish Journal of Political Economy*, 52 (2005), pp. 54–64.

Craik, T. W., (ed.), *The Revels: History of Drama in English*, 7 vols, vol. 6, (London: Methuen & Co., 1975), vol. 7 (London: Methuen & Co., 1978).

Crump, A., *The Theory of Stock Exchange Speculation* (London: Longmans, Green & Co., 1874).

Davies, A. E., *What to look for in a Prospectus Speculation* (London: Allen & Unwin, 1926).

F. T. *Wealth*, 1 (Spring 2008).

Finn, M. C., *The Character of Credit: Personal Debt in English Culture, 1740–1914* (Cambridge: Cambridge University Press, 2003).

Floud, R. and Johnson, P. (eds), *The Cambridge Economic History of Modern Britain* (Cambridge: Cambridge University Press, 2004).

Frith, W. P., *My Autobiography and Reminiscences* (London: Richard Bentley and Son, 1888).

Fun, 31 (23 June 1880).

Gallagher, C., *The Industrial Reformation of English Fiction: Discourse and Narrative Form, 1832–1867* (Chicago, IL: University of Chicago Press, 1985).

Gauci, P., *Emporium of the World: The Merchants of London, 1660-1800* (London: Continuum, 2007).

Grahame, K., *Pagan Papers* (London: John Lane, 1898).

Guiso, L., Sapienza, P., and Zingales, L., 'Does Culture Affect Economic Outcomes? *Journal of Economic Perspectives*, 20 (2006), pp. 23–48.

Hannah., L., The Moral Economy of Business: A Historical Perspective on Ethics and Efficiency', in Burke et al (eds), *Civil Histories,* pp. 285–300.

Hein, L. W., *The British Companies Acts and the Practice of Accountancy, 1844–1962* (New York: Arno Press, 1978).

Hobson, J. A., *Imperialism: A Study,* revised edn (London: Allen & Unwin, 1938).

Innes, J., 'Managing the Metropolis: London's Social Problems and their Control, *c.* 1600–1830' in Clark and Gillespie (eds), *Two Capitals,* pp. 53–80.

Johnson, P., 'Civilizing Mammon: Laws, Morals and the City in Nineteenth Century England' in Burke, et al (eds), *Civil Histories*, pp. 301–20.

Jones, G., *British Multinational Banking, 1830–1990* (Oxford: Clarendon Press, 1993).

Knezevic, B., *Figures of Finance Capitalism: Writing, Class and Capital in the Age of Dickens* (New York and London: Routledge, 2003).

Lambourne, L., *Victorian Painting* (London: Phaidon, 1999).

Landells, W., 'The London Stock Exchange', *Quarterly Review,* 217 (1912), pp. 88–109.

London Corporation, *City of London Day Census, 1911: Report* (London: Simpkins, Marshall, Hamilton, Kent & Co. Ltd., 1911).

Macauley, Lord, *The History of England,* 5 vols (London: Longman, 1848).

McDermott, E., *The London Stock Exchange: Its Constitution and Modes of Business* (London: Railway News and Joint-Stock Journal, 1877).

Manley, P. S., 'Gerard Lee Bevan and the City Equitable Companies' *Abacus: A Journal of Accounting and Business Studies,* 9 (1973), pp. 329–51.

—, 'Clarence Hatry', *Abacus,* 12 (1976), pp. 49–60.

Marsh, N., *Money, Speculation and Finance in Contemporary British Fiction* (London: Continuum, 2007).

May, H., 'The London Stock Exchange' *Fortnightly Review* 1885, p. 566–80.

Michie, R. C. 'The City of London: Functional and Spatial Unity in the Nineteenth Century' in H. A. Diederiks and D. Reeder (eds), *Cities of Finance* (Amsterdam: Proceedings of the Colloquium, 1991).

—, *The City of London: Continuity and Change since 1850* (London, Macmillan, 1992).

—, 'Friend or Foe: Information Technology and the London Stock Exchange since 1700' *Journal of Historical Geography,* 23 (1997), pp. 304–26.

—, 'The Invisible Stabiliser: Asset Arbitrage and the International Monetary System since 1700' *Financial History Review,* 15 (1998), pp. 5–26.

—, 'Insiders, Outsiders and the Dynamics of Change in the City of London since 1900', *Journal of Contemporary History,* 33 (1998), pp. 547–71.

—, *The London Stock Exchange; A History* (Oxford: Oxford University Press, 1999).

—, 'One World or Many Worlds?: Markets, Banks, and Communications, 1850s–1990s' in T. de Graaf, J. Jonker and J. J. Mabron (eds) *European Banking Overseas, 19th–20th centuries* (Amsterdam: ABN AMRO Historical Archives, 2002)

—, 'The City of London and British Banking, 1900–1939' in C. Wrigley (ed.), *A Companion to Early Twentieth Century Britain* (Oxford: Blackwell, 2003).

—, 'A Financial Phoenix: The City of London in the Twentieth Century' in Cassis and Bussierre (eds.), *London and Paris as International Financial Centres*, pp. 15–41.

—, 'The City of London as a European Financial Centre in the Twentieth Century' in *Europäische Finanzplätze im Wettbewerb* (Bankhistorisches Archiv-Beiheft 45, Stuttgart 2006), pp. 51–81.

—, *The Global Securities Market: A History* (Oxford: Oxford University Press, 2006).

—, 'The City of London as a Global Financial Centre, 1880–1939: Finance, Foreign Exchange and the First World War' in P. L. Cottrell, E. Lange and U. Olsson (eds), *Centres and Peripheries in Banking: The Historical Development of Financial Markets* (Aldershot: Ashgate, 2007), pp. 41–80.

—, and Williamson, P. A. (eds), *The British Government and The City of London in the Twentieth Century* (Cambridge: Cambridge University Press, 2004).

Nicholas, T., 'Enterprise and Management' in Floud and Johnson (eds), *The Cambridge Economic History of Modern Britain*.

Nicholson, S., *A Victorian Household* (Stroud: Sutton, 1994).

—, *An Edwardian Bachelor* (London: Victorian Society, 1999).

Noakes, A., *William Frith: Extraordinary Victorian Painter* (London: Jupiter Books, 1978).

Norman, H. and Ashton Johnson, G. C., 'The London Stock Exchange' *Century Illustrated Monthly Magazine*, 66 (New Series Volume 44) (May–October 1903), pp. 177–94.

O'Gorman, F. (ed), *Victorian Literature and Finance* (Oxford: Oxford University Press, 2007).

Oxford Dictionary of National Biography (Oxford: Oxford University Press, 2008).

Peck, J. F. and Smith, J. A., 'Business and Social Mobility into the British Elite, 1870–1914', *Journal of European Economic History*, 33 (2004), pp. 485–518.

Petch, S., 'Law, Literature, and Victorian Studies' *Victorian Literature and Culture*, 35 (2007), pp. 361–84.

Platt, D. C. M., *Britain's Investment Overseas on the Eve of the First World War: The Use and Abuse of Numbers* (London: Macmillan, 1986).

Pollard, A. (ed.), *The Representation of Business in English Literature* (London: Institute of Economic Affairs, 2000).

Reed, J. R., 'A Friend to Mammon: Speculation in Victorian literature' *Victorian Studies*, 27 (1983–4), pp. 179–202

Rintoul, M. C., *Dictionary of Real People and Places in Fiction* (London: Routledge, 1993).

Robb, G., *White-Collar Crime in Modern England: Financial Fraud and Business Morality, 1845–1929* (Cambridge: Cambridge University Press, 1992).

Robinson, A., *Imagining London, 1770–1900* (London: Macmillan, 2004).

Rosenberg, E., *From Shylock to Svengali: Jewish Stereotypes in English Fiction* (London: Owen, 1961).

Roy, H., *The Stock Exchange* (London: Houlston and Wright, 1860).

Rubinstein, W. D., *Capitalism, Culture and Decline in Britain, 1750–1990* (London: Routledge, 1993).

—, 'The Role of London in Britain's Wealth Structure, 1808–99: Further Evidence' in J. Stobart and A. Owen (eds), *Urban Fortunes: Property and Inheritance in the Town* (Aldershot: Burlington, 2000), pp. 131–49.

Russell, N., *The Novelist and Mammon: Literary Responses to the World of Commerce in the Nineteenth Century* (Oxford: Clarendon Press, 1986).

Schwarz, L., 'Hanoverian London; The Making of a Service Town', in Clark and Gillespie (eds), *Two Capitals*, pp. 93–10.

Searle, G. R., *Morality and the Market in Victorian Britain* (Oxford: Clarendon Press, 1998).

Silber, W. L., *When Washington Shut Down Wall Street: The Great Financial Crisis of 1914 and the Origins of America's Monetary Supremacy* (Princeton, NJ: Princeton University Press, 2007)

Slack, P., 'Perceptions of the Metropolis in Seventeenth Century England' in Burje et al (eds) *Civil Histories*, pp. 161–80.

Stone, I., *The Global Export of Capital from Great Britain, 1865–1914: A Statistical Survey* (London: Macmillan, 1999).

Taylor, J., *Creating Capitalism: Joint-Stock Enterprise in British Politics and Culture, 1800–1870* (Woodbridge: Royal Historical Society/Boydell Press, 2006)

—, 'Business in Pictures: Representations of Railway Enterprise in the Satirical Press in Britain, 1845–1870' *Past and Present*, 189 (2005), pp. 111–45.

Thompson, F. M. L. (ed.), *The Cambridge Social History of Britain, 1750–1950* (Cambridge: Cambridge University Press, 1990).

—, *Gentrification and the Enterprise Culture: Britain 1780–1980* (Oxford: Oxford University Press, 2001).

Tucker, H. F., A *Companion to Victorian Literature and Culture* (Oxford: Blackwell, 1999).

Turner, C. C., 'Money London' in G. R. Sims, *Living London* (London: Cassell & Co., Ltd., 1902), reprinted in R. C. Michie, *The Development of London as a Financial Centre* (London: I. B. Tauris, 2000), pp. 33–57.

Victorian Studies, 45 (2002).

Walker, J., (ed.), *Halliwell's Film and Video Guide 2000* (London: HarperCollins, 1999).

Waller, P., *Writers, Readers and Reputations: Literary Life in Britain, 1870–1918* (Oxford: Oxford University Press, 2006).

Weiner, M. J., *English Culture and the Decline of the Industrial Spirit, 1850–1980* (Cambridge: Cambridge University Press, 1981)

Weiss, B., *The Hell of the English: Bankruptcy and the Victorian Novel* (Lewisburg, PA: Bucknell University Press, 1986).

Williams, M., *Round London: Down East and Up West* (London: Macmillan, 1892)

Withers, H., *International Finance* (London: Smith, Elder & Co., 1916).

Wood, C., *Victorian Panorama: Paintings of Victorian Life* (London: Faber & Faber, 1976).

—, *William Powell Frith: A painter and his world* (Stroud: Sutton, 2006).

Wright, R. E., *One Nation Under Debt: Hamilton, Jefferson, and the History of what we Owe* (New York and London: McGraw-Hill, 2008).

Wynne-Bennett, H. D., *Investment and Speculation* (London: Shaw Publishing, 1924)

Unpublished Papers

Michie, R. C., 'Gamblers, Fools, Victims or Wizards? The British Investor in the Public Mind, 1850–1930' (Paper delivered at a conference on investors, Milton Keynes, June 2008).

Munn, C., 'The Positive Depiction of Entrepreneurs and Entrepreneurship in the Novels of Sir Walter Scott'

INDEX